Also by Christiane Bird

A Thousand Sighs, A Thousand Revolts: Journeys in Kurdistan

Neither East Nor West: One Woman's Journey
Through the Islamic Republic of Iran

The Jazz and Blues Lover's Guide to the U.S.

Below the Line: Living Poor in America
(co-author)

New York Handbook

The
Sultan's Shadow

The

Sultan's Shadow

One Family's Rule at

the Crossroads of East and West

CHRISTIANE BIRD

Random House
New York

Published in the United States by Random House,
an imprint of The Random House Publishing Group,
a division of Random House, Inc., New York.

RANDOM HOUSE and colophon are registered trademarks
of Random House, Inc.

ISBN 978-0-345-46940-3
eBook ISBN 978-0-679-60376-4

Printed in the United States of America on acid-free paper

www.atrandom.com

2 4 6 8 9 7 5 3 1

First Edition

Book design by Virginia Norey

When one plays the pipes in Zanzibar,
  they dance on the Lakes [of Central Africa].
  —POPULAR NINETEENTH-CENTURY PROVERB

⚜

Surely in the creation of the heavens
  and the earth;
In the alternation of night and day;
In the sailing of ships through the ocean
  For the profit of mankind . . .
Here are signs for a people who understand.
  —THE QURAN, II:164

Contents

PART ONE

☙

Oman

PART TWO

✣

Zanzibar

PART THREE

✣

Germany and Africa

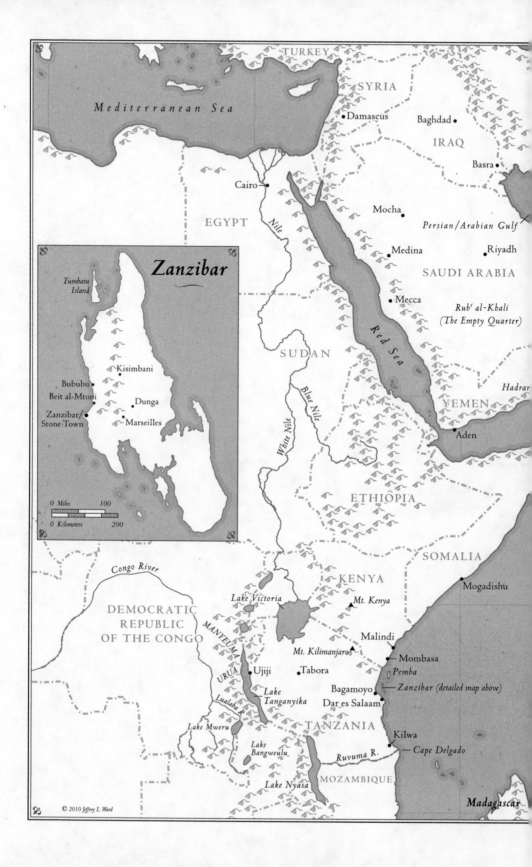

TURKEY

Mediterranean Sea

SYRIA

• Damascus   Baghdad •

                         IRAQ

                    Basra •

Cairo •

EGYPT   Mocha •

              Persian/Arabian Gulf

         Medina •   Riyadh •

         SAUDI ARABIA

         Mecca •   *Rubʿ al-Khali*
                   (The Empty Quarter)

SUDAN

              Red Sea   *Hadrar*

                         YEMEN

                              Aden •

Zanzibar

Tumbatu Island

• Kisimbani

Bububu •
Beit al-Mtoni   • Dunga

Zanzibar/
Stone Town •   • Marseilles

0 Miles   100
0 Kilometers   200

ETHIOPIA

SOMALIA

                         Mogadishu •

Congo River

DEMOCRATIC
REPUBLIC
OF THE CONGO

KENYA

Lake Victoria   ▲ *Mt. Kenya*

MANYEUMA

URUA   • Ujiji   Malindi

Mt. Kilimanjaro ▲   — Mombasa

Lualaba R.   *Lake Tanganyika*   • Tabora   *Pemba*

Lake Mweru   Bagamoyo   — *Zanzibar (detailed map above)*

              Dar es Salaam

Lake Bangweulu   TANZANIA   Kilwa
                              — *Cape Delgado*

         Ruvuma R.

Lake Nyasa   MOZAMBIQUE

                         Madagascar

© 2010 Jeffrey L. Ward

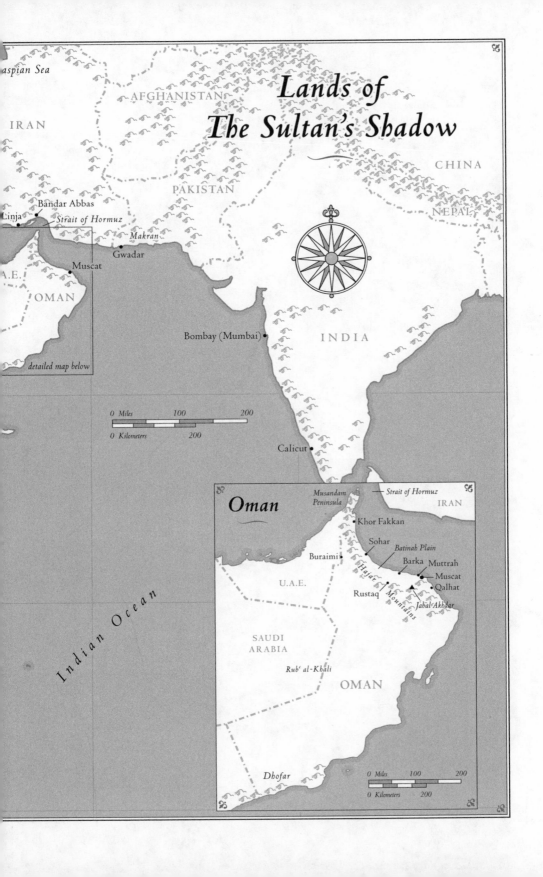

Lands of The Sultan's Shadow

Caspian Sea

AFGHANISTAN

IRAN

PAKISTAN

CHINA

NEPAL

Bandar Abbas

Linja

Strait of Hormuz

Makran

Gwadar

Muscat

U.A.E.

OMAN

Bombay (Mumbai)

INDIA

detailed map below

0 Miles 100 200

0 Kilometers 200

Calicut

Oman

Musandam Peninsula

Strait of Hormuz

IRAN

Khor Fakkan

Sohar

Batinah Plain

Buraimi

Barka

Muttrah

Hajar

Muscat

Qalhat

U.A.E.

Rustaq

Mountains

Jabal Akhdar

Indian Ocean

SAUDI
ARABIA

Rubʿ al-Khali

OMAN

Dhofar

0 Miles 100 200

0 Kilometers 200

Preface

THE INSPIRATION FOR THIS BOOK BEGAN WITH AN ALLUSION TO the "Arab slave trade" in an article I was reading. My curiosity sparked, I searched the Web, when I came across several references to a woman named Seyyida Salme, or Emily Ruete, and a book she had written, *Memoirs of an Arabian Princess.*

Wondering what an Arabian princess had to do with the slave trade, I began to read what proved to be the story of a remarkable nineteenth-century Omani woman, raised in a harem on the African island of Zanzibar. The daughter of a powerful ruling sultan and a Circassian slave, Salme had scandalized the royal family—and the entire island—by eloping with a German businessman, converting to Christianity, and fleeing to Hamburg. Three years later her husband died in a freak accident—trampled beneath a horse tram—leaving her alone in a foreign land with three small children and dwindling economic resources. The strong-minded princess was not one to be undone by circumstance, however, no matter how tragic, and she fought doggedly to regain her status, eventually coming to the attention of Germany's chancellor Otto von Bismarck. He then used her as a pawn in his bid to establish colonies in East Africa.

As for the slave trade, it had been the basis of nineteenth-century Zanzibar's economy. Salme had grown up in the shadow of what was then the busiest slave market in the Indian Ocean. The island had been home to tens of thousands of slaves, imported to work its many clove plantations, and had shipped tens of thousands more slaves farther north to other Muslim lands.

Captivated by the drama and scope of Salme's story, I decided to look for her autobiography. Much to my surprise, it was in print, and I ordered a copy. Later, I learned that Salme had begun writing it in Germany in 1875, when she was thirty-one years old, and had completed it in 1886. The first known autobiography published by either an Arab woman or a Zanzibari, it debuted in Germany that same year. Two years later, two English-language editions appeared. One, published in London, did not name either an author or translator, and the other, published in New York, cited its author as "Emily Ruete, Born Salme, Princess of Oman and Zanzibar." A French translation appeared in Paris in 1905, and a third English translation by Lionel Strachey was published in New York in 1907. Nonetheless, the book soon disappeared from public view.

The edition I initially obtained was the 1888 version published in New York, reissued in 1989. The book began with a brief preface written by the princess: "Nine years ago I made up my mind to write down some sketches of my life for my children. . . . Tired out in body and in mind, I did not then expect to live to be able to tell them, when they had grown up, of the many changes in my life, and of the recollections of my youth. I therefore resolved to write my memoirs for them."

The book went on to describe Salme's years in Zanzibar and the customs that had prevailed there at the time. Chapters covered such subjects as "Daily Life in Our House," "Our Meals," "Schooling in the East," "Woman's Position in the East," and "Slavery." I was intrigued . . . but also frustrated. Salme's account of her childhood was magical, but she gave few details about her elopement or her life in Germany. The book's tone was direct, yet distant, and often seemed to be addressing a wider and less personal audience than just her children. Salme also offered little insight into slavery or the slave trade as it had been practiced in the East. Her "Slavery" chapter was a brief seven pages and did little more than reflect the prevalent attitudes of her day; she called the slaves "great children" who "worked only when compelled to."

Later, I discovered that in addition to her memoirs, Salme had left behind a collection of letters, written while she was in Germany, which shed some light on her life there. Translated and published in English by scholar E. van Donzel, the letters were addressed to an unidentified "dear lady friend" in Zanzibar. It is likely, however, that the letters were never sent, and were never intended to be sent. They are not dated and seem to have been written well after the events they relate. Salme probably used them for catharsis, a way to help her make sense of her strange new world.

The princess's writings left me with more questions than ever, and I began to read more generally—about slavery in Muslim societies, about East Africa, about the Indian Ocean—to soon realize that Salme's story, and the story of the slave trade through Zanzibar, did not begin on the island but in Oman, a tiny country with an extraordinary history. Located on the southeastern edge of Arabia, where it was cut off from the rest of the peninsula by mountains and deserts, ancient Oman had developed a culture that was distinctly separate from that of other Arab peoples. Millennia before the birth of Christ, and again during the Middle Ages, Oman was one of the wealthiest and most powerful nations in the world, trading with other early civilizations such as Mesopotamia, Persia, India, and China. Oman also had its own distinct brand of Islam, Ibadhism, which is practiced virtually nowhere else in the world and is known for its great tolerance of other religions and races.

Salme's father, Seyyid Said Al Busaid, had been Oman's most remarkable modern ruler; with his ascent to power had begun an improbably romantic and ruthless century in Eastern history. During a reign that lasted fifty years, Seyyid Said established a loose commercial empire all along the East African coast, opened up international relations with Europe and the United States, moved his country's capital from the Arabian peninsula to Zanzibar, and transformed that once-sleepy island into both the clove-producing capital of the world and the center of the Indian Ocean slave trade. After Said's death, his legacy was carried on by his sons Seyyid Majid and Seyyid Barghash.

The story of the Zanzibar slave trade also began in Africa—but not just the Africa I was accustomed to reading about. There was also another Africa involved: the Africa of the Swahili, a highly developed people who, during the Middle Ages, established sophisticated, cultured cities all along the East African coast. Like the Omanis, the Swahili were seafarers—they shipped giraffes to Beijing, China, around 1415, to the astonishment of the Chinese, who had never seen giraffes before—

and were heavily involved in the slave trade, acting as middlemen between the Africans of the interior and the Arabs.

The Portuguese arrived in the Indian Ocean in the late 1400s, the English became a presence in the 1700s, and the Americans frequented the region from the 1820s to the era of the U.S. Civil War. Reading the letters and journals of some of the Westerners who were in the area during those centuries, I was struck by how convinced they all were that they knew what was best for the East and for Africa. They had God on their side. The world was their oyster. Shades of our own times.

Other aspects of the Zanzibar-Oman story also resonated in the twenty-first century, drawing me deeper into the historical tale. There was Salme herself—a strong, independent woman who flatly refused to obey the mores of her day. There was her father, Said—a man who not only reached out to the West, but who also took a determined stand against a violent Islamist sect that was threatening to destroy his rule. And there was Salme's brother Barghash, who shared his father's international outlook, only to be betrayed by the British.

Though when it came to betrayal, the Omanis were in no position to complain. Their history is studded with one gut-wrenching, near-unbelievable story of betrayal after another. In the heartless world of premodern Arab politics, it was often deceive or be deceived, kill or be killed.

To the modern sensibility, the violence that prevailed in the Arab region up to and through the 1800s boggles the mind. At times, hundreds and even thousands of innocents were brutally slaughtered—and not always by Muslim hands. The Portuguese were especially savage, at times burning to the ground entire mosques filled with worshippers.

As for slavery, Oman began using slaves sometime in prehistory, as did virtually every other ancient civilization. But because of their seafaring skills, the Omanis were especially complicit in the brutal institution. Their merchants and sea captains were probably involved in the slave trade as early as the 800s, when tens of thousands of East Africans, or "Zanj," as they were known, were toiling in the Euphrates valley of Mesopotamia—where they staged the greatest slave uprising in world history.

During the mid- to late 1800s, Seyyid Said and his sons—along with Arab and Swahili merchants, African chieftains, and Indian businessmen—escalated the slave trade in East Africa to unprecedented levels. During that period, more than a million Africans may have been transported from the interior to Zanzibar.

Oman's slave trade only ended at the instigation of the British, who pressured the Al Busaidi sultans into signing a series of anti–slave trade treaties. The process took decades and involved, directly or indirectly, an interesting cast of Western characters—explorers, missionaries, and journalists—all of whom spent much time in Zanzibar. The British presence on the island grew steadily, and in 1890 it became a British protectorate.

For most of the nineteenth century, the Al Busaidi sultans held sway over a loose empire that stretched for thousands of miles and incorporated dozens of peoples. During the family's rule, Islam reigned supreme in the region, the righteousness of the slave trade went unquestioned, and Zanzibar flourished. But by the time the nineteenth century was over, Christians controlled the Indian Ocean, the slave trade had been abolished, and the power of Zanzibar was no more.

The story of Seyyid Said and his children is both a personal and a public one, tracing as it does the rise and fall of both a family and an empire. It is a tale rich with modern-day themes: Islam vs. Christianity, religion vs. secularism, women's rights, human rights, multiculturalism, and a nation's right to construct its own destiny. The chronicle of the nineteenth-century Omanis is also a chronicle of the Indian Ocean slave trade, which runs like a polluted stream beneath a romantic surface. At times, Zanzibar itself mirrored the dichotomy: from afar, the paradise island beckoned with swaying palms and white-sand beaches; up close, the bodies of dead slaves clogged the harbors, creating an indescribable stench.

My research had begun with a simple phrase. But that simple phrase had been a key that opened many doors, revealing intriguing, complex stories within stories hitherto unknown to me and, I suspected, most Westerners. They were stories, I thought as I delved yet deeper into East African history, that needed to be told.

Author's Note

ALL OF THE DIALOGUE IN THIS BOOK COMES FROM PUBLISHED sources. In the Oman section, I quote from the translations of two traditional Arabic histories: *Annals of Oman to 1728*, which is a partial translation, by E. C. Ross, of Oman's first history book, *Kashf al-Ghummeh*, by Sirhan ibn Said ibn Sirhan; and *Imams and Seyyids of Oman* by Salil ibn Razik (or, more accurately, Humaid ibn Muhammad ibn Ruzayq), translated by George Percy Badger. Both books are a mix of legend and fact; Salil ibn Razik was also the panegyrist, or orator, for Seyyid Said, with prejudices that reflect that connection.

In the Zanzibar and Germany sections, I rely on quotes from Seyyida Salme's *Memoirs of an Arabian Princess* and *Letters Home*, as translated by E. van Donzel in *An Arabian Princess Between Two Worlds*. I decided to use van Donzel's translation of the memoirs rather than earlier editions because it contains passages that Salme later edited out and because his is the only published English translation of her letters. In the East Africa section, I use dialogue quoted in the books of such Western explorers and missionaries as Richard Burton, David Livingstone, and Henry Morton Stanley, and of the Swahili slave trader Tippu Tip.

Since there is no standard transliteration of Arabic into English, I have generally opted to use the simplest spellings available, and/or those most familiar to Westerners, for greater ease of reading. Exceptions include authors' names, which I spelled according to their preferences. I have also opted not to correct spelling and grammatical errors in most quotations, or use "[*sic*]," as I feel that the authors' uninterrupted original language adds texture and a sense of time and place to the narrative.

At the suggestion of Abdul Sheriff, author of *Slaves, Spices, and Ivory in Zanzibar*, I have used the terms "Indian Ocean slave trade" or "East African slave trade" rather than the often-seen "Arab slave trade" or "Islamic slave trade." As Professor Sheriff quite correctly and logically pointed out to me, the phrase "Atlantic slave trade," not "European slave trade" or "Christian slave trade," is common usage, and it is both curious and inaccurate to describe the slave trade of East Africa in ethnic or religious terms; many races and religions were involved.

PART ONE

❧

Oman

1

Beginnings

THE TIME IS 1806. THE PLACE IS A SULTAN'S CASTLE JUST OUTSIDE Barka, Oman, a port on the Arabian peninsula. Inside the castle sit two handsome teenage brothers: the gentle and bookish Salim and the decisive and ambitious Said. Beside them is their adviser Muhammad bin Nasir. Standing sentinel at the door is a tall Nubian slave.

Bedr, the boys' first cousin, enters the room and takes a seat between the brothers. Said admires the scabbard hanging by Bedr's side—a magnificent affair set with semiprecious stones. Yet even more magnificent is the point of the dagger within, Bedr says, and he takes it out for his cousins to admire. Silently, Said reaches for the weapon and then, swiveling suddenly, plunges it into his cousin's breast. The Nubian slave shuts the door.

Screaming with pain, Bedr staggers to his feet and throws himself out a window, to land upon a dung heap. Stumbling to the castle stable, he mounts a saddled horse—one is always at the ready, as is the Arab custom. He gallops toward the desert, where four hundred of his Wahhabi* supporters are quartered. Watching from an upstairs window, Said's aunt Bibi Mouza cries out for Said to go after him, and he does,

---

* Followers of the fundamentalist faith regard the word *Wahhabi* as pejorative; they prefer to be called *Muwahidun* (Unitarians) or just *Muslims* (as opposed to all the other nonbelieving Muslims). And some modern scholars and Islamic reformers prefer the term *Salafi* instead. I have chosen to use *Wahhabi*, however, because it was commonly used in Oman in the 1800s and because it is more familiar to Westerners.

accompanied by his brother, his adviser, other noblemen, and the Nubian slave. Galloping through a copse of date trees, they come upon the wounded man and knock him off his horse. Pouring blood, Bedr doggedly continues on foot toward the Wahhabi camp, now within sight. Said hesitates a moment, then stabs him dead.

Said and Salim are the sons of Seyyid Said bin Sultan Ahmed Al Busaid, who ruled Oman from 1793 to 1804. Bedr was plotting the brothers' own murders and would have succeeded were it not for the boys' perceptive and formidable aunt. Upon discovering Bedr's intentions, Bibi Mouza persuaded Said of the necessity of killing his cousin.

Six weeks after Bedr's murder, Said and Salim are declared the joint rulers of Oman. It will be Said alone, however, who will wield the power. He is fifteen years old—and, legend has it, will be haunted by his vicious act for the rest of his life, so much so that he will rarely sentence a subject to death.

The story of Seyyid Said bin Sultan Al Busaid and his children begins, as all stories begin, in history. But in the case of the Al Busaids, and of the Omanis in general, that history is many centuries old. Though today all but vanished from the world stage, Oman is one of the oldest and most unusual countries in the world.

A small nation, Oman lies at the southeastern edge of the Arabian peninsula, east of today's Saudi Arabia, south of the United Arab Emirates, and northeast of Yemen. A dramatic land of desert, mountain, and sea, Oman is centered on a stark, rugged chain of mountains—the Hajars—and is isolated from its neighbors by the vast, barren reaches of the Rub' al-Khali, or Empty Quarter, the great desert that also blankets much of Saudi Arabia. Geography is destiny: limited contact with other Arabs meant that from the beginning, the Omanis developed their own unique history and culture, including a singular brand of Islam called Ibadhism, and were more focused on the sea and foreign parts than they were on Arabia.

About two thirds of Oman is bounded by the sea. To its south and east are the Arabian Sea and the Indian Ocean, while to its north is the Gulf of Oman, which leads into the Persian Gulf—better known among Arabs as the Arabian Gulf. Directly north of Oman lies Iran, less than thirty-five miles away at the Strait of Hormuz, the narrowest point. As strategically important during Seyyid Said's time as it is today, the strait has witnessed the passage of everything from great argosies headed to ancient Mesopotamia to mammoth oil tankers headed to modern nation-states. As an old Arab proverb goes, "If the whole world were a ring, Hormuz would be the gem in it."

The sea has been central to Oman since the dawn of time. Centuries before the birth of Christ, the ancient Omanis were building boats sewn together with twisted coconut fibers and sailing for thousands of miles with the help of the powerful monsoon winds that blow between India and East Africa. Oman's strategic position at the entrance to the Persian Gulf, midway between India and Africa, also made it a coveted prize for foreign invaders ranging from the Persians to the Portuguese.

"Oman" today refers to the Sultanate of Oman, a modern nation with clearly defined borders, but during Seyyid Said's time, the term was used more loosely, to refer to a broad swath of territory centered on the country's northwestern mountains. The origins of the word *Oman*—or more correctly, *'Uman*—may derive from an Arabic term meaning "to stay in a place."

The forbidding Hajar Mountains, which run in a north-south arc along Oman's east coast, are the country's most striking geological feature. Arid and nearly devoid of vegetation, they rise naked and dark from the earth, the result of a violent upheaval from the ocean bed some one hundred million years ago. Twisted into strange contortions in parts, the largely limestone range changes color with the day—from burnt red to gray, pale green to tan, deep purple to black. In Seyyid Said's time, the Hajars were still well populated with gazelle, wildcat, lynx, and leopard, but already their numbers were dwindling.

In the heart of the Hajars soars the ten-thousand-foot-high Jabal Akhdar, or "Green Mountain," which is green only in relation to the desert. The crucible of Omani culture, the Jabal Akhdar is intertwined with deep valleys and high plateaus that have held small farming communities since as early as the fourth millennium B.C. Later settlements established around the mountain's base grew into some of Oman's most important towns and cities.

Wedged between the northern part of the Hajars and the sea is the fertile Batinah plain, stretching for about 150 miles in length and 5 to

30 miles in width. For centuries, thousands of towering dark green date palms have flourished here, beneath watchful eyes peering out from mud-brick towers and forts. Dates have long been the mainstay of Oman's food supply and economy, used to feed everyone from humans to camels and to purchase everything from spices to slaves. Even today, Oman is one of the world's largest producers of dates, harvesting about 265,000 tons a year.

On the edge of the Hajars south of the Batinah lies Muscat, or "place of anchorage," Oman's capital since the 1780s and one of its few large natural harbors. Muscat is "one of the most picturesque places in the world," wrote one nineteenth-century visitor. "From a distance, immense granite masses of rock, with jagged outline of cliff and crag, are seen rising in gloomy abruptness from the sea. . . . Plastered houses glitter against the somber background like a seagull's wing against an angry sky." A flourishing international port since well before the advent of Islam, Muscat—seductive, reclusive—was, until 1929, accessible only by boat and mountain footpaths.

Lacing the Hajars and the Batinah are the dry riverbeds known as *wadis*. The *wadis* run with water only in the late summer or early fall, when the surrounding mountain slopes gleam with wildflowers and a velvety sheen, and are peppered with oases.

Historically, the *wadis* have been Oman's lifelines, serving as the main transportation and communication routes between the country's interior and its coast, which are otherwise cut off from each other by the mountains. The most important *wadi* is the Sumail Gap, which separates the Western and Eastern Hajars, and is actually a series of several intertwining *wadis*. Guarded by watchtowers—raised fingers along the way—the Sumail Gap is bordered by a mountaintop shaped like a ship. Local legend has it that a group of foreign sailors once tried to depart Oman before paying a young girl for their provisions. She complained to her sheikh, who pulled the ship back against the wind, up the mountain, as a punishment and warning for all to see.

At the northernmost end of the Hajars, jutting out into the Strait of Hormuz, is the Musandam peninsula, where Seyyid Said's father was slain by the so-called pirates who once flourished on this coast. Now separated from Oman proper by the United Arab Emirates, the dark, hulking peninsula rises nearly a mile above the sea and is cut by deep, narrow, fjord-like inlets, similar to those found in Norway. Musandam's easternmost point is known as the Cape of the Graves of the Indians, named for the many Indian merchant vessels that were once shipwrecked on its shores. Treacherous winds and currents meant that those who attempted to sail directly through the Strait of Hormuz—or miscalculated their route, the weather, or the sea—often met their deaths on Musandam, Arabic for "anvil."

To the west and south of the Hajars begins the country's second most striking geological feature—its deserts, which cover about two thirds of today's Oman. Only a small portion of this territory is desert in the classic sense of golden sands and rolling dunes; most is simply barren inhospitable land, with habitats ranging from arid plains to boulder fields to salt flats.

The most famous of Arabia's deserts, the Rub' al-Khali, begins in Oman's far west. The world's largest sand desert, covering 225,000 square miles—most of today's Saudi Arabia—the Empty Quarter receives almost no rainfall and holds few settlements. Along its edges live dozens of Bedouin tribes, known among the Arabs as the Bedu.

Throughout most of human history, Arabia's deserts went largely ignored by everyone but the Bedu. With the arrival of oil companies on the peninsula in the mid-1900s, the desert suddenly took on a far greater importance, but only modest oil reserves have been found in Oman.

Finally, to Oman's far southwest is Dhofar, a large, distinctive region that has at times functioned as a separate state. The Dhofari people differ from the Omani people both physically and linguistically, and their land differs as well. Its rolling hills and plateaus, surrounded by mountains, receive the rains of the summer monsoons and for months every year, Dhofar's slopes are thick with mists. Along its coastal beaches, coconuts, bananas, and papayas grow. Dhofar fell under loose Omani rule about a thousand years ago, but when Seyyid Said rose to power, it was governed by a renegade merchant prince infamous for piracy and smuggling.

Seyyid Said lived most of his formative years and first decades in power on the Omani coast, where he absorbed what was by then a prosperous, cosmopolitan maritime atmosphere. But always at his back were the mountains and the deserts, harboring forces that threatened to bring down his rule, his family, and his empire.

During Seyyid Said's time, and still in many ways today, Oman was a land of fiercely independent tribes. Numbering in the hundreds and varying widely in size, degree of influence, and cohesiveness, most of the tribes were organized around a common ancestor and had a great deal of autonomy, often going their separate ways when they disagreed with the country's ruler. Each tribe was led by a sheikh, who represented it during negotiations or conflicts with outsiders. The sheikh was usually a member of an elite family, but the office was not hereditary. He was chosen by a consensus of his peers.

The tribes of Oman were of two types: the Hadr, or settled, and the Bedu. The Hadr were the country's farmers, craftsmen, teachers, religious leaders, and merchants, living in villages, towns, and cities under the rule of Sharia, or Islamic law. The Bedu were the country's camel breeders, herdsmen, and semi-nomads, living at the edges of the settlements and deserts under the rule of tribal law.

As with most tribal peoples, the Omanis were never an easy people to rule. Wrote one early chronicler: "Now the people of Oman are endowed with certain qualities, which it is my hope they may never lose. They are people of soaring ambition, and of haughty spirit; they brook not the control of any Sultan, and are quick to resent affront; they yield only to irresistible force, and without ever abandoning their purpose."

In the second half of the first millennium B.C., the wealthy Greek and Roman empires began trading with Dhofar, Oman's often-independent southwestern region. Dhofar is one of the only areas in the world where the frankincense tree grows. Then in great demand throughout the lands of the Mediterranean, Dhofar's frankincense was collected by slaves and loaded onto ships that headed north to the Mediterranean through the Red Sea.

The Greeks and Romans used frankincense—believed by the ancient Egyptians to be the sweat of the gods fallen to earth—for religious and medicinal purposes, burning it on altars, using it in embalming and to ward off evil, and flaunting it as a sign of power and wealth. In the first century A.D., the Roman historian Pliny remarked that Emperor Nero had burnt more incense at his wife's funeral than all of Arabia produced in a year. Pliny also noted that the people of southern Arabia—meaning Yemen and Dhofar—were the wealthiest in the world. And wealthy they would remain until the fourth century A.D., when the spread of Christianity, which did not use incense at first, brought about the collapse of the frankincense trade.

Not all of the early frankincense traders transported their cargo on sailing ships; some traveled overland, via camel caravan routes established in Arabia as early as 2000 B.C. These caravans traveled from one oasis to the next, allowing for man and camel to replenish themselves before moving on to the next stop—often weeks away. One of the most famous of these stops was the legendary lost city of Ubar, believed to have been located in southern Oman. Mentioned in the Quran, Ubar dazzled visitors with its precious metals, jewels, and monuments. The city flourished for thousands of years, until God destroyed it for its greed and wanton ways—or so the pious believe. Excavations near Shisr in southern Oman have revealed a walled settlement, surrounded by smaller settlements, which was suddenly destroyed when its underground water caverns collapsed, plunging the town into an enormous sinkhole.

During the sixth century B.C., northern Oman was seized by the Persians, then ruled by the Achaemenid king Cyrus the Great, who established an empire that at one point reached as far east as India and as far west as the Aegean Sea. The Persians would occupy Oman, except for relatively brief intervals, for the next 1,200 years. Their presence was greatly resented by the Omanis, but they gave the country an important gift whose value cannot be overestimated: an ingenious irrigation system made up of underground water channels. Known as *qanat* in Persian and as *falaj* (sing.) and *aflaj* (pl.) in Arabic, the channels were dug twenty yards or more beneath the ground's surface and drained the water from the mountainsides into the arid regions, transforming desert into habitable land. By the time the Persians left Oman, the country boasted about ten thousand *aflaj*, many of which are still in operation today.

* * *

Little is known about the people who lived in Oman when the Persians arrived, but they left behind dozens of fine beehive-shaped burial structures dating back to the third millennium B.C., and may have spoken various dialects of a common language now known as Arabic. The first Omani settlers whose name is recognized today may have belonged to the Yaaruba tribe, of the Azd people, who are said to have begun appearing in the country in the eighth century B.C., trekking north from Yemen's Hadramawt Valley. But the great migration of the Azd occurred later, perhaps during the late second or early third century A.D., and perhaps due to an early collapse of the mighty Marib dam—a seismic event in Arab history.

First constructed around 1700 B.C., and rebuilt about eleven centuries later by the Sabaeans, an ancient people mentioned in the Bible, the Marib dam was located northeast of Sanaa, the capital of today's Yemen. At times measuring about 2,000 feet long by as much as 50 feet high, the dam was built of huge stone blocks held together with metal clamps and contained a two-mile-long lake. Sluices drained the dam's water into a large tank below, where it was used to cultivate the countryside and to provide Marib city with water. During its heyday, Marib city was the largest and wealthiest metropolis in Arabia, home to powerful merchants engaged in the India-Egypt trade.

Signs of the dam's deteriorating condition were obvious for many years but went ignored by local leaders, who were too busy fighting each other to pay much attention to domestic affairs. According to legend, a rat undermined the weakened structure, and it collapsed, causing mile upon mile of death and destruction. Survivors fled to other parts of Arabia, including Oman, and neither the dam nor the city was ever rebuilt. Today, the dam's ruins, still in excellent condition, are Arabia's foremost archaeological attraction.

According to Oman's earliest history book, the *Kashf al-Ghummeh*, or "Dispeller of Grief," the first Azd to arrive in Oman was one Malik bin Fahm. But Malik fled his homeland not because of the bursting of the Marib dam or other disaster, but because of a barking dog—or so wrote the book's author, in a national narrative that includes both legend and lore. The dog belonged to Malik's neighbor, who was under Malik's protection, and was killed by Malik's nephew. Malik's brother defended his son's actions and Malik, a man of great honor, exclaimed that he could no longer live in a country "where a person under his protection suffered such treatment."

Malik then gathered his tribe together and led them across the desert. Many months later, they arrived in Qalhat, a port on the southern Omani coast. En route, Malik was warned of the Persians living in northern Oman and, leaving most of his tribe in Qalhat, he headed farther north in hopes of negotiating peace. But the Persians refused his proposition, saying "we do not wish this Arab to settle amongst us, that our land should become straitened unto us; we have no need of his neighbourship." To which Malik replied, "I must positively settle in the district of Oman; if you accord me willingly a share of the water, produce, and pasture, I shall settle in the country and praise you. If, however, you refuse, I shall remain in spite of you. If you attack me, I shall resist you, and if I prevail against you, I shall slay you, and carry off your offspring, and shall not allow one of you to remain in Oman."

Still, the Persians refused to welcome the Azd. With an army numbering thirty or forty thousand, and a contingent of war elephants, they saw no reason to negotiate with the newcomers. Malik declared war and gathered together his men, numbering only about six thousand. The two forces faced off near the town of Nizwa. Malik mounted a piebald charger and he and his officers headed into battle, clad in body armor and iron helmets worn beneath red robes and yellow turbans.

The Persians advanced, their war elephants in front. The Arabs attacked the animals with swords and spears, piercing their hides until the elephants turned in flight, trampling Persians underneath. The two armies fell upon each other, to "fight with fury, and nothing could be heard but the clashing of their weapons." The battle raged for two days, but on the third day, Malik slew the Persian commander in one-on-one combat, and the Persians withdrew from Oman.

Malik then established the first Arab kingdom of Oman, with Qalhat—later destroyed by the Portuguese—as its capital. He attracted many other Azd tribes to the region until "they became numerous therein, and their power and fame increased." No other Arab leader dared oppose him and he reigned for seventy years, until his accidental death at the age of 120, at the hand of his favorite son.

As the story goes, Malik required his sons to take turns keeping guard over his house at night. His favorite son was Salimah, to whom he taught archery "until he excelled in the art." Salimah's brothers envied their sibling and conspired against him, telling their father that Salimah habitually deserted his post at night in order to sleep. Malik dismissed the accusation at first, saying that he knew his son too well to believe such a thing. But then—oh, fickle human heart!—doubts grew in his mind. He decided to test his son. One night while Salimah was on duty, Malik donned a disguise and left his house. At that fateful moment, Salimah nodded off for a brief nap. He awoke to the neighing of his mare and assumed that an enemy was approaching. Knowing that horses point their ears in the direction of sound, he aimed an arrow between his mare's ears. Malik heard the whoosh of the arrow as it was released and called out, "Do not shoot, my son, I am your father." But it was too late. The arrow entered his heart.

As Malik died, he uttered a verse that has become proverbial among all Arabs, and is all too reflective of their history:

> I taught him every day the bowman's art.
> And when his arm grew strong he pierced my heart.

2

Muscat

DURING THE FIRST THIRTY-ODD YEARS OF HIS FIVE DECADES IN power, from 1806 to 1856, Seyyid Said lived mostly in Muscat, in a whitewashed palace facing the sea. At the time, Muscat was a walled city about a mile in circumference, packed onto a small plain surrounded by sheer, serrated peaks. The city's neat, elegant, light-colored walls contrasted sharply with the darkness of the mountain range.

Hemmed in on all sides, Muscat was a crowded city, with an estimated population of ten to twelve thousand. Built around a web of narrow, crooked alleyways and streets, it contained dozens of tall stone houses, several hundred smaller stone-and-mud houses, and more than a thousand huts built of date tree branches and leaves plastered with mud. Outside the city walls huddled hundreds more huts, housing another three to four thousand people who slept on simple mats, ate out of earthen pots, and burned camel dung for fuel. During the country's infrequent rains, large parts of the city and its suburbs floated away—discarded lives.

But rich or poor, residing in stone houses or mud huts, most citizens of Muscat considered the town's crowded conditions to be a small price to pay for living in what was one of the safest and most tolerant cities in the Middle East. Seyyid Said, like most Omani rulers before him, welcomed all peoples to his capital, and all were free to build houses of worship and live and pray as they pleased. The city was filled with foreigners of every description: Hindus from Gujazat, Parsis from Bombay, Sindhis and Baluchis from the Makran coast, Persians from Bushehr,

Arabs from Syria and Bahrain, Armenians and Kurds from Mesopotamia, and Jews from Baghdad. When Rabbi Jacob Samuel visited
Oman in 1835, he found 350 Jewish families living on the fertile Batinah plain.

Muscat's extraordinary harbor—"the most wonderful that nature
and art could ever devise"—was a deep semicircle surrounded by rock.
On a typical day, it would be filled with a half-dozen merchant ships,
thirty or forty small craft loading or unloading those ships, perhaps
twenty-five small vessels en route to India under the protection of a
frigate, and dozens of fishing boats. Many of the fishermen cast their
nets directly offshore, where the water was sometimes red with crab,
and others stayed right in the harbor, where herring and pilchard were
"thick as gnats on a summer's evening." Hawks, gulls, and sea swallows
circled overhead.

When the sea was calm and smooth enough, it reflected Muscat's
dark hills and two whitened forts near its harbor entrance; when the
water swelled, the picture rolled toward land. At noon, as the day's heat
became unbearable, Muscat fell completely silent. A long, slight canoe
with a lone fisherman might pass by, followed by a *balaga*, a large vessel with an elevated stern, manned by a crew of many races, some
singing and banging on drums as they worked. As the *balaga* passed the
harbor, guns fired, breaking the sun-baked silence. The sounds reverber-
ated in the surrounding hills, rat-tat-tatting in quick succession, and secondary echoes sounded from more distant mountains. Finally, complete
silence reigned once more.

Seyyid Said's palace, built of coral stone and lime, stood just off the
beach near the center of town. Inside, airy apartments opened onto a
central courtyard. Outside, a wide veranda overlooked the sea, and it
was here that Seyyid Said held court every morning and afternoon, receiving everyone from international emissaries to ordinary townspeople
and Bedu. Anybody could come before him with a concern or
complaint—and many did. Like many Arab rulers of his time, Seyyid
Said committed his share of atrocities when dealing with his enemies
but was a just and liberal ruler at home, beloved by his people, especially as he grew older.

An often grave man of average size, Seyyid Said had an open and
pleasant face, light brown skin, and dark and expressive eyes framed

with heavy eyelids and long lashes. When he was a young man, his beard was full and black and his mustache clipped short. Gentlemanly and communicative, polite and generous, and receptive to new ideas and influences, he understood Arabic, Hindustani, and Persian, and later in life, Swahili and probably English.

Seyyid Said dressed simply and elegantly, in a white cotton, ankle-length *dishdasha*. A *furakha*, or short tassel, scented with perfume—an Omani trademark—dangled at the right side of his robe's neckline, while on his head perched a fine blue-checked turban framed by red, green, and yellow threads. At his waist was a cloth belt, into which he tucked a curved dagger, or *khanjar*, which was carried by all Omani men at all times. Sometimes, too, Seyyid Said wore a ruby ring, but otherwise, unlike most Eastern sovereigns of his day, he wore no jewels or ornaments of any kind. During cooler months, he donned a dark-colored embroidered cloak, or *bisht*, over his *dishdasha*.

Westerners who met Seyyid Said were usually very impressed by him, especially as the years went by and he accrued more gravitas and power. One 1819 visitor opined that the ruler had "the most agreeable and polite manner of any Arabian or Persian I have ever met," while a 1835 visitor noted the sultan's "mild yet striking countenance" and said that "he is the most respected prince in the East." A sea captain who met Said in Muscat shortly before his death remarked that he had "so much firmness, honesty of purpose, kind feeling, and decision of character . . . that your esteem is won at once. One of the noblest looking men I have seen in the East." The explorer Richard Burton called the ruler "as shrewd, liberal and enlightened a prince as Arabia has ever produced."

Seyyid Said often held court with only a handful of ministers or family members present. He rose to meet his visitors, and treated both high- and lowborn with equal respect, as did most Omanis. The egalitarian manner of the Ibadhis, practitioners of the Muslim faith unique to Oman, was a quality remarked upon again and again by Western visitors.

Seyyid Said's simple ways did not extend to hospitality, however—he greeted guests with elaborate spreads of fruits, sweetmeats, and drinks, served in cut crystal and laid out on elegant European tablecloths. Tea, sweet and black, was usually served, followed by coffee, bitter and very strong, with a touch of cardamom. Accompanying the coffee were dates, served fresh or dried and sometimes sprinkled with cumin. The Omanis produced more than twenty varieties of dates and used them in everything, from salads to meat dishes to desserts.

Next door to Seyyid Said's palace was the customhouse, where merchants and sea captains brought their cargoes to be recorded and taxed. Seyyid Said used the customhouse revenues to pay all personal and governmental expenses. The Omani citizens paid no country or city taxes.

Crowding the customhouse during daylight hours were hundreds of men of a dozen races; Muscat's thriving trade was even more of an international draw than was its tolerance. Arabs, Hindus, Turks, Jews, Persians, and Baluchis—all were there, packed into a small outdoor square with one side open to the sea. Muscat's most important merchants began assembling at the customhouse in the early morning, just after prayers, some taking seats on benches, some on rusty cannons, and some on coils of rope. Stroking their beards, counting their prayer beads, they appeared to be engaged in idle gossip, but were in fact negotiating deals, some involving substantial sums. Among other things, ships coming into port carried pearls from Bahrain; coffee from Yemen; copper from Basra; gold, ivory, ostrich feathers, and slaves from Zanzibar; and muslin, spices, timber, rice, and porcelain from India and China.

Next door to the customhouse was a partially covered bazaar selling everything from silks and linens to glass beads and bracelets to sugar and dried shark fins. Top-quality produce for sale included grapes, mangoes, peaches, plantains, pomegranates, figs, melons, limes, eggplants, potatoes, and onions.

In the bazaar's open sheds worked Muscat's artisans—blacksmiths, coppersmiths, rope makers, carpenters, and weavers. The blacksmiths sat with their anvils and hammers between two holes in the ground—one for fire, the other for water—and weavers worked their looms while sitting in holes in the ground. Barbers wandered about carrying stools, cups, mirrors, and razors, to give their customers shaves and manicures, or crack the joints of their arms, fingers, and legs. Blind beggars were everywhere.

Most Omani Arab men dressed as simply as Seyyid Said, in white *dishdashas* with scented tassels, open sandals, blue-checked cotton turbans, and *khanjars*. Virtually all men had beards, some wore turquoise rings, and others stained their feet and palms red with henna. Some also applied a narrow stripe of silvery white antimony to the outer edges of their eyes, to increase their sparkle and, it was believed, to improve sight. One admiring European wrote: "The people of Muscat seemed to me to be the cleanest, neatest, best dressed, and most gentlemanly of all the Arabs that I had ever yet seen."

The exceptions were the very poor, of whom there were many. They went about half naked, with "a leathern girdle which keeps their rags together; this ligature is so tight that it forms a cicatrix on the skin of the loins and serves to hold paper, an inkstand, a knife; in short, whatever they possess; for an Arab, like another Diogenes, usually carries all his worth upon his person."

Poorer women went out unveiled, but the rare elite woman on the streets flowed along in voluminous black, her body, face, and hands completely covered. Underneath, however, she wore a bright exotic ensemble consisting of a loosely fitted tunic that fell just below her knees, baggy trousers gathered at her ankles, and a sweeping embroidered headscarf, the *lihaf*, that reached to her calves. Ornate silver and gold stitching embroidered her tunic and trousers, silver bangles clinked on her wrists, and toe rings and platform sandals, called *qurhat*, adorned her feet.

Here and there roamed the Bedu, in town for the day only, to shop for supplies. Regarded by the Muscati people as more foreign than the actual foreigners—"a wild race not to be trusted," some said—the Bedu tended to be smaller and more wiry than the town Arabs, with quick, energetic features and long unkempt hair that hung to their shoulders. They wore coarse shirts tied around their waists with leather cords and carried short spears.

Other peoples could also be identified by their dress. The Baluchis, many of them soldiers recruited by Seyyid Said, were often bare to the waist, and carried daggers, sabers, polished rhino shields, and primitive guns nearly as long as they were. The Hindus, or Banyans, Muscat's largest foreign group, comprising about 10 percent of its population, wore white tunics with long sleeves and red slippers with turned-up toes in winter, and white cloths wound around their waists and legs in summer. Most also shaved their heads, except for the crowns, and wore high red turbans.

According to one nineteenth-century European visitor, Muscat had no public baths, coffeehouses, or mosques—but the mosques, at any rate, did exist. Then, as now, and in keeping with other modest aspects of the Ibadhi faith, the sect's mosques had no domes or minarets and so looked like ordinary buildings to the unpracticed eye. From the outside, only a small angled wall where the *mihrab*, or niche facing Mecca, was located gave a mosque away. Indeed, most Muscat residents were very religious—the Omanis were one of the first peoples to convert to Islam.

By the time of the birth of the Prophet Muhammad in A.D. 570, the Omani coast was prospering. Muscat, Qalhat, Sohar, and a half-dozen other coastal towns were regular ports of call for Indian Ocean–going vessels, and Omani merchants were among the wealthiest businessmen in the Eastern world.

However, the Persians, now ruled by Sasanian kings, were back in the country. Rising to power in A.D. 224, the Sasanians had established their capital, Ctesiphon, in the fertile crescent of today's Iraq, and soon thereafter, sought control of the Gulf of Oman. They had seized the northern Omani port of Sohar, which they renamed Omana, and had developed it into a major market center. A Persian governor and army forces were in residence there, while Persian administrators lived nearby. The Persians allowed the northern Omanis to go about their business much as before, but forced them to pay hefty taxes. Meanwhile, Oman's southern coast and its interior remained in the hands of the Arabs. The two peoples had signed a treaty and peace prevailed.

The Arabs practiced a casual pagan religion. Gods and goddesses were believed to be embodied in springs, stones, trees, and other natural objects, while good and evil spirits were thought to inhabit the shape of animals. The spirit of a murdered man or woman, for example, was believed to haunt his or her grave in the form of an owl, crying out for revenge.

Good and bad witches—both male—also roamed the earth, a belief still held by some Omanis today. The bad witches owned hyenas, which they rode only at night, after summoning them with a special call. The witches dressed in clothes that were eaten by the animals and with-drawn from their anuses.

According to tradition, the first Omani to convert to Islam was Mazin bin Qadhubah al-Tay. One day while making a sacrifice to a stone idol, Mazin heard a voice telling him that a messenger had come to Medina to reveal the "true faith" to humankind. The same thing hap-pened a few days later, causing Mazin to travel to Medina, where he met the Prophet Muhammad, converted to Islam, and asked the Prophet to pray for all the people of Oman.

And so it was that in A.D. 630, the Prophet sent his envoy, Amir bin al-As, to meet with the most powerful sheikhs of Oman, the Julanda brothers. Amir carried with him a letter from the Prophet, the text of which is kept in the manuscript section of the Omani Ministry of Na-tional Heritage and Culture:

> From Muhammad the Messenger of God to Jayfar and 'Abd the sons of al-Julanda. Peace be upon him who follows the right path. To continue, I call upon you both to accept Islam. Become Mus-lims and you will be safe. For indeed I am God's Messenger to all Mankind. . . . If you both accept Islam I will give you authority to rule, but if you refuse, then your sovereignty will pass from you and my cavalry will occupy your country and my prophethood will gain supremacy over your sovereignty.

The Julanda sheikhs agreed readily to Muhammad's terms, perhaps more for political than religious reasons, as word of the Prophet's con-quest of Mecca and the submission of other tribes to Islam had already reached Oman. The brothers then sent out messengers among their people, admonishing them to abandon idolatry and embrace Islam. They apparently did so with little protest. Said the Prophet Muham-mad some time later, "I know one of the Arab lands that is called Oman which is by the sea coast. One Haj [pilgrimage to Mecca] from Oman is better than two from other places."

In contrast to the Arabs, the Persians already had their own religion—Zoroastrianism, founded sometime between 1000 and 700 B.C.—and flatly rejected Islam. Incensed, the Prophet's envoy urged the Omanis to take action against them. They needed little prodding. The

Omanis had been longing to oust their occupiers for over four centuries but had lacked the military and psychological strength necessary to do so. Now, with the force of the Prophet behind them, the Omanis quickly recaptured Sohar and other northern towns, forcing the Persians to withdraw from Oman. By the time of the Prophet's death in A.D. 632, Oman, along with the rest of the Arabian peninsula, was almost entirely Arab and Muslim. The only significant exceptions were the foreign merchants and sailors living in the ports.

The Prophet had appointed no heir, and with his passing, only a year after Oman's conversion, came a critical time for Islam. Civil wars erupted and factions developed as Muslims disagreed as to who should become the Prophet's successor, or caliph. Muhammad's only living child, Fatima, had married the Prophet's cousin and first convert, Ali, and some felt that he was the logical choice for caliph. But instead, the caliphate fell first to Abu Bakr, a close companion of Muhammad, and then to Omar and Othman, two other close companions. Ali did not assume the mantle of the Prophet until 656.

During the reign of the first three caliphs, many leaders in Mecca had become corrupt, neglectful of their religious duties, and enormously wealthy. Ali, in contrast, lived a simple and modest life, preaching that all believers are created equal and speaking out against the social injustice that he saw all around him. Not surprisingly, much of his support came from the poor, whereas many of the elite bitterly resented his growing power. Thereafter, the Muslims would fall into two camps: those who believed that the caliph should be chosen by consensus from Muhammad's clan, as the first three caliphs were, and those who believed that he should be related to the Prophet, as Ali was. The first group became known as the Sunnis, who today comprise between 85 and 90 percent of the world's 1.3 billion Muslims; and the second, the Shiites, who comprise between 10 and 15 percent, and live mostly in Iran and southern Iraq.

A third and infinitely smaller group soon also arose, out of Ali's camp. Shortly after Ali ascended to the caliphate, he became entangled in a bitter civil war with Muawiya, the governor of Syria. As the battles between the two dragged on, with no resolution in sight, Ali agreed to submit to arbitration. That decision outraged some of his followers, who believed that since Ali's authority came directly from God, any sort of compromise meant going against God's will. This group, who became known as the Kharijites ("Seceders"), broke off from Ali's camp, to settle in Basra in what is now southern Iraq.

Rejecting both Ali's and Muawiya's claims to leadership, the Kharijites proclaimed that the imam, or head of the community, should be the person best suited for the job, regardless of his tribe or family. No man had an inherent right to rule; God was the only lawmaker and sovereign. But as promising as this egalitarian precept sounds, the sect also took harsh, uncompromising positions in many areas of Islamic law. They assassinated Ali and any follower who did not meet their strict standards was excommunicated and usually executed—an approach that led to the group's near-extinction only a hundred years later.

From the Kharijite camp, however, broke off several more moderate leaders. Among them was Abdullah bin Ibadh al-Tamimi, who established Ibadhism, the sect that came to dominate Oman. Ibn Ibadh endorsed the Kharijite insistence on electing an imam according to his merits alone, but also advocated a return to Islam's original values, including good personal conduct, strong spiritual values, and tolerance of all creeds and tribes. And such tolerance became the trademark of the Ibadhis, even as they themselves were persecuted, first by other Kharijites and then by the Sunnis.

In the beginning, the Ibadhis were allowed to live peacefully in Basra, where they were organized by an Omani merchant named Jabir bin Zaid. As the sect became more vocal in its criticisms of the reigning Umayyad dynasty, however, persecution began. Many of the group's leaders were imprisoned or sent into exile in Oman, and the movement went underground.

Among those exiled to Oman, in the mid- to late 600s, was Jabir bin Zaid, who is generally credited with spreading the sect's faith throughout the country. Less than a hundred years after his arrival, Ibadhism was the dominant Muslim faction in interior Oman, perhaps spreading so quickly because of a vacuum created by tribal conflict; the faith spread much slower along the country's more cosmopolitan coast. But by the time Seyyid Said came to power in the early 1800s, Oman had become the only country in the world where Ibadhism was widely practiced,* thus reinforcing the country's isolation from the rest of Arabia, and the rest of the Muslim world.

Ibadhism's call for a return to Islam's original values means that, despite its central egalitarian premise, the sect is an Islamist and deeply conservative group. As a peaceful and tolerant faction of Islam, however, it has, in effect, kept other more violent Islamist sects from developing in Oman to this day.

Like Sunni and Shiite Islam, Ibadhism takes the Five Pillars of Islam as its main tenets: Shahada, or pronouncement of faith; Salat, daily prayer; Zakat, almsgiving; Sawn, fasting; and Hajj, the pilgrimage to Mecca, which every Muslim should attempt to make in his or her lifetime. Religious and secular life is lived according to Sharia, or Islamic law, and there is no separation of church and state. For the most part, too, Ibadhis follow the same *hadiths*, or sayings of the Prophet, as do the Sunnis—though there are some separate Ibadhi *hadiths*—and subscribe to similar laws of marriage, inheritance, ritual, and taxation. The principal differences between the Ibadhis and the followers of the two main sects lie in theology, in such areas as the possible visibility of God in this world and man's relationship to God. Sunnis believe, for example, that people can be rescued from hell; Ibadhis, that damnation is eternal. Also, unlike traditional Sunnis and Shiites, who believe the Quran to be the literal word of God, the Ibadhis believe that the holy book can be interpreted.

The Ibadhis regard the Sunnis, Shiites, and all other Muslims as nonbelievers, but do not endorse hostility toward them or toward the followers of any other religion. Hostile action is reserved for one person and one person alone: an unjust imam. In Oman that title is used only for the country's ruler, not for other religious leaders, as is the case in many other Muslim countries.

The traditional Ibadhi imam was expected to be an extraordinarily versatile man—an outstanding military ruler and administrator, as well as religious scholar and spiritual leader. His many duties included supervising tax collection and state revenues, appointing governors and *qadis* (judges), enforcing Sharia, providing for the public's welfare, and

---

* This is still the case today, although small numbers of Ibadhis also live in Libya, Tunisia, and Algeria.

commanding the army. His power was far from absolute, however, as all his duties derived from Sharia, and he was expected to confer with the *ulema*, or religious leaders, and tribal chiefs on all matters of importance. His success, therefore, depended greatly on his skill in dealing with other men. Trickiest of all was maintaining the support of the country's many different tribes, all of which had different agendas.

The early Ibadhis elected their imams in a two-step democratic process. First, the main tribal and religious leaders chose their candidate. He was then presented to the general public, who could in theory veto his appointment, though they virtually never did. Once in office, the imam had to be a good and just ruler. If he was not, it became the community's duty to depose him.

In the uncertain decades following the death of the Prophet, when the center of Islamic government moved from Medina to Damascus to Baghdad, Oman was left more or less alone by the caliphs. But about A.D. 697, the Umayyad caliph Abd al-Malik, the man who built the Dome of the Rock in Jerusalem, sent his armies to Oman, to bring it more directly under government control. His first two onslaughts failed, opposed by the forces of two ruling brothers, Said and Suleiman bin Abbad. But then the caliph tried again, with forces numbering 45,000, causing Said bin Abbad to describe his own small force in comparison with the enemy as "a white spot on the body of a black bull." A terrible slaughter ensued and Said and Suleiman, along with their families and followers, fled to the Land of the Zanj, or "Land of the Blacks," meaning East Africa, where they may have become Oman's first large-scale slave hunters.

The Umayyad dynasty collapsed in 750 and in the ensuing confusion, the Omanis declared their independence, and elected their first imam. Four years later, however, he was killed by the invading armies of Islam's new reigning dynasty, the Abbasids, ruled by Caliph Abu al-Abbas, a.k.a. "The Bloodshedder." According to tradition, Abu al-Abbas began his reign by inviting all the defeated Umayyad males to a banquet. The guests had no sooner taken their seats than they were murdered. The Bloodshedder then threw a leather cloth over their bodies and invited his counselors to partake of a meal spread out on its bumpy surface.

Another forty years passed before the Omanis, during a period of

Abbasid dynastic weakness, were able to elect their second imam. He proved to be an unpopular choice and was replaced two years later, in 795, by Imam Warith bin Kaab, who established Oman's first period of national unity and peace. About twelve years into his reign, however, the imam and seventy men were escorting a group of prisoners on a journey when the prisoners were caught in a *wadi* during a raging torrent. When no one would go to their rescue, the imam reportedly said, "Since they are in my charge and I shall be responsible for them at the day of Resurrection, I shall go across to them." He drowned in the attempt.

Imam Warith's reign marked the beginning of Oman's golden medieval age, during which the country's underground water system was improved; an organized navy was established; Omani ships began sailing as far away as China; and the northern Omani port of Sohar became the largest port in the Islamic world. A city of twelve thousand, it was "the hallway to China, the store house of the East"—and was said to be the hometown of Sinbad the Sailor. "It is not possible to find on the shore of the Persian Sea nor in all the land of Islam a city more rich in fine buildings and foreign wares than Sohar," wrote the medieval Persian geographer Abul Qasim Istakhri.

All the early Omanis wanted was to be left alone to practice their unique brand of Islam and to pursue their mercantile dreams, together with other like-minded peoples, no matter what their color or creed. And so it was, up until the time of Seyyid Said and his sons. Seyyid Said was never particularly interested in building a political empire or in spreading the Muslim word. He was always a merchant at heart, intent on making money for himself, his family, and his people.

3

Slavery

It begins when one finds things happening like a war being waged between one's own country and another: they do not kill the prisoners, but tie them with rope and take them to the town, saying to them, "You stay as our slaves." So they stay and marry among themselves. If they have children, the children are slaves just the same.

Or slavery comes about through a fine for murder. A man has committed a murder, but his people are all poor and he has no money, but he is forced to pay a fine and if he cannot do so he will be taken and sold, going as a slave to the place where the fine is claimed. And if the person he killed is a freeman, then the fine is a big one. If he has a brother or a maternal uncle, he will follow him into slavery.

Or an adulterer has slept with someone's wife, he is made to pay for the offence, and if he has nothing he will become a slave.

Or a witch has killed someone, and the person is known as a witch, so she is killed or goes to where she committed the murder (i.e., to the family of the deceased) and becomes a slave.

Or someone puts his child or his nephew in pawn, but has no money to redeem him, then he (the child or nephew) becomes a slave, but a man cannot pledge his wife nor sell her, even though there be much hunger. If he cannot feed her, she will leave him.

Prisoners-of-war, people in pawn, and adulterers, if their kinsmen have no money to redeem them, they become slaves. When Arabs go up-country or other slave-traders, they buy such slaves and bring them to the coast, and they sell them to other people. This is the origin of slavery.

—Anonymous nineteenth-century East African

JUST DOWN THE STREET FROM SEYYID SAID'S PALACE STOOD A
simple open square—the slave market. The Omanis' humane treatment
of others extended only so far.

Muscat's slave auctions usually took place in the late afternoon,
toward sunset. Then, the latest shipment of Africans, "well-oiled to
show off their smooth skin," were paraded through the streets, while
an auctioneer cried out their attributes and prices: "Number one—
handsome young man, five hundred *piastres*; number two—a little
older, but very healthy and strong, four hundred *piastres*."

After the parade, the Africans, most just off the boat from Zanzibar,
were lined up in rows on either side of the square, the men on one side,
the women on the other. The men were dressed in brightly colored
waistcloths, the women in cloths that covered their torsos. Buyers—all
male, of course—walked among the captives, feeling their bodies and
hair, and making minute, invasive inspections, often while exchanging
witticisms with each other. The slave bazaar was a place to see and be
seen for the Arab dandies of the day, who sauntered among the human
merchandise with their long beards well perfumed, their fine turbans
tightly rolled, and their silver-hilted *khanjars* glinting at their waists.

Nonetheless, once the slaves were sold, most were treated relatively
well—though there can be no such thing as a "good" slave system, of
course. Many became domestics, converted to Islam, and married other
slaves. Some were given small plots of land or taught a profession. "At
Muskat, it is certain, slaves are treated with a degree of humanity that
would do honour in our climes," wrote one visiting Englishman. "The
hardest work in which they are employed, is the plying of the small canoes. . . . They live at their master's, board and sleep under his roof, eating of his dish, and drinking of his cup."

Another Englishman noted that most slaves in Muscat who did not
die young eventually gained their freedom. He estimated that about a
quarter of the town's population were freed slaves and their depen-
dents.

The Omanis' relatively humane treatment of their slaves helped account for the fact, noted with surprise by visiting Westerners, that many
Omani Arabs were part African. The Omani men prized the Abyssinian
women in particular, and often took them as concubines. Under Islamic
law, children born to such a relationship were free and legitimate, and

had equal standing with a man's other children, born to his free wives. Many of Seyyid Said's surviving children, including four of the six sons who ruled Oman and Zanzibar after his death, were born to Abyssinian concubines.

The Arabs' use of African slaves began a millennium before the West's, and continued for more than a century after, with illegal remnants still in operation today. Some historians believe that the Arabs and other Muslim peoples enslaved as many as eleven million Africans over this long, 1,500-year period—almost as many as were abducted by the Europeans and Americans during the much shorter transatlantic slave trade of the 1500s to the 1800s.

During most centuries, however, the Eastern trade was very small scale, with the average dealer handling only a few slaves annually. One rough estimate puts the number of Africans transported across the Sahara, the Red Sea, and the Indian Ocean at about 7,200,000 for the millennium up to 1600—meaning an average of 7,200 a year. Most of those slaves were taken from North Africa by the Egyptians and other North African Arabs. Fewer than 1,000 a year came from East African ports.

During the 1600s and early 1700s, the North African trade increased somewhat, while the East African trade remained the same. But in the mid- to late 1700s, the East African trade jumped exponentially, to 4,000 to 6,000 annually. This was due primarily to French and Portuguese slave traders, who were providing labor for thriving sugar plantations on the French Indian Ocean islands of Bourbon (now Réunion) and Île de France (Mauritius). A growing international demand for ivory had also led to the increase in the trade—slaves were needed to carry the enormous tusks from the interior of Africa to the coast.

Then in the 1840s to 1860s, the East African trade jumped again, to between 15,000 and 20,000 slaves annually. This time, the increase was due to the region's burgeoning clove and grain plantations, accompanied by its assimilation into the world capitalist system. During the mid- to late 1800s, when Seyyid Said and his sons were in power, more than a million Africans may have been abducted from East and Central Africa to Zanzibar, with between a third and a half then shipped farther north—to Arabia, Turkey, Syria, the Persian Gulf, and India.

These figures represent the best estimates of modern scholars, but they remain only estimates. Far less research has been conducted into the slave trade of North and East Africa compared to that of West Africa—mostly because there are far fewer records, but also because much of the Muslim world has yet to confront, or even truly acknowledge, their complicity in the shameful commerce. The subject remains murky on many levels.

Contributing to the lack of clarity is the fact that slavery in the Muslim world was not as clearly defined as it was in the West, where a slave was a possession pure and simple, to be used or disposed of as the master saw fit. Under Islamic law, a slave was both a possession and a person, which meant that he or she had certain inalienable rights that most Muslim masters—though far from all—felt compelled to respect. A master was obliged to give his slaves medical attention when required, teach them about Islam, provide for their upkeep, and support them in their old age. A slave woman could not be separated from her young children or forced into prostitution, and no slave could be severely overworked or mistreated, though the definition of what that constituted was unclear. Masters were admonished to forgive their slaves "seventy times a day" and if they could not get along with them, to sell them to other masters. If a slave felt that he or she was being mistreated, he or she could—theoretically, at least—go before a *qadi* and ask to be sold. A slave woman who bore her master's child could no longer be sold or given away, and upon her master's death, became free.

"As to your slaves, male and female, feed them with what you eat yourself and clothe them with what you wear . . . ," said the Prophet Muhammad. "They are God's people like unto you and be kind unto them." Slaves may have been socially inferior, but they were not inherently inferior.

Social class and color lines were also less rigid in the East than they were in the West. Slaves belonging to the wealthy and powerful sometimes rose to high positions, especially in the military and government. In the 900s, a Nubian eunuch reigned as regent of Egypt for almost twenty years following the death of his master, and in India from the late 1300s through the mid-1400s, black eunuchs served as independent governors of a large province centered on the city of Jawnpur in northeastern India. In the first decades of the 1800s, before Seyyid Said moved to Zanzibar, he appointed two Abyssinian eunuchs in succession to serve as the island's governor.

Although slavery is sanctioned in the Quran, the Prophet urged his followers to free their slaves—to do so was considered to be an especially pious and praiseworthy act. Muslims could also atone for their sins by freeing their slaves, and many chose to do so, especially upon their deaths, leaving instructions behind in their wills. Seyyid Said freed all of his domestic slaves, numbering in the thousands, upon his death.

Slaves whose masters did not release them still had some recourse: they could buy their freedom, usually earning the necessary money by taking outside jobs. A master was not obliged to honor a slave's request to buy his or her freedom, but in the Quran, it is written: "And such of your slaves as seek a writing (of emancipation), write it for them if ye are aware of aught of good in them, and bestow upon them of the wealth of Allah which He hath bestowed upon you" (Surah 24:33).

All of which is not to say that slavery in Islamic societies was a benign institution—or that slaves in the East were content with their lot, as some Western observers, accustomed to the harsher policies of the Americas, believed. Some Muslim masters paid no attention to Islamic law and treated their slaves with savage brutality. Slaves could not marry or own property without the consent of their masters, or testify in court, and had little protection in criminal matters. The slave trade of East Africa—meaning the business of capturing and transporting the slaves—was as horrific as the slave trade of West Africa, with many abducted East Africans never living to reach the slave markets; an estimated 15 to 25 percent died en route. Thousands of other young male slaves, chosen to become eunuchs, died on the castration table. And even those slaves who had kind masters and achieved high status were still degraded citizens, forced to live out lives not of their own making, far removed from their homelands and kin. At times, there were as many recorded cases of runaway slaves in the East as there were in the West.

Despite frequent cohabitation between Arabs and Africans, and their societies' relatively fluid color line, racism was also an issue in the East, especially as the centuries progressed. The earliest Muslims did not seem to regard dark skin as a sign of inferiority. In fact, as the world's first universal religion, Islam actively embraced peoples of all races, with believers from all corners of the world coming together as equals in Mecca for the Hajj: "And of His signs is the creation of the heavens and earth, and the difference of your languages and colours" (Surah 30:22). But as Islam spread, and the religion's newly conquered European and Asian lands proved to be far more sophisticated than its African ones, black skin took on a more primitive and negative connotation. Those black slaves who rose to high positions or gave birth to future Arab leaders were almost always Abyssinians, or Ethiopians, a lighter-skinned and highly developed race that the Arabs had greatly respected since ancient times. Those black slaves who remained trapped in menial labor were virtually all dark-skinned Zanj, or Bantu-speaking blacks from East Africa south of Ethiopia.

But even toward the Zanj, the Muslims never practiced the sort of extreme racial oppression that once existed in the United States. Too many men and women of color held positions of power for such mistreatment to flourish.

Ironically, because the treatment of slaves in Muslim societies was for the most part fairly humane, slavery was harder to eradicate there than in the West. With fewer overt horrors to witness, and the fact that slavery was sanctioned in the Quran, Muslims rarely protested the practice and there was no real abolitionist movement. Many Islamic nations, including Zanzibar, only outlawed the institution in the 1890s or early 1900s—or later—because of pressure from the West. Slavery was not abolished in Oman until 1970; twentieth-century Omanis regarded slaves as essential for the profitable harvest of their date plantations, and the institution ended only after a palace coup that deposed Seyyid Said bin Taimur, himself the owner of hundreds of slaves, most imported from India and Pakistan.

Slavery appears to be as old as the human race itself; it was practiced in all the ancient civilizations of Asia, Africa, Europe, and the Americas. Reference to African slaves in particular can be found in the earliest of human records. Burial sites in Lower Egypt show that some ten thousand years ago, a Libyan race enslaved a Bushman population. But in all of these early societies, most slaves appear to have been prisoners of war—not deliberately ensnared and transported chattel. That custom apparently originated in a far more modern era.

Like their forefathers, the earliest Muslims also took their first slaves through conquest. And well into the Middle Ages, as the new faith spread from Arabia to central Asia, northern Africa, and eastern Europe, the conquerors had no shortage of white, black, and Asiatic prisoners at their disposal.

During the medieval era, most of Islam's white slaves were Slavs; the word *slaves* derives from the late Greek word *sklabos*, meaning "Slavic." Reputed to make excellent soldiers, servants, and eunuchs, the Slavs were transported overland and then across the Black Sea or Mediterranean, often with the help of avaricious Christian merchants from Venice. Centuries later, from the 1500s to the early 1800s, large numbers of Caucasians were abducted from the shores of the Black Sea, to be shipped to the slave markets of Aleppo (Syria) or Mosul (Iraq). Known as Circassians, the Black Sea slaves were highly prized, as they were a handsome people with dark hair and blue eyes.

Seyyid Said's daughter Salme was born to a Circassian slave, and in her memoirs, she describes how her mother was captured:

She had lived peacefully with her parents and her brother and sister, her father gaining a livelihood as a farmer. A war broke out, marauding bands marched through the country, and the entire family fled into a [cellar]. . . . Later, however, a wild horde invaded this place of refuge, slew the parents, and three Arnauts carried off the three children, galloping away on their horses. One Arnaut soon disappeared out of sight, taking away her elder brother; the other two, with my mother and her three-year-old younger sister, who constantly cried for her mother, kept together until the evening when they too parted, and my mother never heard any more of her brother and sister.

After the Middle Ages, as the Muslim conquests died down and the Christian states grew more powerful, supplying slaves to the Islamic world became more problematic. The Christian rulers were cracking down on the slave trade, and the Quran emphatically forbids the enslavement of fellow Muslims (or, at least those who are Muslim before enslavement; those who converted to Islam after enslavement remained slaves). But Africa, where most chiefs had limited power and most people still practiced a pagan religion, was fair and fertile game.

The ancient Egyptians had raided the Sudan for slaves as early as the fourth millennium B.C., and later, the ancient Greeks and Romans had fitfully done the same. But the massive exportation of black slaves only began with the Arabs. It was, notes historian Bernard Lewis, a tragic, "indirect and unintended consequence of one of the most important humanitarian advances brought about by [Islam]"—i.e., Islam's belief that all races are created equal.

The first written record of the deliberate export of East African slaves appears in *Periplus of the Erythraean Sea*, written around A.D. 100 by an anonymous author from Alexandria. The Erythraean Sea is the Red Sea, and the book is a guide to the trade and geography of the Red Sea, Persian Gulf, and Indian Ocean coasts. Describing busy commercial ties between East Africa and the outside world, the author tells of slaves of the "better sort"—meaning Abyssinians—being brought to Egypt in growing numbers. The Abyssinians had close connections with the Arabs, but there was a crucial difference—they were Christian, and thus candidates for slavery.

In the second century A.D., the Greek geographer Ptolemy confirmed the findings of the *Periplus* author, as did Chinese writers from the medieval period. But otherwise, there are few contemporary reports concerning any aspect of East Africa until the tenth century. The slave trade of East Africa must have increased substantially during the intervening period, however, because in the ninth century, tens of thousands of Zanj were toiling in the Euphrates valley of Mesopotamia.

In the Islamic world, both before and after the ninth century, slaves were used primarily for domestic or military purposes. In general, women were in greater demand than men, since there was more work for them—as cooks, wet nurses, housekeepers, maids, and concubines. Men of high rank sometimes had harems numbering in the thousands, while even ordinary tradesmen usually had a concubine or two. The Atlantic slave trade shipped about two men for every woman, whereas the slave trade of the East enslaved about two women for every man. Female slaves often commanded prices 40 to 75 percent higher than did men, and in North Africa, it was not uncommon to see slave caravans transporting only females, usually from the Sudan.

Some of the slave women became singers, musicians, or poets. Every great Muslim family had its own music and dance troupes, some of whose members may have trained in celebrated schools in Baghdad, Medina, or Córdoba.

Male slaves were used for everything from domestic work to pearl diving to agriculture. But in general, most Islamic countries already had their own large underclass to exploit for manual labor and, with limited arable land at their disposal, had little need for field hands on the scale later required by the Americas. However, there were exceptions, and the salt flats of Basra were one. Here, in the 900s, wealthy slave owners forced thousands of Zanj from East Africa to drain the salt marshes, prepare the ground for agriculture, and extract the salt for sale—all brutal tasks. Working together in gangs of five hundred to five thousand, the slaves lived in abysmal conditions, surviving on only a few handfuls of flour, semolina, and dates a day.

Into this arena of misery entered one Ali bin Muhammad. A messianic rebel and a Kharijite—the militant sect from which Ibadhism is derived—Ali had spent his youth wandering the deserts with nomadic tribes, writing poetry, and denouncing the self-indulgence of Islamic rulers. Returning to his hometown of Basra in September 869, he made his way to the slave camps, carrying a banner embroidered with a verse from the Quran, calling the faithful to "fight on the road of Allah." Speaking to the slaves about their deplorable conditions, Ali told them that "God would save them from it through him and that he desired to raise their status and make them master of slaves and wealth and dwellings." Ali bin Muhammad had no qualms about the morality of slavery as an institution—he was a rebel, not a reformer.

Ali's preachings spread rapidly from gang to gang as the Zanj took up his call. The Abbasids sent the black troops of their imperial armies against them, but instead of fighting, the troops deserted to join the movement, enriching it with both arms and trained men. Bedu eager to share in the spoils of war also joined the rebels, as did free peasants in revolt against their landlords.

Impressively, the Zanj and their allies defeated the Abbasid troops again and again, gaining more arms with each victory. No mercy was granted their prisoners; all were put to death—and their heads claimed as trophies. Once, the rebels even floated a whole boatload of heads downriver to Basra. The former slaves also plundered everything in their paths, seizing the houses of the rich and selling high-born women as concubines.

In 871, the Zanj captured Basra, killing everyone who failed to escape. Then the victorious rebels proudly paraded before their leader Ali, each holding the head of a victim by the hair in his teeth.

Ali was now strong enough to build himself a new capital, Mukhtara, or the "Chosen," on the salt flats. He minted his own coins and declared himself to be the new Mahdi, or messianic leader sent by Allah. He became known as al-Burku, or the "Veiled One," and during the next ten years succeeded in spreading his message as far away as Mecca, which the Zanj briefly seized in 880. In 879, the rebels came within seventy miles of Baghdad.

By the early 880s, however, the Abbasids had regrouped. The caliph's brother had recruited an enormous new army, which proceeded to defeat the Zanj in one battle after another, forcing them to retreat to their capital. A long siege began, during which the Abbasids catapulted over the walls by night the heads of those they captured. In 883, the rebels' capital fell and Ali's head was brought to Baghdad on a pole.

During the fourteen-year revolt, the greatest slave uprising in world history, an estimated half a million people died. And afterward, Baghdad and other Abbasid cities began to decline in power, which led to a smaller demand for East African slaves. The demand would not rise precipitously again until the late 1700s.

Many of the Zanj slaves who worked the Mesopotamian salt flats may have arrived in Basra on the Omani sailing ships that traveled with the monsoon winds. Blowing northeast between October and March, and southwest between April and September, the winds could take a ship from as far south as Madagascar on the African coast to as far east as Calicut on India's Malibar coast, and vice versa.

Only the narrow Gulf of Aden, at the entrance to the Red Sea, separates Arabia from the Horn of Africa, and once past its waters, the early

sailors encountered a long string of white sand beaches bordered by barren hills, which were in turn bordered by fertile lands. The East African
coast is a relatively inviting one, and after the coming of Islam especially,
Arabs from various nations began appearing on its shores in increasing
numbers. Some were fleeing upheavals within the Islamic world, others
were bent on trade. Swahili traditions tell of Syrians settling in East
Africa as early as the late 600s; small Arab trading posts popped up all
along the coast from the eighth century onward.

Many of these early trading posts were built on islands, including
Zanzibar and its sister island Pemba. The islands offered protection
from the mysterious, unpredictable Africans and their equally mysterious and unpredictable continent.

Usually built near African settlements, the earliest Arab outposts
were nothing more than a few simple dwellings. With the passing
decades, however, bigger homes, public buildings, and mosques were
built, and the African and Arab neighborhoods began melding together.
Local women were taken as concubines; knowledge was shared. The
Swahili culture, which is an African culture mixed with Arab elements,
was developing.

In the 910s, the Baghdad historian, geographer, and philosopher al-
Masudi sailed from Oman to East Africa. Arriving in Qanbalu, believed
to be Pemba, he encountered a mixed population of Muslims and "Zanj
idolaters." "The Zanj have an elegant language and men who preach in
it," he wrote, in the oldest surviving description of the Swahili. "One of
their holy men will often gather a crowd and exhort his hearers to
please God in their lives and be obedient to him. He [also] . . . reminds
them of their [African] ancestors and kings of old."

After about the year 1000, the Swahili settlements began taking on
a different character. Trade between the continent and Arabia, Persia,
India, and China was growing exponentially, and the demand for
African products, including ivory, gold, and slaves, was high. Islam was
spreading—by the 1300s, it would be the dominant religion on the
coast—and new towns with large mosques and multistory, coral stone
palaces were springing up. By the end of the fourteenth century, there
were thirty-seven East African communities with at least one mosque.
Among them were Kilwa, Sofala, Mogadishu, Malindi, Mombasa, and
Zanzibar.

Wealthiest of all the new breed of towns was Kilwa, located on an island south of Zanzibar. South of Kilwa on the mainland flourished Sofala, the center of the gold trade in East Africa. The precious mineral was mined in what is now Zimbabwe, carried by caravan to Sofala, and shipped north via Kilwa. Between Kilwa and the mainland stretched two superb natural harbors teeming with vessels of all nationalities.

In 1331, the great intellectual Moroccan traveler Muhammad ibn Abdullah ibn Battuta visited Kilwa—now a UNESCO World Heritage Site—and was astonished by what he saw. "Kilwa is one of the most beautiful and well-constructed towns in the world. The whole of it is elegantly built," he wrote. Many of Kilwa's houses were two or three stories tall, with cut-stone borders framing their doorways, and tapestries and decorative niches covering their interior walls. A large stone mosque with five aisles and a domed roof dominated one part of town, while to the north was a huge sultan's palace, built around open courtyards and a circular swimming pool. Surrounding Kilwa were extensive gardens and orchards, tended by African slaves.

The Kilwa sultan, noted Battuta, sent frequent slaving expeditions into the interior, which must have been quite successful, as he once gave twenty slaves to an indigent man from Yemen. The pious sultan also took care to donate one fifth—the traditional Islamic tribute—of the booty he gained through slaving to visiting sharifs, or descendants of the Prophet, some of whom came from as far away as Iraq for the sole purpose of getting their cut.

And the Kilwa sultan wasn't the only Arab sending slaving expeditions into the hinterland. In the twelfth century the historian al-Idrisi wrote: "The Zanj are in great fear and awe of the Arabs, so much so that when they see an Arab trader or traveler they bow down before him and treat him with great respect, and say in their language: 'Greetings O people from the land of the dates!' Those who travel to this country steal the children of the Zanj with dates, lure them with dates and lead them from place to place, until they seize them, take them out of the country, and transport them to their own countries."

A curious medieval tale describing an encounter between Arabs and Africans reflects some widely held beliefs of the earliest Muslims: the basic equality of Arabs and Africans, the possible superiority of a black man over a white man, the ubiquitous nature of slavery and the slave trade, and, most important, the great "benefit" that slavery could bring to an unbeliever. Through slavery, an infidel could be introduced to Islam and allowed to covert, thus becoming both civilized and saved. Slavery was not a savage practice, but rather a humanitarian one—an argument that has also been widely used by Christians.

As the story goes, a wealthy shipowner named Ismailawaih left Oman in 922 to sail to the island of Qanbalu. But a fierce storm drove his ship off course, onto the African mainland near Sofala, the gold port. He and his crew were terrified at first, as the Zanj there were reputed to be cannibals, but to their surprise, they were welcomed ashore by a young chief, "handsome and well made." He assured the sailors that they had nothing to fear and allowed them to stay and trade for several months. When it came time for the Arabs to leave, the friendly chief and seven companions boarded their ship to see them off. And then, the ungrateful Ismailawaih thought: "In the Oman market this young king would certainly fetch thirty *dinars*, and his seven companions sixty *dinars*. . . . Reflecting thus, I gave the crew their orders. They raised the sails and weighed anchor." The chief protested capture but his pleas went ignored, and he and his companions were thrown into the hold, which already contained some two hundred other captured Africans. The chief did not utter a single word during the entire rest of the trip, and when the ship reached Oman, he and his companions were sold in the slave market.

Several years later, Ismailawaih was again sailing from Oman to Qanbalu when his ship was again blown off course, to precisely the same spot on the East African coast. "Fully certain we should perish this time, terror struck us dumb. . . . " Ismailawaih said. "The Negroes seized us, and took us to the king's dwelling, and made us go in. Imagine our surprise; it was the same king that we had known seated on his throne, just as if we had left him there. . . . Ah! said he, here are my old friends! Not one of us was capable of replying. He went on: Come, raise your heads, I give you safe conduct for yourselves and for your goods."

Overcome with gratitude, Ismailawaih tried to give the chief a present of great value, but the African refused, saying, "You are not worthy for me to accept a present from you. I will not sully my property with anything that comes from you."

"But how did you escape and return to your country?" Ismailawaih asked. The chief replied: "After you sold me in Oman, my purchaser took me to a town called Basrah. . . . There I learnt to pray and fast, and certain parts of the Koran." He then told of how he escaped from his master in Baghdad, traveled to Mecca, and arrived in Cairo, where he saw the Nile. Hearing that the river flowed to the Land of the Zanj, he followed its course and, after many adventures, arrived back in his homeland, where he found that his people, like himself, had embraced Islam. "And if I have forgiven you," the African said to the Arab, "it is because you were the first cause of the purity of my religion. . . . As for accompanying you to your ship I have reasons for not doing so."

4

The Portuguese Invasion

GUARDING THE ENTRANCE TO THE MUSCAT HARBOR, WHERE they were easily visible from Seyyid Said's palace, were two brooding forts. Perched on rocks on either side of the deep blue, horseshoe-shaped bay, the sheer, whitewashed structures had been built by the Portuguese in the 1580s. To the right, facing the sea, was Fort Jalali, accessible only by a narrow staircase on the harbor side. To the left was Fort Mirani, with retaining walls three feet thick. Inside both forts were mazes of dark stairways and hallways designed to confuse any enemy who might breach the battlements.

The forts, which still stand today, were a constant reminder of one of Oman's first encounters with the West—and with Christianity.

It was the evening of July 7, 1497, in the port of Belém, Portugal. A stern, strong-faced man was making his way from the waterfront to a chapel built by Prince Henry the Navigator. The man glanced neither to the right nor the left as he walked, but stared straight ahead, a fiery determination in his eyes. A step or two behind him strode three companions. The four men ignored the hushed crowds who parted to let them pass.

In the deep natural harbor behind the men bobbed four vessels, freshly painted with bright colors. Two of the ships rode high in the waters, with tall castles fore and aft, and figureheads of their respective patron saints, São Gabriel and São Rafael, gazing out from their prows. The third ship was a smaller, lighter vessel—a caravel—recently devel-

oped by the Portuguese for exploring unknown ocean waters, and the
fourth was a supply ship. Inside the vessels' holds were enough food sta-
ples to last 150 men three years and all the latest navigational instruments of the day, including astrolabes, compasses, sounding leads, and
hourglasses.

The four men entered the chapel. Candles flickered in the shadows
around them as solemn priests and friars bade them welcome. Barefoot
and dressed in simple tunics, the four men had come for an all-night
vigil of supplication and prayer. Around the neck of their leader hung
the heavy cross of the Order of Christ, a society derived from the Tem-
plars, one of two international orders of knights formed to protect the
Holy Land during the Crusades.

The man's name was Vasco da Gama, and he and his crew were
about to embark on a ten-month journey around Africa's Cape of Good
Hope to Calicut, on the coast of southern India. Da Gama would not be
the first European explorer to circumnavigate the Cape—his country-
man Bartolomeu Dias had done so in 1488—but he would be the first
to reach the Orient, thereby opening up an enormously lucrative trade
route between the two continents.

All of the European powers had been working for years to find alternative ways to reach the East. The old Silk Routes that had been used
for centuries were no longer safe or cost-effective, as they had fallen
under Muslim control.

Portugal was an unlikely country to find an alternative route to the
East. Small and poor, it lay on the western edge of Europe, far away
from Eastern lands. But earlier in the century, Portugal had scored a
spectacular victory, capturing the wealthy Muslim town of Ceuta in
North Africa just across the water from Gibraltar—and its King João
had married Philippa of Lancaster, England, daughter of John of Gaunt.
Both events had boosted Portugal's confidence and its standing. The
Ceuta victory had also ignited Portugal's interest in foreign lands, and
whetted its appetite for battling Muslims.

Vasco da Gama was born circa 1460 in the fishing village of Sines, a tiny
place surrounded by miles of desolate plains. As a boy, he spent his days

with fishermen, becoming an expert sailor and developing a fascination for the sea. As a young man, he joined the Portuguese forces then fighting the Moors in Castile, Spain, where he proved to be an excellent soldier. His ability and courage brought him to the attention of Portugal's King Manuel, who presented him with the cross of the Order of Christ. Da Gama could have chosen to join the king's army or court, but instead returned to his first love, the sea.

While growing up, da Gama had been captivated by tales of Prince Henry the Navigator, who died around the time he was born. A slight and secretive man with a passion for exploration, Prince Henry made a name for himself by sponsoring voyages of discovery along the then-unknown west coast of Africa.

Prince Henry had many reasons for dispatching his expeditions, including a thirst for knowledge, a lust for gold, and a fervent wish to exterminate the Muslims. But his voyages had one result that he could not have anticipated: in 1441, two of his captains, sailing farther south than any Portuguese ship had ever sailed before, returned with stories of an amazing market run by black Muslims dressed in white robes and turbans. The Muslims had given the sailors a small amount of gold dust, and the sailors had seized twelve black Africans to show Prince Henry. Among them was a local chief who spoke Arabic, and who negotiated his release by promising to provide the Portuguese with slaves. The following year, the Portuguese sailed back to Africa and returned with ten more black men. The Atlantic slave trade had begun.

Within the next ten years, thousands more Africans were shipped to Portugal, where most were put to work on the sugar plantations of the Algarve and the Azores islands. And within the next forty years, the Portuguese built West Africa's first slave trading post, São Jorge da Mina, or "Saint George's of the Mine," on Ghana's coast, which would eventually ship over thirty thousand slaves annually to the Americas.

To reach the Cape of Good Hope took da Gama and his crew four long months—three spent without sight of land. To round the Cape took two more terrifying weeks, followed by a raging storm so fierce that for ten days, the world seemed to be in perpetual night. Waves high as mountains swept the explorers' tiny vessels up atop walls of water and crashed them down again. Water flooded the holds.

Once in calm waters again, some of the crew mutinied, demanding to go home. Steely eyed, da Gama replied that even if a hundred of his men died, he would not go back until he had accomplished his mission—he had vowed as much before God.

In early 1498, the expedition arrived in the large and flourishing port of Mozambique, where they found four Arab dhows at anchor—solid proof that they had reached the Indian Ocean at last. Crewman Alvaro Velho wrote in his diary: "We shouted with joy. We begged God to grant us health, so that we might see what we all so desired."

Many of the people in Mozambique were Swahili, a race that few Europeans had encountered before. And the Portuguese were astonished by their wealth and sophistication. "The men of this land are russet in colour and of good physique," wrote Velho. "They are of the Islamic faith and speak like Moors. Their clothes are of very thin linen and cotton, of many-coloured stripes, and richly embroidered. All wear caps on their heads hemmed with silk and embroidered with gold thread. They are merchants and they trade with the white Moors [i.e., Arabs]."

Through an interpreter, da Gama learned that the Arab dhows in the harbor were laden with cloves, pepper, ginger, gold, silver, rubies, pearls, and other gems. Everything but the gold had come from the Orient, where the precious spices and stones were so plentiful that they were collected by the basketful, the informant said.

Da Gama's mouth must have watered at the words, but he grew even more excited when he learned that there were Christian settlements all along the East African coast. Two supposed Christians were then brought before him. Immediately, they prostrated themselves before the ship's figurehead, São Gabriel. Da Gama was delighted.

In actuality, the two prostrate men were Hindus, who had mistaken the saint for one of their gods. Hindu merchants had been living all along the East African coast since at least the tenth century, and since they worshipped before gilded statues and religious pictures, as did Christians, the locals believed the two religions to be one and the same. The Portuguese explorers did not understand that the Hindus practiced a different religion either—they assumed them to be heretical Christians.

Among those who welcomed the explorers to Mozambique was a courteous, elderly sheikh, dressed in long white robes, an embroidered waistcoat, and a silk turban. Never having met Europeans before, he assumed that the strangers were Turks and therefore fellow Muslims. Seeing advantages to be gained in that misassumption, da Gama said nothing to dissuade him. When the sheikh asked to see his copy of the Quran, da Gama replied that he had left it at home because he did not want to bring it on a dangerous voyage.

Completely taken in, the sheikh showered the newcomers with gifts and allowed them to barter for the foodstuffs they needed. But then a local pilot saw some of the crew preparing for Mass, which he recognized as a Christian ceremony. Furious, the sheikh mounted an attack with bows and arrows. The Portuguese responded with crossbows and cannons—and leveled the town. It was the first of many similar sad East-West encounters to come.

Several months later, in April 1498, the explorers reached Mombasa (Kenya), then the largest trading center on the East African coast. Arriving in the port's outer harbor on the eve of Palm Sunday, the crew was eager to go ashore, to celebrate the holy day with the local Christian community that the Hindus had described. But da Gama was leery and refused an invitation to enter the inner harbor because he feared a plot—quite rightly, as it turned out. That night, a boatload of armed men circled his ships and attempted to board, but he held them off.

Regrouping, the fleet sailed on, to arrive a few days later in Malindi (Kenya), a rival port to Mombasa. Founded by at least the twelfth century A.D., Malindi was famed throughout the Indian Ocean for its rich iron mines, cultivated ways, and beautiful women, who dressed in luscious silks and veils of gold lace. Filled with tall, whitewashed houses and about a dozen mosques, the town was surrounded by towering palm groves.

The Malindi people watched with trepidation as the Portuguese approached. Having heard what had happened in Mozambique, they knew the intruders to be ruthless and cruel, clad in impenetrable steel from foot to toe.

Dropping anchor outside the harbor, the Portuguese waited. And waited. All was quiet. No one came out to greet them. Finally, da Gama sent an emissary ashore. He was hospitably received by an elderly, half-blind sultan, who told him that any enemy of Mombasa was a friend of Malindi; the two towns had been at war for generations. The sultan then sent the emissary back to the ships with an invitation to da Gama to enter the harbor.

Still, the commander was hesitant. He had a policy of not going ashore to meet local rulers, as he feared capture. So at last the sultan came out to the foreign ships in his royal barge, seated on two cushioned chairs of bronze beneath a crimson silk sunshade. He wore a damask robe trimmed with green satin and a luxurious turban, and carried a jewel-encrusted dagger at his belt. Accompanying him were his musicians, including two playing on carved ivory trumpets big as men.

Finally convinced of the sultan's sincerity, da Gama and his men went ashore, where they were indeed warmly received. Once again astonished at the civilized nature of the Swahili world, the foreigners tarried in the cosmopolitan town for nine days, resting, feasting, repairing their ships, and enjoying musical and theatrical performances. Horse races were run on the beach, rockets were fired from the ships, and sham fights were staged.

Yet for all the overt manifestations of goodwill, both sides were still deeply suspicious, each regarding the other as damned. The tentative friendship between them was one of necessity, not sentiment. Da Gama and his crew needed a safe haven in which to rest and replenish their supplies; the sultan and his people needed to ward off a possible brutal attack and acquire an ally against Mombasa.

While in Malindi, da Gama also accomplished an urgent goal: he found a navigator, Ahmed bin Majid, to lead his ships to India. A famed Arab mathematician, cartographer, poet, and the author of the most widely used logbooks of his day, Ahmed bin Majid is believed to have been of Omani descent, though he lived in Gujarat, India. Then in his sixties, he may have been coerced into joining da Gama's expedition, but probably went of his own free will, perhaps drawn to aid the Christian enemy through his own hubris. One of his poems reads:

I have exhausted my life for science and have been famous for it.
My honour has been increased by knowledge in my old age.
Had I not been worthy of this, kings would not have
Paid any attention to me. This is the greatest aim achieved.

Without Ahmed bin Majid to guide them to India, the Portuguese might well have been shipwrecked along the way—and disappeared from the Indian Ocean, perhaps for decades. The course of history might have been dramatically different. The navigational skills of the Portuguese were far less developed than those of the Arabs, and they knew little about the region's geography. But, to the disgust of future generations of Arabs, Ahmed successfully took the invaders where they wanted to go, thereby sowing the seeds that led to the decline of the Muslims and the rise of the Christians in the Indian Ocean. The Omanis may have been done in by one of their own.

In one of Ahmed bin Majid's final poems, the *Sofaliya*, probably written in 1500, he speaks of the Portuguese and his gut-wrenching remorse over the irreparable damage he has done:

Oh! Had I known the consequences that would come from them!
People were surprised by what they did!

Da Gama's first Indian Ocean voyage ended, as he had hoped, in Calicut, India, on May 20, 1498, after ten months and two weeks at sea. His plan was to meet the city's zamorin, or hereditary ruler, who was the most powerful man on the Indian coast. King Manuel had instructed de Gama to give the zamorin a letter of friendship.

The Calicut harbor teemed with craft of all shapes and sizes. Behind it spread a vast city, bordered by faraway mountains, dark under gathering clouds. The arrival of the Portuguese caused great excitement, and dozens of small boats came out to meet the vessels, many selling fish, chicken, figs, and coconuts.

Some of the Portuguese crewmen went ashore, where they were overwhelmed by what they saw. A crowded street, lined with trees, led to the zamorin's palace, which covered an area of one square mile and was surrounded by lacquered walls. The city's elite were carried about on litters, preceded by men blowing trumpets; the trumpets of the very wealthy were made of gold.

Arab merchants and shipbuilders, many of Omani or Egyptian descent, controlled the city's maritime trade. The wealthiest of Arabs then living in India, they resided in large stone houses scattered throughout the town. Some owned as many as fifty ships capable of traveling to the Red Sea, to which they carried spices and pilgrims bound for Mecca. "The Moors were very powerful, and had so established and ingratiated themselves . . . that they were more influential and respected than the natives themselves," wrote one contemporary chronicler.

Yet Calicut's Arabs and Hindus lived together in peace. The Hindus respected the Muslims' holy day, Friday, and executed no Muslim without the consent of his community. The Muslims showed respect to cows and never ate beef. Hindu converts to Islam, of which there were many—most converting to escape India's caste system—were not molested.

Da Gama must have felt intimidated by all that he saw and heard. After over ten months at sea, he and his men were a scruffy bunch, with only meager gifts to offer the powerful zamorin. But da Gama had deep faith in the righteousness of his mission. He knew that God was on his side. If he could just get through his first meeting with the Indian ruler, he could return to Lisbon triumphant and sail back later to Calicut, with a much greater fleet at his command.

On the day of his meeting with the zamorin, da Gama dressed carefully in a scarlet cloak reaching to the ground, a blue satin tunic, and a blue velvet hat with a plume. Men carrying palanquins came to meet him and his companions on the shore and bore them toward the palace, to the accompaniment of trumpets and drums. Crowds lined the streets and rooftops along the way.

At one point, the explorer asked to stop at a Hindu temple, which he mistook for a church. Entering, he knelt before a statue of a mother with child—Devaki nursing Krishna. All around, "many other saints were painted on the walls, wearing crowns. They were painted variously with teeth protruding an inch from the mouth and four or five arms," wrote the diarist Vehlo, without expressing any surprise.

At the palace gates, the zamorin watched from a balcony as da

Gama descended from his palanquin. Once inside, the explorer was led through a series of anterooms with huge golden doors, to the royal chamber. The zamorin lay on a green velvet couch beneath a silk canopy, a gold spittoon in his left hand. He was naked above the waist, with his dark hair pulled up into a topknot, and was chewing betel nut, which had turned his mouth and teeth red. Above his left elbow glittered a bracelet studded with jewels, from which hung a diamond thick as his thumb. Around his neck, and descending to his middle, was a double string of pearls large as hazelnuts. Behind him stood a page holding a short drawn sword and a red shield framed with more jewels.

Kneeling, da Gama presented the letter from King Manuel. He had only one wish, he said: to buy spices and depart peacefully. The zamorin replied that he was ready to provide. Then da Gama, who must have been wincing inside, presented the ruler with the gifts that he had brought from Portugal: washbasins, cooking oil, jars of honey, strings of coral, hats. The zamorin said nothing, but his attendants snickered.

The next day, da Gama and his men were heading back to their ships when they were arrested and taken to a hot, airless house, where they were held without explanation for several days. The haughty, impatient da Gama fumed. If he ever got out alive, he swore, he would wreak his revenge.

Behind the men's arrest were the city's Arabs. Unlike the zamorin, they recognized the explorers for what they were: a serious economic and political threat who could turn the whole Indian Ocean world upside down. Also, word of the Portuguese behavior at Mozambique had reached Calicut. The Arabs were lobbying to have the intruders killed. But the zamorin vetoed the suggestion. Calicut was a free port, where foreigners—even ones bearing insulting gifts—were respected. And even if the men in captivity *were* killed, what about the crew left on the ships? They were armed with cannons, and Calicut had no cannons of its own. Hand-to-hand combat would lead to many deaths and serve no purpose, as more Portuguese ships were bound to arrive.

The zamorin ordered the Portuguese released, and sent da Gama lavish presents, along with messages of apology and permission to fill his ships with spices. But the captain-general made no reply. He loaded the spices into his vessels and prepared to weigh anchor. Apprehensive, the zamorin sent another message, imploring da Gama to stay longer; those who detained him would be punished, he promised. An angry da Gama answered by firing his cannons into the air.

Four years later, da Gama returned to the Indian Ocean. This time, he was in command of nineteen vessels and was determined to make the zamorin pay—not only for the insult of his own incarceration, but also for the ruler's treatment of another Portuguese commander, Pedro Alvares Cabral.

King Manuel had sent Cabral to Calicut two years after da Gama's initial visit on an impossible mission: he was to convince the zamorin to expel all Muslims from the city, and make him promise to sell spices only to the Portuguese. The idea had seemed feasible at the time because da Gama, still ignorant of the Hindu religion, had told King Manuel that the zamorin might be a heretical Christian who could be convinced to join the war against Islam.

Undoubtedly relieved not to be under attack, the zamorin welcomed Cabral. A simple treaty of friendship was signed and, under pressure, the zamorin agreed to give preferential bidding to the Portuguese the next time a spice shipment arrived.

But then the monsoon winds perfect for sailing to the Red Sea began and an Arab ship already loaded with spices raised anchor. Furious at what he saw as a breach of contract, Cabral seized the ship. On shore, a riot broke out, and fifty-three of the seventy Portuguese then on land, including three friars, were killed. The Portuguese responded with cannon fire, pummeling the city again and again, and seized ten merchant ships in the harbor, slaughtering most of their crews. The few men who survived were tied up and burned alive in full view of the people on the shore.

Two years later, as da Gama neared Calicut, he overtook an unarmed vessel on its way back from Mecca with six hundred pilgrims and a treasure trove of riches. The ship belonged to the wealthiest Arab in Calicut, a man related to the sultan of Egypt. Seizing the vessel, da Gama sent for the captain, who pleaded for his life and those of his passengers and crew.

"Sir you have nothing to be gained by ordering us killed. . . . Do you put in practice the virtue of knighthood. . . . " The plea fell on deaf ears.

"Alive you shall be burned because you counseled the King of Calicut to kill and plunder the Portuguese," thundered da Gama. "I say that for nothing in this world would I desist from giving you a hundred deaths, if I could."

According to one version of the incident, da Gama then gave the women and children pilgrims the option to be baptized, and fifty agreed to do so. The rest were locked in the hold, and the ship was set on fire. While the victims screamed, da Gama watched from his porthole.

Upon reaching Calicut, da Gama's fleet began bombarding the city and seized the small craft in the harbor, manned by a total of about eight hundred men. Still hoping to negotiate a peaceful settlement, the zamorin dispatched a Brahman messenger disguised as a friar, so that he could pass through the enemy lines unharmed. But da Gama was not interested in negotiation. He commanded his forces "to cut off the hands and ears and noses of all the crews [from the small craft], and put all that into one of the small vessels, into which he ordered them to put the friar, also without ears, or nose, or hands, which he ordered to be strung around his neck . . . with a palm-leaf for the King, on which he told him to have a curry made to eat of what his friar brought him."

Filling another ship with more mutilated crewmen, da Gama set it on fire and sent it toward shore. The victims' families ran into the sea to try to put out the fire, but da Gama drove them away, pulled the survivors off the boat, and hung them from the masts. He then ordered his men to fire arrows at them "so that the people on shore could see."

The subjugation of Oman was next.

When da Gama had first returned to Portugal with news of his success in reaching India, King Manuel, a vain and arrogant man of limited vision, declared his intention to establish an empire, to be called El Estado de India, in the lands all around the Indian Ocean. And to that end, he dispatched three war fleets to the region in 1506. One was bound for southern Arabia—i.e., Yemen and Oman. Made up of sixteen vessels under the command of Tristão da Cunha, the fleet carried with it "the Great Afonso de Albuquerque," who rivaled da Gama in courage, ambition, and Christian zeal.

Born in 1453 near Lisbon, Albuquerque was part Portuguese and part Spanish, and of royal blood. As a youth, he had been a good friend of the Dom João, the future king of Portugal, and together the two young men helped conquer Morocco for their homeland. Afterward, Albuquerque remained in Morocco for ten years, during which time he learned the methods of slaughter that would serve him well in the Indian Ocean, and developed a deep detestation of Islam. He became determined to wipe out the religion no matter what the cost to himself or anyone else.

In 1506, Albuquerque was already fifty-three years old and a seasoned veteran of many campaigns. Of average size, with a long ruddy face, he tended to dress entirely in black, with a jewel-encrusted dagger at his hip. He had a thick gray beard that reached well below his waist and wore it knotted to his belt.

One of Albuquerque's foremost goals was to capture Aden, which guards the entrance to the Red Sea, and close that strategic waterway to Muslims. At first lacking the military strength for this endeavor— though he would acquire it later—he decided to begin his campaign by working his way around the Omani coast, up to the Strait of Hormuz, and gain control of the Persian Gulf instead.

He and his fleet started with the Omani port of Qalhat—said to be the place where Malik bin Fahm founded the first Omani kingdom in the second century A.D. In 1298 Marco Polo had described Qalhat as "a great city . . . a noble city . . . The haven is very large and good, and is frequented by numerous ships with goods from India. . . . They also export many good Arab horses to India."

Qalhat did not resist Albuquerque's initial advances and so was left intact, at least until the following year, when the Portuguese paid a second visit and burned it to the ground. But Albuquerque's next target, Quriyat, did resist—and was annihilated, its men, women, and children brutally massacred. News of the slaughter spread like wildfire along the coast, and by the time the Portuguese reached Muscat a few days later, the town's terrified populace was ready to negotiate. The Muscat governor began to do so, but then heard that reinforcements were on their way and backed out of negotiations. Furious, Albuquerque commanded his troops to slaughter everyone in sight. Later, in a dispatch to King Manuel, he described the "courage" of his men in carrying out his orders: "Antonio do Campo . . . pursued a crowd of women who were retreating to hills, and killed many of them; while João da Nava . . . killed many [men] as well as women and children . . . without sparing any, so that one and all did great execution among them. . . . Finally Alfonso Albuquerque . . . put all the Moors with their women and children, found in the house, to the sword, without giving any quarter."

Over the next few years, Albuquerque would send similar dispatches to King Manuel from all along the northern Indian Ocean coast. One sent from Goa, India, which became the center of Portuguese power in the East, is especially unsettling: "For four days your men shed blood continuously. No matter where we found them, we did not spare the life of a single Moslem; we filled the mosques with them and then set them on fire. . . . We found that six thousand Moslem souls, male and female, were dead. . . . It was a very great deed, sire, well fought and well accomplished."

Yet for all his cruelty, Albuquerque was also a literate and observant man who knew how to turn a phrase. His description of Muscat before he and his crew destroyed it sounds like it belongs in a travel guidebook: "Muscat is a large and populous city. . . . There are orchards, gardens and palm groves with pools for watering them by means of wooden engines. . . . It is a very elegant town with very fine houses and supplied from the interior with much wheat, millet, barley and dates for loading as many vessels as come for them." And later: "The town burned very slowly because the houses in all these places were made of stone and mortar and some of stone and mud, whitewashed and very beautiful and very strong."

From Muscat, the conquistadors moved on up the coast, to capture Sohar and destroy Khor Fakkan, a port on the Musandam peninsula. In a little over a month, the Portuguese had conquered the entire Omani coast.

East Africa also succumbed. The sack of Kilwa, the wealthy city-state known for its gold trade, and Mombasa, which had initially resisted da Gama's attempt to seize it, were especially brutal blows to the Arabs.

After Mombasa fell, its sultan wrote a heart-wrenching letter to his old enemy, the sultan of Malindi: "Allah keep you, Said Ali. I would have you know that a great lord passed here, burning with fire. He entered this city so forcefully and cruelly that he spared the life of none, man or woman, young or old or children no matter how small. . . . Not only men were killed and burned, but the birds of heaven beat down upon the earth. In this city the stench of death is such that I dare not enter it. . . . "

During their reign in the Indian Ocean, which in most places lasted at least 150 years, the Portuguese established about two dozen fortified enclaves around its edges, from Mombasa in the west to Hormuz in the north to Malacca (Malaysia) in the east. From these outposts, they reaped the immense profits of the spice trade, both through their own cargo ships and by heavily taxing all vessels that passed through their ports. Otherwise, however, the Portuguese, like the Persians in Oman and the Omanis in East Africa, had little interest in colonizing or otherwise controlling their new empire. Local populations were left more or less alone, to live as they pleased, as long as they paid tribute to the Portuguese crown.

In the mid-1500s, the Ottoman Turks tried to oust the Portuguese from Oman. Twice they successfully captured Muscat, but neither victory lasted long. After the second short Turkish occupation, the Portuguese built Muscat's Fort Jalali and Fort Mirani.

The story of how the Omanis finally ousted the Portuguese from their country is, as tradition has it, a love story. It is also a story of quick wits, cunning, and courage.

The beginning of the Portuguese end in Oman was the election of Nasir bin Murshid al-Yaarubi as imam in 1624. His tribe, the Yaaruba, was one of the oldest tribes in Oman, and Nasir was the first Omani ruler to successfully unify his country's tribes. He is hailed in Omani literature as the "Just Iman."

At the time of Nasir's election, the Portuguese controlled most of Oman's coast, while independent chiefs controlled the interior. The country was deeply convulsed by tribal wars, and some of the chiefs were bitterly opposed to Nasir's election. However, he had the unanimous support of an elite and learned assembly of seventy men—the "electoral college" that had voted to bring him to power—and immediately after taking the oath of office, went to war.

His first move was to attack the old city of Rustaq, then held by hostile cousins, who surrendered. Next, he marched to nearby Nakhl and, after a siege of several days, captured the town. He and his army then doggedly plowed on, capturing town after town, fort after fort, sometimes by peaceful means, sometimes by force, until most of the country's interior was united. Finally, they turned their sights on the coast and gradually drove the Portuguese out of every town but Muscat and its sister port, Muttrah.

"God bestowed [Nasir] upon the Musselmans, and through him He humbled the infidels, the polytheists, and the evil-doers," wrote Salil ibn Razik, author of *History of the Imams and Seyyids of Oman.* "He drove out the conspirators from their lurking-places, broke up their haunts, overcame their leaders, checked their rebellions, crushed the tyrants and oppressors."

Imam Nasir died in 1649, after twenty-six years in power, but before finishing the task of ridding his country of the Portuguese. Still, after his death, his stature only continued to grow. As is often the case with beloved Islamic leaders, stories about miracles connected to his name began to circulate. One involved the magical sighting of Nasir in a lighted mosque long before he was elected imam. Another concerned the sudden inexplicable collapse of the roof of a house of nobles who had abused him. A single basket of dates or rice was said to have fed one hundred of Nasir's men for several days. It was also said that not one individual great or small had died at the imam's residence while he was still alive, and that not one person was destroyed by wild beasts.

Nasir was succeeded by his cousin Sultan bin Saif al-Yaarubi, and it was under Saif's command that the Omanis finally ousted the Portuguese. As the story goes, Sultan bin Saif pitched his camp just outside Muscat and ordered his army to attack the enemy day and night. But to no avail. The Portuguese had built towers in the mountains surrounding the port and filled them with musketeers. They had also suspended an iron chain between two of the towers, to which were attached iron "cradles" containing more armed men.

The Omanis had begun to despair of ever regaining Muscat when a dispute arose between the Portuguese commander Pereira and a resident foreign merchant named Narutem, "one of the Worshippers of the Cow"—i.e., a Hindu. Narutem had a beautiful daughter with whom Pereira had fallen in love. Through a messenger, Pereira asked Narutem for his daughter's hand in marriage. Narutem refused. Pereira offered him a large sum of money. Still Narutem refused. Pereira's messenger then said to the Indian, "If you do not give your consent to the marriage I am to marry your daughter to him forcibly, and he will punish you and yours. . . . Hence I advise you to yield, for he who disobeys great sovereigns is sure to bring on himself destruction."

Realizing that he had no choice, Narutem went to meet Pereira. He would consent to the marriage, he told the commander, on one condition: that it be delayed for one year. He wished his daughter to wear the traditional gold wedding jewelry of her people, and this could only be made by special goldsmiths in India.

Narutem then offered the Portuguese commander some advice: Imam Sultan bin Saif was hiding in the mountains with "forces as numerous as the drops of rain," and when they attacked, Pereira's men would not be prepared to sustain what could be a long siege. The water in their forts' tanks was foul, and their gunpowder and grain were worthless. Drain the tanks and discard the old supplies now, so that you can replace them with new before the siege begins, Narutem advised.

Overjoyed to have apparently won the object of his desire, Pereira agreed to postpone the marriage and ordered his men to clean out the forts' storage bins. Meanwhile, Narutem sent a letter to Imam Sultan, advising him to attack the following Sunday, the "Christians' feast day," when the Portuguese would be celebrating and their forts empty of supplies. The imam did as Narutem advised, sending in his men disguised as peasants, weapons hidden in their vegetable baskets, and won a resounding victory.

One hundred and fifty years of Portuguese occupation had finally ended. The Omanis were in control of their own once again. Their next prolonged encounter with Christians would not occur until two centuries later, on Zanzibar, where the battleground would be pitched on an entirely different front: the slave trade.

5

The Al Busaids Come to Power

ONE DAY IN 1730, A MERCHANT NAMED AHMED BIN SAID AL BU-
said was traveling from the inland town of Rustaq to Muscat. The son of
a humble camel driver, who had once sold wood to make ends meet, he
was riding on a magnificent she-camel. Languidly, the long-legged beast
picked her way along the dry, rocky *wadi*, sandy hills to either side, the
sheer Hajar Mountains behind. Traveling with Ahmed were a half-
dozen assistants and slaves, the latter leading donkeys and camels laden
with dates bound for Muscat.

A cloud of dust arose in the distance, coming from the direction of
the coast. Ahmed and his companions paid little attention at first, expecting to meet another group of merchants traveling the well-trodden
trade route. But as the dust cloud grew closer, and white-robed figures
began to emerge, the assistants and slaves called excitedly to each other.
Coming their way was their ruler, the young Imam Saif II, and his large
retinue of *qadis*, counselors, servants, and slaves, some mounted on
camels and horses, others on foot.

When the two groups reached each other, their camels dropped to
their knees, and the men alighted. The imam and Ahmed bin Said approached each other, *dishdashas* flowing gracefully around them, their
khanjars blinking in the sun. Ahmed took the imam's right hand in both
of his and bent low. Then he placed his right hand over his heart.

Salaam alaikum, he said.

Alaikum salaam, the ruler replied.

How are you?
How is your family?
How are your children?
How are your sheikhs?
How is your tribe?

The words were the traditional ones exchanged by all Omanis when they met, and to them, Ahmed would have added elaborate compliments appropriate for greeting the ruler of his country. Ahmed and the imam had never met before, but Ahmed of course knew of Imam Saif and Imam Saif had, just shortly before, heard of Ahmed. One of his advisers had recommended the merchant to him, saying that Ahmed was "discreet in judgment and very courageous."

When the traditional greetings were over, the imam drew Ahmed apart from his companions.

"Where are you going?" he asked.

"To your town of Muttrah on business."

"Go, and when you hear of my return to Muscat from Rustaq come to me there."

"I will obey," Ahmed replied.

The founder of the Al Busaidi dynasty, Ahmed bin Said, was Seyyid Said's grandfather. A forceful and daring man, he had grown up in Adam, a walled frontier town on the edge of the Empty Quarter, surrounded by a sandy plain populated with partridges, plovers, gazelles, and hares. Adam was well supplied with water, thanks to three deep *aflaj*, and boasted rich date plantations and a large bazaar. Looming over the town to the north and the east were two stark dome-shaped mountains. To reach the coast from Adam took eight to ten days, traveling along the wide Wadi Halfain, sprinkled with small defense towers.

As a boy and youth, Ahmed bin Said had spent much time with the Bedu, from whom he may have learned his independent and spirited ways. The Bedu came to Adam to shop or to tend to their small gardens at the edge of town, but always left before nightfall, as they believed town air to be poisonous. Their lives lay elsewhere—in the country's open desert spaces—and were centered on their camels, whom they treated with great respect and affection. *Ata Allah*, or "God's gift" they called them.

Ahmed must have traveled with his Bedu friends, or with his father, the camel driver, on journeys over the deserts and through the Wadi Halfain. And, like most camel owners, Ahmed and his comrades would have ridden on their female camels and used their male camels—snarling, roaring beasts when mounted—as pack animals. The Bedu and probably Ahmed, too, liked to ride kneeling, sitting on the soles of their feet, even when galloping—an extraordinary balancing act.

Usually, though, the camels walked, for the men led their treasured beasts much of the time. Upon reaching a well the camels were frequently allowed to drink before the men, and upon reaching bushes or grasses, they were allowed to graze. Not surprisingly, the caravans rarely covered more than three miles an hour. Patience was a virtue that the desert taught well.

In the evening, the caravans would stop near an oasis or sheltered spot. Hobbling the camels' forelegs so that they couldn't wander off, the men let them loose to graze and then stood to say evening prayers, their shadows stretching across the desert floor. Someone would build a campfire, lighting it with flint and the blade of a dagger. Dinner was often a rice dish, accompanied by dates and bread, the latter cooked in the sand beneath the fire's embers. Then came coffee, steaming bowls of camel's milk, and a smoke.

After dinner, the men spread out their rugs and sheepskins, and put their *khanjars* under their saddlebags, which they used as pillows. The camels were pulled in close, made to crouch, and hand-fed dried sardines or other choice tidbits. Light from the dying fire danced over bearded faces and the ponderous heads of the camels as the men talked, sang, or recited poetry, and fell asleep.

In the morning, as soon as it was light, the camels arose, roaring and gurgling. Then someone sang the call to prayer:

Allah is most great, Allah is most great.
Allah is most great, Allah is most great.
I bear witness that there is none worthy of worship but Allah.
I bear witness that there is none worthy of worship but Allah.
I bear witness that Muhammad is the Messenger of Allah.

I bear witness that Muhammad is the Messenger of Allah.
Hasten to the prayer, hasten to the prayer.
Hasten to the true success, hasten to the true success.
Prayer is better than sleep, prayer is better than sleep.
Allah is most great, Allah is most great.
There is none worthy of worship but Allah.

At the time of Ahmed bin Said's encounter with Imam Saif II, Saif was only in his late teens but had just been appointed imam for the third time. His first two terms had been disasters, with regents running things for him and constant warring between the tribes. Now that he had finally come of age, many Omanis were hopeful that this time he would at last succeed in reuniting the country. But it was not to be. Saif proved to be a miserable statesman who would be cast out of the imamate yet again, four years later.

In fact, when Imam Saif met Ahmed, he was already facing the beginning of his final defeat—largely brought upon himself through his own poor judgment. A distant relative, Belarab bin Himyar, who had served as imam between Saif's second and third terms, was leading an uprising against him. Belarab had gained the support of most of Oman's interior and was moving on the coast.

Panicking, Saif had done the unthinkable; he had written to the Omanis' age-old enemy, the Persians, asking for help.

Shortly after Imam Saif's and Ahmed bin Said's first meeting, Ahmed called upon Saif in Muscat, as requested. The imam asked him to conduct some minor business for him. Ahmed acquitted himself well and the imam sent him on another assignment. Yet another followed, and then another, until eventually, Saif appointed Ahmed governor of the prosperous port of Sohar.

Here, Ahmed proved his abilities again; he was a just and able ruler who quickly gained the esteem of both Sohar's citizens and the tribes who lived in the surrounding area. Many came to him with their problems, and he received them all—the rich and the poor, the learned and the illiterate—with gracious hospitality, "so that his renown spread far and wide, all the people obeyed him gladly, and all tongues extolled the justice of his administration."

Imam Saif should have rejoiced at the success of his appointment, but instead, he grew nervous. Still young and inexperienced, he suspected his governor of harboring ulterior ambitions. Abruptly, he summoned Ahmed to Muscat, intending to arrest him. But Ahmed caught wind of the plans en route and returned home. Enraged, Saif sent four warships to Sohar. A truce was declared only when Ahmed agreed to leave his eldest son, Hilal, with Saif as insurance.

From then on, Imam Saif's fortunes slid rapidly downhill. The Persian forces that he had requested landed in northern Oman, to the shocked disbelief of his countrymen. "This is a grievous calamity and misfortune for us and for you," wrote one nobleman to Saif, "since, if [the Persians] succeed they will tyrannize . . . and if their numbers increase they will inflict the sorest punishment upon you, they will slaughter your children and ravish your women. . . . In God's name, are you asleep or awake? Or, has the devil got the ascendancy over you?"

Saif's archrival, Belarab bin Himyar, immediately marched against the Persians, but his forces were badly defeated. The invaders swept inland. Reaching a town called Ibra, they behaved as many had feared and "plundered all they could lay hands on, and slaughtered the children in a most barbarous manner . . . first [binding] them with ropes and then hurling them from the bridges into the streams, regardless of their cries," or so wrote the Omani historian ibn Razik.

Thereupon Saif and the Persians had a falling out. Saif returned to Muscat. More Persian forces arrived, and over the next year they seized one Omani town after another, including Muscat, while making it clear that they had no intention of turning anything over to Saif or anyone else. Ten thousand women and children were said to have been slaughtered and a steep tax was imposed upon the land. Sohar, still under Ahmed bin Said's rule, was placed under siege.

Chastened, Saif went to see his rival Belarab, and the two agreed to join forces to fight their now-common enemy. Under Saif's command, their soldiers held Barka against the Persians and regained the garrison of Behla. Many Persians fled home and others holed up in the southern Omani port of Sur. But the Persian siege of Sohar continued.

Remarkably, Saif still had the support of the Omani people. But the *ulema* had turned against him. They elected a new imam, Sultan bin Murshid al-Yaraabi, whose first order of business was to hunt down Saif.

Once again in a state of despair, poor, weak Saif now made the same mistake twice: he called on the Persians for help, this time promising to give them Sohar in perpetuity if they returned him to the imamate. The Persians sent another large force to Muscat, which they captured, along with other smaller towns. The Persians did not, however, hand over any of their conquests to Saif, as he had rather credulously expected. For the second time, he was betrayed, as he had betrayed.

Finally, secretly, the humiliated ruler fled to his castle in the interior town of Hazm. Here, he told an old comrade: "This is my castle and my grave. I [have] become an eyesore to everyone, and the quiet of death will be preferable to any happiness which dominion has afforded me." He died shortly thereafter, as did his recently elected successor, Sultan bin Murshid, who was killed in a battle.

And so ended the rule of the Yaarubi dynasty in Oman. In power for 120 years, the family that had united the country's tribes for the first time and ousted the Portuguese invaders now came to an inglorious end.

Meanwhile, the Persian siege of Sohar continued. The determined Ahmed bin Said was simply refusing to surrender. Finally, discouraged and at a loss as to who now ruled Oman, the Persian commander approached the Sohar governor. He and his troops would abandon Sohar on the condition that they be given safe passage back to Persia, he said. Ahmed agreed, and made a similar promise, albeit with a more evasive answer, regarding the Persians who remained in Muscat.

In due course, the Persians safely left Sohar and Ahmed invited their remaining compatriots in Muscat to Barka, for a celebration of their final leave-taking. Huge cauldrons of meat and platters of sweetmeats were prepared, much to the indignation of the Omani people, who believed, with reason, that their enemy deserved a far different treatment. Then, on the third day of the celebration, Ahmed invited fifty of the top Persian commanders to a special event inside his fort, while the ordinary troops continued to feast outside. A public crier announced: "Anyone who has a grudge against the Persians may now take his revenge."

By the time the Omanis were finished, only about two hundred ordinary Persian troops were left alive, while all inside the fort had been slaughtered. The remaining prisoners were herded onto ships to sail to

Bandar Abbas, but sailors set fire to the boats while they were still in the harbor and all the Persians perished.

Ahmed bin Said made a triumphal tour through Oman's largest towns, where he was enthusiastically received—all was fair in war. The *ulema* elected him imam, and an official transfer of power from the Yaarubi dynasty to the Al Busaidi dynasty took place. The year was 1743. The Al Busaidi dynasty continues to rule Oman to this day.

Now the legend of Imam Ahmed bin Said Al Busaid, who had no family lineage—so important in the Arab world—to distinguish him, began to grow, as had Imam Nasir's before him. Citizens came forward with stories that claimed Ahmed's greatness was preordained. One concerned his arrival in a town on a festival day. As the story went, after morning prayers and a sermon, a camel race was about to be run. Ahmed was contemplating entering his camel when an old woman took his reins and said, "O, Imam of Oman, it does not become you to run your she-camel with the camels of these people, for they are your subjects, you being their Imam and the Imam of all Oman." Whereupon Ahmed alighted and asked her if she was making fun of him. She answered, "By Allah! I am not; for what I have said shall happen to you shortly." Ahmed did refrain from entering the race, but kept the woman's prediction a secret.

On another occasion, when approaching the town of Manh, Ahmed was said to have heard a voice saying, "Welcome, O Imam of Oman." He looked around to see who was speaking, but could see no one. The same thing happened again and again in different places, and each time, Ahmed kept the voices a secret.

Stories of Ahmed's great heart also began to circulate: After rising to power, he richly rewarded the family of the woman at the camel race (she herself was dead) and granted most requests of ordinary people. Whenever he traveled outside Muscat, he passed out parcels of sweetmeats to poor children along the way. He also ordered his soldiers to march slowly, so that his people had time to salute him and he had time to salute them back.

Ahmed appointed loyal officers to head up the various branches of his administration and established a private army of 1,100 African slaves and 1,000 freemen. Hundreds more slaves—many more than were needed—worked in his household and on his date plantations. Unlike his future grandson Said, Ahmed enjoyed surrounding himself with minions, and always went out with an imposing entourage of *qadis*, scholars, notables, servants, slaves, and executioners—the latter included, per the custom of the day, in case there was trouble.

Ahmed bin Said could not luxuriate in his newfound status for long, however. He faced tremendous troubles. Oman had been devastated by war, and various powerful tribes were hostile to him. In fact, Ahmed had been in power only a short time when Belarab, the leader who had revolted against Imam Saif, led a rebellion against him. Ahmed was absent on an expedition at the time, and upon his return to Sohar, he decided to lay low, to see which of the sheikhs truly supported him. Taking refuge in the hut of an old woman, he allowed his saddled camel to go loose, leading many to believe that he was dead. The strategy succeeded brilliantly. Belarab and other malcontents seized Sohar, and Ahmed and his forces attacked, routing the insurgents. The troublemaker Belarab was killed.

During his thirty-four years in power, Ahmed bin Said rebuilt much of Oman. Consolidating his power through political alliances and marriages, he augmented the navy, strengthened the forts, and secured the ports. Still a merchant at heart, he took a strong interest in trade with East Africa and appointed trusted governors to rule over Kilwa, Zanzibar, and other ports. By the time of his death in 1783, more than half of all the trade conducted between Africa and the Far East was passing through Omani hands. One European who visited Muscat in 1775 wrote: "There are at present such immense quantities of goods in this town that, as there are not warehouses to contain half of them, they are piled up in the streets, and lie night and day exposed, without any watch or guard, yet there never happens an instance that such goods are robbed, or even pilfered in the least part."

Ahmed bin Said Al Busaid set the tone of the Busaidi dynasty for centuries to come. A charismatic and determined man who rose to power on the basis of his merits alone, he had a gift for leadership. Generous and just with his own people, cruel and ruthless with his enemies, pious in his private life, cunning in his public one, he was the rare ruler with the imagination and daring needed to break with the past—always especially oppressive in the Middle East. His grandson Said would inherit many of his qualities.

6

War with the Wahhabis

FOLLOWING AHMED BIN SAID'S DEATH, HIS ELDEST SON, SAID (not to be confused with his grandson Said), was elected imam, and all the towns and forts that had been under the father's control were passed to him, much to the ire of his two half-brothers, Saif and Sultan. A few years earlier, the twosome had plotted against their older brother, and they were now living in ignominious exile—Saif in East Africa, where he died, and Sultan in Gwadar, India.

From Gwadar, Sultan, who was the future Seyyid Said's father, kept a close watch on what was happening in Oman. He was determined to return home one day to usurp his older half-brother, and events seemed to be conspiring in his favor. Said was proving to be a dismal ruler. A very religious man with a great love of poetry, he was shrinking from his administrative duties, and had cornered the textile-dyeing industry by heavily taxing his competition—an extremely unbecoming act for an imam. "His indolence and extortion soon made him obnoxious to the people," wrote ibn Razik.

In the face of such widespread public disapproval, Said's eldest son, Hamed, tried to convince his father to abdicate. Said refused at first, but then gradually allowed Hamed to take over his administrative and military duties. Within three years, Hamed reigned as regent, while Said continued to hold the title of *imam*, a position he would keep for three decades. Hamed adopted the title of *seyyid*, a term used for Muslims of noble lineage. Later, his cousin Said would do the same, never adopting either the title or the religious duties of the imam, not even after his uncle died.

In 1792, Hamed succumbed to smallpox and Sultan bin Ahmed hurried home, to soon take over Muscat and its sister port, Muttrah. Tall, handsome, and courageous, Sultan was said to care "nothing for the number of his enemies, preferring a few select adherents to a multitude of followers." Adept at using his wits, he once fooled an enemy into thinking that he had a great army at his command by lighting a multitude of fires in the hills behind him. But like his father before him, Sultan's methods of war were not always honorable. He acquired one Muscat fort by feigning smallpox, which led the fort's commander to pay him a condolence visit, during which Sultan had him arrested and forced him to surrender.

After securing his rule, Sultan concentrated on overseas expansion— more than any other ruler before him, he understood the importance of maritime power to Oman. Already while in exile he had captured the strategic Persian port of Bandar Abbas, which would remain an Omani dependency for seventy-five years, along with other Persian harbor towns. Now, he took over Bahrain. Sultan's conquests gave him control of both sides of the Strait of Hormuz, and ships en route to the pirate-ridden Persian Gulf began stopping in Muscat to hire Omani protection.

Sultan then ran into his first serious diplomatic problem. The English and the French, who both had sizable presences in the region, began pressuring him to choose sides between them. Oman had maintained fairly good relations with both powers for over 150 years, but now the Napoleonic Wars were under way.

Sultan evaded the issue for as long as he could, but in July 1798, the French army, under the command of a young Napoleon Bonaparte, suddenly arrived in Egypt and quickly defeated the Egyptians. Not surprisingly, Britain's fears regarding France's presence in the region grew exponentially, and three months later a newly appointed East India Company representative came to Muscat to call on Sultan bin Ahmed. A treaty was signed, in which Sultan promised that in times of war

Oman would have nothing to do with the French, and granted the East India Company permission to establish a trading post at Bandar Abbas.

With that agreement, Sultan became the first Arabian ruler to enter into a political alliance with England. Little did he know that this seemingly simple act would lead to a British stranglehold on the Persian Gulf—later nicknamed the "British lake"—or that, less than a hundred years later, Britain would eviscerate Oman by forcing his grandson to surrender its claims to East Africa.

Sultan was too astute a man to completely sever his relations with the French, however. He continued to trade with them and to exchange friendly communications. In January 1799, Napoleon wrote to Sultan: "I am writing this letter to you to inform you of what you have without doubt already learned, the arrival of the French army in Egypt. As you have at all times been our friend, you may be convinced of the desire I have of protecting all the ships of your nation [that you send to Suez]." The letter also asked Sultan to pass along an enclosed letter to the ruler of Mysore, India. The enclosure informed the Indian that the French were on their way to help him throw off British rule.

But the fates had other plans. A British man-of-war intercepted the letters and Cairo fell. Shortly thereafter, Britain signed a second treaty with Sultan that confirmed the provisions of the first. This time, however, Sultan complied with the treaty's terms. Britain had threatened to take away Oman's trading privileges with one of its oldest and most important trading partners—India.

No sooner had Sultan bin Ahmed resolved his difficulties with the British than another, far more violent problem arose—one that would plague both Sultan and his son Said until their deathbeds.

It all began simply enough, with a letter and a booklet. The letter was from one Amir Abdul Aziz Al Saud, and the booklet had been written by the founder of the Wahhabi faith. "In the name of God, the merciful, the companionate!" the booklet began. "This is the book of the *Solution of Difficulties*, written by the sheik Muhammad bin Abdul Wahhab, may God grant him the highest reward, and admit him into heaven without bringing him into account." The booklet then went on to describe the tenets of the Wahhabism, a volatile Islamist movement that had originated in the Najd, the large plateau in the heart of Arabia, about a twenty-day camel ride from Oman. The letter called upon the Omanis to convert to the new religion and to bow to the amir's authority.

Sultan and his advisers paid little attention to the missive at first. The historian ibn Razik wrote that the booklet was nothing more than "a mass of incoherent sentences quite inconsistent with the truth and no one took any notice of it."

In point of fact, Wahhabism, which is still the state religion in Saudi Arabia today, *was* anathema to the Ibadhi faith. A reform movement that called for a return to the simple monotheism taught by the Prophet, the Wahhabi doctrine vowed to purge Islam of heresy—which included Ibadhism—corruption, superstition, and, most strikingly, all innovation that had occurred since about A.D. 950. The sect condemned luxury and accused all non-Wahhabi Muslims of being polytheists who must be either converted or killed, their property and wives seized, and their children enslaved. The polytheist accusation was based on the reverence that many Muslims had for departed sheikhs and fakirs, as well as for the Prophet himself—a veneration supposedly at odds with Islam's most fundamental tenet, "there is no God but God."

"The Christians and the Jews . . . they have their books and must live by them; the Mohammedans alone are guilty and must choose between Wahhabism and death," Abdul Aziz wrote. In contrast, the Ibadhis, though also a fundamentalist sect, had never advocated violence toward any religious group, including followers of other Muslim creeds.

When Sultan received Abdul Aziz's letter, the Wahhabi movement was only about seventy years old. Its founder, Muhammad bin Abdul Wahhab, from a family of Hanbali scholars, had been born in 1703 in the Najd. Hanbalism is the most conservative of the four major schools of Sunni Islamic law, and is followed today by less than 5 percent of the world's Muslims.

Muhammad bin Abdul Wahhab began studying the Quran with his father at an early age, and as a young man he began preaching against the pagan practices of the Bedu. He found some limited support among others who deplored the superstitions of uneducated Muslims, but for the most part provoked widespread antagonism. His call for the destruction of saints' tombs made him especially unpopular.

Many Muslims believe saints to be close to God. A saint can communicate with God on behalf of others and petition Him to relieve misfortune or grant wishes. Since the power of a saint is believed to last even after death, the tombs of saints—usually small domed buildings by roadsides or inside mosques—are regarded as sacred places. A saint's spirit can also dwell in ancient trees, unusually shaped rocks, or gushing springs—often the same natural formations once worshipped by pagans.

Ibn Abdul Wahhab arranged for the destruction of a few sacred trees and tombs in his hometown, creating a huge outcry, with powerful tribal leaders calling for his death. Forced to flee, he took refuge in the neighboring town of Diriyah, where his fortunes and, indeed, the fortunes of the entire Arab world changed dramatically. Diriyah was the seat of the Saud family, a prosperous landowning clan, and its amir, Muhammad bin Saud, embraced the zealot and his faith. Declaring bin Abdul Wahhab to be a deeply sincere man of strong convictions, he pledged to use his power to help him spread the holy word.

By 1775, the Saudis and Wahhabis had control of the Najd. In 1800, they began their campaign against Oman. In 1802, they attacked Karbala (Iraq), the Shiites' holiest shrine, slaughtering all men, women, and children who were in their path and demolishing the great dome of the mosque under which Imam Hussein, the grandson of the Prophet and Shiism's third imam, is buried.

Next, the Wahhabis attacked Mecca, which they captured in April 1803, after its terrified inhabitants had fled. Before entering the city, the Wahhabis performed religious rites and put on the white robes of pilgrims. Then, with the battle cry of "there is no God but God," they destroyed all the tombs of the early Islamic heroes and heroines—only Allah was worthy of worship. The following year, the sect moved on to capture Medina, where they destroyed the tomb of the Prophet.

Muslims everywhere were horrified by the Wahhabis' cruelty and their destruction of Islam's holiest sites. But at the time, the Islamic world lacked the resources to take military action against the sect. The Ottoman Turks, who had inherited the caliphate, were busy keeping Europe at bay; the Persians were fighting the Russians. Not until 1812 were the Ottomans able to send forces from Egypt into Arabia, and not until 1817 were the Wahhabis driven back into the Najd. The city of Diriyah was razed, never to be rebuilt, and Abdullah bin Saud, the fourth Saudi amir, surrendered. He was sent to Constantinople, where he was paraded though the streets for three days before being publicly beheaded.

Amir Abdullah's companions were held in captivity in Cairo for seventeen years. Then in 1834, one of the captives, Faisal bin Saud, managed to escape, using a rope to descend the cliff of the Egyptian citadel and riding off across the desert on a camel. Nine years later, Amir Faisal drove the Egyptians out of the Najd, and thereafter reigned as ruler in Riyadh, the new Saudi capital, until his death in 1865, twenty-two years later. Amir Faisal was the grandfather of the founder of the modern kingdom of Saudi Arabia.

When Abdul Aziz received no answer from the letter that he had sent Sultan bin Ahmed in Muscat, he dispatched a large force on camel- and horseback to northern Oman. "Restless and bold," Abdul Aziz had already taken over the coastal region between Qatar and Kuwait, and subjugated his relatives the Qawasim on Oman's northern coast, demanding that they attack all passing Omani merchant ships. One fifth of all that they confiscated, the traditional Islamic tribute, was to be paid to the Saudis.

A courageous people who earned their living from pearl diving, the Qawasim had fiercely resisted the Wahhabis for years. But now that they had finally succumbed, they embraced the imposed faith with all the fiery enthusiasm of new converts. When an Englishman new to the region asked his Arab servant about them, the man replied:

> God preserve us from them, for they are monsters. Their occupation is piracy, and their delight murder, and to make it worse they give you the most pious reasons for every villany they commit. They abide by the letter of the sacred volume, rejecting all commentaries and traditions. If you are their captive and offer all to save your life, they say, "No! It is written in the Koran that it is unlawful to plunder the living, but we are not prohibited in that

sacred work from stripping the dead"; so saying they knock you on the head.

The Wahhabi forces invading northern Oman were under the command of an able general, a Nubian slave named Salim bin Hilal al-Harik. Winning the support of several Omani tribes hostile to Sultan, he easily captured Buraimi, a strategic oasis straddling major caravan routes. Then the allies began erecting a fort that was to serve as their base of operations for many years to come.

Back in Muscat, Sultan hurriedly assembled troops drawn from friendly tribes—like all Omani sultans before and after him, he had no standing army to speak of. His troops attacked the invaders, only to be badly defeated, and Sultan was forced to negotiate what must have been a humiliating truce.

Over the next two years, the Wahhabis kept a low profile in Oman, solidifying their position in Buraimi but making no attacks. By early 1803, Sultan felt secure enough in his rule to make a pilgrimage to Mecca, leaving his fourteen-year-old son, Salim, Said's older brother, in nominal command. Ever opportunistic, Sultan's nephew Bedr—the same Bedr whom Said would later slay—took advantage of the temporary power vacuum to attempt a coup. But according to historian ibn Razik, his plot was uncovered before it even began. He was discovered hiding inside a large box en route to Muscat's Fort Jalali, which he had hoped to capture. Escaping, he fled for protection to Diriyah, the Wahhabi capital, where he adopted the Wahhabi faith. Learning of his defection, Sultan prophetically remarked, "Had he remained at Habra, or in any other part of Oman, I would have forgiven him. His presence at Diriyah bodes no good to us."

Upon reaching the outskirts of Mecca, Sultan, like all pilgrims, would have shed his worldly identity. He would have purified himself by making ablutions; shaved his head, cut his nails, and trimmed his beard; put on the *ihram*, two simple white sheets, one draped over the torso, the second belted at the waist; and proclaimed: "Here I am, O my God, here I am; no partner hast Thou, here I am; verify the praise and the grace are Thine/and the empire."

Once in Mecca, Sultan would have joined the thousands of other worshippers thronging into the holy area, or *haram*, filled with sacred sites and buildings, including the Well of Zamzam, believed to have been opened by the angel Gabriel to save Hagar and her son Ishmael from a desperate thirst, and a stone imprinted with Abraham's footprint. At the heart of the *haram* was the Kaaba, the sacred black stone, which Sultan, like all other pilgrims, would have circled seven times.

Sultan bin Ahmed may have embarked on his pilgrimage when he did in order to meet with the sharif of Mecca, the traditional steward of the Holy Cities. The Wahhabis had been threatening Mecca and Medina and the sharif had appealed to the Omani ruler for help. Sultan ended up promising him money, ammunition, and some troops. If he couldn't defeat the enemy at home, he could at least help to defeat it elsewhere.

When Abdul Aziz, the Wahhabi ruler, heard of the alliance between his two adversaries, he became incensed. Declaring an all-out war against Oman, he launched a full-scale attack on its Batinah coast. And once again, Sultan was put in a humiliating position. He simply did not have the military might to resist such an attack and was forced to propose a truce. He would pay Abdul Aziz thirty-six thousand Maria Theresa dollars, and permit Wahhabi preachers and a political agent to live in Muscat.

Ostensibly, Abdul Aziz agreed to Sultan's terms. Secretly, however, he used the ensuing months to build up his troops at Buraimi. Then, declaring war on Oman once again, he sent hundreds of horsemen to attack Suwaiq, a prosperous town in the Batinah. Hastily, Sultan gathered together another tribal force, but "the mountains closed in upon them [as] they were assailed with musketry from those who were posted on the heights, and those who were in ambush below." Triumphant, the Wahhabis began marching to Sohar.

Frantically, Sultan convened a tribal conference at Barka. "War threatens us on all sides," he cried. "Those who have heretofore been friends have become our enemies, and those on whom we relied have, under the impending difficulties, proved themselves untrustworthy. The dagger's point is at our breasts."

"We are not dispirited on account of the Wahhabis. . . . " shouted one chief. "Blood is only man's dye, and war, like manna and quails, is as food to us. . . . Let the Wahhabis and their allies prepare for the overthrow which awaits them!"

"We shall be delighted to fight these insolent tyrants," shouted another.

Thereupon, the tribal leaders assembled some twelve thousand men
and Sultan prepared to depart for battle.

Quietly, the Wahhabis waited, assured of their superior military
might. But then came the unexpected: they learned that their leader,
Abdul Aziz, had been killed in a mosque by a Shiite whose children the
Wahhabis had massacred at Karbala. Stealthily, the Islamist invaders
fled their encampment by night, setting fire to their tents before they
left.

Unaware of the death of Abdul Aziz, the Omanis attributed the
retreat to fear in the face of their large numbers.

Sultan bin Ahmed sailed for Basra the following September, having
heard that the Ottomans were preparing to attack the Wahhabis. He
wanted to join their expedition. But when he arrived in the port, he saw
no signs of war. Angry and disappointed, he departed abruptly. Later,
near Linja on the Persian coast, he transferred from his warship to a
smaller vessel, perhaps wanting to sail to Bandar Abbas. It was a fateful
decision.

Around midnight, Sultan's vessel was hailed by three smaller boats
belonging to the Qawasim, the Wahhabi relatives and allies. Not realizing who was on board the Omani vessel, the Qawasim challenged them
to a fight. Boldly, Sultan accepted the challenge and proposed that they
begin at dawn.

The next morning, the battle started, with Sultan fighting bravely
and "roaring . . . at all times like a lion." But then, one enemy, "the vilest
of the vile, fired at him with a musket, and the ball entering his mouth,
he expired on the spot." Lamented a poet sometime later: "Wonders
never cease in these our times, / The lion of lions has been assaulted by
dogs." Sultan was buried at Linja; he had been in power only twelve
years. The date was mid-November 1804.

A slave succeeded in getting early news of Sultan's death to his family at their country home in Fulaij, Oman. Present when the word arrived were Sultan's sons Salim and Said, then ages fifteen and thirteen,
respectively; Sultan's sister Bibi Mouza bint Imam Ahmed, who was

caring for the boys; and Sultan's friend and relative Muhammad bin Nasir al-Jabri, who was the boys' regent.

That same night, the family departed for Muscat. Arriving there the following morning, they quietly commanded forces loyal to them to take possession of the town's fortifications before news of Sultan bin Ahmed's death spread.

At the time, Imam Said, the country's weak religious ruler, was still alive and ruling in Rustaq. A half dozen other powerful Al Busaidi relatives and tribal leaders were also eyeing the Omani throne.

7

Seyyid Said in Muscat

WITH VARIOUS UNCLES EAGER TO UNSEAT IF NOT KILL THEM, AND hostile tribes equally ready to pounce, young Said and Salim were in an extremely precarious position—a state of being that Said especially would become all too accustomed to as he grew older. Too young to rule, the brothers were also at the mercy of decisions made by their regent Muhammad bin Nasir and their aunt Bibi Mouza.

Though little solid historical evidence exists, Bibi Mouza may have been the real power behind the Omani throne in the early 1800s. According to ibn Razik's *History of the Imams and Seyyids of Oman*, she cosigned virtually every order Said sent and accompanied him everywhere. Her nephews also reported directly to her, rather than to the country's many male ministers—an unusual breach of customary Muslim etiquette. Her grandniece Salme speculated many years after her death: "The ministers, who had never thought of such a decision and had rather looked forward secretly to playing the role of masters for a couple of years, had to obey. Every day [Bibi Mouza] summoned them to receive their reports and to give her orders and instruction. She watched over everything and knew about all affairs. . . . She did not care what the world might have to find fault with that but went her way, unperturbed, with skill and energy."

But Bibi Mouza was soon put to a severe test. The boys' uncle Qays, ruler of the northern port of Sohar, made a bid for power. Much older and more experienced than his nephews, he had the support of many members of the royal Al Busaidi family, including that of his brother Imam Said, the country's weak religious leader.

Assembling his troops, Qays marched south and laid siege to Muscat, defended by forces loyal to the deceased Sultan bin Ahmed and his young sons. Most of the area's citizens fled for safety, barricading themselves inside the walled city, but according to Salme, Bibi Mouza put on a man's *dishdasha*, turban, and sandals, and thrusting a *khanjar* into her belt, rode out to inspect the city's outposts and encourage its troops. More than once, she was almost killed, as enemy gunfire exploded in her wake, but the near brushes with death only steeled her determination.

Weeks passed, and still the siege of Muscat continued. The situation was becoming desperate, as famine broke out and the troops were running out of bullets. But then, wrote Salme, Bibi Mouza had a brilliant idea—she ordered that all nails, small pebbles, and metal objects that could be pounded into smaller pieces be collected, and made ready for one final attack. She even had bullets smelted out of her own Maria Theresa dollars. "Everyone and everything was put to use, and lo!, the desperate effort was rewarded. The enemy was luckily taken by surprise and scattered in all directions," wrote Salme.

The threat was far from over, however. Qays's army remained in the vicinity, forcing Bibi Mouza to send a message to another of her nephews, Bedr, now living in Qatar, summoning him home. Despite his earlier attempt to usurp his uncle Sultan, and his conversion to Wahhabism, Bedr was still on good terms with his aunt and younger cousins. Immediately, he returned to Muscat, where Bibi Mouza appointed him deputy minister for two years, until Said turned sixteen. Bedr then appealed to his fellow Wahhabis for help in defeating Qays. They attacked Sohar, and Qays, with his capital in danger, ended his siege to return home.

Why Bibi Mouza, who played such a critical role in Said's rise to power, favored him over his older brother Salim had much to do with genealogy. Said's mother, Seyyida Ghaniye bint Seyf bin Muhammad, was from an influential branch of the Al Busaidi tribe and was closely related to Said's father; throughout the Middle East, marriages between close relatives, and especially between first cousins, are considered to be especially blessed. Salim's mother was of a less important tribe. Furthermore, Said had been pledged to take one of Bibi Mouza's daughters as his first wife—and was a bold, energetic, and ambitious young man.

Salim, in contrast, was gentle, studious, and not particularly interested in power. Very close to his brother, he rose every day before dawn to attend prayers in the mosque and usually took a walk with Said in the afternoon. Friendly with literary men, poets, and judges, Salim liked to memorize reams of Arab poetry and to study the history of Arabian dynasties, often staying up late into the night to discuss such matters with others.

As the years went by, however, Salim became a very fearful man. Perhaps remembering his role in his brother's rise to power and/or suffering from mental illness, he refused to eat anything unless someone else had tasted it first, and whenever a visitor entered the room, "seized the hilt of his dagger, fixed his eyes upon the person, and did not remove them until the close of the interview."

Bedr's arrival in Oman did not put an end to Qays's ambition to rule. The older man bided his time and months later, when Bedr was away in the Persian Gulf, tried to seize Muscat once again. By the time Bedr returned, his uncle had already captured Muttrah, Muscat's sister port. Again Bedr appealed to the Wahhabis for help and again they sent in a large number of troops, along with a fifteen-vessel fleet carrying some four thousand more men. The arrival of the ships caused a huge outcry in Muscat, for from the ships' masts fluttered strips of sacred cloth ripped from Imam Hussein's tomb during the Wahhabis' sack of Karbala. Nonetheless, the Wahhabis forced Said's uncle Qays to retreat and Bedr, Said's cousin, was once again recognized as the ruler of Muscat.

Not without bitterness, however. Most Omanis despised the Wahhabis and felt both enraged and deeply humiliated by their presence on the streets. Proud of their history of tolerance, the Ibadhis resented the Wahhabis' persecution of other religious groups, and the ferocious sanctimony of the Wahhabi preachers, who strictly enforced attendance in the mosques.

Bedr himself may have embraced Wahhabism more for political

than religious reasons. After taking control of Oman, he did nothing to help the Wahhabi cause, and when he got a letter from Amir Saud, head of the Wahhabis, in the summer of 1805 instructing him to spread the holy war to India, he ignored it. To fight India meant to declare war against the British—something that Bedr had no intention of doing. Instead he wrote to the governor of Bombay asking for British help. They were considering his plea when he was killed.

By 1806, Bibi Mouza, Said and Salim, and their regent Muhammad bin Nasir had become suspicious of Bedr's intentions. The deputy minister had started excluding them from affairs in Muscat, sending Said to rule in Barka and Salim to rule in Mesna. And then the brothers' strongest ally, Muhenna bin Muhammad, head of the deposed yet still powerful Yaarubi dynasty, was brutally murdered. Most suspected Bedr of engineering the crime. He had been deeply jealous of Muhenna's friendship with his cousins, and upon hearing gunfire coming from Muhenna's castle on that fateful morning, had reportedly remarked, "I suspect that Muhenna has been killed."

Not long thereafter, on July 9, 1806, Bedr himself was lured to Barka and killed. The Omanis greeted the news of his death with relief, and praised Said for his boldness and courage; he had acted like a true Arab leader. The ruler with the detested Wahhabi connection was gone. Among the first to offer Said his congratulations was his uncle Qays, who from then on supported his nephew.

One of the teenage Said's first acts as ruler, and one probably initiated by his ambitious aunt, was almost as perfidious as the method by which he had risen to power. He sent a letter to Amir Saud, in which he blamed Bedr's murder on his own loyal regent Muhammad bin Nasir. The amir was not fooled—he knew what had transpired at Barka—but he wrote back an apparently friendly letter.

The denunciation of Muhammad bin Nasir, like the murder of Bedr, must have caused Said much anguish, since he was from all accounts a deeply moral man despite these actions—at least when it came to his own people. Vincenzo Maurizi, an Italian doctor who spent some time in Said's service only a few years later, wrote, "His constant love of justice, and distinguished clemency, the effects of which are felt, not only by his own subjects, but even by his domestic slaves, make us endeavor to forget the deep atrocity of that crime which places him on the throne." But in the precarious rough-and-tumble world of Arab politics, it was betray or be betrayed, kill or be killed. Said and his aunt were only too well aware of the fact that the Wahhabis had witnessed Bedr's murder and would, one way or another, at some time or another, retaliate. Perhaps if they blamed the murder on Muhammad, they might have reasoned, they could buy themselves some time.

Less than a month after writing to Amir Saud, Said sent a letter to the British, asking for their recognition. But the British, condemning the way in which Said had risen to power, refused to recognize him. "Begun amidst unfavourable omens," his rule would be a short one, predicted one British civil servant.

The next year, Said and his uncle Qays went to war, attacking Khor Fakkan on the north coast, which had been captured by the Qawasim, the relatives of the Wahhabis, in the confusion following Bedr's death. The Qawasim had built a fort and were using it as a base from which to raid passing ships. The Al Busaids' attack was initially successful, but then the Qawasim regrouped, turned around, and badly routed the attackers. In a deep personal blow to Said, Qays was killed.

Meanwhile, not surprisingly, the relationship between Said and his former regent, Muhammad bin Nasir, had become untenable. Bibi Mouza wanted control of the two forts that were still under Muhammad's command and directed her nephew to write to him and order him to come to Barka. Against his better judgment, Muhammad obeyed—only to be seized and imprisoned until he agreed to give up the forts. Concurrently, Bibi Mouza held Muhammad's wife prisoner in her home.

On his way home after his release, Muhammad suddenly said goodbye to his attendants: "Peace be with you; return home; deliverance from God is near," he said. Then, spurring his camel, he traveled to Diriyah, where he met with Amir Saud and pleaded his case.

Already harboring thoughts of attacking Oman again, Amir Saud was happy to take up Muhammad's cause. He sent his best general into Oman, and together, the general and former regent took quick possession of several towns. Tribes loyal to Muhammad helped him recapture his old forts and seize the ports of the Batinah. By late 1808, Said's authority was limited to Muscat and its immediate environs.

Said's troubles were also escalating on the north coast. Largely through plunder, the Qawasim now commanded a fleet of 63 large vessels and 813 smaller craft capable of carrying a total of nineteen thousand men. With these expanded forces, the tribe was venturing far beyond their traditional haunts, to attack ships from both sides of the Strait of Hormuz and off the coast of India—the heart of British territory.

The Qawasim's capture of the East India Company ship *Minerva* was especially unsettling to the British. After boarding the ship, the marauders perfumed and purified the vessel with water. Then, under "circumstances of horrid solemnity which gave the deed the appearance of some hellish religious rite," they cut the severely wounded captain into pieces on the quarterdeck. Next, the passengers and crew were led forward one by one, "their heads placed on the gunwale, and their throats cut with the exclamation used in battle of Allah akhbar—God is Great."

Finally, the British had had enough. Approaching Said, they proposed sending a joint expedition against the Qawasim. Close to losing what little power he had left, the young ruler must have been ecstatic, and in 1809, the two allies successfully razed their enemy's stronghold and destroyed its flotilla. Upon hearing the news, the Muscati citizenry rallied enthusiastically behind Said.

What exactly the Italian doctor Vicenzo Maurizi, who arrived in Muscat in 1809, was doing in Oman isn't clear. He had apparently left Italy because of his pro-Bonaparte sympathies, which had caused family quarrels, and had lived for a time in Constantinople, where he served as a doctor, and in Mocha, Yemen, where he worked as an agent for the French government. He stayed in Oman for about a year before traveling on to Baghdad and Persia, where he was taken prisoner by the Russians. After the collapse of the French empire in 1814, he returned briefly to Muscat.

Upon meeting the nineteen-year-old Seyyid Said, Maurizi took an immediate liking to him. "Seyd Said is a good looking young man, of moderate stature and florid complexion," he wrote in his *History of Seyd Said*, the first Western book devoted exclusively to Oman. "His manners are lively and agreeable, and he possesses a sound understanding, which always makes him eager to acquire information from the Europeans who arrive at Muscat. . . . "

Maurizi served as both Seyyid Said's physician—an early sign of the ruler's respect for the West—and as the commander of his armies; he had acquired some military experience while living in Constantinople. He accompanied Seyyid Said in his early campaigns against the Qawasim and described the battles that he witnessed as confused free-for-alls, with friends attacking friends by mistake and the British attacking the wrong set of Arabs, as all were dressed alike—probably the norm for that time and place.

According to Maurizi, Oman's economy, already at this early date, was based largely on the slave trade, though it was still quite modest in scale. Maurizi stated that almost all of the country's annual revenue of $75,000 came from slave taxes, with about 2,000 slaves shipped through Muscat each year. Similarly, in 1831, a British visitor estimated that between 1,400 and 1,700 slaves—75 percent from East Africa, 25 percent from Ethiopia—passed through Muscat annually. About half of these slaves remained in Oman to work the country's huge date plantations, each growing between 3,000 and 5,000 palms, and the rest were shipped on to points farther north and east.

After their successful attack against the Qawasim in the north, the British helped Said recapture the port of Shinas in the Batinah from them as well. This second venture incurred minimal losses, and at last Said seemed poised to gain control of Oman. But then came news of approaching Wahhabi reinforcements—a small army mounted on a thousand camels. The British wanted no quarrel with the powerful Wahhabis, and as the reinforcements arrived, they climbed onto their ships and sailed away. Thereupon, the Wahhabis fell viciously upon the Omani troops: "The battle, or rather massacre . . . lasted about two hours, at the end of which time, Seyd Said saw his army completely ruined, 2,000 being slain on the spot," wrote Maurizi. As for Seyyid Said himself, he was already safely on board a ship. "Active personal courage was by no means [Said's] characteristic quality," the Italian doctor observed wryly.

The Wahhabis then mounted a full-scale war against Oman. Collecting an overwhelming force, they marched toward Muscat, burning, looting, and massacring everyone along the way. In greater danger of losing his life than ever before, the desperate Said appealed to the British for help, saying that their joint expedition had put him in an awkward and dangerous position. The British cavalierly responded by urging him to make peace with his enemies. Next Said appealed to the French, who did the same, while also recommending that he embrace the Wahhabi religion.

Said turned to Maurizi for advice, and it is here that his underlying moral character comes into sharp historical view for the first time. "I took the liberty to suggest some steps which, though not quite consonant to the political morality of Europe, except as taught by Machiavelli, would have been rejected by very few oriental despots on that account," wrote Maurizi, without spelling out exactly what steps he was recommending.

> Seyd Said instantly observed that they were contrary to the precepts of the Koran, and the law of God. . . . I replied that when the immediate interest of kings and nations were concerned, it was sometimes necessary to put the divine commands on one side, and the absolute necessity of the case on the other. I had scarcely finished the sentence, when, frightened at opinions so detestable, he exclaimed with energy, that he would sooner lose both kingdom and life, than thus break through the commands of God, and the dictates of his conscience. I might perhaps have suggested, that no crime more grossly violated the laws of the creator than [the murder of a cousin]; but this would have been pushing the discussion to a dangerous point.

Later in the same conversation, Seyyid Said also made it clear that, despite all that had occurred, he still had great faith in the British. Maurizi tried to convince him otherwise, impressing upon him that "when two nations, the one powerful, the other weak, entered into a lasting alliance, the latter, in the course of time, always became subject to the former." But Said paid no attention. Perhaps if he had, the entire history of Oman would have been different.

With no one coming to their aid, Said and Salim had no choice but to negotiate with the enemy. Alone and unarmed, Said went to see General Mutlaq; a slight, smooth-cheeked youth confronting one of the region's most formidable commanders. Said offered to pay the Wahhabis forty thousand Maria Theresa dollars in return for peace. Mutlaq accepted the offer and returned to the Najd, only to have his decision angrily overruled. Amir Saud immediately dispatched another general to Oman, who was murdered on the way, and then sent back Mutlaq, who waged what would be his final campaign. In an early battle, he was shot and killed.

Then, unexpectedly, the Omanis received a reprieve. The Wahhabis retreated. They were having trouble elsewhere: the Egyptian forces, who would eventually drive the sect back into the Najd, had entered Arabia. And shortly thereafter, Amir Saud fell seriously ill and passed away, putting the Wahhabis' expansionist hopes on hold, not to be revived again for another twenty years.

Commented Maurizi: "Philosophers and Poets have alike observed, that when the wheel of Fortune turns, it usually retraces its revolutions with extreme rapidity: it was so on the present occasion. . . . This rapid course of favourable events restored happiness and tranquility to Seyd Said, who so lately appeared to be on the very verge of destruction."

Not all of Said's problems with the violent Islamists had been resolved, however. Back on Oman's north coast, the Qawasim had recovered quickly from the joint British-Omani attack. By 1811, only two years after the assault, they had renewed their raids on passing ships. Another three years, and they were back on India's coast. Another five years, and they were attacking ports on the Red Sea. The British refrained from taking any action while the Wahhabis were still in power, but after the sect's capital fell in 1818, they sent representatives to Muscat to propose another joint expedition. Said received them graciously but hedged his bets, evading commitment until the British sent nine warships to the north coast. Only then did Seyyid Said join in the attack.

The following year, a General Treaty of Peace was signed by the British and the Qawasim sheikhs, and Oman's so-called Pirate Coast became the Trucial Coast, named for the truce. The peace agreement paved the way for the formation of a loose confederation of Trucial States, which in 1971 became the United Arab Emirates.

A year after the treaty, Said's beloved brother Salim died of paralysis, and a deadly cholera swept through Oman, leaving ten thousand people dead. Said might well have regarded the tragic events as fate's revenge for the violent manner in which he had ascended to power.

At last Seyyid Said, now in his mid-thirties, was the undisputed leader of Oman. In 1824, he made a triumphant pilgrimage to Mecca, sailing there on board the *Liverpool*, a vessel of seventy-four guns, specially built for the voyage in Bombay. Muhammad Ali Pasha of Egypt sent officers to greet him upon his arrival with a lavish reception, the sharif of Mecca granted him an audience, and all who met him admired his graciousness and regal bearing, and the generosity of his gifts—the richest that had ever been seen in Mecca.

The first chapter of Seyyid Said's rule was drawing to a close. Five years later, he would make his first trip to Zanzibar.

PART TWO

Zanzibar

8

A Princess Is Born

ON AUGUST 30, 1844, SALME WAS BORN ON THE ISLAND OF ZAN-
zibar. Her father, Seyyid Said, was now overlord of much of East Africa.
Her mother, Djilfidan, was a tall Circassian slave with knee-length, jet-
black hair.

Like all newborn princes and princesses on Zanzibar, Salme was
washed in warm water and bound in a bandage wrapped all around her
tiny body. A mullah recited *adhan*, the call to prayer, in her right ear and
iqama, the introduction to prayer, in her left. Her neck and underarms
were dusted with perfumed powder and she was dressed in a white cotton shirt. Then she was placed on her back, her arms and legs were
straightened, and she was swathed up to her shoulders in another bandage, to be kept on for forty days. Thought to ensure straight posture,
the bandage was only removed for bathing and changing. Her elaborately carved cradle was made of the finest wood from East India.

On the seventh day after Salme's birth, her father came to see her
for the first time, as tradition prescribed. He came bearing gifts from
one of his three treasure rooms, all well stocked with Spanish coins,
guineas, and louis d'ors; toys and trinkets; and jewelry and objets d'art.
Six holes were pricked in each of the princess's ears, and her eyelids
were blackened with antimony to increase the sparkle of her eyes.

On the fortieth day after Salme's birth, dozens of guests arrived for
a joyful ceremony during which her head was shaved by the sultan's
chief eunuch and her hair was buried in the ground, a Swahili tradition,
while an incense of gum arabic was burned. Then her swathing bandage

was removed, and she was dressed in a jasmine-perfumed silk shirt and gold-embroidered *kofia*, or cap with earflaps. Her arms, feet, and ears were adorned with gold rings, and a gold amulet engraved with a verse from the Quran was hung around her neck. Now she was safe from the evil eye and ready to be seen by the world; hitherto, only her mother, father, and a few devoted slaves had laid eyes on her.

When Salme was old enough to sit up, all her brothers and sisters under age ten were invited to the ceremonial party. The princess was dressed in her best and placed in a carriage stuffed with cushions. Then a mixture of soft roasted corn kernels and very small silver coins was gently poured over her head, as all the other children rushed in to claim their share.

At birth, Salme had been given a wet nurse, an African woman who would remain her slave for many years. When she was three or four months old, her father gave her several more slaves, and as she grew older, more still. Salme may have been the daughter of a slave, but she was also the daughter of a free man, and therefore free herself. Similarly, her mother, Djilfidan, could no longer be sold or given away, now that she had given birth, and would be freed upon Seyyid Said's death.

Zanzibar, romantic land of lustrous white sand beaches and swaying dark green palm trees, lies twenty miles off the coast of East Africa, where it is visible from the mainland on clear days. Now part of Tanzania, a nation that was created in 1964 by combining the former Tanganyika with Zanzibar, the island is only about fifty-four miles long and twenty-three miles wide at its broadest point. To its north lies its smaller sister island, Pemba, sometimes known as the Green Island because of its lush vegetation and fertile soil. Much hillier than Zanzibar, Pemba is cut with dozens of small bays and inlets that once provided convenient hiding places for slavers en route from the mainland to Zanzibar.

In contrast, Zanzibar is almost flat—its highest elevation is only 440 feet. Ringed by pink coral reefs and blue-green waters, the island is lush with wild palm, clove, mango, orange, lemon, allspice, and breadfruit trees. To anyone approaching Zanzibar from the sea, these trees are visible long before the rest of the island and seem to float above the horizon, a magical forest-garden.

On the west coast of Zanzibar, facing Africa, is a natural harbor formed by coral reefs. The island's good water supply and ample timber once made this harbor, also called Zanzibar, an ideal central refuge for the Indian Ocean traders, who stopped here to rest, repair their ships, and replenish their supplies. The harbor also offered a huge advantage over other East African ports: thanks to its reefs, it provided a safe anchorage year round. Hundreds of vessels once wintered in Zanzibar annually, awaiting the monsoon winds to propel them back north—to Arabia, the Persian Gulf, India, and beyond.

Zanzibar's original settlers were probably Cushites, an African people of the Late Stone Age, who migrated south from the Ethiopian highlands sometime before 2000 B.C. The Cushites herded cattle and sheep, and may have introduced irrigation to the region. But during the first millennium, the Cushites were either exterminated or absorbed by the Bantu-speaking races from the Cameroons, who came to dominate much of Africa south of the equator.

Also arriving in Zanzibar sometime in prehistory were the Arabs. The first Arabs may have reached the island by the seventh century B.C. and had probably begun trading with Zanzibar by the first century A.D.

One of the early African chronicles—which are essentially oral histories, only later recorded in written form—tells of a large number of Shirazis, or Persians from the city of Shiraz, arriving in East Africa in the 900s. As the story goes, the powerful Persian ruler Hasan bin Ali dreamed that he saw a rat with an iron snout gnawing holes in the walls of his house. Interpreting this as a sign of the imminent downfall of his kingdom, he and his six sons set off in seven different ships for East Africa. Each man landed in a different place, where he founded a town—among them, Mombasa, Kilwa, and Pemba. The chronicle also states that about 150 years later, a Persian ruler ousted from Kilwa took refuge in Zanzibar.

The oldest mosque on the island dates back to A.D. 1107, giving credence to this tale. And, as local tradition has it, the mosque was built by a Shirazi sultan who employed a slave named Kizi as his architect. Kizi's work was so beautiful that a neighboring African chieftain tried to abduct him. But the sultan prayed for divine intervention and a swarm of bees drove the enemy away. The African chieftain attacked again, and this time no help arrived. In desperation, the sultan cut off Kizi's right hand so that he could no longer work, and prayed to be removed from this earth. The ground opened up and the sultan disappeared, a rock appearing on the spot as he vanished. Zanzibaris can still point out the site where the miracle occurred.

Princess Salme was born in Beit al-Mtoni, her father's country palace, which was perched on a small knoll overlooking the sea. Consisting of two square buildings made of coral rock, the two-story residence was cocooned by a whispering grove of coconut palms, mango and orange trees. Through the palace center ran channels of water diverted from a nearby river for which the estate was named. *Mtoni* is Swahili for "river"; *beit* is Arabic for "house" or "palace."

"Of all the most beautiful places that I ever beheld, or ever imagined to exist, this excelled them in natural lovliness and beauty," wrote an American seaman who visited Mtoni in 1847, three years after Salme was born. "The residence (or palace as it is called) is not remarkable handsome, though large and on the whole quite a respectable Arab Palace. But the scenery around it is what attracts the eyes, and renders it magnificent. . . . The Orange, the pinapple and cocoa nut here flourish in a luxurious growth. The walks around the structure are Mc'adamised and layed with sea shells and the sides lined with orange trees. . . . In the rear is a large forest of different kinds of trees layed out in avenues that bespeak no ordinary task to the designer."

A thousand people lived at Beit al-Mtoni, most of them slaves. The palace held hundreds of rooms and was centered on a large courtyard in which peacocks, flamingos, geese, ducks, and ostriches roamed free. The royal children collected the birds' eggs every morning and gave them to the palace cook, who rewarded the children with sweets.

At one end of the courtyard stretched a row of bathhouses, each containing two large baths about five yards long by four yards wide, and ledges upon which to rest. A favorite haunt of the royal family, the bathhouses were usually full from four a.m. until midnight; people spent hours there every day, bathing, praying, working, reading, and even eating and drinking. Each bathhouse was assigned to a specific set of residents, and "woe to the person who took a rather broad view of the differences in this respect," wrote Salme in her memoirs years later. "A rigorous caste spirit reigned at Beit il-Mtoni, to such an extent that high and low alike observed it in all its forms."

Uniting the palace's two main buildings was a *bendjle,* or large round balcony with a cone-shaped roof, built of painted wood, resembling a carousel. The prettiest spot in the palace, with grand views of the sea, the *bendjle* was lined with dozens of cane chairs, while to one side stood a telescope, trained on the horizon. Permanently anchored offshore floated *al-Rahmani,* the sultan's man-of-war, while on the beach below the *bendjle,* small craft came and went, obeying orders from signal flags hoisted on the palace flagpole. Facing the sea gleamed four brass cannons.

In the early mornings, just after first prayers, Seyyid Said usually paced up and down the *bendjle,* deep in thought. Anyone who wished to talk to him in private came to him here. Later in the day, the *bendjle* was his favorite spot for relaxing with his main wife, Azze bint Seyf, and his grown children.

Seyyid Said had three legitimate wives, but only Azze bint Seyf remained with him for decades and was with him when he died. His two other legitimate wives were both Persians, married to Said for political reasons, and they went back to their home country when it suited them. The first of these, Fateh Ali Shah, was a granddaughter of the shah of Persia, and she married Seyyid Said on the condition that she spend every spring with her family in Shiraz. But five years into their marriage she went home and never returned, perhaps because of an argument she had had with one of her stepsons. Omani rumor had it that after leaving Seyyid Said, the Persian princess was driven out of Shiraz because of an affair she had with a muleteer, and that she died while giving birth to a child fathered by a bath-servant.

Seyyid Said's second Persian wife, Shahrazad bint Irish Mirza, was also the granddaughter of a powerful ruler, and she married Seyyid Said just after he moved to Zanzibar. They divorced about a dozen years later, after a fierce argument that Salme would learn about when she grew older, and Shahrazad returned to Persia.

As befitted a ruler of his time and place, Seyyid Said also owned many concubines of various races, with whom he may have fathered as many as 120 children. And, according to one Omani historian, "every time one of his concubines bore a son he put her away so that she should never bear another son to be whole brother to the first. He was afraid that two whole brothers might intrigue against the others who were not their whole brothers."

Superstitious rumor or fact? It is hard to tell. There were no two whole brothers among Seyyid Said's surviving children, though there were whole sisters and whole brothers and sisters. Exactly how many children the ruler fathered is also hard to tell. Salme, too, estimated a high number—100—but many of her siblings must have died quite young. The patriarch was survived by one legitimate wife and 75 concubines, but only 36 children—18 sons and 18 daughters, all born to concubines.

Seyyid Said and Azze bint Seyf lived in the wing of Beit al-Mtoni nearest the sea, where they awoke every morning to the cawing of seagulls and the lapping of waves. But while Azze lived in the palace permanently, her husband stayed there only half of each week. He spent the other half, including Friday, the Muslim holy day, in his Zanzibar town palace of Beit al-Sahel, or "Palace by the Sea."

In another wing of Mtoni lived thirty or forty of the ruler's concubines, or *sarari* as they are called in Arabic (sing., *surie*). The American seaman who visited Zanzibar in 1847 wrote: "They are the most beautiful girls (as far as natural genre beauty are conserned) I ever saw. They are from Persia & Caucasia mostly. Their dresses are of the most gorgeous colours trimmed with silver and gold tinsel and embroidered with fine laces. . . . They are very young, 16 to 25 I should [think]."

Salme was one of her father's youngest children, born when he was already in his sixties, and she hungered for his attention from afar, envying her older brothers and sisters, who had more contact with him. "Above middle-height, his features had something extraordinarily fascinating and engaging . . . ," she wrote. "I never saw him angry or abusive. He mostly had a sense of humour, and loved to joke."

The sultan's main wife, Azze bint Seyf, in contrast, was apparently a tyrannical woman whose presence cast a constant pall over the otherwise charming Beit al-Mtoni. Small and plain, with no children of her own, Azze was "extremely imperious, haughty and pretentious," wrote Salme, and insisted that everyone call her "Highness." All the *sarari* and their children had to visit her every morning to wish her good day and return again in the evening to wish her good night. She never appeared without a retinue, and walked stiffly by family members without uttering a single friendly word. Nonetheless, as is so often the case in such seemingly lopsided marriages, "she possessed an unbelievable power" over her husband, "so that he always willingly submitted to her arrangements."

Salme only lived at Beit al-Mtoni until she was seven, but it was here that she began to develop the outspoken, independent, and impulsive spirit that would get her into so much trouble later in life. She and her siblings were left largely on their own from dawn until dusk—free to roam about the palace and its grounds, play tag among the clove trees, or go down to the beach to swim and sail boats.

Yet the children were also strictly disciplined: "Not one of us was spoiled in any way," Salme wrote. "My father's high sense of justice and unparalleled generosity was combined with an equally firm consistency which did not know any weakness. All of us had to obey our teachers and educators on the strength of their word. If occasionally we complained to our father, we certainly left his presence in tears or shame for our behavior."

Early every morning and again every evening, all the royal children over age five were given riding lessons in the courtyard by one of their father's eunuchs. Horseback riding—done without saddles or stirrups—was a major form of entertainment in Zanzibar, and as soon as a royal child had mastered the basics, Seyyid Said gave him or her a mount. The boys were allowed to choose a horse for themselves from the royal stables, while the girls received large snow-white donkeys—more valuable than horses—imported from Muscat.

Wrote Salme:

What so many people in [the West] believe, namely that sons are particularly privileged over daughters, was unknown in our family

circle. I do not know of one single instance in which father or
mother liked a son better than a daughter, or preferred him merely
because he happened to be a son. Nothing of all that. Though the
law in many cases favours the boy more than his sisters . . . yet the
children are everywhere loved and treated alike. It is, of course,
only natural and certainly also human, that . . . one child, whether
boy or girl, is preferred to the other one, even if not openly but secretly. Thus it was also with our father; only, the favourite children
closest to him were certainly not sons, but rather two of his daughters, Sharife and Chole.

Given the often mind-boggling brutality of Arab succession, and
most especially the propensity of Arab sons to betray their fathers, perhaps Seyyid Said's preference for his two daughters was due at least in
part to prudence. Daughters did not usually murder their fathers.

9

Clove Fever

BEIT AL-MTONI, WHERE SALME WAS BORN, HAD ORIGINALLY been built by a wealthy Omani landowner named Saleh bin Haramil al-Abray. Born in Muscat around 1770, Saleh was an ardent Francophile—though he never visited France. Nevertheless, one French visitor described him as "a perfect Frenchman." Before Seyyid Said's arrival in Zanzibar, Saleh had served as French interpreter to the island's governor.

More important, Saleh was probably the first person to introduce the clove tree to Zanzibar—a simple act that was to have tremendous consequences. Zanzibar, and later Pemba, proved to have the world's perfect conditions for clove production and, under Seyyid Said's direction, became the leading exporter of the spice, yielding nearly four fifths of the world's supply right up until the mid-twentieth century. Cloves brought Zanzibar enormous wealth—and enormous suffering. Clove production requires a prodigious amount of cheap labor. Clove production brought slavery to Zanzibar on a scale never before seen in East Africa.

Clove trees are fragrant tropical evergreens that grow in only a few regions of the world, all bordering the sea. The trees are believed to have originated on the Molucca Islands of Indonesia, where a clove tree was once planted every time a child was born. In the fourth century B.C., Chinese rulers of the Han dynasty required that all who approached them first chew on cloves to freshen their breath; the spice was also highly prized by the Romans. By the seventeenth century, the

Dutch had a monopoly on the clove trade, but in 1770, the French started cultivating the tree on their East African colonies of Île de France and Bourbon, islands to the southeast of Zanzibar. The English word *clove* comes from the French word *clou*, meaning "nail," which a clove bud vaguely resembles.

The Île de France and Bourbon, then busy centers for the slave trade, do not have the best conditions for clove production, but within three decades of their introduction, the French colonists were growing enough for export. Saleh must have noticed that fact during one of his visits to the islands, and in the 1810s, apparently with the help of a French Creole, he introduced the trees to Zanzibar. He established one of the island's first clove plantations at Mtoni and another at Kisimbani, a few miles away. Both were small operations, however—it would take the arrival of Seyyid Said to turn Zanzibar's clove production into a major industry.

Seyyid Said first visited Zanzibar for three months in early 1828, and during that period confiscated all of Saleh's property, including Beit al-Mtoni, which he claimed as his own. He also threw the man in prison. His excuse was that Saleh had violated the Moresby Treaty of 1822, which barred Omani subjects from selling slaves to the subjects of Christian nations. Since the sultan often overlooked transgressions of the treaty, however, the real reason behind Saleh's ouster was probably political. Saleh was the head of one of the island's most powerful political factions and, as such, posed a significant threat to the sovereign.

Seyyid Said may have intended to move to Zanzibar from the moment he saw it. He was captivated by the island's beauty—its soft sea breezes, heavily laden fruit trees, and blue-green waters. He was much impressed with its commercial potential—its strategic location, sheltered harbor, and fertile soils. But with a rebellion going on back in Oman, he sailed away again with the northern monsoons, leaving his son Khalid behind to act as governor. Khalid was only thirteen years old at the time, but he was left in the care of a trusted adviser and relative, Seyyid Suleiman bin Hamed Al Busaid, who later became one of Zanzibar's wealthiest and most influential men.

Over the next twelve years, Seyyid Said returned to Zanzibar many times, spending as much time there as he did in Oman. Not until 1840, however, when he was fifty years old, did he finally move to the island permanently. It was an extraordinary decision that must have shocked many of his followers. But the sultan had his reasons: He wanted to develop commerce in the region—and keep a closer eye on his customs masters, whom he suspected of corruption. He wanted to protect his interests from the Europeans, who were starting to arrive in the area in greater numbers, now that the Napoleonic Wars had ended. And in perhaps the most important, as well as the most private of his concerns, he must have wanted to get away from the constant political intrigue of Oman. On Zanzibar, which had been loyal to Oman's Al Busaidi rulers since the 1780s, he could live in relative peace for the first time in his life.

Nearly a century later, an observer would describe the often startling difference between the Omani Arabs born in Muscat, known as *manga* in Swahili, and those born in Zanzibar: "After a short time one can easily distinguish one from the other; the Arab of Zanzibar has a benign, kindly look in his eyes and moves with deliberation, whereas his brother, born and bred in the mountain fastnesses of Oman, has bright, black, piercing eyes, sharp features and a rapid gait, born of the necessity of ever being wakeful for a foe. . . . It is always said that it is unsafe to wake a Manga Arab suddenly, as he will start up, dagger in hand, and strike out."

Seyyid Said probably chose Beit al-Mtoni for his home initially because of its lovely setting and proximity to the town of Zanzibar, also known as Stone Town, only six miles away. But during one of his many early visits to the island, he also became intensely interested in the plantation's strange crop. Clove trees need about fifteen years to reach maturity, and the plantation at Beit al-Mtoni had produced only a few small harvests. Nonetheless, Seyyid Said intuited the spice's potential for Zanzibar immediately. Taking another unusual step that must have surprised many, he began planting clove trees all over the island. By the time of his death, he owned forty-five plantations, on some of which grew between four thousand and eight thousand clove trees, tended to by as many as five hundred slaves. In 1840, the sultan's plantations produced about 5,500 *frasilas* of cloves (one *frasila* equals 35 pounds), and by the late 1840s, about five times that number. The late 1840s crop was worth $50,000—a fortune for that time and place.

As the story goes, Seyyid Said also ordered all other Zanzibari landowners to join in his project and plant three clove trees for every coconut tree—or risk having their property confiscated. But although the landowners may have hesitated to plant the crop at first, they needed little prodding as time went by. In 1830, when Zanzibar's first small clove harvest was sold, one *frasila* was worth an impressive $10— far more than coconuts. "Almost everyone on the island is now clearing away the coconuts to make way for [cloves]," wrote one observer in 1835. By 1840, Zanzibar was exporting 9,000 *frasilas* of cloves; by 1847, 97,000 *frasilas*, and by 1856, 143,000 *frasilas*—an increase of over 1500 percent in sixteen years.

Clove fever soon spread to Oman as well, and Arab immigrants began arriving on the island in record numbers, though some also came to trade or follow Seyyid Said's court. Oman's economy was then in decline, and easier money, or so it was believed, could be made in Zanzibar. No accurate population statistics for the period exist, but by the mid-1850s, visitors estimated that there were about five thousand Omanis living in Zanzibar, as compared to eight hundred in 1844.

Along with the Arabs came the Hindus, or Banyans, "the bankers of Arabia," who became deeply involved in the slave trade. As in Oman, a handful of the Indian merchants had been living in Zanzibar for centuries, but now the size of their community increased exponentially, to reach nearly two thousand by the mid-1850s. The Banyans not only facilitated trade, but also advanced loans to plantation owners intent on financing mortgages and purchasing slaves, and underwrote caravans heading into the interior in search of more slaves. Some Banyans also became major plantation and slave owners in their own right.

Not surprisingly, the height of the clove boom was short-lived. The dramatic rise in clove production resulted in a sharp decline in price, from $10 per *frasila* in 1830 to $5.50 in 1840 to $2 in 1856. Nonetheless, cloves would continue to be Zanzibar's main cash crop for over a century, and although few new plantations were planted after about 1850, the plantation way of life continued into the early 1900s.

Most of the new plantation owners planted their crops on Zanzibar's fertile west and north sides. In so doing, they may have displaced some indigenous Swahili people, or simply used vacant land—the historical evidence isn't clear. There might also have been some misunderstanding among the Swahili over what exactly was taking place. Like Native Americans, the Swahili regarded land as communal property that could be leased but not privately owned. Like Westerners, the Arabs regarded land as a commodity to be bought and sold.

All of the clove plantations looked more or less alike, though the larger ones were equipped with comfortable villas and the smaller ones with shacks. The clove trees were planted in long, lush rows; most trees grew twenty or thirty feet tall, with foliage so thick that they resembled giant bushes. The leaves of the tree were round and glossy—red on the top, green on the bottom—and gave off a sweet, fragrant smell when rubbed. Straight, dusty roads of packed red earth ran through the dense green. Slave huts dotted the clearings.

To harvest the cloves, which are dried flower buds, from the trees required great precision. The buds had to be handpicked when they were crimson and hard, just before they flowered, and they had to be broken off together with their stems without hurting the branches. Zanzibar's main picking season was November through December, but there was also a smaller harvest in July through August, and during each season, the average tree had to be picked three times because the buds ripen irregularly. The main winter harvest often coincided with the rainy season, meaning that picking conditions were often wet, muddy, and miserable.

But the painstaking nature of clove harvesting was a blessing in disguise—it kept Zanzibar's slaves from suffering the full potential cruelty of slavery. Unlike unskilled cotton pickers in the American South or sugarcane workers in the West Indies, who could easily be replaced when they became old or worn out, experienced clove pickers were skilled laborers who were of great value to their masters. Most took care not to push them too long or too hard. As one European who lived in Zanzibar in the 1870s wrote: "The slave knows very well that there are certain orders that he must obey, and that he must do a certain amount of work for his master, but he knows equally well that the master dare not and would not transgress the understood privileges and acknowledged rights of their slaves."

Zanzibar's younger slaves harvested the cloves while the older, trusted slaves served as supervisors. Men stood on triangular-shaped, scaffold-like ladders to do the picking, while women separated the buds from the stems and spread the buds out on mats to dry. The drying process usually took about a week, during which time the cloves turned a deep chocolate brown. Afterward, the crop was packed into sacks and taken to town to be sold, usually by the women. The process was then repeated again and again, as each tree was re-picked.

During the harvest season, the slaves worked long hours, often picking eight or nine hours a day, seven days a week. But during the off-season, when the plantations needed little maintenance, most slaves worked only a few hours a day four or five days a week—as did most domestic slaves year-round. The simple lifestyle of the Omanis, combined with the island's tropical conditions, meant that many slaves often had time on their hands, especially in the wealthier households, where masters tended to own far more slaves than they needed. To own many slaves was a way of showing off wealth.

The Zanzibar slaves "do less work, on the average, in a month than a Mississippi slave does in a week," wrote one American whaler in the mid-1800s. Another American commented: "Strictly speaking they are not slaves, but are almost as much masters as there owners are. They have three days of the week to work for themselves, and generally the other four, there masters know not where they are. These slaves, many of them have slaves, some three or four. Slaves are owned here because it is fashionable for to have them, not because it is profitable."

When a new male slave arrived on a plantation from the mainland, he was washed and groomed by an old slave and given new clothes, his own hoe and machete, and a plot of land. He was also given enough food to last him until his first harvest, when he was expected to reciprocate by giving his master a gift—usually part of his harvest. Some masters regarded that gift as a one-time offering; others expected a gift every harvest season.

Zanzibar's plantations had no slave quarters as such. Instead, the captured Africans built their own huts, in clearings among the clove trees, using materials provided by their masters. Also unlike in the Americas, a master had no right to enter a slave's hut without first asking permission, except in unusual circumstances, such as when searching for a runaway. Slaves were free to move about as they pleased, and most spent Thursdays and Fridays in town selling their produce, socializing, and observing the Muslim holy day.

Many masters encouraged their slaves to cultivate as much land as they could and keep any profits that they made from selling their surplus in town. Most masters also provided their slaves with simple clothing and took care of them when they were old or sick, as Islamic law prescribes. Credible eyewitnesses reported that few masters whipped their slaves and that cruel punishments were rare, though stocks and chains were used. A master who did kill a slave was not punished, but he suffered some consequences: his other slaves often ran away and others refused to work for him.

All of which is not to say that slavery on Zanzibar was a benign institution. Before the clove boom began in earnest in the 1830s, the island probably held fewer than 15,000 slaves, out of a total population of 100,000 to 150,000. During the height of clove production in the 1840s and 1850s, that number, according to wildly varying contemporary accounts, grew to between 40,000 and 200,000, out of a total population of 200,000 to 300,000. Slavery was big business—no matter what the exact figure. Tens of thousands of men, women, and children had been cruelly torn from their homelands. Tens of thousands were being forced to live degraded lives. "A slave is a brute beast, an enemy of God and the Prophet," went one Arab saying of the day.

Indicative of the fact that something was very wrong were Zanzibar's many runaways. The island had no police, except in Stone Town, and a slave's escape was often successful. The bigger problem a runaway faced was where to go after fleeing—as an island, Zanzibar had few hiding places. Some sold themselves to slave traders, in the hopes of gaining kinder masters, and some stole canoes and escaped to the mainland, where, knowing no one, they were often recaptured or killed. Others fled to Pemba, where escaped slaves had established a settlement on the island's wild north end that the sultan's soldiers dared not attack.

In addition, the relatively humane treatment of slaves in Zanzibar had an insidious side: the island's paternalistic system tied the slaves to their masters in ways that did not exist in crueler slave societies. As owners of their own homes and gardens, with weekends off and the right to at least some freedom of movement, slaves in Zanzibar had less incentive to rebel than did many of their counterparts in the Americas. The kind master took even as he gave.

Slavery in Zanzibar endured long after the profitability of the clove industry declined. Not until 1897, forty-one years after Seyyid Said's death and seven years after the island became a British protectorate, was the institution finally abolished.

Saleh bin Haramil al-Abray, the wealthy Arab landowner who first introduced the clove tree to Zanzibar, eventually escaped from prison and fled to the African mainland, where he was later pardoned by Seyyid Said. But even as thousands of other Zanzibaris profited handsomely from Saleh's agricultural experiment, he suffered a fate more akin to that of the slaves imported to harvest the spice. Far removed from the cultured French lifestyle he so admired, he died a pauper. "None obtains but what is granted to him," wrote one Omani historian of Saleh's fate, before citing a chilling poem:

> *How many have [been] seen, noted for good fortune*
> *Whom fortune has left, unnoticed*
> *forgotten, knowing not where to turn. Who climbs may fall;*
> *   be not unaware.*

10

The Move to Town

DJILFIDAN, SALME'S MOTHER, WAS NO BEAUTY, ACCORDING TO her plainspoken daughter, but she was tall and strongly built, with dark black eyes and hair. A very gentle and pious woman, she spent much of her spare time caring for the sick, and was a great favorite of Seyyid Said, who always rose to meet her—an honor he did not extend to many of his concubines. Salme was her only child.

Djilfidan had been purchased in a slave market by one of Seyyid Said's men when she was only seven or eight years old, and had grown up playing with his oldest children. Attending school with them, she learned to read, which gave her an advantage over most of the other *sarari*, who had entered the harem as teenagers. Djilfidan encouraged Salme to go to school as well, but she herself seems to have made little use of her literacy. "Intellectually speaking, my mother was not exceedingly gifted, but on the other hand she was very clever with needlework," wrote Salme in a statement that probably did not sound quite as derogatory in the 1800s as it does today.

One of Djilfidan's closest friends was Sara, another Circassian concubine. The two women had an agreement: should one of them die, the other would take care of her children. Sara passed away first, when Salme was seven, leaving behind a seventeen-year-old son, Majid, and his sister, Chadudj. Both were already considered to be grown and were living in Majid's new home in Stone Town, Beit al-Watoro. All of Seyyid Said's sons received their own homes when they turned seventeen or eighteen—along with servants, horses, and a monthly allowance—and often took their mothers and single sisters to live with them, as is still customary throughout the Muslim world.

Although they were now considered adults, Majid and Chadudj begged Djilfidan to join them in their new abode. Djilfidan was reluctant at first—Mtoni had been her home since childhood. But her promise to her deceased friend weighed heavily on her mind, and in the end she agreed to their request.

Her friends at Beit al-Mtoni were devastated. "Do you have no heart left for us?" they cried. Djilfidan replied, "Oh, my friends, it is not my own will to leave you; it is my fate to go away." Of which the adult Salme later observed: "In a real Arab house, two things above all are unknown: the word 'chance' and materialism. The Muslim . . . is convinced that not his will, but the will of the Lord is done, in little things as well as in great ones."

Mother and daughter prepared to leave. After packing up their few belongings, and alerting their slaves, they went to bid goodbye to Azze bint Seyf. The first wife received them standing—a rare honor—and permitted them to kiss her hand.

Outside, on the beach, hundreds gathered to see Djilfidan and Salme off. The spatial distance they were traveling wasn't far—only six miles—but the symbolic one was. Beit al-Mtoni was the country; Beit al-Watoro was the town. Beit al-Mtoni was a backwater; Beit al-Watoro stood next door to Beit al-Sahel, Seyyid Said's town palace, in which he held court twice daily, receiving everyone from laborers clad in scanty waistcloths to landowners flaunting fine *dishdashas* and elaborately rolled turbans.

Two cutters arrived, one for Salme and her mother, the other for their belongings and slaves. The first boat was manned by a crew of fourteen oarsmen and filled with dozens of green, red, blue, silver, and gold silk cushions. At its stem and stern fluttered the deep red flags of Seyyid Said.

Tears ran down Djilfidan's and Salme's cheeks as eunuchs helped them into their boat. "*Weda, weda!*"—farewell, farewell—everyone cried. Twilight had fallen and the boats' colored lanterns cast a magical glow over the darkening waters. Waves lapped whispers against the shore.

The boats began to move, the oarsmen keeping time with melancholy song. Salme listened for a while, watching the shore slip past, black shapes in the darkness. Then she fell asleep, to awake to the sound of voices calling her name. Already they had reached Stone Town and were passing beneath her father's town palace, its small high windows ablaze with lights. Lining the windows were dozens of heads, bobbing beads on a wire. Everyone was peering out to catch a glimpse of Salme and her mother, whom they'd never met before.

But the cutters didn't pause, and a few moments later they arrived at Beit al-Watoro, where Sara's daughter Chadudj was waiting for them at the bottom of the stairs. A stern and practical young woman, she briskly escorted the newcomers up to her room, where her personal eunuch served them simple refreshments. Then she sent word to her brother Majid to come up and greet the arrivals. He could not enter the women's quarters without a specific invitation; the higher the rank of women in the Muslim world, the more they are secluded from men. Only Seyyid Said could enter all the palaces' harems without an invitation.

Salme dozed again as the grown-ups drank tea and talked, and drank more tea and talked. But finally, the welcoming party was over and Djilfidan and Salme were taken to their new quarters, a moderately sized room overlooking a mosque. Like many Arab rooms of the day, it was carpeted with plush Persian rugs and enclosed by thick whitewashed walls complete with deep recesses for displaying objets d'art. Large, floor-length mirrors imported from Europe sparkled on the walls and a divan ringed most of the room. In between the mirrors—and indeed, all over the house—ticked-tocked portentous clocks, also imported from Europe and then all the rage in Zanzibar. In one corner stood a double bed made of carved rosewood and mounted on high legs. Beneath the bed was a space large enough for sleeping; it could be used by a nurse attending to a young child or an invalid.

At first, Salme was miserable in her new home and spent her days moping about, pining for the country and her family there. Beit al-Watoro was tiny compared to Beit al-Mtoni and she had no place in which to sail her boats and no white donkey to ride. But then her half brother Majid, a gentle youth, took her by the hand to see his many animals, including dozens of white rabbits and fighting cocks. And before long, Salme had her own squadron of fighting cocks, which she pitted against Majid's almost daily—perhaps with little bloodshed, as she writes only of the entertainment they provided. Later, Majid also taught Salme how to use a sword and how to shoot, to the great distress of Djilfidan, who tried, without success, to interest her daughter in needle-work.

Majid suffered from epilepsy and could not be left alone. Even when he was bathing in the royal bathhouse, his sister Chadudj or some other trusted family member always waited by the door, to periodically call out, "Are you all right?" He would answer teasingly, "Yes, I am still alive."

Until, that is, one day not long after Salme's arrival. Chadudj heard a heavy thud coming from the bathhouse, and rushing in with several slaves, she found her brother lying on a raised platform and convulsed with a terrible attack—the worst he had ever had. Frantic, she sent a messenger to Beit al-Mtoni to fetch their father. Majid's convulsions stopped. He lay senseless.

One hour later, Seyyid Said arrived, alone and in a dugout canoe—an unheard-of mode of transport for an Arab ruler. But he had not wanted to waste time by saddling a horse or assembling a retinue. He knelt at Majid's bed, tears streaming down his face. "More than forty children the old man called his own, and yet he was deeply affected by the illness of a single one! . . . " wrote Salme. " 'O Lord! O Lord! pre-serve my son for me!' he incessantly prayed. His prayer was granted by the Highest, for Majid was spared."

By the time Salme and her mother moved to Stone Town in 1851, it was a bustling trading port of some 30,000 to 40,000 inhabitants, mak-ing it the largest settlement in all of East Africa, especially during the winter months, when the monsoon winds caused its population to swell by the thousands. Most of the town's inhabitants were African or Swahili, about 5,000 were Arab, and another 2,000 were Indian. A handful of Westerners, including Americans, Englishmen, and French-men, also lived in the town.

Stone Town's most impressive buildings stood along the waterfront—a tidy, lustrous row stretching for about one and a half miles. Largest among them were the royal palaces and the Old Fort, the latter built by the Omanis around 1700, on a site earlier occupied by a Portuguese church and a merchant's home. Flanking the palaces and the fort were utilitarian American, British, and French consulates, and the large but outwardly plain mansions of the Arab landowners—two- or three-story boxes with few windows and flat roofs topped by crenellated walls. Built around large central courtyards open to the sky, the mansions' beauty lay on the inside, hidden from prying eyes, like the beauty of the Arab women.

From the street, Seyyid Said's main palace, Beit al-Sahel, was also a modest affair. Two stories high and about 130 feet long, it had only one unusual outward feature—a red-tiled roof. Rows of high, small windows framed by pale green shutters ran along the harbor side, and it was from here that the *sarari* and their children watched the comings and goings of the outside world. Next door to Beit al-Sahel stood Salme's new home, Beit al-Watoro, and another small palace, Beit al-Tani, while separating the residences was the Al Busaidi family burial plot, where runaway slaves could sometimes be found lying in the shade, chained together at the neck. Behind Beit al-Sahel reigned the royal mosque, and farther inland were the royal stables, housing about two hundred horses.

Set into the plain, whitewashed walls of many of the better houses in Stone Town was the Zanzibari door—an all-important architectural feature that continues to characterize the port today. Usually made of teak imported from India or mainland Africa, the tall, heavy portals were elaborately carved, most often with motifs of the sea. Waves and fishes climbed up doorposts and danced on panels, while chain designs, symbolizing security, entwined the borders. Some doors were embellished with frankincense and date palms—symbols of wealth—and some with Indian floral designs. Many doors were also dotted with brass studs and spikes, and over most hung inscribed verses from the Quran. "The higher the tenement, the bigger the gateway, the heavier the padlock, and the huger the iron studs which nail the door of heavy timber, the greater is the owner's dignity," wrote the explorer Richard Burton when he visited the island in 1857. It was even said that wealthy Zanzibaris ordered their doors first and built their houses second.

Stone Town was—and still is—largely built of coral stone, whitewashed with *chunam*, a mixture of coral lime and mortar. Coral stone is easy to quarry and to build with, but it retains water for long periods, meaning that even the best-built homes often suffer from gaping cracks and mushrooming patches of blue, yellow, and green mold, especially during the rainy season. Nineteenth-century visitors were often singularly unimpressed by the town's sometimes shoddy appearance, which they attributed to the Arabs' "natural" indolence.

To the immediate east of the palaces stood the Old Fort, which, though small by European standards, was the town's biggest structure, with high walls topped by towers. The Omanis had once used the fort to defend themselves against the Portuguese, but by Seyyid Said's time it was no longer needed for defense and was sliding into disrepair. Even its cannons were rotting—another sign, many visiting Westerners agreed, of the Arabs' inherent laziness.

Inside the fort lived about a hundred of Seyyid Said's soldiers and their families, their huts jammed closely together into tiny courtyards separated by mud walls. Some of the soldiers were African slaves, but most were Baluchi mercenaries—often handsome men with silky henna- or indigo-dyed beards, originally from what is now western Pakistan and eastern Iran. The soldiers—free or slave—dressed in a motley array of uniforms, including cast-offs from corps in Bombay, and carried a motley variety of weapons, including muskets, two-edged swords, heavy sticks, and shields made of rhino hide.

Seyyid Said's forces elsewhere in East Africa were equally unimpressive. At the time of Salme's birth, he had only about four hundred men stationed along a 2,000-mile-long coastline—including those at Zanzibar—and none at all in the interior. Seyyid Said did not rule East Africa by force, but by trade and mutual economic self-interest, a network that linked himself and his family with the region's Arab, Indian, and Swahili businessmen, as well as the African chieftains of the interior. But just because Seyyid Said's control of East Africa was "only" economic, and thus subtle and indirect, did not mean it wasn't real. The Swahili and Africans knew very well who was behind the caravans snaking in and out of their continent and were wary of the economic ruin that might befall them if they crossed one of those caravans' leaders. Later, many Europeans believed that since the Al Busaids had no military force to speak of in East Africa, they had no true power there, but this was not the case. As a popular proverb of the day went, "When one plays the pipes in Zanzibar, they dance on the Lakes [of Central Africa]."

The Old Fort also housed a small jail, which was rarely occupied by more than a handful of prisoners. Serious crime in Zanzibar was rare, and Seyyid Said seldom chose to incarcerate petty criminals. But for those who were imprisoned, the jail was miserable—dark, dank, and malodorous. Rumor had it that even a stay of three or four days led to high fever, dysentery, and death.

Beyond the Old Fort stood the customhouse, a long, low-slung, and unimpressive shed where, nonetheless, tens of thousands of dollars changed hands each year. Every ship that arrived in Zanzibar had to bring its goods to the customhouse to be taxed, and from dawn until dusk twin streams of slaves went to and from the shed, staggering beneath enormous loads of sacks, bales, and baskets. The waters directly in front of the customhouse teemed with small craft unloading and loading their wares, and the beach was jammed with more sacks, bales, and baskets, along with sprawling piles of animal hides, woods, and ivory tusks. Farther out in the harbor bobbed dozens of larger vessels of every description, from lateen-sailed dhows from Arabia to high-riding *balagas* from India to square-rigged merchant ships from Salem, Massachusetts.

During the winter months, the number of vessels in Zanzibar's protected harbor swelled even more, as hundreds of ships came to rest, "silent wanderers of the sea all herding together with no order or system, patiently awaiting the southern breezes to blow them back to their homes." Conversely, during the spring months, when the northern monsoons arrived, hundreds of dhows carrying thousands of marauding Arabs from the Gulf and the Hadramawt arrived—much to the despair of the Zanzibaris. Seyyid Said managed to keep these Arabs more or less in check during his reign, but after his death in 1856, they laid a virtual siege to Zanzibar each year. Christopher Rigby, the British consul to Zanzibar in the late 1850s, recalled their ominous arrival:

Each boat is crowded with armed men; they bring nothing for sale; and they take no cargo back. . . . Their sole object in coming to the coast is to procure slaves either by kidnapping or by clandestine sale.

During the times the Northern Arabs are here, Zanzibar resembles a city with a hostile army encamped in its neighborhood;

every person who is able to do so sends his children and young slaves into the interior of the island for security; people are afraid to stir out of their houses, and reports are daily made of children and slaves kidnapped in the outskirts of town; they even enter houses and take children by force. . . . Arabs have been found carrying kidnapped children through the public street in large baskets during the day, their mouths being gagged to prevent them from crying out.

Seyyid Said, who could speak Hindustani, farmed out the management of the customhouse to an Indian businessman named Jairam Sewji. Like other Omani rulers before him, the sultan had the greatest respect for the Indian people's business acumen, and he encouraged them to settle in Zanzibar, granting them the same trading rights as Arabs.

Jairam Sewji paid Seyyid Said an enormous annual rent—$150,000 in the mid-1850s—in return for complete control of the customs system. In effect, this meant that it was Jairam Sewji, and not Seyyid Said, who benefited most directly from Zanzibar's burgeoning trade. Seyyid Said obtained most of his revenues from the rent that he received from Sewji. This unusual system forced the ruler, and later his sons, to draw frequent advances from the customs master, to whom they were frequently in debt. During Seyyid Said's time, this scarcely seemed to matter, as revenues were expanding exponentially, but after his death, as the clove industry and the slave trade declined, the system began to undermine the Al Busaids' power.

As Seyyid Said borrowed money from his Indian customs master, his Arab subjects borrowed money from other, more ordinary Indian financiers, usually repaying their debt with interest after the clove harvest. And as the Zanzibari ruler's revenues suffered with the decline of the clove industry, so did his subjects'. Many Zanzibari Arabs were deeply in debt to "the bankers of Arabia" by the 1860s.

Traffic to and from the customhouse wasn't the only activity taking place on the Stone Town beach during Seyyid Said's reign. Slaves were also busy washing and scraping ivory, shredding copra (dried coconut meat), and cleaning cowrie shells, which German merchants exported to West Africa, where they were used for currency. Brahman bulls wandered about at will, while large circular fires flickered at night, neatly built from rings of coral rag alternating with wood. Burnt coral produced the lime needed for making mortar and *chunam*.

A few years before Salme's move to Stone Town, the harbor's waterfront had also been known for something else: dead slaves. Most had died while being transported from the mainland and were thrown into the harbor by traders wishing to avoid paying the $1 per head customs tax. Washing ashore, sometimes by the dozen, the bodies were left unburied, to be devoured by dogs, or to rot, creating an unbearable stench.

That horrific practice more or less ended in the mid-1840s, thanks to the efforts of Colonel Atkins Hamerton, the first British consul to Zanzibar, who convinced Seyyid Said to have the corpses buried elsewhere. Nonetheless, evidence of the earlier practice remained in place for decades; to trip over "bleached and ghastly skeletons, peering here and there from the chambers of their graves" on the beach was not at all unusual.

11

On the Streets

BEHIND THE WATERFRONT, STONE TOWN—PORT OF BRILLIANT
sunshine, dark alleyways, narrow staircases, and massive doors—
beckoned with mysteries that Salme and the island's other well-born
women never got the chance to explore. Tiny winding streets led past
square stone houses, most two to four stories tall, with the bottom floor
used as a storehouse or sleeping quarters for slaves. Thoroughfares were
often so narrow that residents could gossip from their upper windows
on opposite sides of the street while people, horses, donkeys, and carts
flowed by below. Throughout most of the day it was possible to walk
from one end of town to the other without ever having to leave the cool
shadows of the buildings for the brutal rays of the tropical sun.

Most of the streets were crowded with Africans—some free men
and women, but most slaves. The men wore white or checked cotton
cloths that tied above their hips and fell almost to their knees, while the
women wore similar cloths wrapped around their bodies from their
armpits to their knees or ankles. The *khanga*, a brightly colored cloth
with a bold design that is popular throughout East Africa today, had yet
to be widely adopted, though some Swahili women may have begun
using it as early as the 1700s.

Both the African men and women often bore tattoos or other tribal
markings such as raised bumps or beauty slashes, and the women's ears
were often pierced with a half-dozen holes, in which they wore rings or
studs of tin or silver, sticks, or cloves. Some also slit and stretched their
earlobes and lower lips in order to flaunt silver-dollar-sized wooden

disks—much to the horror of visiting Westerners. Silver buttons glinted from the sides of many noses—a Muslim tradition—and rings adorned many wrists, thumbs, and ankles.

Male slaves in service to Seyyid Said and other influential Arabs often carried spears and other weapons—another astonishing sight to Westerners, who were all too aware of the slave uprisings that had occurred in the New World. But the Arab masters had complete confidence in their slaves—often more confidence, in fact, than they had in their own countrymen, who might be allies of an enemy clan, or even in members of their own family, who might try to usurp their position. The slaves, in contrast, were usually extraordinarily loyal. Far removed from their homelands, they had no one to depend on but their masters.

Zanzibar's poorer Arab and Swahili men dressed in simple waist-cloths, while the more well-to-do dressed as they did in Oman—in the traditional long white *dishdasha*, or *kanzu* as it was known in Swahili, girded at the waist with a sash made of cashmere or raw silk. In the colder months, the men donned an embroidered brown or black *bisht* over the *dishdasha*, and on their heads sat white skullcaps topped with turbans. Made of Omani silk mixed with cotton, the turbans were usually of a fine blue-and-white check fringed with broad red borders, and were worn with their ends hanging over one shoulder. Some men also reddened their palms with henna and blackened their eyes with kohl.

As in Muscat, all of the Omani men, rich or poor, carried the curved *khanjar* at the belt. Among the wealthy, the weapon's hilt was often made of rhino hide adorned with gold and silver filigree, and its sheath, of leather or brocade. Many carried rhino shields as well, sometimes covered with the scarlet cloth that was emblematic of Oman.

Also as in Muscat, the Omani women rarely appeared on the street in daylight. Those who did came out completely draped in black, with face masks through which only eyes showed. Often walking beside the black shrouded forms were light-skinned slave women dressed in brightly colored silk or cotton gowns. These women were regarded as the town beauties and they flaunted their looks—staining their eyelids black and lengthening their eyebrows with paint, and sometimes shaving their heads, smoothing them with oils.

In among the local population strutted a handful of Europeans. "How ghastly appears his blanched face, and how frightful his tight garb!—stalking down the street in the worst of tempers, and using his stick upon the mangy 'pariah dogs' and the naked shoulders of the 'niggers' that obstruct him," wrote the explorer Burton. And then, there were the wild "half-breeds from the western shores of the Persian Gulf," who looked like "bundles of fibre bound up in highly-dried human skin" and the Hadramawt Arabs who "hobbled along in pairs," carrying huge packets of goods or hides suspended from a pole and "kicking out of the way the humped cows that are munching fruits and vegetables under the shadow of their worshippers, the Banyans."

Arabs and Westerners alike tended to refer to all Indians in Zanzibar as "Banyans," but the term was inaccurate. The Banyans were a specific Hindu merchant class from Kutch, who initially dominated trade on the island. Zanzibar had a large Shiite Muslim Indian population as well, most of them Khojas, also from South Asia, and their numbers eventually exceeded those of the Banyans. Caste restrictions did not allow the Banyans to bring their families to East Africa; during Seyyid Said's time, no Hindu women were allowed on the island and scandals involving Hindu men and slave girls were common. In contrast, the Khojas began to settle Zanzibar in the 1840s, and by the 1870s, there were nearly seven hundred Khoja women on the island. The Banyans lived together in makeshift dormitories or in rooms behind their shops, while the Khojas built spacious homes above their businesses, many fronted by long latticework verandas, which still overlook Stone Town's streets today.

In the southern part of the city teemed its largest marketplace, the Manioc Bazaar, where the Africans and Swahili came to buy and sell fruits, vegetables, grain, cloth, and other goods. Manioc, the bazaar's namesake—also known as white cassava in English and as *muhungo* in Swahili—grew everywhere on the island and was the chief food of the poor. Full of gluten, it could be prepared dozens of ways: boiled and served with a sauce of groundnut cream, mixed with water into a paste and baked into biscuits, placed raw in plantain leaves and cooked in coals.

Directly behind the Manioc Bazaar was a fish market, while to the north, in the Malindi district, a meat market bustled. Arabs rarely frequented any of these markets, preferring to send their slaves instead.

The one market that the Arabs did frequent was the Salt Bazaar. Located between the customhouse and the Old Fort, it made a good stop for seamen just off the boats, merchants waiting for the customs master, and soldiers from Seyyid Said's army. Plenty of local produce, salt, sugar, fish, and fritters were for sale, along with live steer (usually purchased by the Banyans, 5 dollars each); Muscovy ducks (a favorite food among the Africans, 10–12 cents each); guinea hens, a.k.a. "Abyssinian cocks" (trapped by slaves on the mainland, 6–8 cents each), and pretty civet cats, which the Zanzibaris kept as pets.

Lining the edges of the Salt Bazaar were the narrow, hole-in-the-wall shops run by Indians, who sat cross-legged on the floor from dawn until dusk, gossiping with friends, keeping books on their knees, and seducing would-be buyers with their wares—Persian rugs, Madras cloth, combs, beads, spoons, knives, coffee, and spices. On various street corners blacksmiths were at work, forging spearheads, horseshoes, and farm implements; and in one back alley, blindfolded camels powered a millstone that pressed oil from coconuts. Every neighborhood had at least one well, usually unprotected by barriers and frequented by children, who filled coconut shells and earthen jars with water to carry home on their heads.

Sometimes the routine activity of a marketplace or street would be interrupted by the unexpected appearance of an erect figure with bright, piercing eyes and a bushy white beard—Seyyid Said. The sultan was usually accompanied by a small retinue of noblemen and foot soldiers dressed in white pantaloons and secondhand red coats from Bombay. A few slaves followed behind.

Scattered throughout the town, and flanking it to the north and south, were hundreds of traditional African dwellings—small, square mud huts thatched with coconut leaves—housing a mixed population of slaves, freed slaves, and poorer Arabs and Swahili. Adjoining the huts were shelters for cooking, and over each doorway, as in the wealthier homes, hung a passage from the Quran, these written on paper. Inside, the huts were simply furnished with low beds, tables, and chairs.

Also scattered throughout the town were perhaps thirty mosques, most Ibadhi or Sunni and raised a yard or more above the street to symbolically elevate the worshippers above the distracting noise of the world. As in Muscat, the Ibadhi mosques had no minarets and were distinguishable from ordinary buildings only by a small square protruding on the north side. Facing Mecca, the square housed the *mihrab*, or prayer niche, where the imam stood to lead prayers. Most Ibadhi mosques were also quite small, built for only one family or clan, and broad, so that as many worshippers as possible could sit in the first two rows, an especially coveted position from which to pray.

Behind the mosques were *madrassas*, or traditional Islamic schools, where children were taught the Quran and *hadiths*, or sayings of the Prophet, and the sounds of young voices chanting at the tops of their lungs could often be heard in the streets. Peeking in through a *madrassa* window, a visitor might catch a glimpse of young boys sitting in a semicircle in front of a bearded teacher. Before them would lie a copy of the Quran, open on a two-foot-high stand, so as to be situated above the seated scholars' waists.

A few Shiite mosques belonging to the Indian Khojas also graced the town, and these, like most Shiite mosques, included sections for women, usually located behind a partition or on an upper floor. The Ibadhi and Sunni mosques did not have sections for women; they worshipped at home.

Many of the town slaves, who probably numbered about ten thousand in the mid-1800s, served as domestics. Virtually every household—be it Arab, Swahili, or Indian—had at least one slave to cook, clean, run errands, fetch water, and guard the house, and most had many more. Often, the domestics had been born and raised in their masters' homes.

A female domestic usually worked in the kitchen and served the family's meals. She might also carry a parasol over her mistress when she went out in the hot sun or hold a water jug for her master when he washed his hands and feet. Female domestics accompanied their mistresses to weddings and mourning sessions, and at the mourning sessions it was often the old female slaves, experts in the art of bereavement, who wailed the loudest.

Male domestics guarded the house, ran the household errands, and accompanied their masters on journeys. Many learned how to sew their master's *dishdasha* and embroidered outer garments, and some learned how to make shoes and caps. A male domestic could rise to a position of great trust. There was even a category of slaves known in Swahili as *watumwa wa shauri:* "advice-giving slaves."

Other town slaves worked as artisans, laborers, soldiers, sailors, and concubines. As in the Western hemisphere, the artisans had the most autonomy. As skilled carpenters, masons, tailors, door carvers, and boat builders, they were allowed to work for others after their work for their masters was done and could keep part of their pay. They often lived independently and owned their own houses and shops.

More surprisingly, many of Zanzibar's laborer slaves had a similar arrangement. Hired out by their masters to do everything from unloading ships to sailing them, from working as caravan porters to serving as caravan leaders, they, too, were allowed to keep part of their pay and live independently. They often found their own work and chose their own employers. Their only real obligation to their masters was to give them the bulk of their wages.

A laborer slave often lived right next door to free slaves and poor Arabs and Swahili, and the temptation to break completely loose from an owner must have been tremendous. However, the laborer slave was also excruciatingly aware of the fact that if he failed to deliver his master his due, he would be found and severely disciplined. In Zanzibar, there were few places to hide.

The laborer slave system made it possible for everyone, including other slaves, to make money. A poor man or a slave could purchase a laborer slave for about $30, borrowing the money from a moneylender if necessary. The new master could then hire that slave out and keep at least half of his wages for himself. Through such an arrangement, a master could earn $1–2 per month and a slave-owning slave could earn enough to buy his freedom in about two years. Purchasing a laborer slave was a "safe, easy, and profitable investment" for the lower classes in Zanzibar, commented one British official in 1873.

A slave always walked behind his or her master, never sat down in his presence, and, if living nearby, saluted him every morning and evening. *Shikamuu*, "I embrace your feet," the slave would say; *marahaba*, "welcome," the master would reply. Masters usually called their slaves *watoto*, "children," or *watu wangu*, "my people."

As in the case of Salme's mother, concubines were often bought as children and treated like the master's freeborn offspring until reaching puberty. Then they were put in the seclusion of a harem, where each was given her own room. Under Islamic law, a master could sleep with his concubines every fourth night, unless he had no legitimate wife, and then he could sleep with them every night. A son could not have a concubine while living in his father's house, and a slave girl could refuse to become a concubine. Few did, however. The alternative—working as a domestic—was far less attractive.

Most ordinary Arabs in Zanzibar owned concubines, and they often had more children through these relationships than they did with their legitimate wives. Seyyid Said's family composition was the norm, not the exception. Every child born to an Arab father and a concubine was regarded as an Arab, and was treated, in theory at least, as the social equal of their freeborn siblings.

In a society where the size of a person's family mattered enormously, such a system made sense. The more people a master or clan leader could count on in times of trouble, the better. Masters also encouraged their slaves to marry and to have children to add more numbers to their party, and often bought an appropriate spouse for a slave if none was available in-house. To marry off one's slaves was a duty in Islam.

Zanzibar was far from a color-blind society, however. White Circassian concubines cost more than light black Abyssinian concubines, who in turn cost more than dark black African concubines. But color was regarded as only one aspect of a person's identity. Far more important was family and clan affiliation.

Sometimes the line between a master or mistress and his or her slaves became blurred. One of Salme's closest playmates when she was young was her half sister Shewane, the daughter of an Abyssinian concubine. As an adult, Shewane preferred the company of her slaves to that of her family and "tried to possess the most handsome and selected slaves, and loaded them with the most costly weapons and jewels . . . ," wrote Salme. "When, in a favourable moment, I now and again told her how people found fault with her because of her high expenses, in particular because of her numerous train of slaves, she quite passively answered she knew very well that she would not have long to live and that she wanted, during her lifetime, partly to give her fortune to the poor, partly to dissipate it as quickly as possible, so that there would be nothing for us to inherit." Shewane did indeed die young, and in her will not only set her slaves free, but also bequeathed them all her costly belongings and jewels.

As in Muscat, manumission, or the freeing of one's slaves, was common in Zanzibar. Some visitors reported that many island-born slaves, who had greater status than newly arrived slaves from the mainland, were freed after only a few years of service. Other visitors estimated that 50 percent of the slaves brought to Zanzibar from the mainland were eventually freed.

Also as in Muscat, and throughout the Muslim world, masters freed their slaves for many reasons—to atone for a major sin such as homicide, to give thanks for recovering from an illness, to reward exceptionally loyal service, or, most commonly, to do a good and pious act that would be noticed by others. In fact, even after slavery in Zanzibar was abolished and the government was offering former slave owners money in return for freeing their slaves, many still chose to liberate them after their deaths for no compensation. A heavenly reward was coveted more than an earthly one.

Once freed, a slave received a certificate from a *qadi*, which he or she usually wore around the neck, encased in a locket. Technically speaking, freed slaves had the same legal rights as freeborn men or women, but many remained closely tied to their former masters, whose family and lineage they usually adopted. All were also looked down upon by the society at large, which never forgot their origins—a stigma that continues to exist in Zanzibar today.

For many Africans, too, being freed meant little; once they had been violently separated from their families and villages, they could never be truly free again. Wrote one missionary to East Africa: "In my continual endeavours to translate, I have often tried to get a rendering for giving a man his freedom, and there seemed to be a great difficulty, but as I grew impatient I began to realize that the natives were getting impatient too at my questions. 'What is this you are asking about?' they said in effect. 'How can an Arab or a white man who has taken a man away from his home give him his freedom? The only people who can give him his freedom are his own kindred, if they come to redeem him."

Around the time of Salme's birth in the mid-1800s, another child—to be later known as Rashid bin Hassani—was born into the Bisa tribe in what is now Zambia. Over fifty years later, Rashid was interviewed by a

German anthropologist, and today his is one of the only existing accounts of what it was like to become and be a Zanzibari slave.

As Rashid told it, his father had three wives, all of whom had children, and the three families lived together in relative harmony in separate mud huts in a village of about four hundred huts. The villagers
spent their days tending to their fields and animals, hunting everything
from eland to elephants, and doing business with the passing traders of
the Yao tribe, who gave them cloth, beads, axes, and hoes in exchange
for ivory and slaves. The village's largest slave owner was its chief; most
of his slaves had either been born in the village as slaves or been condemned to slavery after committing a serious crime.

A few had become slaves through witchcraft. When a villager died
suddenly, a suspect was found and a witch doctor consulted. The witch
doctor heated water in a large medicine pot until it bubbled ferociously,
and put a stone inside. The accused was told to thrust his hand into the
water. If he found the stone, he was innocent. But if he did not, he was
seized and bound, and a bamboo collar was squeezed around his forehead until his eyes nearly popped out. At that point, he might name his
associates, in which case, all would be seized and sold as slaves. Or he
might continue to hold back, in which case he would be forced to build
a fire, and would be tied above it, flames licking his legs, until he confessed. Then all of his clan, sometimes numbering as many as sixty people, would be seized and sold as slaves.

When Rashid was about thirteen years old, the Angoni raided his
country. Most of his family and neighbors were slaughtered, but he and
about twenty other villagers were captured and marched to an Angoni
camp, their village burning behind them. The children and women were
allowed to walk free, but the men were bound together at the neck with
wooden yokes.

The next day, the Angoni captured the Bisa tribal leader, Sultan
Mtisa, and told him that he would be taken to see their ruler. He refused, saying that he preferred to be killed. The Angoni then cut a long,
thick pole, whittled one end to a sharp point, and buried the other end
in the ground. Around the pole they built a stage about six feet high and
sat the chief on the pole's point. Some held his arms and some, his legs.
All pulled hard. At the first heave, the pole passed into the sultan's

stomach; at the second, it went as far as his chest; and at the third, his head fell back and the point came out of his throat. Throughout the execution, neither Sultan Mtisa nor any members of his watching family made a sound.

A day or two later, the prisoners were marched to the Luangwa River, where Rashid was purchased by a man who later sold him to a Yao trader. The trader took him to Kilwa, where he was sold again—this time to an Arab from Zanzibar. The Arab smuggled him and six other slaves across the channel to Zanzibar on a small open boat.

Once on the island, Rashid was purchased by Bibi Zamzam, one of Salme's oldest sisters and a wealthy woman who owned a reputed five hundred to six hundred slaves. Rashid was sent to one of her plantations, where a headman beat a drum and called out, "Anybody who has not got a child and wants one, can choose one from this lot." A woman from the country south of Kilwa stepped forward and claimed Rashid.

He stayed in his new home for the next three years, during which time he was circumcised and taught KiSwahili, the basic principles of Islam, and how to read the Quran. Then Bibi Zamzam hired him out as a house builder. His wages were eight *pice* a day, of which he was allowed to keep one.

A few years later, Rashid had earned enough money to buy his own home. He married one of Bibi Zamzam's slave women and the couple had a daughter. Rashid was still a slave, but he was now working a variety of jobs of his own choosing and was allowed to keep most of his wages. He was also making many of his own decisions, and considered himself to be not so much in servitude to Bibi Zamzam as under her protection.

One day in Stone Town when his daughter was about five years old, Rashid saw an amazing sight: Swahili men drinking wine and cognac, and throwing money around as if they were wealthy Europeans. Joining them at their table, he learned that they had been porters on a caravan that had traveled to Uganda. Two days later, he signed up for the same kind of work. He was to be paid ten rupees a month, half of which he had to give to Bibi Zamzam.

That very day, Rashid sailed to Mombasa, where he embarked on a year-long journey into the African interior. Later, he became a soldier in the Omani army, fought against rebels in Mombasa, and took up residence there. When Bibi Zamzam died, leaving behind a will that freed Rashid and all the rest of her five hundred slaves, Rashid requested and received leave to attend her funeral in Zanzibar. By the time he arrived, however, it was over. He returned to Mombasa, to live much as he had before.

12

A Day in the Life

BEIT AL-SAHEL, SEYYID SAID'S TOWN PALACE, WAS ONLY A HUN-
dred yards away from Salme's new home of Beit al-Watoro, but her first
visit there was one of much ceremony. Just after dawn one Friday morning, her mother wrapped herself in her *shele*—a large black silk shawl
with golden borders—took Salme by the hand, and went to knock on
the patriarch's door. An elderly Nubian slave received them crossly. He
had been on his feet for the entire last hour admitting nothing but lady
visitors, he grumbled.

Since Seyyid Sultan was still in prayer and could not be disturbed,
Djilfidan and Salme were taken to a waiting room, already filled with
many other black-shrouded women, most newly arrived from Oman.
The women were distant Al Busaidi relatives who had come to ask
Seyyid Said for financial aid—Oman was much poorer than Zanzibar
and many Omanis were destitute. Illiterate, the women had no choice
but to make the long sea voyage to see their sultan in person. And
Seyyid Said hardly ever turned anyone down; he gave generously to all
according to their rank.

His prayers finished, Seyyid Said received Djilfidan, Salme, and the
Omani women in a long, plain hall overlooking the sea.

"Salme, tell me, how do you like this place?" he asked his young
daughter. "Would you like to return to Beit al-Mtoni? Do you get your
milk soup here?"

Salme's fondness for *farni*, a cold soup made with rice flour and sugar, and generally more popular among toothless old ladies than among young children, was a joke between them.

Between nine-thirty and ten a.m., other family members arrived, with the women congregating in the hall, the men outside on the stairs, and all dressed in their Friday best. "Our mothers walked about, stood together in groups, and talked eagerly," wrote Salme. "They laughed, jested, and were in such high spirits that a stranger, unfamiliar with the circumstances, would not have believed these were all wives of one and the same man."

People were much happier in Beit al-Sahel than they were in Beit al-Mtoni, Salme observed as she grew older. Here, there was no imperious main wife to throw her weight around. Here, no one gave orders except Seyyid Said, by now a benevolent older man with crinkly eyes and a bushy white beard.

Breakfast was served, and Salme was invited to eat with her father and siblings—an honor granted only to those royal children over age seven. Everyone moved to a long, low table and sat down on woven mats on the floor. Seyyid Said reigned at the table's head, his oldest children beside him, his youngest at the table's foot. Djilfidan and the other *sarari* were not invited to join the party. Only legitimate wives were allowed to eat with the sultan.

About fifteen different rice dishes, all piled up pyramid style, sat on the table. Some were mixed with mutton, some with chicken, and some with fish. Breads, cakes, and a few vegetable dishes were also laid out. Eunuchs dressed in *dishdashas* and blue-and-white turbans stood at attention against the walls.

"In the name of God, the merciful and compassionate, who has intended this as food for my body to give strength to live. Praise be to God who has given me this food. I eat for His glory and that of Muhammad His apostle," everyone prayed in an undertone and then dug in, using their fingers. Spoons were used only for soups, and forks and knives only when Westerners were present. Hardly anyone spoke while eating, as is customary throughout the Middle East, and afterward, slaves appeared with washbasins, towels, and perfume for the hands. Thick, unsweetened coffee was served in small cups nesting in gold or silver holders.

Meanwhile, Djilfidan ate downstairs in a noisy dining room with the other *sarari*. When in the presence of Seyyid Said, the women spoke only Arabic, but here, a loud cacophony of languages swirled—Persian, Turkish, Circassian, KiSwahili, Nubian, Abyssinian. Djilfidan ate at a table filled only with Circassian wives, while the Abyssinian *sarari* ate together at another table, and the Africans, at yet another table still. Generally, the palace's many races got along well together but, true to human nature everywhere, each preferred to stick largely with its own kind, with many members of each race believing themselves to be superior to members of other races. Rivalry was especially strong between the Circassians and the Abyssinians.

As the daughter of a Circassian, Salme held that the white-skinned women were "without a doubt much more distinguished in appearance than the Abyssinians," but was forced to admit that "among the latter also quite unusual beauties are to be found." She described the Abyssinians as fiery and hot-tempered, and declared that they had "no decency" when they were angered. In turn, the Abyssinians jeeringly called Salme and the other Circassian children "cats" because some had blue eyes.

The eunuchs, or castrated males, who attended to the royal family— serving the meals, guarding the harem, overseeing the African slaves, and assisting Seyyid Said in his administrative tasks—were an integral part of the Al Busaidi household, as they were an integral part of elite nineteenth-century Arab households everywhere. Westerners who visited the region may have regarded the neutered males with a mixture of repulsion and fascination, but to most Arabs, they were simply a part of life, as common as multiple wives. And far from being pitied or reviled, eunuchs were usually regarded as privileged people, since they often held positions of responsibility and sometimes accrued considerable wealth.

The Arabs were not the first to enslave eunuchs. The earliest records of intentional castration come from the Sumerian city of Lagash in the twenty-first century B.C.; Queen Semiramis, who ruled Assyria from 811 to 808 B.C., was another early proponent. Eunuchs were used in China, where castration was a traditional form of punishment, at least as early as 781 B.C., and at the end of the Ming dynasty, there were more than seventy thousand eunuchs in the Imperial Palace. The custom was also known in ancient Persia, ancient Greece, and ancient Rome, with the Roman emperors employing eunuchs as everything from personal groomers to human shields. During the Middle Ages, Prague and Verdun were the castration centers for Europe, while Kharazon near the Caspian Sea was the center for central Asia.

Mutilation is forbidden in Islam. A *hadith* states, "Whoever cuts off the nose of a slave, his nose will be cut off; and whoever castrates a slave, him also shall we castrate." But the Arabs became familiar with the custom after conquering parts of the Roman Empire, and as the size of their wealth and harems grew, they began to see the advantages of using eunuchs. Robbed of their libido and separated from their natural families, eunuchs could be trusted to guard harems—and coffers and holy sites. Believed to have allegiance only to their masters, eunuchs were also trusted to serve as administrators, diplomats, and confidants.

In the 1820s, when Seyyid Said was still living in Muscat, a Swiss explorer named Johann Ludwig Burckhardt visited Mecca, where he found richly attired black eunuchs, along with a few "copper-coloured" Indian ones, guarding the city's mosque. All were married to black slaves and had male and female slaves as servants, as well as a large income garnered from the revenues of the mosque and donations from pilgrims.

Traveling on, the Swiss explorer found a similar situation in Medina, only there, the eunuchs were even "more richly dressed . . . they usually wear fine Cashmere shawls and gowns of the best Indian silk stuffs, and assume airs of great importance. When they pass through the Bazar, every body hastens to kiss their hands; and they exercise considerable influence in the internal affairs of the town. . . . They live together in one of the best quarters of Medina, to the eastward of the mosque, and their houses are said to be furnished in a more costly manner than any other in the town."

Since Muslims also could not perform castration, centers were established just outside the borders of Muslim lands. After the operation, the average healthy eunuch was worth two to ten times as much as before he went in—due in large part to the eunuchs' low postsurgery survival rates, probably less than one in ten.

In the early centuries of Islam, the Slavic region was the Muslims' main source for eunuchs, who were usually transported from their homeland to Islamic Spain, where Jewish merchants performed the operation. Later, in the nineteenth century, one of the largest Muslim castration centers was in Abu Tig, on the caravan route between the Sudan and Egypt. Between one hundred and two hundred boys ages eight to ten were castrated there each year, most for the ruling Egyptian family and wealthy Turks. The operation was performed by skilled Coptic priests.

After breakfast at Beit al-Sahel, the day began. Seyyid Said retired to his audience room to receive his many supplicants and guests, and some of the sarari took seats at the windows to watch who was coming and going through the main palace door. Other sarari tended to their children, visited the sick, or did needlework, embroidering cambric shirts for their sons and brothers or clothing and face masks for themselves.

All the sarari, no matter what their country of origin, wore the colorful women's costume of Oman: a long silk tunic of a brilliant hue, pantaloons gathered at the ankles and tied at the waist with rich tassels, and an elaborately embroidered headscarf reaching to the calves. Around their ankles they wore silver and gold bracelets, one hung with gold coins that tinkled when they walked.

Even while at home and in the harem, the sarari also often wore face masks because of the presence of unrelated males, such as the sultan's sons by other wives. Elegantly made of black satin trimmed with lace of colored silk, gold and silver, the mask covered the nose and part of the cheeks but left the eyes and lower face bare. The mask was attached with silk strings interwoven with gold or silver chains, which were twisted around the head several times, thereby also helping to keep the headscarf in place.

Royal girls under age nine—the age at which, under Islamic law, girls begin covering their heads—wore their hair in small braids, numbering perhaps fifteen or twenty, which were gathered together with elaborate ornaments, often made of gold and set with precious stones. No young child was allowed to approach Seyyid Said until his or her toilette was complete, as Salme learned one day when she ran to get the "French sweetmeats" that her father gave his children every morning before her hair was done. She was promptly sent back to the harem—*sans* treat.

Beit al-Sahel was smaller than Beit al-Mtoni, but more stylish and luxurious, with many of its most coveted rooms overlooking the sea. It was built around a large covered courtyard, whose roof was supported by thick pillars several stories high. All the doors on the upper floor, which held the living quarters, opened onto a wide inside gallery lined with railings and chairs overlooking the courtyard. From the roof hung many colored lamps, which cast a golden glow over the palace at night.

Two large interior flights of stairs connected the courtyard to the first floor, and these were always jammed with people coming up or going down. Children of all races and gradations of color swarmed everywhere, running, laughing, shouting, and shoving, while the *sarari*, rattling about on wooden sandals two to four inches high, clapped their hands for service.

In one corner of the courtyard, butchers slaughtered cattle. In another, barbers shaved the heads of African slaves. Nearby, water carriers rested—until, that is, a eunuch arrived and ordered them back to work. Basking in the sun were the African nursemaids, telling the youngest royal children traditional Swahili folktales about lions, leopards, and elephants, and good and evil witches.

Near one of the courtyard pillars stood the kitchen, where food was cooked in wide range of styles, including Arab, Swahili, Persian, and Turkish. Smoke from various fires swirled in all directions as the cooks—male and female—shouted orders at assistants, slapping them when they moved too slowly. Into the cooks' tall black four-feet-wide cauldrons went an enormous amount of meat, the animals often cooked whole. Perspiring cooks wielding six-foot-long spoons stirred the food and ladled it out.

Meanwhile, "fish of so large a size that they had to be carried by two sturdy negroes, were often seen disappearing into the kitchen." Small fish were accepted by the basket only and poultry by the dozen only. As for fruit, "thirty to forty porters, sometimes even as many as fifty, came in daily laden with fruit, not to count the many small boats which brought deliveries from the seaside plantations."

A long wall protected the palace from the sea, and every day at low tide, several of Seyyid Said's best horses, imported from Oman, were tied to the wall with long ropes so that they could exercise and roll about in the sand. The sultan took great delight in his thoroughbreds, visiting them daily and tending to them personally when they were sick, which was often. Horses did not thrive in Zanzibar's hot and humid climate.

At one p.m., when the Zanzibari sun was at its hottest, a slave announced that it was time for second prayers and everyone retired to a private spot to pray. Afterward, all rested on soft mats, into which were woven sacred texts from the Quran. Some fell asleep, some daydreamed, and some talked quietly together while munching on cakes and fruit.

At four p.m., it was time to rise and say third prayers, after which everyone put on his or her "splendid afternoon-dress." Members of the royal family called upon Seyyid Said again to wish him good afternoon, with the grown-up children addressing him as "father," and the littler ones and the *sarari*, as "*hbabi*," or "sir." The second main meal of the day—basically the same as the first—was served.

After dinner, eunuchs carried European-style chairs for the adults onto the wide gallery in front of the sultan's apartment. Children remained standing, and the eunuchs lined up against the walls in well-dressed rank and file, slim spears and rhino-hide shields blinking in the setting rays of the sun. Coffee and fruit syrups from France were served while one of the eunuchs turned the crank of an enormous barrel organ or a singer with an enchanting voice performed.

An hour or two later, the family gatherings broke up, and some family members retired to their rooms to chew betel nut, the seed of the betel palm, a stimulant that produces a mild euphoria. "Arabs born in Arabia proper do not take a fancy to it. But we, who had seen the light of the world on the East coast of Africa and had grown up with negroes and mulattoes, readily took over this habit," wrote Salme.

At sunset, gunshots and a drumroll reminded the royal family of fourth prayers, which were always said in a great hurry because afterward, the day's social hour began. Seyyid Said retired to his audience hall for another session of business; more ordinary men and women went visiting. Coffee and lemonade, fruits and cakes were shared, as people joked, laughed, read aloud, played cards, sang, and listened to "negro music played on the *sese*," a one-string instrument built of a coconut shell. "People over there are quite easily satisfied," Salme wrote while in Germany. "The feverish rush of this country in search of continuously changing amusements and pleasures is unknown to them."

Children over the age of two were not forced to go to bed and so often fell asleep in the middle of the floor, to be tenderly picked up by slaves, who took them home. As the hour grew late, the *sarari* dismissed their male servants, who adjusted the coconut oil lamps, kept burning all night, before they left. Women who had no visitors usually went to sleep at about ten p.m., while others stayed up until just before midnight, often sitting out on the palaces' flat rooftops, gossiping and laughing beneath a sky packed with stars. Light winds scented with cloves brushed their faces, while in the distance could be heard the sound of slaves playing upon calabashes, banjos, brass pans, buffalo horns, and drums made of goatskins stretched over ends of hollowed logs.

The last prayers of a Muslim's day are supposed to be said at around seven-thirty p.m., but can be postponed until midnight, which many in Zanzibar did. And when it came time for a well-born Omani woman to go to bed, she usually found two slave girls waiting for her. One gently massaged her limbs—an "indescribably agreeable" custom adapted from the Swahili—while the other bathed her feet with eau de cologne and water, and swung a fan to and fro. The girls then sprinkled their mistress's wardrobe with jasmine and orange blossoms, ambergris and musk, and slipped out of her room as she fell asleep, fully clothed, as was, and in many places still is, the custom in the Arab world.

13

Gatherings

SEYYID SAID'S AUDIENCE HALL, OR *BARAZA*, OCCUPIED A CORNER
of the ground floor of his palace, close to the sea. Waves lapped against
the room's foundation walls at high tide and its glass-paned windows
looked directly out onto the water. Sparsely furnished with Persian carpets, floor-to-ceiling mirrors, clocks, and dusty chandeliers, the room
was where Seyyid Said held court twice daily, once after breakfast and
again after fourth prayers. His male relatives, ministers, male subjects,
and visiting male foreigners could attend the sessions, and since many
traveled with large retinues, the hall was usually packed.

Seyyid Said's sons were allowed to attend their father's court beginning at age fourteen, and were obliged to do so daily after age sixteen.
Important men were also obliged to attend the court daily. If a notable
Arab was absent for several days in a row, a slave was sent to his house
to ask what was wrong. If the man was sick, Seyyid Said would pay him
a visit. But if the man stayed away for some other reason, ill intent—
meaning disloyalty—was assumed.

The sultan's *baraza*—the word was used for both the event and the
place—usually lasted between one and a half and three hours, with
most of that time devoted to hearing petitions and lawsuits. Seyyid Said
sat on a simple chair, surrounded by his advisers, and each approaching
supplicant knelt before the ruler. "*Seyyid Na!*" "My lord," he said and
kissed the backs of the sultan's hands and knees. Men could leave during the *baraza*, and if a man of rank departed, Seyyid Said rose, with

everyone else following suit, and walked with him a few steps as he headed to the door.

Seyyid Said decided major disputes himself and sent more minor ones to his *qadis*, who held court in private homes or in ad hoc assemblies on the streets—Zanzibar had no courthouses. Seyyid Said tried hard to appoint good *qadis*, but corruption among them was rampant. "From His Highness the Imam alone a poor man can obtain justice"; he "is truly every man's friend; he wishes to do good to all," wrote the British consul Hamerton. The explorer Richard Burton agreed: "Under Sayyid Said torture was unknown, death was inflicted according to Koranic law, and only one mutilation is recorded."

To Westerners unfamiliar with Arab culture, the government of Zanzibar seemed simple: Seyyid Said was the unquestioned ruler, and his wish was everyone's command. But the reality of the situation was quite different. As in Oman, Seyyid Said was obliged to rule by consensus. His followers regarded him more as an administrator than as an absolute sovereign. The various Arab clans on the island—most notably the powerful al-Harthi, who'd settled on Zanzibar generations before Seyyid Said arrived—did not welcome interference. Regarding themselves as Seyyid Said's social equals and his near equals politically, they expected to be consulted on all major policy issues. Seyyid Said may have had fewer enemies in Zanzibar than he had had in Oman, but he still had to tread carefully. Whenever he left Zanzibar for an extensive period, he took the al-Harthi leader with him, as insurance.

While Seyyid Said held his evening court with other powerful men, most of his more ordinary subjects were also busy socializing. Nearly every house in Zanzibar had its own *baraza*, where men could visit with friends over cups of coffee and other refreshments—including, in some homes, alcohol, a habit that Seyyid Said condemned.

Among the wealthy, the *baraza* was often a cool downstairs room with a floor paved with white-and-black marble slabs imported from France. Among the middle class, the *baraza* was usually a heavy stone bench built into the walls encircling a courtyard or flanking a front door. And among the poor, the *baraza* was often just a plain wooden porch or wooden bench.

Barazas can still be seen all over Zanzibar today. Now usually lining outside walls, they serve as front porches, where people congregate to gossip, play games, drink coffee, or simply relax in the sun. Prior to Zanzibar's revolution of 1963–64, when African nationalists overthrew the island's foreigner-dominated government, the *barazas* also served a political purpose, as places where people met to exchange ideas and foment rebellion.

Arab women of rank seldom appeared on Zanzibar's streets during the day. Everything changed, however, after the sun went down. Then everyone—young and old, married and single—either went visiting or else received visitors. Those who went out were often accompanied by large processions, which could include troops of ten to twenty armed slaves, marching two by two, and gaggles of women slaves. The soldiers usually marched in front of the Arab ladies, the slave women behind, but all were just for show. The slaves' weapons, adorned with silver and gold, looked better than they functioned, and on the safe streets of Zanzibar ladies needed little protection.

Pedestrians often had to step aside to let the ladies' processions pass, because they carried with them enormous lanterns, some two yards in circumference. Zanzibar had no streetlights and the lanterns were needed to illuminate the way. Salme's favorite lamp was shaped to resemble a Russian church, complete with a big cupola in the center and four small towers in the corners. In each tower burned a candle, throwing light out onto the dark, narrow streets through red, green, yellow, or blue panes.

When a procession reached its destination, a slave announced its arrival, and the visiting ladies were immediately ushered into a sitting room or, on moonlit nights, onto a clean flat roof surrounded by a parapet. The hostess would be sitting on her *medde*, a cushion made of fine brocade, and reclining against her *tekje*, a similar cushion placed against the wall. She would rise to greet her guests, and if they were of rank equal to hers, they would shake her hand and sit down on nearby cushions. If they were not of the same rank, they would kiss her hands or head or the hem of her shawl, and sit down on mats or carpets some distance away. Face mask and *shele* remained in place. Only shoes were removed and left at the door.

Coffee was served, followed by fresh fruit and cakes, as the women talked and gossiped, laughed and joked, sang songs and played games for hours. The master of the house was not allowed to enter the women's quarters during visiting hours and the lanterns were kept burning throughout. When it was time to leave, the slaves were summoned and the hostess was given a small present. Then the procession headed home, leaving a trail of incense, perfume, gossip, and laughter in its wake.

In her memoirs, Salme writes defensively of the Arabs' leisurely lifestyle. Her German acquaintances apparently often asked her, in a rather superior tone, "Do tell me, please, how can people in your country manage to live without being occupied with anything?" To which, Salme eloquently replied: "Natural circumstances differ everywhere; our views, customs and habits develop in different ways. In the North, one has to work just to exist, or rather to be able to enjoy life; for the blessed Southerner it is completely different. Yes, I [use] the word 'blessed,' because contentedness is a great and priceless boon for a people, and because the Arab, so frequently described in books as lazy, possesses a great contentedness. . . . Nature itself brings about that the Southerner *may* work, while the Northerner *must* work."

Salme soon made new friends at Beit al-Sahel, where she was brought every day for schooling. That arrangement was unpleasant for her at first, accustomed as she was to running free at Beit al-Mtoni, but she soon settled into her new routine.

The girls were taught to read, and the boys to read and write using bamboo quills dipped in ink, with the bleached shoulder blades of camels for their tablets. Their schoolroom was an open gallery with views of the busy courtyard to one side, the sea to the other. The children sat cross-legged on the floor, and their slaves, who learned the lessons alongside them, took seats behind.

Together, all recited the first *surah*, or verse, of the Quran:

Praise be to Allah, Lord of the Worlds,
The Beneficent, the Merciful.
Owner of the Day of Judgment,

Thee (alone) we worship; Thee (alone) we ask for help.
Show us the straight path,
The path of those whom Thou hast favored;
Not (the path) of those who earn thine anger nor of those
  who go astray.

Afterward, the pupils chanted in chorus the verses from the Quran that they had memorized the day before. Then the teacher gave them new verses, with no explanation of what they meant, and those, too, were memorized in chorus, as is still the teaching method in the traditional Muslim world. When a girl knew a third of the Quran by heart, usually by age nine, her schooling was considered over. Most boys continued studying for only two or three years more.

The children were also taught a little arithmetic, learning how to write figures up to one hundred and how to recite up to one thousand. But they were taught very little grammar, and no history, geography, physics, or math. Salme learned something about those subjects later, as a grown woman living in Europe. "But it still remains an open question to me whether, with the little wisdom laboriously acquired here, I am now better off than the others over there," she wrote in Germany. "That I have never been more deceived and swindled than in the time of my greatest knowledge, this is certain. Oh you happy people at home!, not even in your dreams do you surmise all that is connected with holy civilization!"

Further comparing the East's and West's approaches to education, Salme observed with a touch of upper-class bias, but also with some insight: "In my opinion, learning [in the West] is carried much too far. Through education, everyone wants to climb higher and higher until in the end no workmen are left any more; the greatest importance is attached to education, to knowledge. The majority's needs and just and unjust claims to life increase of course with the superficial education thus attained; consequently also the increase and aggravation of the struggle for life with all its contingencies. Indeed, the mind is educated in an extraordinary way, the heart is left disregarded and put aside unheeded."

After lessons, which ended about noon, just before second prayers,

Salme and her siblings prowled around the palace, often playing pranks on unsuspecting adults. The old Nubian slave who manned the front door was a frequent target—they liked to hide his enormous collection of keys—and on one occasion, the children took a strong dislike to a young Circassian concubine newly arrived from Egypt. Judging her to be haughty and indifferent to them, the children decided to find "an appropriate punishment for her." An opportunity arose one day when they passed by her room and saw her seated on her simple Swahili bed, made of four posts held together by coconut rope and a mat, and singing a "national song" at the top of her lungs. "In a thrice we took hold of the legs of the bed, hoisted it as high as we could together with its inmate, to drop it then suddenly to the fright of the unsuspecting person. It was a very childish trick indeed, but it was successful. . . . Henceforth she was amiability personified," wrote Salme.

Always filled with irrepressible high spirits, Salme also played pranks that were entirely of her own making. One morning when she was about seven or eight and the family was visiting a clove plantation, she slipped away from the others to climb a towering coconut palm without a *pingu*, a thick rope that is used to anchor the feet and "without which even the most skilled climber cannot be prevailed upon to ascend a palm-tree," she wrote. "In full bravado I began calling out to the unsuspecting passers-by and wishing them good morning in a loud voice. What a fright! Immediately a full throng of people stood below, entreating me to come down very carefully. . . . I was, however, quite happy up there and only when my mother stood below me, in despair, wringing her hands and promising all kinds of beautiful things, did I slowly slip down and arrive below happily and unhurt."

Salme would display a similar courage and obliviousness toward the opinions of others all her life.

Salme and her mother, Djilfidan, lived happily in Beit al-Watoro for two years, but "such times, unfortunately, as a rule, do not last long," wrote a world-weary Salme years later. Aashe, a distant family relative from Oman, married Salme's brother Majid. She was young, gentle, and charming, and got along with everyone—except Salme's half sister

Chadudj. In theory, Aashe was now the mistress of the house, but Chadudj refused to instruct her in the household duties and patronized her so much that Aashe often went running to Djilfidan in tears.

Why Majid didn't interfere and reprimand his sister for her behavior isn't clear, but Djilfidan was now in a difficult position. She couldn't side with Aashe without antagonizing Chadudj, or vice versa. Finally, she decided to leave Beit al-Watoro altogether. Majid and Aashe begged her not to go, but Chadudj voiced no opinion, cementing Djilfidan's decision. She and Salme decamped to another nearby palace, Beit al-Tani.

After Djilfidan and Salme left, Aashe sued for and obtained a divorce, and returned to Oman to live with an old aunt. To return to one's family is always an option for unhappily married women in Muslim society, although once back home, divorcées are often treated as second-class citizens. Remarriage is an option, but many women never have that opportunity and live out their years as virtual servants to their father's or brothers' families.

Salme's new home, Beit al-Tani, connected to Beit al-Sahel by an overhead walkway, had once belonged to Seyyid Said's second legitimate wife, the Persian princess Shahrazad, whom Salme refers to in her memoirs as "Shesade." Entrancingly beautiful but extremely extravagant, Shesade had come to Zanzibar accompanied by a large personal retinue, including her own private executioner, and dressed in sumptuous clothes embroidered with pearls from head to toe. When her slaves cleaned her rooms in the morning, they often found loose pearls scattered on the floor. The Persian princess never wanted them back.

Shesade had kept a cadre of 150 Persian cavaliers, who lived on the ground floor of her palace. With them, she hunted and rode about in broad daylight—scandalous behavior as far as most Arabs were concerned. She was also adept at using her dagger and was said to have an "intense relish of seeing her people ride men down in the bazaar." Persian women, Salme commented, were generally much freer than Arab women, especially when it came to physical exercise. However, they were also "more rude in mind and action."

Although Salme was very young when Shesade left Zanzibar, she was convinced that the Persian princess had married her father only for his position and money. In her memoirs, Salme also accused the woman of breaking many strict commandments; she did not explicitly say which, but did write, "Her heart belonged to someone else, and she made no secret of it." One day when the princess returned home with her retinue from an outing, Seyyid Said met her in a rage. He raised his sword to strike her but, luckily, a slave stayed his hand. "Such a scene could, of course, only end in divorce," wrote Salme, and Shesade, childless, returned to Persia. Later, when Oman was at war with Persia, Shesade was apocryphally rumored to have been seen among enemy troops, taking aim at members of her former family.

Had Shesade committed adultery? Probably. At the very least, she had apparently been involved in a serious flirtation. But curiously, even as Salme thoroughly condemned the princess's behavior, she did not seem to realize that it was a mirror of her own adult life. Like Shesade, the grown-up Salme became involved in an illicit romance. Like Shesade, she unabashedly exerted her will over that of her male relatives. Both women flew boldly in the face of Muslim mores—and paid the price.

Beit al-Tani was much more crowded than either of Salme's earlier homes, so much so that the *sarari* often had to share rooms. Only when someone died did space open up and, Salme observed, "it often was revolting indeed to see how one or the other woman, spying on the slightest coughing of her neighbor, immediately believed that she could smell out the malignant consumption; she then at once began in her mind to arrange to her taste the room that was to be inherited."

But Salme and her mother were lucky. Long before their move to Beit al-Tani, Djilfidan had become good friends with Chole, one of Seyyid Said's oldest daughters and his favorite child. Chole was the head of the Beit al-Tani household and moved the newcomers into their own fine private room right from the start.

While living in Beit al-Tani, Salme taught herself how to write—inspired perhaps, despite all her reservations, by the independent spirit of the palace's former Persian resident. Working in secret, Salme started by copying letters from the Quran on the bleached shoulder blade of a camel, and later paid an educated slave to be her writing teacher. When news of her acquired skill became known to her father and brothers, she was reprimanded, but probably not too harshly, as "this did not trouble me much," she wrote. In the short run, Salme's writing skills would get her into serious personal and political trouble. But in the long run, "oh how often have I, in the course of time, blessed this decision, which has enabled me . . . to be in correspondence with those loyal to me in my far-away home!"

14

The Slave Trade

AS AN ADULT, SEYYIDA SALME WAS AN APOLOGIST FOR SLAVERY.
She referred to Africans as "big children" and complained about their
laziness and dishonesty. Slavery was a necessary institution in the Orient, she wrote, and one must be careful not to judge it "by what one has
heard about it in North America or in Brazil. The slave of a Muslim is in
a quite different, incomparably better, position." Even Salme was forced
to admit, however, that the slave trade, as opposed to slavery itself, was
an entirely different matter; getting slaves from the mainland to Zanzibar was an extraordinarily cruel business in which "innumerable people perish from the hardships, from hunger and thirst."

The East African slave trade began in earnest in the mid- to late 1700s.
The international demand for ivory was growing steadily and slaves
were needed to transport the huge precious tusks to the coast. Slaves
were also needed to tend to the booming sugar plantations of the
French Indian Ocean islands of Bourbon (Réunion) and Île de France
(Mauritius), whose slave population exploded from virtually nothing
in the mid-1700s to 100,000 by 1800. Most of those slaves were provided by French and Portuguese traders, with the latter operating out
of what was by then the only Portuguese colony left in East Africa—
Mozambique.

　　For much of the eighteenth century, Kilwa—on the coast south of
Zanzibar—was the region's primary port of export for both slaves and

other goods, but after the Omanis took control of Kilwa in the 1780s, they began diverting most of its trade through Zanzibar. In the 1830s, the number of slaves arriving at the island was an estimated 6,000 to 9,000 annually. In the 1840s and 1850s, that number grew to between 13,000 and 18,000, and in the 1860s—when the trade was at its peak—to over 20,000. Most of the slaves remained in Zanzibar to work its huge clove plantations or were sent to what is now the Kenyan coast to work grain plantations, while between a third and a half were shipped on to points farther north.

But these numbers tell only part of the story. As on the west coast of Africa, many more East Africans died evading capture and defending their villages than were actually enslaved. One witness to a recently raided village recalled:

> The sight and smell of dead bodies everywhere. Ghastly living forms of boys and girls, with dull, sad eyes, were crouching beside some of the huts. . . . Human skeletons were seen in every direction, and it was painfully interesting to observe the different postures in which the poor wretches breathed their last. A whole heap had been thrown down a slope behind a village. . . . Many had ended their misery under shady trees, others under projecting crags in the hills, while others lay in their huts, with closed doors, which when opened, disclosed the mouldering corpse with the poor rags round the loins—the skull fallen off the pillow—the little skeleton of the child, that had perished first, rolled up on a mat between two large skeletons.

Tens of thousands of other East Africans who were captured died en route to the coast. Some historians estimate that one out of every ten slaves captured never made it out of the continent alive—and others put that figure significantly higher. The missionary Dr. Livingstone and several of his contemporaries believed that four or five lives were lost for every slave delivered safely to the coast.

The march to the coast was brutal, sometimes taking months through difficult terrain. The slaves were usually roped, chained, or yoked together at the neck with thick pieces of wood, and their hands were often tied behind their backs. Sometimes they were gagged with

pieces of wood. The amount of food and water they received was piti-
fully small and many slaves fell ill, whereupon they were either killed
on the spot or left behind to die.

One ex-slave captured in the Sudan in 1874 later bore witness to a
march similar to those endured by Zanzibar's slaves:

> The wicked end of the lash curled round the face of the poor
> wretch [yoked to a pole in front of me] and drew from him a wild
> scream of agony. . . . I could see the blood gushing from his cheek
> down on his shoulder, and in a moment or so his legs gave beneath
> him and he hung a dead weight on his yoke. And as he hung he
> twisted half-round, his feet dragging on the ground, and I saw that
> one eye had been neatly flicked out by the end of the lash, and was
> hanging down on his cheek. . . . And then I saw one of [the Arabs]
> drive a spear right through the poor wretch's stomach. . . .
>
> I was just thinking that the Arabs were, at least, a little kinder
> to the women . . . when [they took an infant from a young woman
> who] was slower than all the rest. . . . As casually as though it
> were part of a day's work (as, in fact, I suppose it was!) the driver
> who had unfastened the baby drew his long, curved knife and slit
> its throat before the woman's eyes! . . . Its still-twitching little
> body [was] flung carelessly aside.

Nor was the East Africans' ordeal over once they reached the coast.
A mere twenty miles separated the mainland from Zanzibar, but for
many new captives, that short passage, across a sea most had never seen
before, was as terrifying and tragic as the far longer Middle Passage
across the Atlantic.

Wrote one observer:

> The Arab dhows are large unwieldy open boats without a deck. In
> those vessels temporary platforms of bamboo are erected, leaving
> a narrow passage in the centre. The negroes are then stowed, in the
> literal sense of the word, in bulk, the first along the floor of the ves-
> sel, two adults side by side, with a boy or girl resting between or on
> them, until the tier is complete. Over them the first platform is
> laid, supported an inch or two clear of their bodies, above a second

tier is stowed, and so on till they reach above the gunwale of the vessel. The voyage, they expect, will not exceed 24 or 48 hours; but it often happens that a calm or unexpected land-breeze delays their progress—in this case a few hours are sufficient to decide the fate of the cargo. Those of the lower portion of the cargo that die cannot be removed: they remain until the upper part are dead and thrown over. From a cargo of from 200 to 400 stowed in this way, it has been known that not a dozen at the expiration of ten days have reached Zanzibar.

Initially, most of the slaves captured by the Zanzibari caravans were taken from what is now Tanzania. But as the demand for the slaves grew, the coastal areas became depopulated and the traders were forced to move inland. Traveling along well-established trade routes forged by the Africans a century earlier, they began decimating the region around Lake Nyasa and then Lake Tanganyika.

Initially, too, most Zanzibari slavers obtained their captives through traditional means, by buying them off African traders such as the Yao, a people who had long been known for transporting and selling prisoners of war captured during legitimate tribal conflicts. But as the demand for slaves grew and grew, a new sort of slave trade developed. Greatly aided by the introduction of firearms—most provided by the fledgling United States, then one of Zanzibar's primary trading partners—the Arab traders would promise the African chieftains a certain number of muskets in return for slaves, and then encourage them to attack their neighbors, with whom they had hitherto been living in peace. One common tactic was for a trader to go into an area, stir up trouble, and then wait for the victor to come to him with the spoils—i.e., prisoners of war.

Not surprisingly, the practice led to a huge increase in tribal warfare, until it seemed as if the whole country was being destroyed. After attacking a village and rounding up all who had not escaped or been killed, the marauders would burn the place to the ground. Cattle and other livestock were confiscated or driven off, and crops were cut down, burned, or left to rot. Any villager who managed to survive and creep back found only smoldering, blackened ground strewn with a pitiful collection of broken belongings and the bodies of loved ones.

The destruction often stretched for miles. Regions that just a few years earlier had been teeming with life turned into huge silent grave-yards virtually overnight.

With no livestock and no one left to tend to the crops, famine be-came widespread, which in turn led to even more people becoming en-slaved. A desperate, starving tribe would sell its own people, even its children, for food. Sometimes a young child went for as little grain as it took to fill a hat.

When the Omanis began diverting the East African slave trade from Kilwa to Zanzibar in the late 1700s, Britain had virtually no presence in the region. No British ship had landed at Zanzibar for decades, and Britain basically regarded the entire Indian Ocean as the territory of the East India Company; British merchants with no connection to the com-pany were even discouraged from sailing there. In turn, the East India Company had little interest in East Africa—its focus was India and points farther east.

Then came the Napoleonic Wars of 1799 to 1815. Napoleon's hopes of destroying British rule in India were shattered, and the British cap-tured the Seychelles and the Île de France from the French. The British navy began policing East African waters—and Britain began noticing the region's slave trade.

Less than ten years earlier, in 1807, the British Parliament had passed the Slave Trade Abolition Act, which made it illegal for a British subject or British ship to engage in the slave trade. Any infraction thereof was a felony, punishable by three to five years' hard labor, and the law was strictly enforced, so much so that by end of the Napoleonic Wars, the British slave trade was all but nonexistent.

British abolitionists then tried to suppress the slave trade elsewhere in the world—in part, through bribery. In 1815, Portugal agreed to limit its slave trade to the southern half of Africa and its transatlantic colonies in return for 300,000 pounds and the cancellation of its 400,000-pound war debt. Spain made a similar agreement in return for 400,000 pounds. And in 1818, bowing to pressure from the British, France passed a law prohibiting the slave trade, though it had little effect, as it did not make the trade a criminal act and let offenders go virtually un-punished.

Britain's first anti–slave trade campaign in the East was directed at the trafficking between Oman and India. Oman had been shipping a small number of slaves to India for centuries. Now, however, thanks to the Slave Trade Abolition Act, that trade was illegal. India was a British possession.

In 1812, the Bombay governor wrote to Seyyid Said, then still living in Muscat, to complain about the trade—and to make the astonishing suggestion that the sultan follow Britain's example and abolish slavery altogether. Not surprisingly, the governor received no answer. Three years later, he wrote again, this time using more urgent language, as a horrific event had occurred: a vessel containing hundreds of slaves, en route from Zanzibar to Muscat, had been seized by Gulf pirates who "barbarously put to death" every soul on board. But again, the governor received no answer.

Then in 1821 rumors reached the British governor of Mauritius that the French, despite their anti–slave trade law, had recently sent twenty-four slaving ships to East Africa and that they planned to establish a slave depot on the island of Providence, between Madagascar and the Seychelles. Immediately, the governor dispatched Captain Fairfax Moresby of the HMS *Menai* to investigate. Cruising the waters between Madagascar and Zanzibar, Moresby concluded that no depot as yet existed, but that the slave trade was thriving. In one three-week period, he said he saw eight ships flying French colors sailing out of Zanzibar, each carrying two hundred to four hundred slaves and probably bound for the West Indies.

Whether Moresby's observations were strictly accurate is hard to tell. He was an ardent abolitionist who, like many other Westerners then in the East, tended to exaggerate in order to promulgate his point of view. But at least Moresby was a relatively straight shooter; many of his British compatriots were not. Like the British government itself, they took an antislavery stance as much out of political self-interest as out of humanitarian concerns. At the time, Britain was in a position to domi-nate East Africa's "legitimate" trade—meaning the export of such prod-ucts as ivory, cloves, copal, and rubber—and the demise of the slave trade would free up workers for that kind of work. International capitalism was the new world order; slave-labor colonies were declining in profitability. The British could both take the moral high ground and reap considerable economic profit.

One day, Moresby saw the French ship *Industrie* boldly loading slaves off Zanzibar's shore. The ship's captain was a notorious criminal and murderer named Mongin, who had a $2,000 price tag on his head. Moresby ordered two boats under the command of his first lieutenant to take the *Industrie*, and they found 140 slaves on board. But before any further action could be taken, Zanzibar's governor sent the British a message, demanding that they release the French ship, which was in Oman's territorial waters.

"The governor might blow away and be d——d," the British first lieutenant defiantly declared, and forced Mongin to pilot the vessel out of the harbor at gunpoint. Zanzibar did not open fire—all but one of its cannons was in disrepair. Later, the British asked Seyyid Said to overlook the unauthorized incident.

Following Moresby's investigations, the British again wrote to Seyyid Said, asking him to cooperate with them to end the slave trade. Said was deeply troubled by the request. Much of his revenue came from human trafficking and, more important, virtually all of his most powerful subjects, on whose political support he depended for survival, were heavily involved in the trade. He realized, however, that if he did not cooperate with the British, he would be in an even more untenable position. He still desperately needed Britain's help in his struggles against the Wahhabis in Oman.

And so it was that in 1822, Captain Moresby arrived in Muscat to negotiate what became known as the Moresby Treaty. The "external slave trade," meaning the export of slaves to "Christian markets," was now illegal; only the "internal slave trade," meaning human trafficking within the sultan's dominions, could continue. Zanzibari vessels could no longer transport slaves south of Cape Delgado in Africa, thereby preventing their sale to Mauritius, or east of a line drawn from Diu Head in India to near the island of Socotra south of Arabia, thereby ending the trade to India. Britain was also given the right to seize and search those Zanzibari vessels they suspected of transporting slaves, and to punish the offenders. As both sides recognized, Seyyid Said did not have the power to enforce the treaty—that job would have to be done by the British.

Seyyid Said could not have been happy at the turn of events, yet managed to send an upbeat letter to his local governors: "Whosoever receives this letter at Zanzibar, at Kilwa, or any ports within my dominions, this is to let you know that I have permitted my friends, the English, to keep an agent in any part of my country they may choose; and you are to give a house to the English Agent, and wherever he may stay, you are to pay him great respect, and nobody must refuse to receive the Agent."

In return for signing the Moresby Treaty, Seyyid Said was offered 2,000 pounds annually for three years—a pittance compared to the 400,000 pounds Britain had given Spain and the 700,000 pounds they had in effect given Portugal. Perhaps offended, the Omani ruler refused the offer. By his own estimation, the Moresby Treaty cost him $40,000–50,000 a year in lost slave-trade taxes.

Seyyid Said did appear to be sincere in his efforts to enforce the treaty, however. When Commodore Nourse of HMS *Andromache* visited Zanzibar in 1822, he observed: "the Imam of Muscat had issued the most positive orders forbidding the traffic in slaves with any Christian whatsoever; and from all the intelligence I could obtain those orders had been most strictly attended to by the Governor of Zanzibar."

The Moresby Treaty was only the first of a series of anti–slave trade treaties that Seyyid Said and his successors were forced to sign. But the treaty was also a victory of sorts for the sultan, as it was the first to recognize his territorial claim to East Africa.

In the end, however, the treaty had much less effect than anyone had anticipated. The Indian Ocean was simply too vast, the East African coast too long, and the British patrollers too few—their antislavery patrol usually consisted of no more than a half-dozen ships.

The treaty also had one completely unexpected side effect: the restriction of the slave trade to foreign markets led to a burgeoning demand for slaves within East Africa itself—primarily Zanzibar and what is now the Kenyan coast. The Arab, Swahili, and Indian businessmen had to make up for their lost revenue somehow, and if they could no longer profit from the foreign slave trade proper, they could at least profit from slave labor by growing products for foreign markets—

something that the British not only tolerated, but encouraged. Zanzibar's economy rapidly transformed from one based on maritime trade to one based on agriculture, as everyone from merchants to caravan leaders got into clove production. The planting of other crops such as rice and cereals fell off precipitously, and by the 1860s, Zanzibar was no longer economically self-sufficient.

Not long after signing the Moresby Treaty, Seyyid Said sent a fleet to the powerful but rebellious port of Mombasa. Once under Al Busaidi protection, Mombasa had declared itself independent more than seventy years earlier and had caused the Omani rulers constant trouble ever since, mostly by trying to take over other East African ports under their control.

Sailing into Mombasa one early winter's day, Seyyid Said's forces laid eyes on a most peculiar sight: 25,000 African warriors standing at arms beneath a homemade British flag. Just days earlier, British ships surveying the East African coast had been in the port and its Mazrui ruler had appealed to them for protection against the Al Busaids. The British naval commanders had made no commitment, but the Mazrui ruler had ordered the flag hoisted anyway, "for beneath its protecting shade we may defy our enemies; as the lamb trembles at the lion's roar, so will the Imaum shrink from that which is the terror of the World." The flag had the desired effect—Seyyid Said's fleet did not attack, though it remained anchored outside the harbor.

Meanwhile, another British survey ship, the HMS *Leven*, under the command of Captain William Fitzwilliam Owen, was making its way up the African coast. A strident abolitionist, Owen considered the destruction of the slave trade to be an intrinsic part of his surveying mission. And he had been appalled by what he had thus far witnessed along the East African coast—namely, the intense slave trafficking taking place at the Portuguese ports of Sofala, Mozambique, Ibo, and, especially, Quelimane. A dozen or so ships, each containing four hundred to five hundred slaves, set out from Quelimane for Rio de Janeiro each year.

When the Portuguese were at the height of their power in the Indian Ocean, they had had little interest in slave trafficking there. They were busy reaping the region's profits of spices, silks, and precious gems, and obtained all the labor they needed from Africa's west coast, where the slave trade was then in full swing. Only in the nineteenth century did the Portuguese turn seriously to slaving in East Africa. By then, they had lost most of their power in the region, the West African slave trade was under fierce attack, and better boats that could more easily navigate the Cape of Good Hope had been developed. Between 1815 and 1830, Mozambique was sending an estimated ten thousand slaves to Brazil annually and another seven thousand annually to the French Indian Ocean islands. In the 1820s Quelimane may have been the most important slave port in Africa, exporting about ten thousand slaves a year.

Captain Owen was forced to leave East Africa in order to sail to Bombay to refurbish his ship. While in the Indian port, he met some Mazrui envoys from Mombasa, in town to talk to the Bombay governor about their desire to live under British protection; the Bombay governor oversaw British interests in East Africa. Owen embraced the Mazrui proposition wholeheartedly, telling the governor that it was "the surest, if not the only, means of putting an end to the diabolical traffic in slaves." The governor rebuffed the proposal.

But Owen was not a man to take no for an answer. Certain that he was right, despite his limited knowledge of the region, he "made up his mind to take possession of [Mombasa] until the pleasure of His Majesty should be known." And with that in mind, he sailed to Muscat, landing there on Christmas Day 1823.

A day or two later, Owen met with Seyyid Said, whom he described as a man of "mild and gentlemanly manners and very communicative." A few pleasantries were exchanged, and then Owen launched into an attack on the sultan's trading practices. No one is enforcing the Moresby Treaty along the coast, he said bluntly, to which Seyyid Said replied, equally bluntly, that he would give Owen the authority to punish any slave traders he encountered. Seyyid Said then returned to a more pleasant subject—the friendship between their two nations—only to be rudely interrupted by the young man. There is but one key to Britain's friendship and that is to totally abolish the slave trade within the next three years, Owen said. Furthermore, he was sailing to Mombasa immediately to give the Mazrui the British protection they desired.

Expert in diplomacy that he was, Seyyid Said reacted only by saying that he would be happy to see British possessions blanket the world, from the rising to the setting of the sun, and that he would be especially pleased to see them take rebellious Mombasa. ("I thought I observed symptoms of insincerity," noted Owen at this point in his journal, in one of his few perceptive moments.) "But," the ruler went on, "to put down the slave trade with Muslims, that is a stone too heavy for me to lift without some strong hand to help me."

Thereupon, Owen huffily drew himself up and left for Mombasa, where he did indeed draw up an agreement with the Mazrui. The completely unauthorized document stated that the British would recognize the Mazrui's sovereignty, a British agent would reside in the port, Britain would receive half of the port's customs, and, most important to Owen, the slave trade would be abolished. The Mazrui accepted this last provision with great reservations, but were too intent on obtaining British protection to object too strenuously. They also planned to disregard the provision as soon as Owen departed.

His audacious mission apparently successful, Owen left Mombasa shortly thereafter, leaving behind a half-dozen men under the command of a twenty-one-year-old third lieutenant named John James Reitz. The Mazrui gave the Englishmen a plantation on the mainland opposite Mombasa, on which they would later establish a colony of freed slaves. But Reitz was too restless a man to be interested in farming. He wanted to see the country, and especially Pangani Falls, located in what is now northern Tanzania.

This is not the time to visit the falls, the Mazrui warned him. True, big rains have just fallen and we have good weather now, but those big rains were only the false monsoon. The real monsoon is about to begin.

Reitz didn't listen. The Mazrui were wrong, he was convinced, and he set out for the falls one sunny morning with seventy men. The very next day, torrents of rain began to fall and the party spent a miserable night in the shelter of shallow caves. They missed the boats on which they had intended to travel down the coast to the entrance of the Pangani River, and climbed aboard local canoes instead. Deluged by the rain, the canoes drifted out to sea, out of sight of land. By incredible good fortune they made their way back, but Reitz, still convinced that he was right, insisted that they try again, this time in open boats. The rain was coming down in floods and the tide brought all but Reitz's boat back to shore. Nine hours later, in the dark, his party reached the mouth of the Pangani River, from which they could hear the falls. But it was too late. The next day, Reitz came down with a high fever. He died "in a most awful state of delirium" and was buried in Mombasa.

Reitz was one of the first Englishmen to be buried in East Africa, but he was far from the last. "Wave may not foam, nor wild wind sweep,/ Where rest not England's dead," reads the inscription from the famous poem by Felicia Hemans that marks the entrance to the British cemetery at Grave Island, Zanzibar.

When Seyyid Said received word of Owen's actions in Mombasa, he was incensed. But the British quickly appeased the ruler by disavowing Owen's actions and the unauthorized treaty. They needed Seyyid Said's help to control the region almost as much as he needed theirs.

Ignorant of local customs and unable to see the world through anything but their own ethnocentric eyes, Reitz and Owen made fatal mistakes. Reitz lost his life; Owen, his credibility. The East African slave trade was far too complex an institution to be ended with a few simple treaties. To get rid of it would take many more decades, and much more economic and political change.

As the 1820s and then the 1830s progressed, the British slowly began to realize the obvious: far from curtailing the East African slave trade, the Moresby Treaty was actually encouraging it. The demand for slaves within Africa had increased dramatically.

Moreover, the slave trade to foreign markets such as Mauritius and India was still flourishing, with many slavers openly flouting the treaty by passing off captured Africans as crew members or wives of crew members. Language and cultural barriers made it extremely difficult for patrolling British seamen to know who was who on board the Zanzibari ships, and the slaves, beaten or frightened into submission, with no idea of who the British were, rarely spoke up. In 1838, one British captain estimated that as many as ten thousand slaves were being illegally shipped out of Zanzibar every year.

Things finally came to a head in June 1841, when Britain's foreign office sent a letter to Bombay, saying that the illegal trade would no longer be tolerated. The letter was forwarded to the newly appointed first British consul in Zanzibar, Lieutenant Colonel Atkins Hamerton.

Hamerton read the letter aloud to Seyyid Said: he was to "forbid all slave trade by sea and to permit British ships of war to search, seize and confiscate all native vessels found with slaves on board wherever navigating." The sultan "muttered about one thing and another," Hamerton wrote, but eventually capitulated, saying, "It is the same as the orders of Azrael (the angel of death)—nothing but to obey."

Still, the Omani ruler was not going down without a fight. He assembled a delegation to go to England to protest the crackdown. Bearing gifts for the queen—two pearl necklaces, two emeralds, an ornament shaped like a crown, ten cashmere shawls, four bottles of attar of roses, and four horses—the delegation also carried a letter. "That these countries will be totally and entirely ruined, and no revenue nor any income, saving and except a trifle, will remain with me; the loss of the whole world is as one shore," wrote Seyyid Said.

Seyyid Said also protested repeatedly to Hamerton. He would lose the support of his subjects, he argued over and over again. The Arabs were not "like the British and other European people who were always reading and writing," and so could not understand the antislavery point of view, he said.

Hamerton was sympathetic. "The Sultan has neither officers nor seamen, only five empty ships . . . ," he wrote to his superiors. "I do not believe he has one officer in his service who would do his duty and carry the Imam's orders fairly into effect if sent upon any service for the suppression for the slave trade."

But the foreign office was adamant—and impatient. Foreign Secretary Lord Henry Temple Palmerston wrote one brusque, condescending letter to Seyyid Said, and another to Hamerton: "You will take every opportunity of impressing upon these Arabs that the nations of Europe are destined to put an end to the African Slave Trade, and that Great Britain is the main instrument in the hand of Providence for the accomplishment of this purpose; that it is in vain for these Arabs to endeavour to resist the consummation of that which is written in the book of Fate, that they ought to bow to superior power."

The irony of the West invoking Fate—as opposed to the East, which is so often ridiculed in the West for its reliance on "God's will"—was apparently lost on the foreign secretary.

In the end, a new treaty, known as the Hamerton Treaty, was drawn up. Taking effect on January 1, 1847, the treaty put an end to the legal export of slaves from Africa to Arabia, the Persian Gulf, and Asia. Only the slave trade within the sultan's African dominions, meaning primarily from the interior to Zanzibar and the mainland coast, could continue.

Seyyid Said had won only one concession. The anti–slave trade cruisers could not search any vessel belonging to him or any other member of the royal Al Busaidi family. His steady supply of "Abyssinian girl-slaves and eunuchs" would still be safe from prying eyes. Harem life could continue as before.

Unlike virtually all of his subjects and other Muslims in the region, Seyyid Said understood that he had no choice but to accept the Hamerton Treaty. Britain was a powerful country with a growing presence in the East, and the world was changing. If he refused to sign the treaty, things might continue as they were for a time, but eventually, he would be destroyed. The fierce opposition of others to the treaty, however, meant that the Al Busaids would become ever more isolated and dependent on the British as time went by.

For most of his life, Seyyid Said probably never questioned the existence of slavery, but as he grew older and the horrors of the slave trade became more apparent, he may have seen it as an evil, albeit a necessary one. As with the Moresby Treaty, Seyyid Said was apparently sincere in his efforts to enforce the Hamerton agreement. He destroyed at least one village notorious for its slaving, and in 1850 when a Turkish Arab, said to have been sent from the sharif of Mecca, arrived in Zanzibar to "remonstrate with the Imam for the injury he had inflicted on the Moslem world" by signing the Hamerton Treaty, the Omani ruler refused to listen, saying that he meant "to meet the views of the British government as long as he lived."

Three years after the new treaty went into effect, Hamerton reported that the export of slaves from the sultan's dominions had decreased by 80 percent. But that same year, a German Protestant missionary named Johann Ludwig Krapf reported that the stream of "slavers bound for forbidden Arabia" from Kilwa was as steady as ever, and that new slave-trade routes were opening up as soon as old ones closed down. Slaves were also being kidnapped in Zanzibar and smuggled northward, to considerable profit.

Salme was only a young child when the Hamerton Treaty was signed, but she heard much about it as she grew older and wrote bitterly about the hypocrisy of the West's attitude toward slavery: "In my time a good many Europeans in Zanzibar kept slaves themselves or bought some when their interests were at stake . . . ," she wrote. "Nor are these European slave-keepers always humane enough to set the purchased slaves free later, as the Arab so frequently does; on the contrary, if they are no more useful to the master, he simply resells them."

15

Americans in Zanzibar

WHEN SEYYID SAID FIRST SET FOOT IN ZANZIBAR IN 1828, HE found an angry New England merchant eager to talk to him. Edmund Roberts, of the vessel *Mary Ann*, out of Salem, Massachusetts, had landed on the island three months earlier, hoping to make a tidy profit by exchanging a cargo of textiles, gunpowder, and arms for such products as ivory, tortoiseshell, and gum copal. But instead of making the speedy and profitable getaway that he had anticipated, Roberts had been detained by one difficulty after another. First, he had been told that unlike the British merchants in port, who could trade with whomever they pleased, he could trade only with Seyyid Said's agents, who were offering less-than-favorable terms. Then he had been told that he would be subject to heavy trade and export taxes—again, unlike the British.

Roberts must have watched with a mixture of impatience and hope as the sultan's fleet, fresh from a military skirmish in Mombasa, sailed into the Zanzibar harbor on that 1828 day: one 64-gun warship, three 36-gun frigates, two 14-gun brigs, and about 100 dhows. In all the arriving Omani force totaled over six thousand soldiers—an impressive sight that might have intimidated a less assured man.

But Roberts was not one to be put off by a show of power, or much of anything else. He had a great deal riding on his East African venture, having recently lost much property back in his home state of New Hampshire. He had even had to borrow money from friends to charter the *Mary Ann*.

Seyyid Said and Roberts met a few days later. The obligatory pleasantries were exchanged and then the American pleaded his case. The
Omani replied that Zanzibar and Britain had a trade agreement—that
was why the English merchants enjoyed preferential treatment. In reality, no such agreement existed, but the suggestion led Roberts to propose that Zanzibar sign a similar agreement with the United States,
exactly as Seyyid Said had hoped.

Once back home, Roberts wrote to his senator, Levi Woodbury, soon
to become secretary of the navy, suggesting that the United States both
negotiate a treaty with Oman and appoint a consul to Zanzibar. Woodbury began to work on the idea, but it would take six more years before
Roberts, traveling incognito as a captain's clerk so as not to arouse
British suspicion, returned to the Indian Ocean bearing a draft of the
treaty. Seyyid Said agreed immediately to its terms. "To the most high
and mighty Andrew Jackson, whose name shines with so much splen-
dour through the world," began his letter of acceptance, dated October 7,
1833.

Written on parchment in Arabic and English, the U.S.-Oman treaty
was the first agreement ever signed by a Gulf ruler with a Western
power and the second U.S. treaty signed with an Arab state. The oldest
U.S. treaty with an Arab country was signed with the sultan of Morocco
in 1787.

The British received the news of the U.S.-Oman treaty with "the reverse of pleasure" and immediately dispatched one Captain Hart to
Zanzibar. Welcoming him, Seyyid Said "commenced by saying how
pleased he was to see an English ship. . . . He always considered the
English as his best friends, and was happy to see them at all times." Captain Hart replied that the feeling was mutual, but also expressed his
country's displeasure over recent developments. The United States was
a rising power; the sultan should have consulted with the British before
taking such a big step. Seyyid Said, who had undoubtedly been angling
to negotiate a trade agreement with Britain all along, said that he would
revoke the American treaty if the British wanted.

"Mr. Edmund Roberts was an old, fat blustering man, and I was glad
to sign the treaty to get rid of him, as I did not think it of any importance . . . ," the ruler said. "[I] am willing to give the English everything

even [my] country if they wished it. As for the Americans, [they] are nothing to me, [my] attachment is to the English."

But Seyyid Said was only telling the British what they wanted to hear. His later close friendships with Americans belied his words.

In the end, Britain did not ask the sultan to revoke the U.S. treaty, probably because they couldn't find any grounds upon which to annul it. But Britain did negotiate its own treaty with Oman, similar to the U.S. one, and Seyyid Said promised never to sign another agreement with a foreign nation without consulting the British first.

In the decades that followed, Oman signed other treaties almost identical to the U.S. and British ones with France (1844) and Germany (1859). The treaties allowed the foreigners to buy and sell as they pleased within Seyyid Said's dominions, to reside at his ports without paying taxes other than those payable by the citizens of other favored nations, and to appoint consuls who could settle any suits involving their nationals in the region. The U.S. treaty had placed no restriction on trade with mainland Africa, but all the subsequent treaties did—an issue that later created much contention, with the Omani sultans declaring that Americans had no right to trade directly with the mainland either.

After the treaty was ratified by the U.S. Congress, Roberts returned to the Indian Ocean on board the USS *Peacock* with a completely executed copy. He was en route from Zanzibar to Muscat, where Seyyid Said was then residing, when "a disaster befell the *Peacock*, which proved nearly fatal," he wrote in a letter. The vessel ran aground on a coral reef near the island of Masirah, off southern Arabia. No help was nearby, Muscat was four hundred miles away, and "numerous piratical vessels" were "using every stratagem to plunder us, their numbers hourly accumulating for the purpose without doubt to destroy us." The intrepid Roberts volunteered to go to Muscat for help. Traveling in a small open boat, he and his crew were chased by pirate dhows for five harrowing hours before finally escaping during the night and, after an ugly storm and 101 hours at sea, reaching Muscat.

Seyyid Said received the Americans with open arms. He ordered the crew of his warship *Sultana* to prepare to go to sea and sent a message to a governor near Masirah to proceed to the *Peacock* with four armed

dhows and 300 men. He also sent 350 armed Bedu overland on camel-
back to warn the chiefs along the coast that they would be held "responsible with their heads for the safety of every individual of the crew,
& the property of the ship." The *Sultana* sailed south the next day, and
two days later the *Peacock* and its crew arrived safely in Muscat, where
Seyyid Said replaced the American cannons that had been thrown overboard in the panic.

It was the beginning of a close and mutually profitable relationship
that would last until the U.S. Civil War, when American ships stopped
frequenting the region in significant numbers. Interestingly, the only
portrait of Seyyid Said, probably painted by an American lieutenant
around 1831, hangs in the Peabody Essex Museum in Salem, Massachusetts, Roberts's home port. And for years, much to the chagrin of the
British, most Zanzibaris believed that all Westerners came from Salem
and that England was a suburb of Salem.

American vessels had begun venturing into the Indian Ocean in the late
1600s—well over a century before Roberts's arrival—but their numbers
were few. In fact, during colonial times, American merchants, like private British merchants, were expressly forbidden to trade with the East,
due to the East India Company's monopoly of the region. But following
the War of Independence, the American presence in the Indian Ocean
grew rapidly, so much so that before the start of the nineteenth century,
Americans were conducting more trade in the area than any other nation except Great Britain. The American "star-spangled banner may be
seen streaming in the wind where other nations, not excepting even my
own country, would not deign to traffic," observed one visiting Englishman.

Most of the early American Orient-bound ships sailed out of either
Boston or Salem, Massachusetts. The Boston ships usually sailed around
South America, up the coast to Alaska, across the Pacific Ocean to
China, and home through the Indian Ocean. The Salem ships went the
other way, sailing across the Atlantic Ocean and up the East African
coast to India, the East Indies, and the South Pacific, before turning
around and sailing home the way they had come.

At the time, Salem was a thriving commercial seaport with a population of about eight thousand, filled with sailors and entrepreneurs from all over the world. Its harbor air smelled of cinnamon, sandalwood, pepper, and ginger. Its streets were lined with lovely sea captains' homes. Presidents and dignitaries made stops in the town, concerts and exhibits were held there, and the first elephant to arrive in America—from India—stepped ashore in Salem in 1797.

In the 1700s, the American ships were very small, seldom over 100 tons, but after about 1800, the vessels began to increase in size, ranging from 100 to 500 tons. This put Salem at a disadvantage, as its harbor was not deep enough to handle the bigger ships. And then came the War of 1812, which dealt the small port another devastating blow—many of its ships were captured by the British or lost in battle. Of the 200 vessels registered in Salem before the war, only 57 survived to restart trading after hostilities ended. Salem's period of maritime prosperity appeared to be over; "the great tide of the East India trade had ebbed away, leaving Derby Street stranded, its brown wharves given over to rats and the slow lap of water among the dull green piles, the toppling warehouses transformed into Irish tenements and the harbor sadly empty," wrote one resident.

But salvation was at hand. The first Salem vessels arrived in Zanzibar, where the resourceful New Englanders discovered that East Africa—hitherto all but ignored by the Americans—produced many interesting items: animal hides, which they began bringing home to be processed in Salem's growing number of tanning factories; dried beef, which they took to Cuba to feed slaves; gum copal (resin taken from copal trees), used in the making of rubber and varnish; ivory, for producing billiard balls and piano keys, among other things; and tortoiseshell, used to make combs.

In two further strokes of good fortune, Zanzibar's harbor proved to be tailor-made for the Salem ships—its waters, too, were shallow, keeping out the competition—and gum copal proved to be a most profitable new business, thanks to one Jonathan Whipple, a Salem resident who discovered that the resin could be cleaned by letting it stand in alkali baths overnight. Before, it had been laboriously scraped clean with knives. Whipple established a small gum copal factory in Salem not far from Nathaniel Hawthorne's House of Seven Gables, and for twenty-five years monopolized the industry. At the time of Whipple's death in 1850, his factory employed thirty-five to forty men cleaning over 1.5 million pounds of gum copal a year.

A few New England entrepreneurs also managed to wedge their way into the East African slave trade, though not in Zanzibar—those who succeeded in entering the business bought slaves in Mozambique and took them to Brazil and Spanish America. The number of East African slaves exported by the New Englanders was probably quite limited, although in 1849, one American captain commented that:

> the east coast of Africa, which, being considered safer than the west coast for the slavers, owing to the number of cruisers on the latter station, although the distance was greater, was for a long time the favourite coast for shipping the slaves, both with the Spanish and American traders. These vessels were generally disguised as whalers until a fitting opportunity presented itself, and when they thought the road was clear they would anchor at the entrance of a river and, aided by the dhows, in one night would take in cargoes of several hundreds of slaves, and be far off the coast the next morning.

Many genuine American whalers were in the region as well. At the time, schools of whales frolicked in the southern waters of the Indian Ocean, migrating north every winter to the Red Sea in search of food. In some years, between thirty and sixty pounds of ambergris—part of the whale's intestinal lining, once used in the making of perfume—were found washed up on Zanzibar's beaches.

In return for their cargoes of gum copal, hides, ivory, ambergris, and other East African products, the Salem merchants traded muskets, gunpowder, brass wire, "Yankee notions" (chairs, nails, rope, crockery, mirrors), and, most important, textiles. The cloth was manufactured in the humming mills of Salem, Lawrence, and Lowell, Massachusetts, and by the mid-1830s, almost every Salem ship heading East carried hundreds of bales of cotton. Hitherto, East Africa had obtained most of its cloth from India and England, but the unbleached American cloth proved to be a more durable product and became a bestseller not only in East Africa, but in Arabia and Persia as well. For a time, the English even tried to pass off their cloth as American-made by stamping it with similar marks, but they were soon found out. *Merkani* became the region's word for "cloth."

The Omanis used the American-made cloth, muskets, and powder to trade with African chieftains, often in return for slaves. Americans were therefore key players in the slave trade on the east coast as well as the west coast of Africa. Early Americans also had a virtual monopoly on the coffee and gums of Aden, the dates and hides of Muscat, and the ivory of Mozambique. Most ships couldn't obtain enough cargo in Zanzibar alone and so made multiple stops before returning home.

But American dominance in the region was short-lived. With the Civil War, the production of *merkani*, dependent upon cotton grown in the American South, ground to a halt, and muskets and gunpowder were no longer available for trade. Even the gum copal business ended, as a stiff import tax was imposed on uncleaned resin and the Salem factory closed.

After the Civil War, some Americans tried to regain their former position in East Africa. But England, Germany, and France had made great inroads into the region in the intervening years, and the New Englanders never recaptured their former prominence.

Of the 41 foreign ships that called at Zanzibar between September 1832 and May 1834, 32 were American, with 20 shipping out of Salem, 3 out of Boston, and 3 out of New York City. Of the 80 foreign ships that called at Zanzibar in 1859, 35 were American. Between 1825, when the Salem brig *Spy* sailed into Zanzibar, and 1870, when the *Glide* returned home, 189 Salem-based ships conducted trade with Zanzibar. The *Glide* was the last vessel to arrive in Salem from beyond the Cape of Good Hope.

Not surprisingly, the first U.S. consul posted to Zanzibar, Richard Palmer Waters, was from Salem. He was also a classic New Englander, devout, reserved, astute, and canny—traits that would serve him well in his exotic new position.

Richard Waters was the younger brother of John Waters, a sea captain who had met Seyyid Said in Zanzibar in 1832, five years before his
brother's arrival. The sultan had taken a great liking to Captain John
Waters and had given him a letter to publish in the American papers,
inviting all U.S. citizens to come and trade in Zanzibar. But when Captain Waters presented the letter to his vessel's owners, all Salem men,
they told him, "No, Mr. Waters, if we allow this to be published, everybody will know of the place and we shall lose our trade."

Born in 1807, Richard Waters opened his own retail shop at age
twenty-five. As a young man, he became an outspoken critic of slavery,
an unusual and courageous act for the time. Joining the Essex County
Anti-Slavery Society, he became good friends with Reverend James
Trask Woodbury, brother of Levi Woodbury, now secretary of the navy.
It was through this connection that Waters was appointed consul to
Zanzibar. The United States offered no formal consular training at that
time, and Roberts, a largely uneducated man, apparently startled many
who met him. An American who visited the island in 1840 wrote this
cryptic note to a fellow merchant: "I expect you will be greatly astonished & amused with the American Consul. . . . Mr. Waters is not the
right kind of man to be placed here. . . ."

Waters set sail for Zanzibar in October 1836, on board the brig *Generous*. Much like other Westerners heading to the Indian Ocean before
him, he had a hidden agenda: "I have desired to be made useful to the
Souls of these pagans among whom I am called to reside. That my going
to dwell with them for a season, may be the means of introducing the
gospel of Christ to them," he wrote in his journal.

The *Generous* sailed across the Atlantic and around the Cape of
Good Hope without incident, to arrive in Mozambique four months
after leaving Salem. Waters was immediately appalled by what he saw,
though he had the sensitivity to realize that as an American, he had no
right to cast stones. "This city is a depot for slave Vessels . . . ," he wrote.
"I can see from the deck of our Vessel that the decks of these Slavers are
filled with Slaves, mostly with children, from 10 to 14 years of age. This
sight called up many unpleasant feelings. What can I say to those engaged in this trade, when I remember the millions of Slaves which exist
in my own country?"

One month later, the *Generous* arrived in Zanzibar, where it was greeted with two thirteen-gun salutes—one from another Salem brig, the other from an Omani vessel. Zanzibari officials then boarded the *Generous* to extend a more personal welcome. Waters invited them to share in a glass of wine, but they refused, saying that it was against their religion.

The next day, Waters went to see Seyyid Said, who received him with great courtesy, even insisting that he sit in the chair that he usually occupied and offering to pay the consul's rent. "I left the Sultan quite pleased with my first interview. His Highness is a fine looking man about 50 years old," wrote Waters.

Some time later, Seyyid Said invited Waters to ride out with him to Beit al-Mtoni, an excursion that the American thoroughly enjoyed:

We were preceded by a guard of 16 soldiers, dressed in red coats and white pantaloons. . . . Our horses were first rate Arabian. The road was very good, and the appearance of the country most delightful. The birds were singing. . . . His Highnesses country Seat is a most delightful place. . . . One of the most beautiful sights I ever beheld was the extended plantation of Clove trees. His Highness has *two hundred thousand* on this plantation. . . . The air, for some distance round, is strongly impregnated with Cloves. I was reminded of Bishop Hebers "Spicy Breezes," in his beautiful Missionary Hymn, "From Greenland's icy mountains."

During their visits together, Seyyid Said and Waters spent much time talking about religion. Waters hoped to convert the sultan to Christianity, and the sultan—who had no intention of converting—loved argument and discussion. Seyyid Said also admired Waters's religious devotion and allowed him to distribute Christian tracts and Bibles among the Zanzibaris—undoubtedly knowing full well that they would fall upon deaf ears.

Despite his admirable views on abolition, Waters was a man of little perception and even less tolerance, and he was often confounded by the Zanzibaris' response to his preaching. "These people remind me of those spoken of in Holy Writ," he wrote. " 'They honor me (saith the Lord) with the *lip*, while their *hearts* are far from me.' I often talk with them on the interest of the Soul, and they most always reply by saying—'Our book (the Koran) speaks all the same as yours (the Bible) and we pray plenty.' "

Waters's main duties were to settle disputes between American and Arab merchants, oversee transactions between the same, and report to the U.S government. Occasionally, too, he was expected to intervene in cases of desertion or mutiny on board whaling ships.

As a Salem man backed by Salem merchants, Waters understood that he needed to do all that he could to maintain his hometown's monopoly of Zanzibar's trade. His sea captain brother had even hammered that point home to him before he left by telling him that insofar as "honorable" means permitted, he should not give competitors (i.e., non-Salem men) too much information and should try to prevent them from forming profitable relationships in Zanzibar.

A shrewd businessman, Waters scarcely needed that advice. Soon after his arrival in Zanzibar, he entered into a complicit arrangement with the Banyan customs master, Jairam Sewji. The arrangement gave Waters priority over all other merchants when it came to American cargo, while Sewji, as was his wont, dictated to which local vendors and at what price all the foreign traders could buy and sell. The supremacy of the Salem merchants was thus maintained and the two business partners profited handsomely. When Waters left Zanzibar in 1844, after about seven years of service, he had a reputed $80,000 in his pocket; Sewji was said to have made an annual profit of $100,000 for many years.

Other Americans complained about Waters's behavior, and four years into his tenure, Seyyid Said himself even wrote a letter of complaint to U.S. president Martin Van Buren. But the letter never reached its intended audience. As one witness stated:

Capt. Hassan & the Imaun secretary came in [to Mr. Waters's house] with a letter from the Imaun, for *Martin Van Buren, President of the U. States.* After they were gone Mr. Waters said he did not wish the letter to go as he feared it contained charges against him, and he had no time to write home to conteract their effect, and that he did not think it any harm to destroy the letter as it was not the work of the Imaun, but wrote at the instigation of the native merchants who wished to drive him from the Island, so that they could again get the American business, or words to that effect. He then asked me to throw the letter overboard when at sea, which I declined. He then ordered all the servants out of the Cook room. When they were all gone he went with the letter, tore it in halves and hove it in the fire.

Even if the sultan's letter had reached the president, however, chances are that little would have been done. The U.S. authorities were too far away to intervene in local matters, and the consuls of that era, paid no salary to speak of, were expected to make their positions profitable in whatever way they could. In fact, twenty years after Waters's departure, when William Speer, the first noncommercial consul appointed to Zanzibar, tried to get some answers as to how trade on the island was conducted, few merchants would talk to him. "The Consul is supposed to have too much delicacy to ask questions," he wrote bitterly, calling Zanzibar a "receptacle of secrets," full of spies. He left the island after only a short term and was replaced by another, and presumably more understanding, commercial man.

The man who did break the Waters-Sewji stranglehold on the island's trade was British consul Hamerton. Shortly after arriving on the island in May 1841, Hamerton was deluged with complaints from the port's Indian and British traders. He went to speak to Seyyid Said about the problem, and as soon as he sat down, got a sense of what he was up against. Behind the sultan hung two paintings. In one, a British ship was being captured by an American one, and in another, the ship's Union Jack was being hauled down, to be replaced with the Stars and Stripes.

Nonetheless, Seyyid Said listened attentively to Hamerton's complaints and took them to Waters, who began spreading a false rumor: Hamerton represented the East India Company, not the British government, and the East India Company was nearly bankrupt, meaning that Hamerton had virtually no power. Seyyid Said believed the rumor at first, but one day a British ship, the HMS *Grecian*, arrived in port to greet Consul Hamerton with full diplomatic honors.

So ended the Waters-Sewji monopoly.

After leaving Zanzibar, Waters returned home to Massachusetts, where he became a gentleman farmer and ardent supporter of many re-form movements. But he and Sultan Said parted on friendly terms and remained in touch, with Waters apparently trying to extend his influence over Zanzibar even from afar. A letter he received from Seyyid Said on November 29, 1845, read: "Respecting the letter appointing you my agent in America. My dear friend, I do not feel like sending [it], as it would be necessary for me to write to the U.S. Government. And as I have within a short time written the Government four letters and have never received an answer to [any] of them, I do not feel like writing more. In regard to the new Consul appointed to Zanzibar, it would not be right for us to interfere. Please God we will shew him proper respect. . . ."

Traffic between Zanzibar and the United States did not only go one way. On April 30, 1840, the first Arab ship ever to arrive in the United States dropped anchor in New York harbor. On board was Ahmed bin Naa-man, a small, plump man dressed in a flowing *dishdasha*, black *bisht* trimmed with gold, and multicolored turban. A representative of Seyyid Said, Naaman was the first Arab emissary ever sent to the United States.

The arrival of the *Sultana* in New York harbor created an extraordinary sensation. Reporters from all ten of the city's papers rushed to the docks, along with hundreds of residents, all eager to catch their first sight of Arabs. The *Morning Herald* called the ship's arrival "a perfect wonder," and the city marshals had to be summoned to protect the crew—and the two women on board, who were rumored to be slaves and gifts for the U.S. president. In reality, one of the women was the wife of an English trader and the other, her maid.

The crewmen were indeed a curious sight. Eighty-seven days out of Zanzibar, they were gaunt and haggard, having survived on one meal of curried rice a day for months. The Americans were fascinated—by the men's long unkempt beards, by their scanty clothes, by the endless clicking of their prayer beads—and stalked the visitors' every move for their entire three-month stay. One sympathetic official noted after their visit: "They were tormented continuously by the mob crowding the vessel to see the Arabs, looking on them as a curiosity—their privacy was intruded on, they were pulled by the beards, and otherwise insulted." Some New Yorkers even thrust alcoholic drinks into the crewmen's hands, to laugh uproariously when the offer was accepted and the Muslims—unaccustomed to alcohol—began to stagger; or to take umbrage when the offer was turned down. "The Arabs look around, curl up their mustaches, look at each other and wonder at the depravity of the natives," reported the *Morning Herald*.

As it happened, many of the *Sultana*'s crewmen were not Arabs, but impoverished Banyans or Khojas from western India, and others were African slaves. Dressed in coarse cotton garments made of *merkani*, the men had little education and smelled of the coconut oil that they had rubbed all over their bodies during their voyage to keep away the cold.

In contrast, envoy Naaman and his officers—most of whom *were* Arabs—were sophisticated and well-groomed men. They had fared somewhat better than the crew during the *Sultana*'s long voyage, often dining on curried rice with meat or mangoes, drinking Mocha coffee, and smoking the hookah. Naaman and the officers were fêted everywhere they went. Lavish lunches and dinners were held in their honor, and special tours were given—of the penitentiary on Blackwell's Island, City Hall, Castle Garden, and the Battery. At the Brooklyn Navy Yard, the foreigners were met with a thirteen-gun salute and a reception at the commodore's home, complete with a band and iced punches.

Naaman charmed everyone he met with "his naivete and intelligence," and was invited to take up residence at the commodore's house. Shortly after he had settled in, the *Morning Herald* reported: "[He] . . . looks quite cool and contented. He strokes his beard—watches movement in the Navy Yard—says his prayers morning, noon and night and takes a siesta every day." When asked which were more attractive, American women or Arab women, Naaman gallantly defended his country's fairer sex.

The *Sultana* had brought many items for trade: 1,300 bags of dates, 21 bales of Persian carpets, and 100 bales of Mocha coffee shipped on at Muscat; and 108 ivory tusks, 81 cases of gum copal, 135 bags of cloves, and 1,000 dried hides shipped on at Zanzibar. These goods were sold to New York merchants in exchange for 125 bales of *merkani* cloth;

24 bolts of scarlet cloth; 13 cases of red, white, and blue beads; 300 muskets; and 300 25-pound bags of gunpowder. Items purchased for Seyyid Said's personal use included four decorated rifles, several boxes of gold thread, 20 reams of paper, 50 boxes of refined sugar, a box of perfume, 10 boxes of sheet music, a case of candies, some red soap, and almond and pineapple extract.

The Americans had not forgotten Seyyid Said's help in rescuing the USS *Peacock* and its crew after its shipwreck on the Arabian shore. To express their gratitude, they spent $5,000 repairing his ship, the *Sultana*—the same vessel that had rescued the *Peacock*—and equipped it with a new water closet.

Naaman had hoped to meet with President Van Buren while he was in the United States, but it was not to be. Van Buren was busy with a reelection campaign, and Naaman's mission was not of high priority— he had come as a businessman, not a diplomat.

Nonetheless, Seyyid Said had sent many gifts for Van Buren: two fine stud horses from the Arabian Najd (which were much admired while stabled at Tattersall's on Broadway), a string of pearls, 120 brilliants, a small gold bar, a Persian carpet, a jar of attar of roses, six cashmere shawls, and a gold-mounted sword. The gifts threw the U.S. Congress into a tizzy. Under the still-new Constitution, the president could not accept presents, and the fledgling nation had no precedent for such a thing. John Quincy Adams argued adamantly against taking the presents, while others brought up Seyyid Said's rescue of the *Peacock*. He could not be insulted, they said. Finally, Congress decided to take the gifts, but to sell them and give the proceeds to the U.S. Treasury.

After six weeks in New York, the *Sultana*'s crew was moved to new accommodations where it would be easier to keep an eye on them. Abolitionist activity had led to the desertion of seven of the ship's slaves, and more were feared. But surprisingly, most American abolitionists paid little attention to the *Sultana* and its crew. The *Nationalist Anti-Slavery Standard* didn't even mention the ship until three months after its arrival, and then only to praise the New Yorkers' treatment of its "colored crew." When the *Sultana* left New York, two more slaves jumped overboard, hoping to swim to freedom, but they were quickly apprehended and returned to the ship by the New York police.

Naaman's portrait hung in New York's City Hall for many years, and is now owned by the Peabody Essex Museum in Salem, Massachusetts. Like Seyyid Said's portrait, also in the museum, it portrays a dignified, courtly, and intelligent-looking man. American demonization of Arab rulers was still a century away.

16

The Swahili

SEVERAL TIMES A YEAR, THE *SARARI* AND THEIR CHILDREN MADE an excursion to one of Seyyid Said's *shambas*, or plantations. The patriarch owned forty-five of them, scattered all over the island, some tended to by as many as five hundred slaves. However, only two of the plantations had villas, as opposed to simple houses or shacks, and these were the only ones deemed suitable for a visit from the royal family.

Just after dawn on the day of an excursion, with hypnotic calls to prayer still echoing over Stone Town, the royal women and children assembled with their slaves outside the palace walls. Here waited their donkeys, hung with rich trappings of embroidered red cloths, tasseled cushions, and jingling gold and silver plates.

Some of the slaves helped the *sarari*, older children, and more delicate eunuchs onto the donkeys, while others began to walk, some carrying young children on their shoulders. Slowly, the procession filed out of the still-hushed town, passing only a handful of early risers—mostly pious men on their way home from prayers at the mosques. The Banyan shops were still shuttered, and the empty marketplaces, littered and stained.

As the sun began to rise, the procession passed by the large graveyard and racecourse on the edge of town. Shrubs sparkled with dew and a golden light flooded the day. A fringe of coconut trees nearly a mile long swayed along the beach in the distance, while to either side lay grassy plains and dark green, sun-dappled forests thick with mango and orange trees. Following a mix of beaten red dirt roads and crooked winding paths, the procession passed in and out of shadows and over streams. The air was fragrant with wildflowers. The whole of Zanzibar stretched ahead.

On their way to and from the plantations, the royal family passed Swahili villages. Compact settlements filled with homes built of mud and coral stone, with coconut-leaf thatched roofs, the villages were usually centered on a simple mosque, a few shops, an open market, and a well. Homes were adjoined by small gardens and clutches of coconut, mango, and orange trees, while nearby stood chicken huts, elevated on legs to keep the mongooses and civet cats away. Surrounding the villages stretched small cassava, millet, maize, and sweet-potato fields.

Many Swahili villages also boasted a *mkahawa*, or coffee shop, a gathering place for men only, and a theater, where dances were performed, to the accompaniment of huge *ngomas* (drums made of hollowed tree trunks), *siwas* (giant crescent-shaped horns often made of black wood or ebony), *zezes* (one-stringed instruments made of calabashes), *tamburs* (lutes), and other instruments.

Like the residents of Stone Town, the Swahili villagers were awakened just before dawn by the call to prayer, sung by village muezzins. Especially pious men scurried off to a mosque while the villages filled with light, and smoke rose from huts.

After breakfast, most of the men left the villages, to plant seed—blessed earlier by a mullah—hoe fields, tend to crops, pick coconuts, or cut firewood. Skilled carpenters and boat-builders left for the shore, to repair dhows and canoes, while merchants, blacksmiths, and other artisans opened up their shops.

The Swahili women spent the early morning cleaning the huts and fetching water at the communal wells. But around mid-morning, most of the women also left the villages, usually to help their husbands in the fields, sometimes with a child in a sling on their backs. Other women went down to the shore to catch shellfish and crabs with a basket, or to net small schools of fish with a piece of cloth, which was held by two women while a third drove the fish into it.

Unless, of course, it was clove-harvesting season. During that period, all able-bodied men and women headed to the plantations of the wealthy, to work alongside slaves for weeks for minimal pay.

Around noon, the women returned home to grind maize or millet and pound flour for the evening meal. Later, they gathered wood and dead coconut leaves to build fires, and revisited the communal wells.

The men stopped working at about four p.m. and returned home. Changing from work clothes into spotless *dishdashas*, they went calling on their friends, to talk, snack, and perhaps drink palm wine or play a game of *bao*, an East African board game that involves moving seeds around four rows of eight holes. At dusk, the women served the evening meal on the *baraza*, and afterward, the men went to the headman's house to discuss local affairs and tell stories.

After sundown, and especially when in the vicinity of Beit al-Mtoni, Salme's first home, everyone took care where they stepped. An old Swahili superstition had it that it was dangerous to kick baskets left outside after dark, in case the basket was actually a wizard who had transformed himself for the night. The roads near Mtoni were said to be a favorite dwelling place of such shape-shifting beings, as well as the haunt of ordinary human criminals, who would hide in the baskets in order to attack and rob unsuspecting travelers.

When the Al Busaidi Omanis first began arriving in Zanzibar in the late 1700s, they found it occupied by two Swahili populations, the Hadimu and the Tumbatu. The Hadimu were the predominant group, living in most parts of the island, while the Tumbatu occupied the northwest coast and an island just off the coast, also named Tumbatu. Both groups made a significant part of their living from the sea, but most of their settlements were located inland, for they feared the "black birders," i.e., pirates in dhows who kidnapped women and children for the slave trade. However, the Hadimu and Tumbatu were themselves slave owners. Their captives were Africans from the mainland.

The Swahili are different from all other African peoples. Living along the East African coast, where they today number about half a million, they are and have long been Muslim, their culture has long been literate, and their centuries-old civilization, which reached its zenith during the 1300s and 1400s, was primarily urban until the Portuguese destroyed their cities and trade routes in the 1500s, leaving only villages behind. The Swahili culture did revive somewhat after the Portuguese left, but then the Omanis arrived.

Never enslaved themselves, the Swahili were once both slave owners and slave traders, acting as middlemen between the Africans of the interior and the peoples of the Indian Ocean. Up until the nineteenth century, the Swahili traders transported relatively small numbers of slaves, but as the trade escalated and the Swahili helped to depopulate large sections of the African interior, they, like the Omani Arabs, became feared and hated by many other African peoples.

The Swahili people speak Swahili or, more correctly, KiSwahili—the Bantu prefix *ki-* indicates it is a language. During the nineteenth century, the Zanzibari caravans, venturing deep into Africa in pursuit of ivory and slaves, spread the language far and wide, so that today KiSwahili is East Africa's lingua franca, spoken by about seventy million people, some as far west as the eastern Congo.

KiSwahili is a Bantu, or African, language. But in the nineteenth century, again through the influence of the Omani Arabs, many Arabic words entered the language, and today its vocabulary is about 25 percent Arabic—a fact that has given rise to much confusion. Throughout most of the twentieth century, most scholars believed that the Swahili culture, like its language, only began with the mixing of African and Arab peoples, with the Arabs providing the all-important "civilized" part of the mix. More recent scholarship, however, has revealed that the Swahili culture and its language began developing before the arrival of the Arabs, meaning that the Swahili are a predominantly African people who only later in history absorbed many Arab elements, along with a smattering of Persian, Indian, and Indonesian influences.

However, the Swahili only truly became the Swahili with the coming of Islam, which was introduced by the Arabs. The new religion first took hold on the Somali coast, directly across the Red Sea from Arabia, in the 700s and spread gradually down the East African coast as far south as Cape Delgado (the northernmost point of Mozambique), a thousand miles away. By the eleventh century, over a dozen small Swahili settlements dotted the shoreline; by the fourteenth century, there were at least 30 communities with at least one mosque. In all, before the decline of their civilization, the Swahili built an impressive total of 173 towns—20 with populations over eight thousand.

The word *Swahili* comes from the Arabic word *sawahil*, meaning "coast" or "edge"; the Swahili are the "People of the Coast" or the "People on the Edge" of Islamic civilization. The term existed as early as the thirteenth century, but only came into widespread usage in the eighteenth century, when the Al Busaidi rulers began applying it to their East African subjects.

In most places, the Swahili coast is only about ten miles wide. Bordered by the *nyika*, or bush, to the west, it is a fertile swatch of agricultural land dotted with tidal estuaries in which flourish mangrove forests. The Swahili once exported the mangrove wood as building materials to Arabia, Persia, and beyond. Early on the Swahili, like the Omanis, became expert ship builders, though most Swahili vessels only traveled up and down the African coast, conducting local trade, rather than across the high seas.

At no point in history did the Swahili have their own political state. Rather, local rulers reigned independently over small coastal cities and towns, which were linked together economically and culturally. Most of the cities and towns stood on the sites of older African settlements, which the Swahili had rebuilt with fine new houses, mosques, and public buildings constructed of coral stone whitewashed with lime.

In the stone houses resided the Swahili elite, who, during the Middle Ages, had a standard of living that was comparable to that of the upper classes of Europe, the Middle East, and India at the time. With the whole world at their fingertips, they dressed in luxurious clothes, dined off Chinese porcelain, adorned themselves with Indian jewelry, and used perfume and rose water stored in bottles from Persia. A literate people, they were well versed in the Quran and Islamic law and could recite reams of Arabic and Swahili poetry by heart.

Strict observers of Islam, the Swahili elite also secluded and veiled their women, endowed mosques, and built *madrassas* and large tombs in the Islamic tradition. Cut off from the African interior by their religion and sophistication, they felt their closest connection to be with other Muslim peoples. Many elite Swahili traveled to other Muslim countries and, in turn, received Muslim visitors from all over the Indian Ocean world.

At first, the Omani settlers arriving on the east coast tried to keep separate from the Swahili people. They saw themselves as political leaders and temporary colonizers, in the region to make money, not to build towns or develop full-scale societies. But before long, the Omanis found that they needed the help of the Swahili elite—to trade with the mainland, navigate the slave trade, and control the poorer African peoples. And so, gradually, the Omani Arabs and the Swahili elite began to intermix and intermarry, though it was only the Arab men who married into Swahili families; the Arab women never did. The two cultures began to take on characteristics of each other, even as the Arab culture began to predominate. Omani governors replaced Swahili rulers; official judges replaced local religious leaders; Sharia was more strictly enforced; and the Arabs built ever more mosques and *madrassas*. KiSwahili became the informal idiom of Arabs and Swahili alike, while Arabic remained both peoples' formal and religious language. Salme and her siblings spoke KiSwahili with each other and their mothers, but only Arabic with their father.

However, the Omanis never lost their sense of superiority over the Swahili, so much so that many Swahili fervently disliked them. Ibadhism is a tolerant religion, but it is also a strict and an exclusionary one, since one cannot convert to Ibadhism but must be born into it. And in that complicated way that subjugated peoples often internalize the value systems of their oppressors, the Swahili themselves began to see their own culture as inferior, and to claim an Arab lineage—no matter what the color of their skin.

Zanzibar, or "Unguja," as it is known is KiSwahili, is seldom mentioned in early travelers' accounts of East Africa and so was probably not an important Swahili center during the Middle Ages. But by the time the Portuguese arrived in the region in the early 1500s, Zanzibar and Pemba were flourishing. "The kings of these isles live in great luxury, they are

clad in very fine silk and cotton garments, which they purchase at Mom-
baca from the Cambaya merchants," wrote one Portuguese sailor in
1512.

In the 1570s, the Portuguese established a permanent trading post
near Zanzibar's harbor, but it was very small until about 1600. The Portuguese had built their major stronghold of Fort Jesus in Mombasa in
1593; the fort made the Portuguese position in the region much more
secure and their presence in Zanzibar grew exponentially. Traders and
vicars arrived, and Zanzibar's first church was built.

In 1649, the Omanis attacked the Portuguese in Zanzibar, destroying their settlement and killing their vicar. The island's Swahili ruler at
the time was a woman, Mwana Mwema, who was married to an Arab
from Yemen; Swahili history is rich with stories of ruling queens, some
of them mythical only, who were often married to immigrant rulers,
thus providing an important link between the Swahili's two worlds—
Africa and Arabia/Asia. Mwana Mwema was on good terms with the
Portuguese but, upon their defeat, quickly transferred her allegiance—
a mistake, as it turned out. Oman was too far away to control the island
for long, and the Portuguese soon returned.

Mwana Mwema was succeeded by her brother Yusuf, who reigned
for many years. Upon his death in the late 1600s, his kingdom was divided into two parts, with the southern half going to his son Bakiri and
the northern half, including the harbor, to his daughter Fatima.

Throughout her reign, Fatima, unlike her grandmother, remained
steadfastly loyal to the Portuguese, even as their control of East Africa
slipped dramatically. Then in 1698 the Omanis conquered Fort Jesus
and the Portuguese departed from Zanzibar. In their wake came the
Omanis, who appointed a governor and began to settle on the island in
small numbers. Fatima could have left with the Portuguese, but instead
chose to remain with her people—and pay the price. The Arabs arrested
her and her son and carried them off to Oman. They were allowed to
return some years later, but for the rest of her life, Fatima lived with an
Omani cannon trained on her residence.

When Seyyid Said arrived in Zanzibar, the island's Swahili ruler, known
as Mwenyi Mkuu, or "The Great Lord," was Hassan bin Ahmed, Fatima's

great-great-grandson. He lived in the center of the island, at a place called Bweni, but probably came into Stone Town to meet the Omani sultan, whom he recognized as the island's overlord.

The two rulers came to terms. Mwenyi Mkuu was to provide Seyyid Said with as many laborers as he needed, and collect a yearly tax for each of his married male subjects. In return, the sultan was to pay Mwenyi Mkuu an annual pension. Otherwise, Mwenyi Mkuu was free to rule his people as he pleased. Throughout the Omanis' occupation of Zanzibar, both before and after the arrival of Seyyid Said, they had virtually no contact with the ordinary Swahili.

At first, Seyyid Said's needs in Zanzibar were limited: he required only a few men now and again for cutting timber, building houses, and the like. But before long, thanks to the island's exploding clove industry, he needed the labor of hundreds of men—as did Mwenyi Mkuu himself, who was also in the clove business. Every village headman was ordered to round up a quota of workers, who were paid no wages, only a supply of grain.

Around 1845, a new Mwenyi Mkuu, Muhammad bin Ahmed al-Alawi, took over the Swahili throne. He demanded complete submission from his subjects. Any Swahili who approached him had to fall on his or her knees and crawl, singing the ruler's praises, and whenever he went out, coconut and clove pickers had to slide hurriedly to the ground, because no one's head was allowed to be above the Great Lord's. Anyone who did not obey these rules was severely punished. Near Mwenyi Mkuu's residence was a pit where slaves convicted of drunkenness and other crimes were slaughtered and buried.

Nonetheless, Muhammad was highly respected by his people, as the following story reveals: Tradition has it that sometime after Seyyid Said's death, Mwenyi Mkuu was arrested, for reasons that are unclear. That same night, the Swahili ruler miraculously disappeared from his prison, to appear the next day on the mainland, where he remained in exile for several years. And throughout his absence, not a single drop of rain fell on Zanzibar. Only when the Omanis pardoned Mwenyi Mkuu and allowed him to return did rain fall once more.

A year after coming to power, Muhammad began building a heavily fortified palace at Dunga, located in the lonely, isolated center of the island. The ruins still exist—giant slabs of stone standing sentinel in a silent green wood. The palace took a decade to complete and was a magnificent affair, with its own mosque, bathhouse, and separate quarters for retainers. Fifty armed slaves stood guard at each palace door.

Had Mwenyi Mkuu built his fortified palace because he felt himself and his family to be in danger from the Omanis? Perhaps. By the time the palace was finished, the Swahili ruler—who died a few years later—was out of touch with much of what was going on in Zanzibar. His power and that of his people was on the wane, snuffed out by the increasing weight of Omani rule.

Almost immediately after the Dunga palace was finished, rumors began to swirl. The Swahili said that it was haunted by *masheitani* (sing., *sheitani*), or devils, while the Europeans said that it was haunted by an Arab woman with a black dog. A sacred *siwa*, or giant horn, was supposedly buried in its walls, in a spot known to only one man, who would tell another of its location only upon nearing death. The sound of this horn was said to carry far and wide, and to have the power to rally together all of the island's Swahili. The Hadimu of Zanzibar actually did have a great *siwa*, made of wood and five feet in length, that is now housed in Zanzibar's national museum.

The last time the museum's *siwa* was blown was three days after the death of Mwenyi Mkuu Muhammad bin Ahmed on June 25, 1865—a date that also marked the end of the island's Swahili monarchy. Muhammad bin Ahmed left behind a young son who was recognized as his successor, but the boy never got the chance to rule. The Al Busaids forced him to move to town, to live under their close watch, where he died of smallpox in 1873.

17

Seyyid Said's Last Journey

IN 1853, WHEN SALME WAS NINE YEARS OLD, HER FATHER PRE-
pared to depart for Oman, as he did every three or four years, in order
to maintain control over his home country. But this time, the sultan also
had a more specific reason for going: the Persians had seized control of
Bandar Abbas, the port on the Persian mainland that had been under
Omani rule for over seventy years.

Preparations for Seyyid Said's journey took more than two months.
Enough biscuits had to be baked to feed a thousand people for ten
weeks, and sheep, a dozen milk cows, and other livestock had to be collected. The Omanis had not yet discovered salted beef or cod, but even
if they had, it would have been *haram*, forbidden by Islamic dietary
laws.

But at last, everything was ready: the three-masted *Kitorie*, or *Victoria*, named after the queen of England, on which Seyyid Said, several of
his sons, a couple of *sarari*, and his advisers were to sail; and two smaller
boats, to carry the royal retinue, slaves, luggage, and gifts for the many
Al Busaidi relatives in Oman.

All of Seyyid Said's wives and daughters were free to travel with
him to Oman, but most did not care to do so, partly because of the in-
conveniences of travel but mostly because of the cool reception that
they knew they would receive there. "The proud Omani ladies treat
those of Zanzibar as uncivilized creatures," wrote Salme. "This arro-
gance even prevailed among our brothers and sisters; a member of our
family born in Oman felt and imagined herself particularly aristocratic

vis-à-vis us 'Africans.' They are of the opinion that we, who grew up among the negroes, must have something from them. Our greatest uncouthness, they think, is that we, (how awful!), speak another language besides Arabic."

Before leaving Zanzibar, Seyyid Said, his son Khalid—who was to rule Zanzibar in his absence—and a contingent of elite Arabs went to visit the British consul. Hamerton had been in Zanzibar for over a decade now, and although he and Seyyid Said had had their differences, they had also become friends. They shared a love of horses, often racing their steeds on the beach at low tide, and whenever the consul was sick, Seyyid Said visited him. Hamerton, in turn, understood the difficult position that the British anti–slave trade treaties had put the Omani ruler in, and had great respect for him. "Setting aside what I know to be my public duty, the kindness which I have experienced from the Imam would have restrained me or any other man of proper feeling from intentionally offering to His Highness the slightest possible disrespect," he wrote at one point.

In earlier years, Hamerton had traveled with Seyyid Said on his journeys to Oman, but in the early 1850s France had increased her presence in the region and the sultan was worried about her designs on Zanzibar. He therefore asked Hamerton to stay behind to keep an eye on things and advise Khalid in his absence. The consul agreed to do so. Seyyid Said then "placed his son's hand in mine," Hamerton wrote, "and desired him in all difficulties to be guided by my advice and to do nothing without consulting me. The Arabs then rose and came and kissed my hand, saying, 'we are now satisfied through the favour of the Almighty and the powerful destiny Her Majesty Queen Victoria all will go well with us.' "

On April 15, 1854, the day of Seyyid Said's departure, his servants and slaves and the ordinary seamen embarked on the ships at five a.m. Next boarded a handful of women and finally, at about noon, Seyyid Said and his sons. Tearful goodbyes were said and the visitors debarked. As the small fleet sailed away, a twenty-one-cannon salute bade it farewell.

Back in the royal palaces, an immense quiet fell. With the head of family no longer at home, "there reigned a kind of loneliness," wrote Salme, that was to last for many months.

Khalid, now the ruler of Zanzibar, lacked his father's ways. A man in his twenties, he put his principles before his people. One day not long after the sultan had left, a fire broke out at Beit al-Sahel. Panicking, the royal women rushed to the doors, only to find them locked and guarded by soldiers. Khalid had ordered that the women should not expose themselves to "the eyes of the population in broad daylight," no matter what the possible danger. Fortunately, the fire was soon put out.

Khalid was not to reign for long, however. He died of smallpox seven months after his father's departure, and Majid, the sultan's next oldest son in Zanzibar, became deputy ruler. Then only nineteen years old, Majid was the opposite of Khalid in almost every way. Salme described him as a gentle and compassionate man, who soon "succeeded in winning hearts everywhere through his amiable character." And two years after Majid's ascent to power, Hamerton wrote: "The Prince Majid has given the fairest possible promises from the way in which he has acted on various occasions and under some very trying circumstances of his perfect fitness and aptitude for the duties it was his father's intentions should devolve upon him. He has frequently shown a sense of justice and fair dealing in his decisions in difficult cases which has elicited the admiration and astonishment of all."

Months and then years passed, and still Seyyid Said did not return, though the family received news of him from arriving ships—he was busy with affairs in Bandar Abbas and Oman. Not until three years after the patriarch's departure did word finally come that he was about to leave Oman. At long last! With great excitement and joy, everyone began to make ready for the royal return, planning the greatest of all possible feasts. Then they waited. And waited. The time in which a ship could have reached Zanzibar from Muscat came and went. Uneasiness descended.

The royal family prayed. What could have gone wrong? Had the sultan's ships been lost in a storm? Had they been attacked by pirates—or evil spirits?

Swahili clairvoyants were called in. Many lived in the most remote areas of the island, but they were tracked down by slaves and brought to the palace by boat, horseback, or foot.

Among them was a prophetess "of a quite unnatural corpulence," who claimed to have an unborn child inside her who could foretell the future. Arriving at the palace one afternoon, the woman told the worried family that her omniscient child, who had been living under her heart for years, could see from the tops of the mountains to the depths of the seas. And then, in a high, squeaky voice, the "child" described three sailing ships, from the vantage point of the tallest mast, and outlined in detail what every single person on board was doing. Apparently, Seyyid Said was still alive and well. The family rejoiced and the prophetess ordered that a myriad of sacrifices be made. Gladly, the family obeyed, slaughtering animals and distributing meat, cloth, and rice among the woman's followers and the poor.

At the time, Salme and everyone else in the palace believed in the miraculous child. Only later, while living in Germany, did Salme realize that the woman was a ventriloquist.

In the nineteenth century, most Zanzibaris, be they African, Swahili, Indian, or Arab, believed in the spirit world. The island's educated elite all but ignored the possibility of another realm during times of prosperity and peace, but during times of strife, when worlds turned upside down, all turned to the spirit world for solace, hope, and relief.

The Swahili spirit world was—and still is—enormous, composed of both spirits of Muslim origin and spirits of African origin. The Muslim spirits tended to be more closely connected with the towns and with the dichotomy between good and evil, while the African ones inhabited the countryside and were usually more mystical in nature.

The Swahili believed that human behavior could affect the physical world. Moral acts and religious observance led to harmony and prosperity; immoral acts and religious negligence led to famine and death. The Swahili spirits fell into two main categories: the *mizimu*, who were ancestral spirits, and the *majini* (sing., *jinni*), who were non-ancestral ones. The *mizimu* were usually associated with rocks, trees, ruins, or caves, and believers often built them small shrines or altars in which offerings were made.

In contrast, the *majini* were much more complicated characters. Believed to be the first inhabitants of the earth, they were said to have been created from fire, while humans were made from dust or clay, and angels from light. The *majini* lived in paradise with God until their leader, Iblisi, said that he was superior to Adam. At that heresy, God expelled him and all his kind from paradise and made them invisible.

The *majini* could be good or evil, male or female. And reflective of the values of Swahili civilization, the good *majini* knew Arabic, accepted Islam, and usually lived in the towns. The evil *majini* spoke no Arabic, did not accept Islam, and lived in the bush.

Among the most populous of the *majini* were the *pepo*, personal spirits who could possess people and send them into trances by sitting on their heads. Not really harmful, a *pepo* would often jump onto a person who passed too close to a large tree, and thereafter, possess her or him.

Sometimes, an entire family of *pepo* moved into a Swahili house, where they were heard but not seen. They would offer the family protection against evil if they were treated well, and so the owners of a *pepo*-possessed house kept themselves and their house spotless, sprinkled with rose water, and perfumed with incense.

Other kinds of *majini* included the *masheitani* and the *rohani*, both of whom could become visible to humans. The *masheitani* were malevolent and the *rohani*, benevolent, but both were very powerful and potentially dangerous. They often lived in trees, and if a person wished to cut down a *jinni*-inhabited tree, he or she needed to carefully carry out a prescribed ritual: first, read certain verses from Quran; next, clean his or her room and sprinkle it with rose water; then, burn incense and wait—for the sound of wings late at night. If the sound of wings was heard, the *jinni* had moved to another tree and it was safe to cut down the old one.

The *rohani* were especially unusual spirits who often became visible to only one person—usually a woman. And that woman often conjured her *rohani* into being by shutting herself in a room, hanging white sheets all around, burning incense, strewing rose water, and reciting certain verses from the Quran for four to seven days. On the last night of her vigil, a lion, snake, or other beast suddenly appeared and, if the woman showed no fear, transformed itself into a tall man wearing magnificent robes and a turban.

The *rohani* could be of any race, including European, and often made exorbitant demands, such as being kept in expensive essences, like rose water. Nonetheless, even well-educated women sometimes chose to become possessed by *rohani*; the connection gave them a kind of power and prestige that was otherwise difficult for women to acquire.

Childless and divorced women were especially likely to become possessed by *rohani*.

Zanzibar was also said to be home to humans who could turn others into zombies and use them as secret laborers. In the early morning before the cock crowed, according to popular belief, a person could meet bands of zombies returning home under the guard of their Arab masters. The zombies, who would resume their human forms at daybreak, had been forced to work throughout the night.

As they returned home, the zombies sometimes ran into the *pinga*, spirits whose job it was to fold up the night and spread out the day. Or, they sometimes met one of the many spirits who dwelt at the crossroads—the same spirits who would soon be appearing a continent away, brought over by slaves, in the blues songs of the American South.

When the *majini*, malevolent or benevolent, got out of hand, they could be brought back under control by various specialists. A male or female *fundi*, or spirit controller, could appease a *pepo* with gifts, or exorcise it through music, dance, recitations, and various potions of leaves and roots.

The *fundi*'s power was only temporary, however. For more permanent control, the possessed person had to join a *chama*, or association, all of whose members were also possessed by the same *pepo*. These *chama*, or "possession cults," were usually composed mostly of women, who didn't really want to exorcise their *pepo* as much as they wanted to control them. Possession cults—as well as a general belief in the spirit world—still flourish in Zanzibar today, much to the disapproval of more orthodox Muslims.

The more powerful *rohani* and *mashaitani* could only be controlled, and then only nominally, by the *waganga*, or witch doctors. Male or female, the *waganga* could catch evil spirits, cure the sick with herbs and medicines, protect people with good-luck charms, make charms for catching slaves, and divine the future with a *bao* board, onto which cowries and other objects were thrown.

As useful members of society, the *waganga* practiced their art openly. But their evil counterparts, the *wachawi*, or wizards, did not. These nasty beings could turn themselves into animals and attack unsuspecting humans, create potent poisons, raise the dead, become invisible, and pass through the tiniest of openings. In the 1920s, and probably earlier as well, the East African headquarters of the *wachawi* was Pemba, Zanzibar's sister island, where the cost of entry into a *wachawi* guild was said to be a child, who would be sacrificed and eaten by the other members of the guild.

At times, people hired the *wachawi* to put curses on their enemies. One Westerner gave the following account of a *wachawi* dance in Zanzibar in the 1920s, performed to cause the death of a man who had refused to pay the wizard for healing him:

> I proceeded about midnight in the direction the dance was to be held. I was wearing the white *kanzu* of an Arab, barefooted, with a cap and a beard and a brown face. . . . I saw some way ahead a pale blue light go vertically up in the air and with no report seem to burst and fade away. Soon after I heard a weird calling as of dogs, and the hooting of owls, and presently came on some lonely mango and cotton trees, which appeared to be the scene of the dance. There was a species of 'follow-my-leader' in progress: a chain of about a dozen young men and women dressed in black were following each other silently but quickly in and out round the trees, uttering no words, but slapping their bare arms in a peculiar way, and every now and then barking or hooting.
>
> Not only did the barking and hooting come from the procession, but every now and then it would be from the trees, and forms would drop with a rustle through the leaves and join in the procession darting about among the trees. Although I was right in the midst of it in a very white *kanzu*, on a moonlit night, not the slightest notice was taken of me, and I stayed for over an hour, till the procession moved away in the distance, though I could still hear the clapping, the barking and the hooting.

Salme was exposed to the spirit world from birth. As a very young child, she listened to the Swahili folktales of her wet nurse, and as she grew older, she absorbed a multitude of beliefs and superstitions from the many peoples living around her—Muslim, Swahili, African, Indian, and perhaps even Catholic, as at least one of the *sarari* is believed to have been Christian.

Zanzibar's most popular sacred spring was Chemchem, located a few hours outside Stone Town. Its waters were believed to possess miraculous powers, and its spirit, living inside it, to have the ability to grant wishes. Hundreds of offerings from the poor—small strips of fabric tied to bushes, eggshells, *halvah*, and incense—marked the miraculous spot, but if a supplicant wanted to be absolutely sure that his or her voice was heard, only the spilling of blood would do.

Salme visited Chemchem often as a child and young woman, but one occasion in particular was etched in her memory. Her sister Chadudj—the one who had refused to accept her brother Majid's young wife—had been very ill. Praying for her recovery, her family vowed that if she got well, they would make a sacrifice to the spirit of Chemchem. Chadudj recovered and preparations for the sacrifice began.

Everyone, including slaves of both sexes, was outfitted in fine dress and jewelry, some of which had been specially designed for the occasion. Riding equipment was fiercely polished and mounts carefully brushed.

On the day of the celebration, Salme and her slaves left their palace at five-thirty a.m. to meet Chadudj. It wasn't easy to reach her, as a great crowd had already gathered, but at last they got through, and the party took off, riding two by two for several hours.

Reaching Chemchem, the ladies found that their slaves had already turned the otherwise lonely and deserted spot into a fairyland. They had cut the area's long grasses, spread out carpets and cushions beneath the trees, and nailed mirrors to the trunks of mango trees. The cooking and roasting of food had also begun.

About two hours later, the party prepared to make its offering. An enormous number of raw eggs were broken on the water's edge and hundreds of sweets were strewn about. Two flags were dedicated—one scarlet red, signifying the Al Busaidi dynasty; the other, white, signifying peace. An older female slave approached the spring and made a short speech about Chadudj, her serious illness, and the beneficence of the Chemchem spirit who had restored her to health.

Then a beautiful bull was brought forth and slaughtered—dark red blood spurting through the air, to be carefully collected and sprinkled over the spring and its surroundings, along with the bull's organs, cut up into small pieces. Donations of rose water were made, and musk and amber were burned in silver incense burners. The ceremony concluded with prayer.

One stormy morning in 1856, not long after the ventriloquist's visit to the royal family, a drenched fisherman arrived at the palace with exciting news: he had seen ships in the distance flying the sultan's flags. Joyfully, the family began making final preparations for a grand celebration—slaughtering, cooking, baking, perfuming the rooms, and getting dressed in their best. From the fisherman's report, Seyyid Said should reach the island in two or three hours.

Braving the heavy storm, Majid and his retinue set off in two cutters to meet the arriving ships. They hoped to be back with their ruler by seven p.m. "But man proposes and God disposes," wrote Salme. Seven p.m. came and went, with still no trace of the ships. Unrest took hold of the town, followed by foreboding. Perhaps Majid and his companions had drowned. Perhaps all the ships had foundered. No one went to bed.

Then suddenly a rumor flew about the royal palaces, which at first no one believed. The palaces were said to be surrounded by hundreds of soldiers. Salme and the others rushed to the windows, where, to their astonishment, they could see the soldiers' muskets glimmering in the pitch black night. What had happened? Why were they locked in? A few courageous women pressed to the door separating the harem from the guardroom, and spoke with the guards. But the men refused to provide any information. A dreadful confusion ensued. Women shrieked and wailed. The pious prayed.

Morning dawned, and still the women and children had no answers. "But then, who could describe our horror, when at last we clearly saw our fleet cast anchor, flying mourning flags," wrote Salme. "Lamentation was immense when early in the morning our gates were opened and our brothers came to us, without our father!"

Seyyid Said had died at sea on Sunday, October 19, 1856, in the vicinity of the Seychelles. The cause of death was an old gunshot wound in his thigh, inflicted many years before in Oman. The wound had begun to swell a few days out of Muscat, and had led to abdominal hemorrhaging. Seyyid Barghash, traveling with his father, had ordered that the patriarch's body be washed and wrapped in a shroud, but had not allowed it to be buried at sea, as Muslim tradition prescribed. Instead he had the body placed in a coffin and transported to Zanzibar.

Seyyid Said may have had some premonition of his death. When taking leave of his mother, who would outlive him by many years, he had reportedly said, "Good-bye Mother, I do not think that we shall meet again in this world. I have a feeling that this is my last voyage, so I am taking my shroud with me so that death may not come on me unprepared." In that era, Arabs of a certain age always took their burial shroud, or *kafan*, with them when they embarked on long journeys.

By the time Majid and his retinue reached Seyyid Said's ships that night, Barghash was already gone—en route to having their father's body secretly interred in the family plot and to surrounding the royal palaces with men loyal to him. Barghash had hoped to seize power from his older brother Majid by capturing him, but with Majid at sea, his plans were foiled. Afterward, Barghash defended his actions by saying that he had wanted to prevent a possible revolution. Majid was probably not fooled, but he accepted the explanation.

On November 10, Hamerton wrote his home office: "I have the honour, but with the profoundest distress and the sincerest sorrow, to communicate for your Lordship's information the melancholy intelligence of the death of His Highness the Imam of Muscat. . . ." Seyyid Said had asked for Hamerton on his deathbed; Hamerton himself died a year later, apparently from fever.

The royal family now changed out of the elaborate clothes they had donned in honor of Seyyid Said's return and put on simple black. They refrained from using perfume—usually applied liberally, but now deemed disrespectful—and from sleeping in their beds. With the sultan deep in the earth, they should not enjoy such ease.

For the next two weeks, paupers and princes, slaves and masters, Arabs and Swahili, Africans and Indians—all came to Beit al-Sahel to mourn their ruler and to eat their fill, as custom prescribed. The sultan's favorite dish was prepared by the cauldronful and served to all.

The sultan's main wife, Azze bint Seyf, and all of his *sarari* were now widows and had to observe a period of mourning that lasted four months. The mourning was done in a dark room, which the women were not allowed to leave during daylight hours. Consequently, when the four months were over, the women could only gradually re-expose their eyes to light.

A *qadi* formally introduced the women to mourning and formally released them. And after he had done so, each woman had to wash herself from head to toe, while a female slave stood behind her, beating two swords over her head. This ceremony usually took place in the privacy of a family's home, but because of the large number of Seyyid Said's wives, this time it took place on the beach—and "a very peculiar, lively, curious spectacle it was," wrote Salme. Afterward, the women put on fresh clothes, and could begin to think about remarrying.

The death of Seyyid Said marked the end of Salme's innocence. Though she was only twelve, she—like her father in his youth before her—would from now on be swept into the endless fray of alliances and betrayals that characterized life in the royal Al Busaidi family.

18

The Explorers

ON DECEMBER 19, 1856, TWO MONTHS AFTER THE DEATH OF
Seyyid Said, two English explorers—Richard Francis Burton and John
Hanning Speke—sailed into Zanzibar with the southwest monsoon. A
sultry wind was blowing, carrying with it the heavy perfume of cloves,
and from afar the men were awed by the beauty of the island. "Earth,
sea, and sky, all seemed wrapped in a soft and sensuous repose, in the
tranquil life of the Lotus Eaters, in the swoon-like slumber of the Seven
Sleepers, in the dreams of the Castle of Indolence," wrote Burton. The
inner harbor, however, was a different story: it was congested, as usual,
with dozens of dhows, a handful of Western sailing ships, an aging fifty-
gun warship, and a thick, sloshing bath of filth that included at least a
body or two. The problem that had plagued Seyyid Said's reign for
decades had still not been resolved.

Burton and Speke had come on a mission: to travel into Central
Africa, where they hoped to discover the source of the Nile—a mystery
that had intrigued humankind for millennia. No one knew where the
Nile began. Longer than any other river in the world, it flowed through
a harsh, broiling desert for over a thousand miles, receiving no tribu-
taries and hardly any rainfall, and yet its wide waters never dried up,
never diminished. It even flooded the Nile Delta in September, the
hottest month of the year in North Africa.

The first known Westerner to search for the source of the Nile was
Herodotus, the Greek "father of history." Arriving in Cairo in 460 B.C.,
he followed the Nile upriver for about six hundred miles, to come to

what is now known as the First Cataract. But he couldn't go any farther—pounding water, cliffs, and jungle blocked his way. Five hundred years later, Diogenes, a Greek merchant, reported that when he was returning home from India one year, he landed at Rhapta (an ancient marketplace on the East African coast), traveled inland for twenty-five days, and came to two great lakes and a snowy mountain range from "whence the Nile draws its twin sources." The geographer Ptolemy used Diogenes' description when drawing his famed map of the world in A.D. 140. It showed the Nile flowing out of two round lakes, which were in turn watered by streams descending from the "Mountains of the Moon."

But still the site of the river's source remained unknown, and in the first half of the 1800s party after party of amateur Western explorers set off to solve the puzzle. Most were English—this being the period of British imperialist expansion—and most, like Herodotus, trekked upriver from Cairo, only to be defeated, many by death. Then in 1848 Johannes Rebmann, a German missionary and one of the first Europeans to enter the African interior from the east coast, said that he had seen a towering mountain, Kilimanjaro, capped with snow. His news was ridiculed—there couldn't be snow so close to the equator, he must have seen sun reflecting off a rocky peak, many scoffed. But the next year, Johann Ludwig Krapf, another German missionary, saw Mount Kenya, just north of Kilimanjaro, also capped with snow.

Rebmann's and Krapf's reports encouraged the British Royal Geographical Society to send a major expedition, headed by Burton and Speke, to East Africa. Entering the continent from the coast opposite Zanzibar, the explorers would travel about a thousand miles inland, to reach Lake Tanganyika in Central Africa in February 1858.

The arrival of Burton and Speke in Zanzibar was a harbinger. The island was about to become a stepping-stone for dozens of Western explorers and missionaries eager to plunge into the continent to map its rivers and lakes, convert its peoples, harvest its natural resources, and/or expose and eradicate the East African slave trade. Missionaries would soon be taking up residence on Zanzibar as well. Five years after the explorers' visit, the French Roman Catholics opened a school and hospital on the island, and in 1864 Britain's Universities' Mission to Central Africa arrived. The Universities' Mission laid the first foundation stone for an enormous Anglican church on the site of the old slave market on Christmas Day 1873 and established Zanzibar's first freed slave community in 1874.

In many ways, Burton and Speke could not have been more different. Burton, then thirty-six years old, was almost six feet tall, handsome, intimidating, and muscular, with savage scars from a Somali spear wound disfiguring his cheeks. He had dark brown, almost black eyes—"questing panther eyes," wrote a friend—thick eyebrows, a granite jaw, and an impressive black mustache. Born in Devon, England, he had spent much of his childhood in France and Italy, and had studied briefly at Oxford—from which he was expelled for attending a steeplechase race.

As a young man, Burton served seven years in the Indian Army, living first in Bombay, where he perfected his already excellent Hindustani, learned Gujarati and Persian, explored the city's brothels and bazaars, and began collecting his first journals of ethnological notes. Languages would prove to be Burton's passion—he would know twenty-nine by the end of his life—and he was an acute and scholarly observer, who compiled and published a vast amount of anthropological, linguistic, scientific, and economic information about the many lands to which he traveled, including Zanzibar.

From Bombay, Burton was posted to Baroda, India, a walled, medieval city surrounded by jungle in the province of Gujarat. Only a few other officers were stationed there, and Burton avoided them as much as he could, spending his time exploring the city's narrow, exotic, and often dangerous streets. He took an Indian wife, and frequented courtesans and prostitutes—a practice he would continue everywhere he traveled. Burton published the first English translation of the *Kama Sutra* (1883) and was an outspoken advocate of the sexual emancipation of Englishwomen—a position that earned him no friends back in Victorian England.

From Baroda, Burton—nicknamed the "White Nigger" by his fellow officers—was ordered to investigate Karachi's homosexual brothels. He did so with his usual thoroughness, only to have his reports in effect end his army career. The reports implicated his fellow officers and raised questions about Burton's own sexuality—questions that would follow him throughout his life, despite his huge appetite for women.

By the time Burton and Speke arrived in Zanzibar, Burton was already famous. Three years earlier, he had disguised himself as an Afghan and entered the holy city of Mecca, forbidden to non-Muslims. His three-volume account of his adventures, *Personal Narrative of a Pilgrimage to El-Medinah and Meccah*, became a huge bestseller in England, as did a book he published shortly thereafter, *First Footsteps in East Africa*, which described a similar adventure to the forbidden holy Abyssinian city of Harar.

Speke, in contrast, was a tall and slender thirty-year-old with fair hair and blue eyes. Born into the English gentry, he had an outwardly quiet and gentle manner, but was also an insecure, vain, and often boastful man—claiming, for one thing, to have been the first white man to have penetrated Tibet, when in fact many had been there before him. Extremely fastidious and methodical, Speke drank little and never smoked, and kept himself in excellent physical condition. He hated book learning; his passion was the outdoors—exploring, collecting flora and fauna, and especially hunting.

Like Burton, Speke served in the Indian Army and rather than spend his free time drinking and gambling, as did his fellow officers, he traveled to remote regions in India, the Himalayas, and Tibet in search of exotic game. He was a ruthless, cruel hunter with an unsettling proclivity—he liked to eat the unborn fetus of his kill.

But Burton and Speke also had much in common. Both were restless loners driven by an intense hunger to explore the world. Both felt suffocated by the restrictions of Victorian England, and both were determined to live life on their own terms. Both were excellent fighters. Both were exceptionally bold and brave.

Near the beginning of his two-volume book *Zanzibar: City, Island, and Coast*, Burton writes:

Of the gladdest moments in human life, methinks, is the departure upon a distant journey into unknown lands. Shaking off with one mighty effort the fetters of Habit, the leaden weight of Routine, the cloak of many Cares and the slavery of Home, man feels once more happy. The blood flows with the fast circulation of childhood. Excitement lends unwonted vigour to the muscles, and the sudden sense of freedom adds a cubit to the mental stature. Afresh dawns the morn of life; again the bright world is beautiful to the eye, and the glorious face of nature gladdens the soul. A journey, in fact, appeals to Imagination, to Memory, to Hope—the three sister Graces of our moral being.

It was a sentiment with which Speke would have agreed whole-heartedly.

Upon arriving in Zanzibar, Burton and Speke proceeded straight to the house of British consul Hamerton. He welcomed them enthusiastically and promised to help them in any way he could, even though he was by then exceedingly ill, with an anomalous disease that afflicted many Englishmen posted to the East. Burton wrote: "I can even now distinctly see my poor friend sitting before me, a tall, broad-shouldered, and powerful figure, with square features, dark, fixed eyes, hair and beard prematurely snow-white, and a complexion once fair and ruddy, but long ago bleached ghastly pale by ennui and sickness. Such had been the effects of the burning heats of Maskat and 'the Gulf,' and the deadly damp of Zanzibar, Island, and Coast. The worst symptom in his case—one which I have rarely found other than fatal—was his unwillingness to quit the place which was slowly killing him."

Hamerton's support of the explorers was crucial, for they needed him to recommend them to Seyyid Majid, in order to obtain the protection of the African chieftains through whose country they would be traveling. They also needed Hamerton to help them collect the enormous amount of equipment and supplies they required for their expedition: camping necessities, scientific instruments, stationery supplies, books, weapons, ammunition. The expedition would also take with it many items to be used as gifts and payment to the Africans, including dozens of bolts of cloth and thousands of beads. About four hundred varieties of beads were in use in East Africa, varying from a simple round white porcelain bead to a fine, enameled scarlet-and-white bead called *samsam*. It was said that women would happily ruin themselves and their husbands for a few pieces of *samsam*.

Before heading into the African interior, the explorers journeyed along the coast for two months, in order to familiarize themselves with East Africa. On their way back to Zanzibar, they stopped in the port of Pangani, where Burton visited ancient Swahili ruins and both men traveled up the Pangani River to view its impressive waterfalls. It was near Pangani, too, that the explorers hired Sidi Mubarak, an African man with filed-down teeth who later became an established figure in East African exploration. Short and stocky, and extremely hard-working and knowledgeable, Sidi Mubarak was better known as "Bombay." He had been captured as a youth and sold into slavery to a Banyan, who took him to India. After his owner's death, Bombay was freed and made his way back to Africa, where he joined the Zanzibari army.

In general, neither Burton nor Speke had much sympathy for or understanding of Africans. In his writings, Burton—who did have a great appreciation of Arabs—railed against the Africans, calling them everything from ignorant, childish, and immoral to insolent, dishonest, and savage. They have no culture or civilization, and no real religion; they are "an undeveloped and not to be developed race"; they are always drunk on *pombe*, native beer, he wrote. Speke had little empathy for any people of any color—or indeed, for anyone but himself.

But the one African whom Burton did come to greatly respect was Bombay: "He works on principle and works like a horse. . . . With a sprained ankle and a load quite disproportionate to his chetif [puny] body, he insists on carrying two guns; and after a 30 miles' walk he is as fresh as before it began. He attends us everywhere, manages our purchases, carries all our messages, and when not employed by us, is at every man's beck and call."

As Burton spent more time in Africa, he came to appreciate its people to at least some degree. A careful observer and recorder of their customs and languages, he was appalled by the widespread poverty he saw and by the British government's general indifference to the Africans' plight. He also took a fierce stand against the Arab slave trade, which he compared to "a flight of locusts over the land."

Finally, on June 16, 1857, Burton and Speke were ready to depart. Boarding Seyyid Majid's *Artemise*, an eighteen-gun vessel built in India, they set off for Bagamoyo, the beautiful, palm-tree-lined town on the coast opposite Zanzibar. Traveling with them was Hamerton, who had come to say good-bye, even though he knew that he was near death. His last advice to Burton was to avoid "walnut and velvet-slipper men" and to placate the Arabs as much as possible. He died only a few days after returning to Zanzibar.

The explorers started off, into huge, mysterious, forbidding Africa, which would test them both to the breaking point. Burton's account of their expedition, *The Lake Regions of Central Africa*, is filled with one harrowing passage after another; both men were near death at least a half-dozen times. Burton's earlier journeys to the holy cities of Mecca and Harar, as dangerous as they had been, could not compare to the near-disastrous *safari*—a Swahili word that he introduced into the English language—that lay ahead of him and his companions.

Most of the caravan routes leading inland from the Bagamoyo region headed first to the town of Tabora in what is now western Tanzania, and from there, fanned out farther west. Burton and Speke's destination was the town of Ujiji, an Arab settlement on Lake Tanganyika in Central Africa that had been established some thirty years earlier by an Arab trader from Zanzibar.

The terms *Arab settlement* and *Arab trader* were misnomers. Most of the merchants and traders operating in East and Central Africa in the 1800s were Arab-African—i.e., Swahili. They wore Arab dress and practiced Islam, but they often looked more African than Arab and sometimes had no Arab blood at all.

Ujiji was just one of about twenty so-called Arab settlements then in operation in the African interior. An ever-growing demand for ivory and slaves had increased traffic along the traditional caravan routes and thus the need for Arab outposts. And most of the Africans welcomed their new neighbors, as the Arabs brought them gifts, purchased crops and livestock, and paid often-hefty tolls, or *hongo*, for permission to pass through tribal lands.

Ruling over each outpost was a powerful Arab trader who had a close affiliation with Zanzibar but no formal ties—an arrangement that suited the Al Busaidi sultans just fine. As long as a steady supply of ivory, slaves, and other goods flowed from the interior to the coast, they were content.

The Burton-Speke expedition began what would become its daily routine, similar to that of all caravans traveling inland from the east coast: Up every morning at four a.m., while it was still dark and cold, for a light breakfast and morning prayers. Herd together the cattle and goats, and parcel out the loads the porters were to carry. Begin the day's march, led by a guide clad in a six-foot-long scarlet robe and headdress of animal skins and feathers, and carrying the scarlet Omani flag. No one could walk ahead of the guide—anyone who made that mistake had to pay a fine.

After the guide came a man banging on a kettle drum, followed by a "disorderly mob" of porters carrying bulky bundles on their heads, and their wives and children, all also carrying bundles of some kind. The procession started and stopped, started and stopped, but then gained momentum and, like a monstrous land-serpent, wound its way over hill, dale, and plain, making an immense racket. "The normal recreations of a march are, whistling, singing, shouting, hooting, drumming, imitating the cries of birds and beasts, repeating words which are never used except on journeys . . . and abundant squabbling," wrote a delighted Burton. Every man carried a weapon of some kind, and the Baluchi guards were spread out along the caravan's length, each bearing a musket, saber, and huge cow horn filled with ammunition. Bringing up the caravan's rear were Burton and Speke, riding on donkeys, or, if sick—as was often the case—being carried in hammocks.

The caravan usually stopped briefly at mid-morning and then halted for the day between nine and eleven a.m., when the heat of the day began, after covering six to ten miles. The explorers spent the rest of the day resting, writing in their journals, reading Shakespeare aloud to each other, making scientific observations, and—in Speke's case—hunting. Meanwhile, the head porters purchased food from nearby villages and everyone else set up camp. At four p.m., dinner—usually a rice and meat dish—was served.

Night was ushered in with the settling down of the animals. And then, if the moon was brightly shining, and there was no trouble, a furious drumming and a loud clapping of hands ensued, summoning "the lads and lasses of the neighboring villages to come out and dance." The men danced in one group, the women in another, someone sang, everyone else hummed, and a hundred pairs of heels sounded like one.

Around eight p.m., the cry of *"lala, lala,"*—sleep, sleep—was heard and the exhausted camp fell asleep.

Less than a week after the expedition left the coast, the first of many mutinies occurred: the Baluchi guards were demanding more money. There were troubles with the pack animals as well; they kicked and reared every time the porters tried to attach their loads, and frequently bolted. A few more days in, and Burton and Speke both came down with malaria. The porters began to desert, usually in the night, carrying precious equipment and supplies with them.

The expedition was traveling through Africa's variable coastal lowlands, which stretched for about ninety miles. At times, the explorers found themselves trudging over sandy soil, thick with thorns and bush; through grassy swamplands, where they sank knee-deep in mud; over parkland where herds of gnu, antelope, and hartebeest grazed; and through forested areas with cultivated clearings "where modest young maidens beckoned" and crops such as rice, sweet potato, beans, and maize were grown.

The rains began, heavy showers falling every day. The pack animals slipped continually, often losing their loads, and the encampment was stalked at night by lions, hyenas, and other animals of prey. Three times, the wild beasts successfully felled a donkey—a loud wrangling shriek was heard, followed by the sound of torn flesh.

Then the expedition entered an area known to the Arabs as Wady el Maut—"the Valley of Death." It was a thick, dark, nightmarish place, filled with fetid vegetation and "a mortal smell of decay . . . emitted by dark, dank ground." Black clouds scudded across the sky, tall stiff trees groaned, birds screamed, and the mud deepened. Black, greasy bogs stretching in length from a hundred yards to a mile appeared, followed by open spaces of twelve-foot-high tiger and spear grass.

Burton and Speke recovered from malaria, only to be struck with marsh fever. Debilitated for twenty days, Burton tossed and turned at night with feverish dreams of "animals of grisliest form, hag-like women and men with heads protruding from their breasts."

Still, the two men never considered turning back. Pushing on, they entered a part of Africa that no Westerner had ever seen before. Bedraggled village followed bedraggled village, and the rain poured relentlessly down. More pack animals died, more porters and slaves fell ill, and food supplies ran low.

Then at last, the expedition began to climb, onto the great plateau that is Central Africa. Stretching for hundreds of miles in all directions, the open, dun-colored grasslands were speckled with tall tamarind trees, lacy acacia trees, and patches of scrub. In the distance rose hazy purple mountain peaks. In the foreground grazed herds of elephants, zebras, giraffes, antelopes, and wildebeests. The climate was cool and the skies, clear blue. The beams of the equatorial sun danced upon the earth.

On November 7, 1857, after traveling 134 days and six hundred miles, the explorers reached Tabora, a major crossroads, where they were met by a welcoming crowd and led to a vacant house to rest. The next day, a dozen Arab merchants came to call, bearing goats, tamarind cakes, and other gifts. They were delighted to have the two Westerners among them, and Burton was overjoyed to be among Arabs again.

Before reaching Tabora, Burton and Speke had had their differences, but generally got along well together. Now, however, they began to get on each other's nerves. Among other things, Speke resented the fact that Burton, who was the expedition's official leader, did not let him hunt unless food was needed. Burton, meanwhile, began to eye his fellow explorer with contempt.

The expedition rested in Tabora for about five weeks before continuing westward. Speke had wanted to travel north instead, to the place where a large lake that might be the source of the Nile was reputed to lie, but Burton insisted that they stick to their original plan and continue to Lake Tanganyika.

The caravan proceeded, following a route that led through yet more difficult, variegated terrain. Problems with mutiny and desertion continued, and both Burton and Speke fell extremely ill with malaria. Burton also developed an ulcerated jaw and had what he called "an attack of 'paraplegia,'" meaning that he was paralyzed in all four limbs. Speke was in even worse shape. Both men had to be carried in hammocks.

Finally, on February 13, 1858, seven and a half months after leaving the coast, the expedition reached Lake Tanganyika. The guide Bombay was the first to see it.

"What is that streak of light which lies below?" Burton asked Bombay upon noticing that the caravan had suddenly stopped.

"I am of the opinion," said Bombay, "that that is *the* water."

Burton gazed in dismay. He could see but one sliver of light through the trees and began to lament his folly in having risked so much for so poor a prize. But then he advanced a few yards and the full lake burst into view, filling him with wonder and delight. The longest freshwater lake in the world, Tanganyika stretched to both the northern and southern horizons.

Their spirits renewed, the party continued on to the lake's main settlement, Ujiji, arriving there the next day. From the Tabora Arabs' description of the place, the explorers had expected a major port. But Ujiji in 1858 was nothing more than a collection of miserable beehive huts and a simple local bazaar. Upon arrival, the explorers were "mobbed by a swarm of black beings, whose eyes seemed about to start from their heads with surprise," according to Burton, and given a damp, cold hut in which to stay.

The men remained in Ujiji for three months. Both were still too ill to do anything strenuous and they spent most of their time languishing in their hut. Many of their books rotted, many of their journals became illegible, and many of the botanical specimens they had collected fell apart. The inhospitable locals made repeated demands for more *hongo*, or tribute, and their only two remaining donkeys were repeatedly stabbed with spears.

Time was running out for the explorers. Their supplies were dangerously low and they had little left in the way of trading goods, needed to ensure their safe passage back. Their only hope was to try to explore the lake by local canoes. And so they set out, Speke in one canoe and Burton in another, accompanied by a surly African chieftain, his forty paddlers, and his harem, who passed the time by blowing on reedy flutes and beating on iron sheets—and driving Burton crazy.

They never reached the northern end of the lake. The canoes leaked, and there were several violent storms. En route, too, Burton learned that the river they had hoped to reach, which they had thought might be the source of the Nile, flowed into the lake and not out of it. "I felt sick at heart . . . ," he wrote, and later commented, "the mystery remains unsolved . . . we failed."

They started back to the coast. But they were sicker now than ever, and were forced to stop in Tabora to recuperate. After several weeks, Speke felt significantly better and, with Burton's blessing, decided to travel farther north to look for the rumored great lake that he had wanted to explore earlier.

It was a fateful decision that would lead to the end of their friendship.

The first leg of Speke's trek took him through ugly scrub dotted with villages where everyone seemed to be drunk on *pombe*, local beer. But then wide, sunlit plains flecked with granite boulders appeared, followed by a dark green forest filled with mango and flamboyant trees. A lake came into view—a body of water as large as a sea—and Speke, making an astonishing leap of imagination, immediately *knew* that he had discovered the source of the Nile. "I no longer felt any doubt that the lake at my feet gave birth to that interesting river . . ." he wrote.

Back in Tabora, Speke told Burton about the lake he had seen, which he had named Lake Victoria, in honor of their queen. But he didn't mention his "discovery" until the following morning. "We had scarcely, however, breakfasted," wrote Burton, "before he announced to me the startling fact that he had discovered the sources of the White Nile." Naturally, Burton asked to hear more—how did Speke know? what proof did he have?—only to learn that Speke had no real evidence. He had not followed the lake's outlet, or circumnavigated its shores, or taken any measurements. He had spent only three days at the lake.

Still, Burton did not dismiss Speke's theory out of hand. Lake Victoria might be the source of the Nile, he agreed, but more investigation was needed. Lake Tanganyika might be the source as well—they hadn't explored it sufficiently. He suggested that they simply present their findings to the Royal Geographical Society when they got back and take things from there.

But that answer was not good enough for Speke, whose months of simmering resentment toward Burton were now coming to the fore. "Jack changed his manners to me from this date . . . ," Burton wrote. "After a few days it became evident to me that not a word could be uttered on the subject of the Lake, the Nile, and his *trouvaille* generally without offence. By tacit agreement it was, therefore, avoided."

Four months later, the explorers were back in Zanzibar, where they rested for three weeks before continuing on to Aden. But their health was still precarious, and a British doctor who examined them there advised them both to rest for a while before continuing north. Speke, however, was eager to return to London and left on the first available ship.

At that time, the two men were still on speaking terms and, according to Burton, Speke promised him that he would wait for him before revealing their findings to anyone. But Speke did not keep his word. Once in London, he immediately went to see the president of the Royal Geographical Society, to report that he had discovered the probable source of the Nile. He then lectured before the society's membership, and the impressed assembly voted to send him back to Central Africa to get proof. This time, he would be in charge of his own well-funded expedition. Headlines blared out the story, and Speke was fêted by a public eager to believe that the age-old mystery of the Nile had finally been solved.

On May 21, 1859, only twelve days after Speke's return to London, Burton arrived, to discover to his astonishment that "everything had been done for, or rather against me. My companion now stood forth in his true colours, an angry rival." No one at the Royal Geographical Society, or anywhere else, was interested in what Burton had to say. He had only carefully researched reports to present—no astonishing discovery to proclaim—and was not invited to join the new expedition.

The Burton-Speke saga did not end there. For five long years, a feud between the two explorers raged, as they attacked each other in speeches, articles, and books. Speke accused Burton of "incompetence, malice, cowardice and jealousy," and more, and Burton said that Speke was a fool "unfit for any other but a subordinate capacity," and worse. Speke departed to further explore Lake Victoria in Central Africa. Burton traveled to North America, got married, and spent three years on the West African coast.

Returning to London from his new expedition in June 1863, Speke proclaimed that the question of "the Nile is settled"—he now had proof that Lake Victoria was the river's source. All of London rejoiced, but only briefly, as it quickly became apparent that things were not so simple. Once again, Speke had failed to collect any concrete evidence, and now others aside from Burton—who was still touting Lake Tanganyika as the Nile's probable source—were beginning to take notice.

And so it was that a public debate between Burton and Speke—dubbed the "Nile Duel"—was scheduled to take place on September 16, 1864. Sponsored by the British Association for the Advancement of Science, it was to be held in the Mineral Waters Hospital in Bath, which housed the only auditorium in town large enough to hold the expected crowd.

On the day before the debate, the president of the Royal Geographical Society delivered opening remarks before an electrified audience. Burton and Speke were both seated on the speaker's platform. It was the first time they had seen each other in five years, and Speke seemed overcome with emotion. Wrote Burton's wife, Isabel, "He looked at Richard and at me, and we at him. I shall never forget his face. It was full of sorrow, or yearning, and perplexity. Then he seemed to turn to stone. After a while he began to fidget a great deal, and exclaimed half aloud, 'Oh, I can't stand this any longer.' " He got up and left.

The next morning, the Bath auditorium was again packed, but Burton and his wife were the only ones on the speaker's platform. Neither Speke nor any official from the Royal Geographical Society was there. The time set for the debate to begin—11:00—came and went. The audience fidgeted. Then, at 11:25, the doors of the auditorium swung open and the president of the Royal Geographical Society and a half-dozen other men filed grimly in. They took their seats on the platform and the president waited for the crowd to hush.

"I have to apologize but when I explain to you the cause of my being a little late in coming to take the chair you will pardon me," he finally said. "Captain Speke has lost his life."

Burton staggered visibly and sank into a chair. "I saw by the workings of his face the terrible emotion he was controlling and the shock he had received," wrote Isabel. "When called upon to speak, in a voice that trembled, he spoke of other things, and as briefly as he could. When we got home he wept long and bitterly, and I was for many a day trying to comfort him."

Speke had gone hunting the afternoon before with a cousin who lived near Bath. He had fired several shots at a partridge and then lodged his rifle, a double-barreled breech-loader Lancaster, into a low stone wall before climbing over it. That movement had apparently jarred the gun, which fired directly into his heart. He bled to death ten minutes later.

The attending doctor ruled the death an accident. But there was a question of suicide, which has never been resolved. Speke's state of mind that day is unknown, but it does seem strange that a hunter of his experience would have made such an elementary mistake.

Today, Speke is credited with having discovered one of the sources of the White Nile. (The Nile is fed by both the Blue Nile, which begins in Ethiopia and supplies 83 percent of the Nile's waters, and the White Nile, which provides only 16 percent of the waters but has a far steadier flow—without it, the Nile would dry up every May.) However, Lake Victoria was not actually proven to be a source of the Nile until eight years after Speke's death, and the lake has several important feeder rivers. Those that are farthest away—and thus the ultimate sources of the White Nile—originate in Burundi, Uganda, and Rwanda. Ironically, the stream in Burundi begins very near Burton's Lake Tanganyika.

19

Rebellion

WHEN BURTON AND SPEKE RETURNED TO ZANZIBAR IN MARCH 1859 after their twenty-month expedition, they found the place in turmoil. Though Seyyid Said had passed away two and a half years before, the question of who was to succeed him still had not been resolved. There is no law of primogeniture in Islam—which helps account for the extreme violence that has often erupted after the passing of an Arab ruler.

Seyyid Said's oldest son, Tueni, ruling in Muscat, refused to recognize his younger brother Majid, who had taken over as the sultan of Zanzibar after their father's death. The island was a much more lucrative possession than was the home country, and Tueni coveted it—so much so that in the month before the explorers' return, he dispatched a large expedition to invade Zanzibar. Alerted, Majid gathered together his own formidable force, which included Swahili warriors and "African tribes from the interior of the opposite mainland—wild men who had never before approached the sea."

But before the two armies could meet, Britain intervened. A regional war, especially one between two powerful brothers, was against their interests. Intercepting Tueni's fleet, they forced it back to Muscat. The Omani ruler could do little to object. He was as dependent upon the British as his father had been.

Two years later, Britain settled Tueni's claim on Zanzibar altogether by negotiating what became known as the Canning Award. The agreement declared that henceforth Oman and Zanzibar were to be separate states, though Majid was to pay Tueni $40,000 annually to compensate for his loss of trade revenue. Majid did pay his brother for a few years, but then stopped, and Tueni was too busy fighting the Wahhabis to do much about it. The longer-lasting effect of the agreement was to make the Al Busaidi dynasty more dependent on the British than ever before.

For Tueni, the Canning Award had an even more fateful repercussion. Several years after its enactment, with no money arriving from Majid and in dire need of financing for his military operations, he levied taxes—an unheard-of practice in Oman, where people were accustomed to their rulers paying all state expenses out of import duties. Omani citizens raised a huge outcry, which did not go unnoticed by Tueni's oldest son, Salum.

One day, Tueni came home after a long and exhausting meeting, and threw himself onto a divan. Salum entered the room moments later and, in Seyyida Salme's words, "so categorically demanded the reversing of the tax decrees that his father had to reprimand him energetically. Salum flew into a rage, drew a hidden revolver and shot down his own unsuspecting father!"

Retribution was swift. Salum had scarcely taken power when his brother-in-law Azzan bin Qays attacked Muscat by surprise one night. Few took up arms to defend the wayward son—patricide went beyond even the Arabs' usual liberal attitude toward violence—and wild hordes broke into the royal palace to carry off everything of value. Salum managed to escape on a man-of-war, saving nothing but his life.

Azzan bin Qays was in turn driven out of power by Turki, Seyyid Said's third-oldest son, who was in turn driven out by his younger brother Abdul Aziz. But then Turki returned to rule, and Abdul Aziz fled to Baluchistan, where he lived in exile for many years. "Surely a sad picture, these family feuds, which one can only understand if one has come to know personally the innate lust for power of Oriental princes and the passions of the Oriental in general," wrote Salme. "Such sad situations were not to remain strange to me either, I equally have had to struggle through in the first line."

One oppressive night, around the time of Tueni's thwarted invasion of Zanzibar, Salme lay in her bed at Beit al-Tani, unable to sleep. It was the hottest time of the year. No wind stirred the trees, and the air was thick and sticky. Salme's entire body was bathed in sweat. Finally, she moved onto a woven grass mat on the floor, where it was cooler, and fell into a fitful sleep. A few hours later, she awoke to the sound of whimpering, and was horrified to discover her mother at her feet, writhing in pain. A devastating cholera epidemic was then sweeping the island, and Djilfidan had fallen victim. She wished to die near her daughter, "if it had to be," wrote Salme. Two days later, she was gone.

Salme was beside herself with grief. Sobbing uncontrollably, she threw herself onto her mother's corpse and clung to it tightly, kissing the beloved face over and over again. Family members and slaves tried to pull her away—the disease was so contagious, she might fall victim too, they cried. But she paid no attention—let me go, let me go, I want to die too, she sobbed.

But the disease spared her and left her an orphan; in less than three years, she had lost both her father and mother. "At the age of barely fifteen, I now stood there in the world, fatherless and motherless, similar to a ship which drifts away without rudder on the sea waves, moved by the storm," she wrote.

The turtledoves sang their song, which the Swahili interpret to mean: "Mother is dead, father is dead. I am left alone by myself."

The deadly cholera epidemic that ravaged Zanzibar in late 1858 and early 1859 claimed at least twenty thousand lives. The plague decimated the island's African population and took many thousands of poorer Banyans and Arabs as well. Mortality rates among the wealthier were lower—Djilfidan was one of the unfortunate few. Cholera is transmitted through contaminated water and food, and those who were better off had access to cleaner water and a healthier diet.

James Christie, a medical practitioner who was living in Zanzibar at the time of another, equally deadly cholera epidemic ten years later, described the plague's effect on the island in the most extreme of terms: "some two thousand cholera corpses, in various stages of decomposition, lay in their shallow graves within the city, in its immediate precincts, or exposed on the sea-beach. . . . Zanzibar could be compared to nothing but a beleaguered city, the inhabitants of which were daily falling in hundreds under the rifles of an unseen foe."

According to Christie's now-classic work, *Cholera Epidemics in East Africa*, both epidemics had begun in Mecca three or four years before reaching Zanzibar. Mecca was an ideal incubator for disease, as it brought together tens of thousands of pilgrims from all over the world and crowded them into unhealthy living conditions. Many of the pilgrims had traveled hundreds of miles to reach Arabia and so arrived in an exhausted, weakened state, which then became exacerbated by the excitement of attending the Hajj, making them even more susceptible to disease.

From Mecca, the epidemics traveled down the Blue Nile through Abyssinia to the River Jub, through Galla country to the Pangani River, through Masai country and on into Central Africa and Zanzibar. Only six weeks before the 1869 outbreak exploded in Zanzibar, there was as yet no documented case of cholera on the island. Only a month before the epidemic arrived did advance warning from the mainland even filter in.

Both epidemics spread throughout the island in more or less the same way. At the start of the 1869 epidemic, a dhow from the coast reached a small Zanzibari village in late October, and some passengers alighted during the night. A death from cholera was said to have occurred the next day, and during the next few weeks, a number of other sudden deaths were reported.

Then, in late November, the epidemic broke out in full fury in Malindi, a northern section of Zanzibar town, inhabited by poor Arabs, free blacks, and slaves. Described by Christie as "the filthiest quarter in Zanzibar," Malindi was bordered by a beach that sloshed with raw sewage and by a deposit of old dung heaps so solid that they never washed away with the tides. Once a collecting point for slaves to be shipped north, Malindi also held the salt and fish bazaars, and was a slaughtering ground for goats.

At first, Christie questioned the veracity of the reports of cholera that he received—he thought them exaggerated, as they described sudden seizures resulting in near-immediate death, with some victims collapsing in the streets. Christie soon found out, however, that he was wrong. His first cholera patient was an Abyssinian slave, and her death was unlike anything he had ever witnessed before. In his book *Cholera Epidemics in East Africa*, he wrote:

She was a remarkably handsome woman, about nineteen or twenty years of age, and had all the appearance of being otherwise in perfect health. There had been no vomiting, no diarrhea, no cramps; in short, none of the usual symptoms of cholera. She complained only of having been suddenly seized with vertigo, and the sensation experienced was of such a peculiar nature that she told her master that she was certain she had been attacked with cholera, and that she would die. When I saw her, I examined her most carefully, and there was then no nausea, no abdominal tenderness, no pain in any part of the body, no coldness of the extremities, and no apparent depression in temperature of the surface of the body. There was only a certain wildness in the expression of the eyes, a restlessness of manner, and an anxious aspect of countenance. . . .

Turning to her master, she said, "Oh, my master, I am dying;" and she threw herself down upon the cushions on the floor. She said that she felt herself getting worse and worse every minute. . . . In a very short time there was a marked change in the temperature of the body; a peculiar coldness . . . the cold clamminess of death which, when once felt, can never be forgotten. . . .

The pulsation of the temporal arteries ceased, and the carotids throbbed laboriously and spasmodically; the plump rounded form of the body began to be effaced; the skin of the fingers, toes, hands, and feet became shriveled; the features pinched; the eyes sunken, and glaring; and the entire aspect of the countenance changed. The voice became hollow in its tones, and sepulchral; the pulsation of the carotids entirely disappeared; the breathing became laborious, and the breath was as cold, or colder than a current of atmosphere air, and the heart's action began rapidly to fail. . . .

She was dead in four hours from the first recognized accession of the symptoms.

For Salme's sake, one can only hope that her mother died more peacefully.

Zanzibar's slave population suffered the brunt of the epidemics' devastation in more ways than one. Even while members of their community were dying in disproportionately high numbers, others were forced to spend entire days doing nothing but burying the dead. From early in the morning until evening, new corpses were always waiting. At first, the slaves dug shallow graves for the victims, but as the horror continued—and continued, and continued—they simply threw the bodies on the beach or over the bridge that connected the town to the main part of the island.

Some slaves also took a heartbreaking precaution against the disease: "Believing as they did that death was inflicted by the hand of the destroying angel, and that the black race was doomed, but the European exempt, some endeavoured to save their lives by giving themselves a coating of white-wash, to lead, as they said, the evil spirit to believe that they were Europeans."

Yet throughout the outbreaks, there was surprisingly little panic among any of the island's populations. The Zanzibaris "acquitted themselves nobly in the unequal struggle with death," wrote Christie. "In the history of almost every epidemic there are accounts of the flight of a third or a half of the population, of the sick being left neglected, and the dead unburied. . . . No such scenes as those . . . were witnessed in Zanzibar."

After her mother's death, Salme continued to live in the room that she and her mother had shared at Beit al-Tani, and as the days and weeks passed, she grew very close to the palace's mistress, her older half-sister Chole, whom she had admired since childhood. The daughter of a "prudent and clever" Assyrian concubine who had probably been Christian, Chole was cheerful, charming, generous, and kind—at least in her youth. She was also very stylish, and received many offers of marriage, all of which she refused, for reasons that are unclear.

During Seyyid Said's lifetime, Chole had been one of his two favorite children, and had suffered the consequences—bitter, corrosive envy from the rest of the harem. Then in charge of overseeing her father's town palace, Beit al-Sahel, she had been blamed for everything, from rotten fruit and spoiled fish arriving from the countryside to the dearth of rose water and attar of roses available from Turkey one year.

But most of all, Chole had been blamed for the fact that Seyyid Said took her with him into his treasure chambers, and even worse, sometimes allowed her to go there by herself. One time, too, he gave her a specially ordered present from Persia—a splendid precious crown made of pure gold, richly set with diamonds. Ironically, the crown's shape made it impossible to wear with the Omani woman's headdress, but as far as the rest of the harem was concerned, that was beside the point.

Chole had taken care of Salme when she was a child, and now that the girl was almost grown she became her best friend and surrogate mother. The two were together day and night, sharing meals and secrets, gossip and dreams.

In the years immediately following Seyyid Said's death, Chole had been on good terms with his successor Seyyid Majid. However, her favorite brother had always been Seyyid Barghash, the forceful, determined man who had tried to grab the throne after their father's death. And so, it was probably inevitable that tensions between Chole and Majid soon arose. She began to avoid him, and to curse him in Salme's presence. Salme tried not to take sides, but as time went on, that became impossible:

"For months I found myself between two fires . . . ," she wrote. "I vacillated to and fro between two beloved persons, and when I could no longer stand aside from a decision, I took Chole's part for, although in the wrong, she was closer to my heart and ruled me more and more. For what is there in the world which we finally do not offer to our beloved ones, though not without struggle with ourselves? In the face of their supplications and entreaties, our views, our principles, even our most sacred convictions drop from us like the withered leaves of a tree in autumn. . . ."

Barghash had moved into a house directly across the street from Beit al-Tani. He began dropping by to visit Chole and before long, the two hatched a plot to capture Majid and proclaim Barghash sultan of Zanzibar. Majid had the support of the majority of the Zanzibari people, but tribal alliances are always fluid and Barghash worked at playing one sheikh off against another. Many meetings took place, always in the dead of night.

Hearing rumors of what was going on, Majid sent a messenger to Salme, his former playmate, warning her not to get involved—it was dangerous and she could only get hurt. But the headstrong sixteen-year-old, probably flattered to be included in adult affairs, paid no heed. She had already pledged her word to Chole and Barghash—and taken on a key role in the planned revolt. "On account of my ability to write I, the youngest female member of the conspiracy, became as it were the secretary-general of the alliance and I had to take charge of the entire correspondence with the chiefs," she wrote. "I was of course already old enough to be tormented by bitter pangs of conscience. It did not weigh lightly on my soul that the bullets, the powder, the muskets which I had to order, were intended to kill totally innocent people. But what to do? Was I to break my word and let my beloved sister down at the very moment in which the danger grew day by day? Never!"

Barghash started skipping Majid's *baraza*, or daily assemblies, thereby throwing down the gauntlet. Majid could have had him arrested then and there but didn't have the heart. Instead, hoping that his brother would come to his senses, he let things take their course, though he did place Barghash's home and Beit al-Tani under surveillance.

The day for the rebellion was finally set when suddenly one morning, several hundred soldiers surrounded Barghash's house. Salme and Chole fully expected Beit al-Tani to be next, but nothing happened. Later, they learned that Majid's ministers had wanted to surround Beit al-Tani as well, but that Majid had vetoed the suggestion. He wished to spare his sisters the fright and humiliation.

Chole, Salme, and several other conspirators then conferred with Barghash through their upper-story windows—their houses were so close together that they could talk over the narrow streets, despite the soldiers below. Barghash refused to even consider the possibility of surrender, and new plans for the revolt were quickly made. The conspirators would assemble at Marseilles, a plantation about ten miles from town that belonged to two sympathetic nieces. With its many rooms, thick walls, and floors paved with black-and-white marble, apropos of its namesake, Marseilles was already "like a little fortress" and could easily hold several hundred people and a large cache of arms.

The only trouble was—how to get Barghash to Marseilles? It was up to Chole and Salme to devise a plan, and they succeeded brilliantly. On the night of October 6, 1859, they left their house, along with the two sympathetic nieces and a retinue of female slaves, and approached Barghash's house. Guards stopped them, whereupon Chole and Salme stepped forward, went up to the unsuspecting officers, and gave them "a good talking-to." Such behavior was unheard of in Muslim society, and the poor dumbfounded guards let the royal women pass.

The sisters' plan was to have Barghash don the *hejab* and leave the house disguised as a woman. He resisted the idea at first—wasting valuable time—but at last consented, concealing multiple weapons under his *shele*. The group then left the house in a leisurely fashion, so as not to arouse suspicion, with Barghash walking between the two tallest women. The guards respectfully made way.

With their hearts in their throats, the group walked through the rest of the town at an ordinary pace, but once on its outskirts, began to run. Wrote Salme:

> Like a fleeing column we began to traverse the fields with our otherwise so delicate feet. We hurried up hill and down dale, totally unconcerned about our slippers, so beautifully embroidered with gold. The softly whispered warnings of our servants to run more carefully because we were crossing a thorn field fell on deaf ears; moreover the night was dark and we had our lanterns extinguished as soon as we were outside the town.
>
> All of a sweat and completely out of breath, we finally received news from our forerunner that we were right in front of the meeting place [with other Barghash supporters]. Now we women had to show more reserve. We moved more slowly and soon heard slight coughing and throat clearing, signals of those who were waiting. . . . A soft and careful voice came across to us: "Your highness, is that you?", and an affirmative answer was followed by a general, soft: "Praised be the Lord!"

Immediately, Barghash threw off his disguise, bade his liberators farewell, and joined his new male companions, to continue on to Marseilles. The women stood still for some time, panting and speechless, watching the retreating figures. But the hour was late. Silently, they started back.

Upon nearing the town, they separated, to arrive home without incident. They were exhausted. But there was no question of rest. Far too agitated to sleep, they lay awake all night, listening fearfully to every noise—and anticipating arrest, punishment, even death.

But when the new day dawned, everything was as it had been before. Guards were still pacing to and fro in front of Barghash's home, and the call to prayer was wafting over the town. Anxiously, Salme and Chole said first prayers together, and wondered. . . . Had Barghash reached Marseilles safely?

Two hours later, they knew. They had been discovered. A Baluchi soldier had recognized Barghash as he left the house, but had waited for hours before alerting anyone, out of respect for the late Seyyid Said. The Baluchi had also assumed that Barghash would flee Zanzibar, and that therefore no immediate action was necessary.

Majid sent several thousand soldiers to Marseilles, and their cannons reduced the once-magnificent plantation house to rubble. Hundreds of insurgents were killed, but Barghash and the other key coconspirators escaped unharmed.

Salme and Chole paced Beit al-Tani, worrying and wondering. What would happen next? How would Majid react? Time crawled.

A few mornings later, Salme was astonished to learn that Barghash was once again living next door—this time as a fugitive. Majid had no idea his brother was back, and Barghash hoped to remain undiscovered for as long as possible. Yet that very day, news of his arrival spread throughout the town. Many believed that he had returned to give himself up, but Barghash had no such intention, and turned down his brother's offer of clemency.

Fed up, Majid, with the approval of the British consul, ordered a gunboat to be anchored in front of Barghash's house. Hours later, it opened fire.

Wrote Salme:

Panic seized our house. . . . Everybody, high and low, young and old, ran around purposeless and in confusion. Here people took farewell from each other forever, there people asked each other's forgiveness for injustices caused in happier days. . . . Many prayed. . . . Their example was followed by other members of the household, and gradually the intense agitation was replaced by the so marvelously soothing consciousness that it is not the will of man, but that of the Lord which is done, that our fate is destined by the All-good and All-wise since the beginning of the world. All were now plunged in prayer and bent their forehead to the ground in token of deepest humility before the Lord. In enlightened Europe one may call this fanaticism, or whatever else, but such a faith certainly brings indescribable peace to those who adhere to it.

In the end, Chole persuaded Barghash to surrender, and Majid banished him to Bombay, on the advice of the British, who probably wanted to keep an eye on him there. Barghash remained in India only two years, however, quietly returning to Zanzibar in October 1861, in the company of a new British consul. Not surprisingly, Majid received his brother coolly and with conditions: Barghash could remain on the island only if he attended Majid's *baraza* and lived in seclusion.

"Thus ended our enterprise, which had started with such high expectations," wrote a wiser Salme years later. "It had cost us dearly. . . . Many of our best slaves had fallen and others, maimed invalids, reminded us continuously of the disaster we had conjured up. But this was the least we had to expect from our evil seed. Much more oppressive was for us the burden caused by the fact that [we] were conspicuously avoided and ignored by all our right thinking brothers, sisters and relatives, and that I, in the bottom of my heart, was not able to blame them for it."

20

Elopement

NOW EVERYWHERE SALME TURNED, SHE MET WITH DISAPPROV-ing faces. Her brothers and sisters, her aunts and uncles, even her slaves—most could not understand how she could have taken part in Barghash's rebellion. And so, she decided to retire to the countryside for a while, to live on a plantation that she had inherited from her father until the "high waves of enmity and hatred had abated."

Seyyid Said had left all of his children sizable inheritances, out of an estate that had included dozens of plantations, a half-dozen palaces, a man-of-war, coffers full of precious jewels and gold coins, and much more. Most everything had been equally divided among his offspring, although, as per Islamic law, his daughters' shares were one half the size of his sons'; each daughter had received 5,429 pounds and each son, 10,859 pounds.

The sun was just beginning to reach over the horizon on the morning that Salme left Stone Town, mounted on a small white donkey and accompanied only by her slaves and many pets. Covered in her black *shele*, which she would remove as soon as she reached the countryside, she was headed for Kisimbani, about ten miles north of the harbor. Kisimbani had been the second plantation on Zanzibar to be planted with cloves, and held a fine, luxurious mansion. Her mother, Djilfidan, had loved it there, and as Salme rocked gently to and fro on her embroidered saddle-cushion, her donkey picking its way over Zanzibar's red earth, she thought about her mother—how much she missed her!

How much of what had occurred had been due to Salme's youth? How would she have reacted to Chole if her mother had still been alive? Would she even have been aware of Barghash's plot? Chances are good that she would have known nothing; her life could have taken a far different course.

Salme enjoyed much about her new quiet life, writing: "My domestic animals, whose number I increased continuously, gave me much pleasure. Several hours every day I was busy with them. I greatly enjoyed visiting old and sick people in their small, humble huts and giving them, through my servants, a share in the abundance of my kitchen. Every morning I had the slaves' little children—a sort of 'dividend' of the masters—come to me. . . . Afterward these children were fed copiously. . . . I rejoiced with all my heart at having reached this coziness, away from the troubles of the town."

But Salme was not one to hide away completely. She missed the constant activity and intrigue of her family. Every day she sent two messengers into town to scout out the daily news, and every two or three days she sent a servant to one of her siblings' homes to discover the latest Al Busaidi family gossip.

Salme also missed the sea, whose sound she had awoken to nearly every morning of her life. Neither Kisimbani nor any of the three other plantations she had inherited bordered the sea, and so she set about trying to acquire one that did. That was easier said than done—then, as now, most people preferred estates on the sea—but at last, through the help of a *dellal*, or broker, she found the perfect place: Bububu. Named for the bubbling sound of a nearby spring, Bububu had a small river running through it, reminding Salme of her beloved childhood home, Beit al-Mtoni.

Regrettably, Bububu's owner did not wish to sell. But he did agree to rent the estate. Salme signed a contract and moved a week later. Now she spent her days sitting in her new courtyard, watching her animals drink from the Bububu stream, or strolling along the beach, watching the ships heading to or from Zanzibar town.

Bububu was much closer to Stone Town than was Kisimbani, and soon three of Salme's brothers were visiting her almost daily. They were only a few years older than she, and the four teenagers spent many happy days on the beach, talking, picnicking, playing cards, and setting off a myriad of fireworks. It was a joyful, carefree few years that Salme would later remember with great wistfulness: "Thinking back on these beautiful days of my youth, when I knew the world only from its good, glorious sides and still had no idea of the numerous thorns which later would threaten to block my path through life everywhere, my heart turns heavy. But in the hours of distress, those holy remembrances of my youth, the remembrance of my parents, brothers and sisters, of my home country, again and again are a comfort to me and almost daily I bask in them."

However, Salme's stay at Bububu was cut short. One afternoon while she was sitting in her usual spot, gazing through a telescope trained on the sea, she saw a small boat approaching, bearing only one brother. One look at his face told Salme that he had bad news. Majid had sent him to ask her to give up Bububu for the British consul. If anyone else had made that request, Salme would have refused him or her. But after all that had occurred, she felt she had no choice.

A short time later, Salme was back in Stone Town—a move that was to define her fate. Her brothers found a house for her in a section of town that was inhabited by many Europeans, and more important, by a certain German gentleman.

One night after moving, Salme was on her roof, enjoying the night air. African drums were sounding in the distance, palm trees were rustling, and a bright moon was floating in the sea and sky.

A servant appeared with a message: Chole had come to call. Disconcerted, Salme asked her to come up. The two sisters had barely seen or spoken to each other in the four or five years since Barghash's aborted rebellion.

Chole had no sooner taken a seat and sipped a taste of tea when she began to berate her sister. "Oh, Salme, I never thought you were so bad as all that!"

"Good evening, Chole, what ill have I done to you?" Salme asked, surprised.

"You really pretend you have done nothing to me?" Chole exploded.

"It is just nothing that you have given up Bububu to oblige Majid and the godless *kafir?*"

"But my dear sister . . . That is my own business, and besides I explained the matter to you the other day in my letter."

"I suppose you wished to insinuate yourself with the damned," Chole said.

"No, you are altogether mistaken about that; I do not need to insinuate myself with anyone. . . ."

"Well, I see now that you are against us," Chole said, rising abruptly. "From now on you have to choose between Barghash and myself on the one side, and the servant of the Englishman on the other!"

And with that, Chole disappeared. Salme never saw her again, even though they lived just a few blocks apart. Reconciliation came only years later through letters, when Salme was living in Germany, and it was short-lived, as Chole died soon after under mysterious circumstances. Wrote Salme: "The much-loved, much-envied and much-hated Chole is no more of this world. . . . It is said that she fell victim to a treacherous poisoning, on which no true light could ever be shed. She always remains close to me in spirit."

Not long after Chole's visit, Salme received another surprise caller—Seyyid Majid, who came accompanied by a large retinue of noblemen, *gadis*, servants, and slaves, as befitted his status. It was now the mid-1860s, and the young man had been in power for about eight years. A gentle and amiable person who continued to suffer from severe epileptic fits, he lacked the charisma and force of character of his father, but was an effective and steady ruler, and Zanzibar was flourishing under his reign.

Like his father before him, Majid had a close relationship with the British, whose influence over Zanzibar had been growing steadily, especially when it came to the slave trade. Britain had increased the number of anti–slave trade vessels it had patrolling the Indian Ocean and, for a period, allowed its navy to destroy all suspicious dhows on the spot—much to the outrage of the Zanzibaris, who mobbed Majid's palace in protest. A new British consul, Christopher Rigby, had also declared that Zanzibar's Indians were British subjects and so could not own slaves, leading to more than eight thousand slaves being emancipated almost overnight. As laudable as Rigby's action sounds, its abrupt enactment had had harmful effects. Suddenly, the Indians' plantations were worthless, the Indian financiers lacked capital to make loans, and the newly freed slaves had no source of economic support. When Rigby left the island after only three years of service due to ill health, his decree was quietly forgotten.

One of the reasons for Britain's growing power over Zanzibar was the island's straitened operational budget. Because Seyyid Said's fortune had been dispersed among his many children, the state coffers were not as full as they had once been. As early as 1860, Zanzibar's customs master had told Majid that he must henceforth "confine his payments to sums absolutely required for the service of the state and for his household expenses."

"Good morning, Salme," Majid called out to his sister in a hearty voice on that day following her move back to Stone Town. "You see that, though being your senior, I am the first to come to express my thanks that you have not wished to make a fool of me before the Englishman."

"Oh, my brother, that was nothing, really nothing," Salme stammered, astonished and no doubt terrified to see Majid standing before her.

But during the visit that followed, her brother did not mention Barghash's conspiracy. Instead, Salme wrote, he told her stories that seemed designed to put her at ease.

"You will, I hope, come and see my sister Chadudj soon, will you not?" he asked as he was leaving.

"Yes, surely I will," said Salme, with sinking heart. Good manners dictated that she must return Majid's visit with a visit to his sister, but she knew that Chole would hear of it and hold an even greater grudge against her. "I was to pay dearly for this simple act of courtesy . . . ," she wrote years later. "The two parties existed as before, and intrigues continued likewise, only more secretly and with less stir than before."

In the mid-1860s, when Salme moved back to Stone Town, it held a community of sixty-six Westerners, mostly men, but also a few women and children. Of these, twenty-two were British, twenty-five were French, seven were Americans, and twelve were German.

The Germans had been a presence in Zanzibar since the late 1840s, when Wilhelm O'Swald & Co. of Hamburg opened up an office on the island. Initially, the O'Swald firm specialized in the unusual business of transporting cowrie shells from Zanzibar to West Africa, where they were used as currency. Later, the firm traded in more traditional items such as copal, ivory, and cloves. Other Hamburg companies soon followed suit, and by the mid-1850s, about twenty Hamburg ships were calling at Zanzibar annually. Seyyid Said signed a trade agreement with the Germans in 1859, and by the time Salme left Zanzibar in 1866, the Hamburg Germans were second only to the British in the amount of goods they were importing to and exporting from Zanzibar.

Directly next door to Salme's new residence stood a high-ceilinged, two-story home inhabited by a tall, blond German businessman named Heinrich Ruete, whom she probably met sometime after July 1865. The son of a schoolmaster, the twenty-eight-year-old had begun his career in the office of a Hamburg merchant and was in Zanzibar as "the head, if not the sole representative of the modest yet flourishing house of Ruete & Co.," according to the acting British consul Edwin Seward. Ruete had been "adequately educated," spoke French and English as well as German, and was regarded as an intelligent and able man who had "borne a character for a very blameless life, so far as is known in Zanzibar."

Though it went against the usual etiquette of Muslim women, Salme had been friendly with the handful of European women living on the island for some time. Like her father before her, she was deeply curious about the world and, together with Chole, had at times received Western women at home. And now, still estranged from much of her family, the princess started to turn to the Westerners more and more. Salme "knows a little English, is very anxious to get to Europe and to Europeanize in every possible way," noted the island's Anglican minister.

It was therefore not altogether surprising that Salme struck up an acquaintance with Heinrich Ruete. But what was surprising was that this acquaintance took a romantic turn—an astonishing development for that time and place.

Salme describes her courtship and elopement in her memoirs, but

gives disappointingly little detail about what occurred, leaving it to the
reader to fill in between the lines:

> During this troubled time [after the death of Seyyid Said], in
> which discord and dissension reigned in our family, I was made
> happy by the affection of a young German who lived in Zanzibar
> as representative of a Hamburg mercantile firm and who later be-
> come my husband. Untrue descriptions of the events which were
> connected with this affection and which were of so great impor-
> tance to me, have already often been made public. I therefore feel
> the need to report briefly on the entire connection. . . .
>
> I made the acquaintance of my husband soon after my removal
> from Bububu. My house was next to his; the flat roof of his house
> was below my own, and from a window on the upper floor I often
> was a witness to joyful gentlemen's parties, which he arranged to
> show me the way in which European meals are organized. Our
> friendship, from which in time deep love developed, was soon
> known in the town and my brother Majid also learned about it; I
> have not had to experience hostility on his side, much less impris-
> onment about which there has been gossip because of this.
>
> I was, of course, desirous of leaving my home secretly, where
> the union with my beloved would have been completely impossi-
> ble. A first attempt in this respect failed; but a more favourable op-
> portunity soon presented itself.

And from this brief description of that most momentous period of
her life, Salme leaps into an account of how the acting British consul's
wife, Emily Seward, helped her flee Zanzibar. Emily secured passage for
Salme on board the HMS *Highflyer,* a British man-of-war commanded
by a Captain Pasley, traveling from the island to Aden on the Arabian
peninsula.

Heinrich Ruete recorded no account of his courtship with Salme,
and the Europeans living on Zanzibar at the time left behind only a few
tantalizing details. The Anglican minister recalled: "There had long been
half a joke and half a scandal about Ruete's attention to the princess,
and it had been said that they had met in the country and had been seen

walking together." The future British consul John Kirk wrote: "She'd have been killed, I think, sooner or later, had she remained [on Zanzibar]."

Kirk's dire prediction stemmed from the rumors that Salme was pregnant and that Majid, upon hearing the news, sent a female relative to examine her and report on her condition—a six-foot-four African executioner at the ready. Wanting to protect Salme, or so the rumors went, the relative did not tell Majid the truth, but he suspected it anyway and sent Salme a letter offering her the chance to leave Zanzibar on a pilgrimage to Mecca on board his chief eunuch's ship. Other girls in similar predicaments had mysteriously disappeared on such sea voyages, and Salme declined the offer.

No historical evidence exists to indicate that Majid had any intention of harming Salme whether she was pregnant or not, and she herself vigorously defends her brother in her memoirs and letters. And although Majid was undoubtedly under great pressure from his fellow Muslims to punish his sister in some way, it is doubtful that he would have executed her. For one thing, fornication outside marriage is forbidden in Islam, but it is punishable by flogging, not death. For another, he was deeply fond of Salme.

And yet . . . Why did Salme elope with Heinrich Ruete? And why wasn't she already married? In 1866, the year that she eloped, she was twenty-two years old—on her way to becoming an old maid by the standards of her time and place. Had Majid, all her protestations to the contrary, impeded her marriage prospects in some way? Was she so lonely and estranged from her family that she felt desperate to escape Zanzibar? Or had she simply fallen so deeply in love that she cared nothing for consequences?

For Salme to fall in love and then elope with Heinrich took extraordinary courage. She was breaking all the mores of her society and leaving behind everything she had ever known. And she was doing so carefully, deliberately, making rational decisions every step of the way. She wasn't a naïve, flighty woman in love with love. Her eyes were wide open; she was strong, determined, and in control.

A photograph of Salme taken circa 1868, two years after she left Zanzibar, depicts a slim young woman with a direct gaze. The expression on her face seems to be part astonishment, part apprehension, part determination, and, perhaps, part suppressed glee. She is dressed in an elaborate Omani costume, complete with a half-dozen heavy bracelets on each forearm, a necklace of large gold coins that reaches her chest, a headdress that hides her hair and falls below her knees, ankle bracelets, and elevated wooden sandals. Her tunic appears to be velvet, embossed with a swirling design, and her solid-colored leggings feature stiff embroidered cuffs.

By the end of July 1866, Salme had sent many of her things to Germany on one of Ruete's ships, and was beginning to sell off her slaves and property on the pretext of wishing to finance a pilgrimage to Mecca. Secretly, however, she was waiting for a propitious moment to flee—a moment that came in late August with the arrival of the Persian New Year. Nairuzi, or "New Day," was and still is widely celebrated in Zanzibar, a legacy from the Shirazi Persians who arrived in the region during the medieval period.

On the evening before Nairuzi, it was customary for Zanzibari women—be they Arab, Swahili, or African—to bathe in the sea, cleansing off the sins and troubles of the old year in preparation for the new. Salme told her household that she would be celebrating the ritual with a sister who lived in another part of town and so would not be home until the following day. Then that night, carrying several boxes filled with money and jewels, she made her way down to the beach near the British consulate. With her were two slaves who had no idea what their mistress was up to. The women attracted little notice—hundreds of other revelers were also on the beach.

Near the consulate, a cutter from the *Highflyer* was waiting. Salme waded nonchalantly toward it, and then, with a sudden rush, was pulled on board. Her slaves screamed. A blue-jacketed sailor covered the mouth of one and hauled her in after her mistress, but the other one got away and ran "bellowing up the street." Still, no one paid any attention and the *Highflyer* steamed away.

The next morning, people noticed that the *Highflyer* had left Zanzibar without having notified either the Arab authorities or the British consulate, as protocol demanded. Seyyida Salme was also missing, and it didn't take long for her family to put two and two together.

Majid wrote a letter of protest to Seward, the acting British consul, who declared that he knew nothing about the matter. His wife, Emily, recognizing that the British could not officially condone Salme's escape, had acted without his knowledge. Majid accepted Seward's plea of ignorance. Secretly, he was probably greatly relieved that Salme had gotten safely away. In fact, when the *Highflyer* returned to Zanzibar a few months later, Majid gave its Captain Pasley a very friendly reception, much to the astonishment of many of his subjects, who expected some sort of retribution. Majid also allowed Heinrich Ruete to remain in Zanzibar for months after Salme's departure, in order to wind up his affairs.

The *Highflyer* reached Aden, strategically located at the entrance to the Rea Sea, without incident. Built on volcanic rock on the edge of a desert, the ancient port—rumored to be the burial site of Cain and Abel—was a desolate place, notorious for its flies, wind, and torrid heat. Not even a blade of grass was said to survive there.

From the sea, Aden towered with sharp peaks, gothic spires, and craggy cliffs, all made of bleak, black rock. Connected to the mainland by a sandy isthmus with harbors on both sides, the town itself was hidden from view, as it lay in the crater of an extinct volcano. Occupied over the centuries by everyone from the Egyptians to the Romans to the Persians to the Ethiopians to the Turks, Aden had been acquired by the British in 1839.

Once in town, Salme took up residence with Bonaventura Mass and his wife, a Spanish couple whom she knew from Zanzibar. A former employee of the French consulate, Bonaventura was a major player in the slave trade, facilitating operations between a large Marseilles-Barcelona trading company and the Arab-African slavers. The Masses had been forced to leave Zanzibar precipitately a short time earlier, due to Bonaventura's illicit activities, but these don't seem to have bothered Salme at all, as she makes no mention of them in her memoirs.

Salme adjusted quickly to life with the Masses. She started studying Christianity, began wearing European dress, and accompanied her hosts to whatever social events the town's small Western community had to offer.

Under Islamic law, Majid was still Salme's guardian, as she was not yet married, and he sent her a letter telling her that she was free to re-turn to Zanzibar if she wished but that she must not leave Aden for other parts without consulting him first. He also sent a message to Aden's British political agent requesting that Salme be convinced to live a quiet life and "on no account be permitted to leave for Hamburg, or be allowed on any pretext whatever to have intercourse or correspondence with any European or English-speaking European or English-speaking German who may visit Aden."

To which the British political agent could only helplessly reply:

> Every effort has been made to induce the Bibi Suleyma to quit her present quarters and adopt a more secluded life. But I regret with-out avail; indeed I have endeavoured to work upon the lady's feel-ings through the most respectable Arab families resident in Aden and have offered her a private apartment and establishment, but the Bibi seems determined to adhere to the step she has taken and to renounce her former life entirely and become Europeanised. To use her own words, she cannot, she says, after wearing the dress of Europeans revert to Arab dress, nor will she certainly for the present quit Mr. Mass' house. Under the circumstances further attempts would be useless.

Throughout this time, Salme and Heinrich were in constant corre-spondence. However, Heinrich did not arrive in Aden until nine months after Salme's departure—it took him a half year to finish up in Zanzibar and then he spent another three months conducting business in the Seychelles.

When the couple did finally reunite, they quickly made up for lost time. On the same day as Heinrich's arrival—May 30, 1867—Salme was baptized in the town's Anglican Christ Church, where she took the Christian name of Emily, in honor of the woman who had helped her flee Zanzibar. Immediately afterward, she and Heinrich were wed, and that very afternoon they departed for Europe.

Six months before Heinrich's arrival in Aden, Salme had given birth to their first child. The European rumor mill had been right on that count at least. The child was baptized on April 1, 1867, and named

Heinrich, but his name is not mentioned in Salme's memoirs or letters, and he probably died before she left Aden.

Had Salme fled Zanzibar primarily because she was pregnant? And if so, did she wish herself back after she lost her child? What was she doing, giving up everything for a man she scarcely knew? What would life with him be like? Would his family and friends accept her? Would she be happy living in the West?

❧

PART THREE

Germany and Africa

21

Hamburg

THE AFTERNOON SUN WAS SETTING OVER THE HAMBURG SKY-line, its long summer rays glinting off the spires of the city's many churches. Hamburg's narrow, winding canals, linking three nearby rivers, also caught the sun's setting rays and sent them scattering across pewtered surfaces lapping with waves.

Clip, clop, clip, clop. Salme and Heinrich were seated in a horse-drawn hackney carriage that swayed from side to side, its tall wheels jolting over cobblestone streets crowded with other horse-drawn carriages, wagons, carts, and trams. Gripping Heinrich's arm, Salme stared incredulously out at the passing scene. She had never seen so many light-skinned, blond-haired people before—or so many people in such a hurry. The sidewalks were packed—with gentlemen in long jackets and tall hats; matrons in dark high-necked dresses, bustles in back; maidservants in short sleeves and white caps; and laborers in simple shirts and pants. Digging her nails into her husband's arm, she tried to ignore a desperate, mocking voice crying out within her: "And here you wish to pass the rest of your life?"

Situated on the River Elbe in northern Germany, about seventy-five miles from the North Sea, Hamburg was and still is one of the most important ports of Europe. A mercantile city-state, it was a founding member of the medieval Hanseatic League, which held a trade monopoly over the North and Baltic Seas and most of northern Europe between the thirteenth and seventeenth centuries. Hamburg's greatest period of growth, however, occurred between 1870 and 1900—just after Salme's arrival—when its population more than quadrupled to over eight hundred thousand, thanks to its burgeoning trade with the Americas.

As a prosperous mercantile city in the second half of the nineteenth century, Hamburg was a practical and cosmopolitan place, with a population renowned for its discretion and reserve. Its Old City dated back to medieval times and was surrounded by a girdle of green that had once been an encircling wall. Laying so low that it at times flooded, the Old City was picturesque and crowded, packed with warehouses and tall, narrow, half-timbered homes. Salme and Heinrich were to settle not far from the Old City and they spent much time there, with Salme sometimes shopping for fruits and vegetables in the Hopfenmarkt, a large public square, and marveling at the ice skaters on the canals in winter—"It was as if they had invisible wings," she wrote.

But as the newlyweds drove through the Old City on that late afternoon in 1867, all Salme felt was fear. The emotion had been virtually unknown to her in Zanzibar, but would soon become her constant companion.

The journey from Aden to Germany had been difficult for Salme. Their ship had traveled north through the Red Sea, where the temperatures had been unbearably hot. It was too sweltering to stay either on the deck or in the cabins, so most of the first-class passengers had whiled away the days in an upstairs saloon. Socializing with so many strange men and women for hours on end had been excruciating for Salme—though it hadn't compared with the torture of mealtimes. Suspecting pork in every meal, she survived on next to nothing—despite her conversion to Christianity—eating only biscuits, boiled eggs, and fruit, and drinking only tea. Too embarrassed to tell Heinrich the real reason for her lack of appetite, she claimed she wasn't hungry.

On the hottest of nights, most of the first-class passengers also slept in the saloon—men, women, and children all snoring away in flimsy white nightshirts on mattresses side by side. The practice went against everything that Salme had been brought up to believe, and at first she refused to join the other travelers, saying that she would rather sleep below. But then a French lady from Mauritius, discerning the cause of her discomfort, offered to sleep next to her so that she would not have to lie beside a strange man, and she reluctantly joined the others.

From the Red Sea, the ship passed into the Mediterranean and stopped in Cairo, where Salme and Heinrich visited the Muhammad Ali mosque. Perched high above the city in the ancient citadel, the mosque's shiny alabaster domes and lacy minarets spun a fairy tale against the sky. But it was here that the enormity of what Salme had done sank in for the first time. The mosque's caretakers refused to let her in until she had covered her feet with felt slippers—only Muslims could enter without them. "Here it became clear to me what I really was," wrote Salme sadly, in words that reflected what would be a life-long ambivalence toward her conversion. "In my eyes no sacrifice is greater than changing religion. Position, wealth nor the highest secular rank can appear to us as irreplaceable as our sacred religion."

The ship's final stop was Marseilles, where it docked on a summer's day so cold that Salme had to borrow a shawl—none of her own clothes were warm enough. Waiting for her belongings to clear customs, she heard a heated argument escalating behind her, and turned to see Heinrich quarreling with the customs officials. They wanted him to pay import taxes on the jewelry that Salme was bringing into the country; they said there was so much, she must be intending to sell it. Heinrich couldn't convince them otherwise, and finally, losing patience, Salme strode over to the men and mentioned her family's name. The startled officials then allowed the jewelry to pass through untaxed.

Salme and Heinrich spent the next week visiting with Bonaventura Mass and his wife, the Spanish couple from Aden, who were now living in a Marseilles suburb. Salme was overjoyed to see her old friends again, but couldn't completely enjoy their visit together. The thought of what lay ahead of her kept intruding, setting her heart pounding, her palms sweating, until by the time she and Heinrich finally left Marseilles, she was in a state of full-blown panic:

"I was seized by such fear, otherwise unknown to me, that I would have preferred to cry aloud . . . ," she wrote in a letter addressed to a "dear friend" back home. "My soul was crying out for all of you and seemed to blend with a thousand voices from my beloved island, calling me back with one warning: 'Go no further! Instead come back!' I fought a terrible fight with myself. Mechanically I mounted the train whose purpose it was to bring me as quickly as possible to an unknown country, to perfect strangers, as if I too were in the greatest hurry to reach my future destination as soon as possible—and so we drove on and on towards the North."

When the newlyweds arrived in Hamburg, Heinrich's family welcomed Salme "in the kindest manner," she wrote, and helped them settle into a small villa near the Alster River in the heart of the city. Salme loved the villa's location, but before long, she grew to dislike her new home. Its vast amount of needless furniture, its thick curtains, its uncomfortable chairs, its bed comforters made of "horrible chicken feathers," and most of all, its lack of fresh air—all made her feel suffocated and oppressed. The front doors were always closed—even in the summer, even in the daytime. She hated the bathtub, too, though she did like the indoor plumbing, the gas lighting, and the four-poster beds, which reminded her of the Indian beds she had slept on in Zanzibar.

Salme's first year in Hamburg passed like a bad dream. Everything, everything was so different—the houses, the streets, the clothing, the food, even the air. She was often filled with "a slight feeling of horror" that she was unable to shake off, and except when in her husband's presence, she felt constantly afraid.

Good manners dictated that Salme and Heinrich pay courtesy calls on his many friends and acquaintances, and the process drove the princess to despair. She spoke next to no German, and whenever she entered a drawing room, everyone stared at her, raking her over from head to foot with such naked curiosity that she had to lower her eyes. She couldn't tell one person from another—they all looked alike—and their names were unpronounceable.

Dinner parties were especially unbearable. No one said prayers before eating, as was customary in Zanzibar, and her hosts loaded her plate with piles of strange food that she was afraid to eat—something might contain pork. Everyone conversed rudely throughout the meal instead of waiting politely until they were done eating, as in Muslim society, and the ladies' low-cut, short-sleeved evening dresses offended her. Worst of all was the drinking of wine. People drank much more than they ate, even when they weren't thirsty, and then began to talk in loud voices, vying to dominate the conversation. Thereafter came the unavoidable toasts, when various gentlemen stood up and praised their hosts, "rightly or wrongly," and everyone clinked their glasses together much too loudly. "Such a situation is called here an 'animated gathering,' " sniffed the princess.

Early on, Salme was struck by the Germans' "endless smiles," and mentioned them to Heinrich, calling Germany a "cheerful nation." But to her astonishment, he told her that the smiles were a matter of politeness, not cheerfulness, and did not mean much of anything. So acting natural is socially unacceptable in Germany—here people wear figurative face masks rather literal ones, Salme thought to herself.

Heinrich left the house to go to his trading company's office every morning at nine-thirty a.m., leaving Salme on her own until four p.m., when he returned. At first, she passed the time by reading and rereading her Arabic-language books, special-ordered from Alexandria, and by hugging and kissing and talking to the clothes, jewelry, and other belongings that she had brought with her from Zanzibar. Often Heinrich came home while she still had everything unpacked, and when she saw him, surrounded by her beloved objects, she sometimes believed for just a flash that they were back in Zanzibar, living happily together. One day, Heinrich brought her home a pomegranate and at the sight of the tropical fruit she burst into tears.

But Salme soon realized that if she were ever to become comfortable living in Germany—and prove to her new acquaintances that Arabs were not stupid, as most seemed to believe—she needed to learn the German language. And so she hired a tutor, who came every day from one to three in the afternoon. After about a year of study, she was able to carry on simple conversations, communicate effectively with servants, and keep the household books—a skill that she found to be held in curiously high regard in Germany. "If at home you are accustomed to put your yearly revenues in a coffer . . . here the matter is totally different . . . ," she wrote in a letter home. "A precise account has to be rendered of everything, and woe to him who lives carelessly without much ado. Even the ministers, that is to say the real government of each land, have to account for almost every penny they spend."

Despite being an international port, Hamburg was a xenophobic city with a very small foreign population, and Salme often suffered from its lack of "exotic people," as she put it. That first year, people stared at her everywhere she went, and on more than one occasion, she saw ladies kneeling on the seats of their carriages to catch a glimpse of her as they passed by. The craziest of rumors abounded: she was as fat as a barrel, her hair and complexion were African, her feet had been bound Chinese-style and she could not walk. Feeling angered and humiliated, she started riding in closed carriages and refusing invitations whenever she could. "In fact I led two lives: a mental one, encircled by the eternally blue sky and animated by . . . beloved forms, full of high spirits and mischief, and the real one, as had been allotted to me," she wrote.

Salme took solace in gardening and in her pets. Her beautiful white cat from Mecca, a gift from a cousin, had been stolen, but Heinrich had given her a poodle, a whippet, a singing canary, and a goat, which she milked herself.

And her marriage was happy. Every second or third Sunday, she and Heinrich—who called her "Bibi," a KiSwahili term of respect and affection—took a walk along the Elbe, down to the harbor, to watch the boats. The princess loved seeing them, especially if they had African crew members. Sometimes, she and Heinrich went to the Circus Rentz, where she enjoyed watching the horses, or to a concert or show, though here she was often offended by the skimpy dresses of the female performers, and the European music "badly knocked" her "unmusical head."

A photograph of Salme and Heinrich taken in early 1870 depicts a serious young woman with large soulful eyes and a long nose, and a sturdy young man with round cheeks and a dark beard and mustache. Salme's hair is black and shiny, parted in the middle and perfectly coiffed, and she wears a heavy, satin dress with a long string of beads and dangling earrings. On her face is a look that is half beseeching, half defiant, while Heinrich, dressed in a dark jacket and lighter-colored pants, has a solid, comforting presence.

Heinrich seems to have been a perceptive and sensitive man who was attuned to Salme's needs and very patient in the face of her often-overwhelming homesickness, which scarcely abated throughout their marriage. Years later, Salme would write: "Oh, how often did my husband tease me when I wanted to go to bed somewhat early. He then always said: 'Aha, Bibi, do you want to travel so early to Zanzibar today? Please remember me to our friends there.' "

Winter arrived, and Salme experienced the magic of her first snow. But she felt cold all the time and hated wearing the requisite layers of heavy clothing. Hamburg's liveliest social season also began and invitations that could not be avoided poured in.

Wrote Salme with an almost audible sigh:

With the sadness of winter arrives the time of the so-called social life. . . . And so there begins for innumerable people, who find cosy family life much too tedious, an existence which is not unlike a hunt. Some do not seem to be happy unless they have, on one and the same day, taken breakfast with A., lunch with B., and dinner with C. I myself used to know a very ailing lady who during the day was mostly confined to her bed but who in the evening "had" to go out. Every time she "had" to go out—as she expressed herself—she took several glasses of champagne to strengthen herself before leaving the house. . . . But what does that matter, if only one "has a good time" and has "enjoyed" oneself.

To make matters worse, good manners dictated that Salme and Heinrich return others' hospitality with invitations of their own, a prospect that filled Salme with dread. If she didn't get everything just right, she worried, the Germans would think badly not only of her but of the whole Arab race.

One day, about two weeks before Salme's first dinner party, a huge sea turtle from Zanzibar arrived. With no place else to put it, she and her maids half-pushed, half-pulled the animal into the bathtub—from which it had to be removed, with great difficulty, every time someone wanted to take a bath. Salme spent many hours sitting beside the turtle, stroking its shell and dreaming of her beloved island so many miles away. The "most melancholy reflections took possession" of her soul and she imagined that the turtle understood her innermost thoughts. His

presence made her feel a little less lonely . . . but also horribly guilty.
The turtle was to be killed to make soup for the dinner party.

Salme and Heinrich did not usually go to church, but one Sunday he
asked her if she would like to attend. She said that she would, yet when
the couple reached the church door, she suddenly felt as if she was
about to do something terribly wrong. Taking a deep breath, she forced
herself to go inside, only to be gripped with anguish. She hated seeing
the figurative images on the walls—forbidden in Islam—and hearing the
sermons and hymns, which dragged on and on. No one seemed to be
showing even the slightest humility before God; they barely bowed
their heads, and she found the passing of the offering plate highly of-
fensive. Asking for money in a place of worship!

Salme had received some instruction in Christianity in Aden before
she converted, but it had been perfunctory, and no one there had
seemed to care whether she understood even the little she'd been
taught. The pastor officiating at her baptism had asked her yes-or-no
questions in a language she barely understood, waiting only for her to
answer everything in the affirmative. "Nothing else was required," she
wrote, amazed. "From that moment onwards I belonged to Christianity;
all the rest I should in any case manage all by myself."

Though Salme never says so outright in her memoirs or letters, having perhaps never completely admitted it even to herself, she had converted to Christianity only for the sake of her husband and would
remain a Christian only for the sake of her children. She never acquired
anything approaching true conviction—"Conviction? Indeed, from
whom and from where should I have gained the conviction?" she wrote
at one point—and was continually tormented by the choice she'd made.
As late as 1886, nearly twenty years after her conversion, she commented: "I left my home a complete Arab woman and a good Muslim
and what am I now? A bad Christian and somewhat more than half a
German."

At first, and probably for many years, Salme continued to say her
Muslim prayers in private. Always, she seems to have yearned to return
to the faith of her birth. Her descriptions of Muslim celebrations and

rituals resound with warmth and life; reading them, one suspects that she was always a Muslim at heart.

Despite Salme's close relationship with Heinrich, she never confessed to him the depth of her religious doubts. Perhaps doing so would have felt too much like an assault on him and her decision to leave everything for him. Or perhaps she already knew that such a discussion would have been fruitless. "Why discuss a problem when views are so diametrically opposed?" she wrote. "In youth, one hardly has a presentiment how strongly one remains lifelong attached to one's education, however much circumstances change in the course of time."

Salme had hoped that her Christian convictions would grow once she got to know other Christians. They would guide and teach her, initiate her into their ceremonies, and make her "into one of them internally," she thought. But quite the contrary occurred. In letter after letter addressed to her "dear lady friend" in Zanzibar, Salme described her profound disillusionment with the Christians she met. No one in the West seemed to take their religion at all seriously—and certainly not as seriously as Muslims in Zanzibar. "I found so few good examples among many Christians that I felt neither fish nor flesh . . . ," she lamented in one of many similar passages. "For how should I, as a Muslim, feel attracted to the new religion if people, who had been born and brought up in Christianity themselves, dealt so disdainfully with their religion?"

Salme's first Christmas approached with all its usual promise of good cheer. But the foggy and sunless days of a Hamburg winter, when the winds were often cutting and the temperatures severe, saddened the princess, and the holiday bustle only depressed her all the more. She felt like crying all the time, and when Heinrich asked her what she wanted for Christmas, she couldn't understand the question and replied that she already had everything she wanted.

On Christmas Eve, Heinrich and Salme drove to his parents' house. His younger brothers ran out to meet them and, laughing and whispering, escorted them inside. Don't look in the dining room! they commanded Salme. A short while later, a gong sounded and everyone ran in to see a lovely Christmas tree decorated with burning candles and sweets. Then the family led Salme to a table laden with gifts just for her. Most prominent among them was a long velvet coat trimmed with ermine from top to bottom. Salme was astonished—and repulsed. In Zanzibar, ermine was regarded as "cat's hide," and was worn by only the poorest of Africans.

Salme had been eagerly awaiting Christmas Eve—she had hoped to learn more about the "Occidental rites" at last. But the ermine-trimmed coat marked the beginning of what turned out to be a crushingly disappointing evening for her. No prayers were said and no religious ceremony was conducted, causing her opinion of Christians to plummet even more. "I was very disillusioned. . . . From that moment onwards it appeared so evident to me how superficial the concept of being a Christian is," she wrote.

One wonders how Heinrich's family responded to Salme's reaction to their most beloved of holidays. Her horrified astonishment at the sight of the costly coat and lack of enthusiasm throughout the evening must have been glaringly apparent. Young and newly arrived from Zanzibar, she was incapable of dissembling.

In the spring of 1868, Salme gave birth to a daughter, Antonie. A little over a year later, her son, Said, later known as Rudoph Said-Ruete, was born, and a year after that, her daughter Rosalie. With the births of her three children, the lonely Arabian princess felt more complete. She was a devoted mother and throughout her life would make many decisions based almost exclusively on the welfare of her children.

22
Alone

ON JULY 19, 1870, THE FRANCO-PRUSSIAN WAR BROKE OUT. FIGHT-
ing on the side of the Prussians were men from the North German Confederation, which included Hamburg, and the South German states of
Baden, Württemberg, and Bavaria. The war lasted less than a year and
when it was over, the Prussians were victorious—an outcome that led to
the final unification of the German Empire under King William I of
Prussia.

Salme marveled at the scale of the military operation—"You, on
your peaceful island, have no idea," she wrote home—at the patriotism
of the Germans, and at the enormous sacrifices that had been made by
both sides. She also felt overwhelmed by the Westerners' lust for power.
"European states all suffer more or less from a very severe illness,
namely jealousy," she wrote. "None of them grants the other anything,
and every state continuously endeavours to surpass the other at any
cost. . . . All try to invent the most frightful instruments of wholesale
murder."

Under such circumstances, Salme went on, in a questionable jump
of logic, Europe had no right to protest the institution of slavery in
Africa on the basis of humanitarian principles:

> For what does it mean if a negro state wages war against another one
> and robs it, in comparison with one single war in the North. . . .
> Why do they raise the alarm when we keep slaves, who are by far
> much better off than many people here. You know that we are by

no means all social democrats, yet I have often thought that it would be more suitable for Europeans to spend the uncounted millions on their own poor population, who are starving so much, especially in winter, rather than to spend them on the so-called 'liberation' of the negroes. . . . The contrast between rich and poor nowhere comes to light more than right here in the cold North, where such plenty and luxury are found on the one hand, but such heartrending poverty on the other.

One day not long after the Franco-Prussian War began, Salme lay in bed with a fever, ice packs on her head. Heinrich came home at four p.m. as usual, ate an early dinner, and then went to visit his father, who was ill in his summerhouse, just outside Hamburg. After he left, Salme fell into a heavy sleep. When she awoke, it was already dark. The nanny brought the children in to her to say good night and Salme remained in bed, dozing until about nine, her head full of dreams of Zanzibar. But then suddenly she jolted awake, seized with acute anxiety. The hour was growing late—where was Heinrich? He was always on time. Holding her breath, she listened to the whistles of the steamboats on the nearby Alster River. Otherwise, all was quiet.

Salme shivered . . . and waited. The clock struck ten . . . eleven . . . midnight. Heinrich still had not returned. A thousand disastrous scenarios flashed through her head. Something must have happened—Heinrich would never deliberately frighten her by coming home this late and not sending word. She wanted to run out into the streets to look for him, but forced herself to remain in bed.

Finally, the doorbell rang softly. "The Lord be praised! There he finally comes," Salme said to herself, and listened for her husband's footstep. A minute or two passed, but she heard nothing more. That was strange. Heinrich usually passed from room to room looking for her as soon as he entered the house.

Thoroughly frightened now, she jumped out of bed and ran down the hall, her long nightgown, still so foreign to her touch, flapping against her legs. Leaning over the banister, she called out—"Heinrich?"

No one answered.

A maid came rushing up the stairs.

"Where is the master, where is my husband, Anna, where is my husband?" Salme screamed.

A man's voice replied, "Reassure yourself, Madam; the master is still alive, but he is badly injured!"

Salme fainted.

When she came to, the man—a doctor—was hovering over her. He had just come from the hospital, where he had attended to her husband, he said. On his way home from visiting his father, Heinrich had jumped off a horse tram before it had completely stopped, and had fallen, to be dragged and then run over by the still-moving vehicle.

The doctor said nothing more about Heinrich's condition, but Salme could tell from his manner that it was serious, and demanded to go to the hospital immediately.

"No, Madam, that is impossible," the doctor replied. "So late at night you are not allowed into a hospital."

"Then I will go on foot!" Salme shouted.

Finally, reluctantly, the doctor agreed to take her to the hospital and they climbed into a carriage.

"Oh my God, what a drive!" Salme wrote years later in words so full of anguish that they could have been written that night. "Everything seemed to proceed so slowly, the horse, the carriage, even the cabman appeared drowsy to me."

But when they reached the hospital, the supervisor refused to let Salme in. She fell to her knees. "Oh, Mister Supervisor, please be merciful and let me go to my poor husband," she begged.

"It is not permitted. The sick may only be visited on certain days and hours," the supervisor said.

"How is this?" she cried. "Am I not permitted to see my own husband soon?"

Feeling as if she were about to go out of her mind, she began pacing up and down the corridor, wailing in KiSwahili. She would not go away until she saw her husband! They would have to carry her out before she did.

At last, the supervisor took pity. Salme could visit with Heinrich for fifteen minutes, if she promised to stay composed, he said. She agreed, but was forced to wait another long half-hour for a surgeon to dress Heinrich's wounds. While she waited, the supervisor, tears welling in his eyes, tried to comfort her—despite his reluctance to break hospital rules, he was a soft-hearted man.

Finally, Salme was allowed into a darkened sickroom. Shaking in every limb, she forced herself to approach the bed. She couldn't utter a word.

"*Bibi, roho jangu!*"—"Bibi, my soul, my life"—Heinrich said in a hoarse whisper. "You have come so late, be brave, my life, and don't cry like this."

"Does it hurt much?" was all she could say.

"Yes, very much."

"How did it happen?"

"*Amury ja mungu*"—"Owing to God's will."

Salme didn't dare say anything more. She could hardly make out Heinrich's face in the darkness, but she could hear how hard it was for him to talk. He took one of her hands in his. Unbeknownst to her, his other hand and arm were completely crushed.

A half hour later, the supervisor came to escort her out. Tomorrow, he said, you can stay all day. She embraced him.

Salme had to be half-carried back to the carriage and then into her house. She spent the rest of the night on her balcony—she couldn't bear to stay inside the stifling, airless house. The summer night was bitterly cold, but she wrapped herself in a heavy shawl and, lost in misery, watched as the stars spilling across the sky grew pale in the dawning light. Then she went inside and waited for her three young children, all still under age three, to wake up. At the sight of their innocent faces, she burst into tears.

At nine a.m. Salme took a carriage back to the hospital, where she was forced to wait a long hour until a surgeon arrived to change Heinrich's bandages. Standing outside the sickroom door as the doctor worked, she tried to prepare herself for whatever she might find within.

At last, she entered the room. Now that it was light, she could see that Heinrich looked terrible. A large wound ripped down the entire length of his torso and his head was wrapped in bandages. One of his ears was missing and his nose, chest, and one arm were severely crushed.

Trying not to show how shocked and frightened she felt, she sat down at the bedside. Surprisingly, Heinrich was in less pain now than he'd been the night before and didn't seem to know how badly he was injured. His mind was lucid and he talked about all sorts of things, including Zanzibar. For a few hours, Salme felt almost happy.

At about two p.m., however, Heinrich grew feverish, and then, toward evening, delirious. The doctors told Salme that it was time for her to go and, worried that they might revoke her visiting privileges, she obeyed. She longed to see her children anyway—though by the time she got home, they were asleep. Sitting by their beds, she stroked their heads. Without Heinrich, the house felt empty and desolate.

The next day, the hospital supervisor greeted Salme with a beaming face. Heinrich had slept well and wanted to eat. He was still free of fever and pain, and in good spirits. Salme felt encouraged and even asked if she could take her husband home.

But that evening, Heinrich took a turn for the worse, and the next day, he was very ill. His temperature had soared and he was again delirious. Nonetheless, he immediately recognized Salme as she walked in, and implored her to take him for a walk. Again and again he begged, adding in KiSwahili, "Wait a minute, Bibi, I am almost ready dressing." He tried to jump up; it took three orderlies to keep him down.

His crushed arm and leg had turned a deep blue. Inflammation had set in, which in those days meant a death knell. But no one informed Salme of that—"Whom did I have to prepare me gradually for what was coming?" she asked plaintively in her memoirs. "Nobody at all." She begged the doctors to let her stay the night, "But this was, alas, to no purpose, because clever doctors mostly have neither heart nor pity."

Leaving the hospital, Salme was stopped by an old gentleman whom she did not know. He asked about Heinrich and as she closed her carriage door, she saw big tears running down his cheeks. Somewhere inside her, she knew that it was the end.

That evening, the doctor who had first examined Heinrich came to see Salme, but he would not meet her eyes or answer any of her questions. Over and over again, she begged him to tell her the unvarnished truth until finally he blurted out, "Pull yourself together, Madam, there is no hope left."

That night, Salme sat still for many hours, and prayed. If there is truly no more hope left, God, she begged, please release Heinrich from suffering.

When Salme arrived at the hospital the next morning, her husband was already slipping away. Still, he recognized her as she came in and said, "*Heli gaeni, Bibi*"—"How are you, Bibi?" Then he lapsed into unconsciousness. He was conscious again for a short time at midday and, again recognizing her, asked for fresh cherries. But by the time they arrived, he had slipped away once more, and this time did not return. It would take many years before Salme was able to eat cherries again, and for decades, she distributed the first cherries of the season among the poor—a customary way of remembering departed loved ones in Islam.

Heinrich died at five-thirty p.m. on August 6, 1870.

For the first six months following Heinrich's death, Salme was completely lost. She felt indifferent toward everything, even her children, and lost her faith in God.

Half-crazed with grief, and suffering from severe headaches, she sometimes searched the house from top to bottom, calling out her husband's name, while an insidious voice whispered in her head: "Just go to the hospital to fetch your husband, for he is still alive. It cannot be true that he has left you forever in this foreign country, hurry over there, hurry over there!"

Salme's small son, Said, grieving for his father, called out for him all day long, breaking her heart. And when her oldest child, Antonie, only two and a half years old, noticed that her brother was upsetting their mother, she whispered to him to be quiet, breaking Salme's heart even more.

At night, the princess tried to find peace on her balcony. In nature, all was as it had been before. But the calm of the darkness, the rustling of the leaves, even the shining of the stars only disturbed her.

"The mere thought of having to live from now on with my children in a foreign country without my husband threatened to deprive me of the rest of my brains," she wrote. "In the whole of Germany, indeed in the whole of Europe, there was not a single soul upon whom I might have leaned and rested. . . ."

"Off, off, homewards!" cried her soul, but she fought against its siren song. Heinrich had wanted his children to grow up in Germany, and she wanted to honor his wishes.

During this difficult time, Salme learned that Majid had died—on

October 7, 1870, only two months after Heinrich. The news crushed her. Despite all that had occurred, Majid had been her favorite brother, her playmate, her defender, her friend.

Salme had written to Majid shortly after Heinrich's death, asking for permission to return to Zanzibar for a visit and for an allowance that she felt was due her. But Majid never replied, and it is quite possible that her letter didn't arrive until after his death.

Then just when Salme thought that things couldn't get any worse, they did. The import-export business between Hamburg and Zanzibar, still the core of Ruete & Co. business, fell apart, thanks to the economic repercussions of the Franco-Prussian War. Heavy losses were expected, and Heinrich's lawyers informed Salme that she would have to reduce her living expenses considerably. She would have to leave the villa that she and Heinrich had settled into together.

"Nowhere was there a ray of hope, neither inside nor outside my soul," she wrote.

The dismal winter days passed, foggy and gray, damp and cold. Salme dismissed her parlor maid, leaving her with just one general maid and a nanny; had the laundry done at home rather than sending it out; and cut back on grocery expenses as best she could. She felt anxious all the time, her financial worries exacerbated by her shaky grasp of arithmetic and by the fact that no one could tell her exactly how much money she had. Sometimes she felt so insecure about the dangers lurking outside that she locked herself and her children in her bedroom for hours on end.

But that winter did bring with it one bright spot: One day while Salme was attending to some business in town, she noticed a gathering of at least a hundred people. Crossing the street to get a better look, she saw that they were sailors from the *Ilmedjidi*, out of Zanzibar, which had just docked in Hamburg. Overwhelmed with emotion, she longed to go to them. But then she thought about how the Germans would stare, and what the German newspapers—always curious about her—would say, and held herself back. Quickly she caught a carriage and returned home.

Two weeks later, she was in her sitting room when the maid entered and said that there were twenty black men outside wishing to see her. Salme had them enter, and "hardly had we exchanged greetings in Arabic, when all of them fell to my feet and kissed the floor in deference, starting to cry heartily," she wrote. Salme started to cry too and, in one of her few truly democratic moments, she "saw only one thing in these people, namely that they were from Zanzibar."

Seemingly in one voice, the men exclaimed: "Praised be the Lord, our God, that we have found you again! *Oh Bibi tua.* How long we have been looking for you!"

Salme asked the men how they had found her, and they replied that they had asked about her as soon as they arrived, but nobody knew anything. Finally they met a tobacconist who had read about her in the papers and looked up her address.

Then the men asked, over and over again: "Bibi, how can you live in such a country? Please come back to us, all people yearn for you."

Sadly, Salme shook her head. "Not yet, not yet."

"But then when, Bibi?"

"When the children have grown older," she replied with a heavy heart, wondering if she would ever be able to return to Zanzibar.

Every day until the *Ilmedjidi* departed, the sailors were Salme's constant guests. They told her Zanzibar's latest news and gossip, and played with her children while regaling them with Swahili folktales. They preferred the baby Said to his sisters "naturally, because [Salme] had named him after [her] noble father," and liked to push his extraordinarily large pram—big enough to hold three children, Salme thought—around in the garden. Often a crowd of spectators gathered to watch the unusual scene.

Salme served the sailors coffee in big European cups—she didn't have enough small Arabic ones—which they called "tureens." When offered food, they always hesitated to accept it, asking, "does it contain pork?" just as she had done three years before.

As the days passed, many of the sailors pulled Salme aside to beg her to employ them as a nurse for her children. She fervently wished that she could, "but as is well known, wishing and being able are two quite different things, the simultaneous control of which is allotted to privileged mortals only," she wrote. When some of the crew threatened to desert their ship whether she voluntarily hired them or not, Salme felt obligated to notify their captain, and he retained them on board the day before the ship's departure.

A few years later, Salme was deeply saddened to learn that the *Ilmedjidi* had sunk at sea, probably during a storm. The whole crew had perished.

23

Changes

WITH HEINRICH'S DEATH, SALME'S POSITION IN HAMBURG SOCI-
ety devolved overnight from that of an exotic, mysterious princess married to a wealthy, well-respected businessman to that of a lonely and
needy widow with three small children to support. Many so-called
friends fell by the wayside and most of the once-dreaded invitations
dried up as Hamburg revealed its true, xenophobic colors. "I had now
taken a thorough dislike of the place of my former family happiness, the
more so because in many circles of that city on the sea I did not find as
much consideration as I thought I might have expected," wrote Salme.

Her financial situation was also deteriorating. After liquidating the
Ruete company in Zanzibar, Heinrich's agent—despite being one of his
oldest friends and the son of a prominent clergyman—embezzled most
of its funds. In addition, by Hamburg law, the remainder of Salme's inheritance had to be managed by two male "assistants." Unlike Muslim
women, German women of that era were not permitted to handle their
own financial affairs. Salme asked two gentlemen she knew to assist her
and they invested her money in Russian and American government securities, in Hungarian railway bonds, and in mortgages. One of the men
was a family doctor whom Salme trusted implicitly but who knew little
about finance, and the other, a well-known, business-savvy lawyer. The
lawyer therefore handled most of the transactions, and told his Omani
client little about what he was doing. Salme never knew exactly how
much was in her accounts and had to incessantly beg the lawyer to give
her household money. Often, she had next to nothing in her purse.

In the spring of 1871, less than a year after Heinrich's death, Salme and her children moved into simpler and cheaper accommodations. It was the first of many, many moves that the young family would be forced to make in the next decade or so.

"I experienced for the first time in my life the pungent feeling of beginning poverty," wrote the unhappy princess, a woman who just a short time before had had the whole world at her fingertips. How sad Heinrich would have been to see her like this, she often thought, as she struggled to do even the most mundane of tasks, such as lighting the morning fires and getting her children dressed and fed. Her headaches worsened, but her doctors, less than sympathetic, suggested only that she get more exercise.

No sooner had Salme settled her family into their new home than she began to think of moving again. Hamburg was an expensive city, and with Heinrich gone, she had nothing to keep her there. She had no real friends in the city, and Heinrich's family, whom she almost never mentioned in her memoirs or letters, do not appear to have been much help, either financially or emotionally. A surviving letter from her father-in-law does express his pleasure in being a grandfather and his surprise in Bibi's being "an able housewife" and "amiable daughter-in-law," but little else is known about their relationship. The senior Herr Ruete may not have been in a position to support the princess, and other members of the Ruete family may have shunned her.

Salme spoke to various acquaintances about her desire to leave Hamburg, only to be met with blank stares. No one had any suggestions as to where she should go, and some querulously, self-righteously, told her that other people with far less money than she managed to get by— why couldn't she? Insightfully, Salme commented: "Most people, though having taken the term 'freedom' as a principle, are little inclined to make the same allowance to others. Very rare is the understanding that people must be dealt with individually and not simply—as is the usual practice here—in keeping with accepted norms."

Finally, a woman suggested that Salme move to Darmstadt in central Germany, where it was warmer and somewhat less expensive, she said. So one morning, Salme left for Darmstadt by train, traveling in a bare, uncomfortable third-class carriage for the first time in her life. Tears slipped down her face as the train pulled out of the station, and she fingered her new pince-nez, set in gold. A friend had criticized her for buying it, saying that she could no longer afford such extravagances. "Lord, God, protect me from my friends," Salme sighed.

The next morning, Salme began searching for suitable accommodations, only to be met with even ruder stares and more invasive questions than she had encountered in Hamburg. Where was she from? Where was her husband? Did she have references? And why did she want to move to Darmstadt anyway?

Discouraged, she returned to Hamburg. How different Germany was from Zanzibar, she thought. On her beloved island, every European, whether "an honourable person or a swindler," was warmly welcomed. Sadly, she remembered an old Zanzibari proverb: "He who does not know you, cannot value you."

Not long thereafter, and still intent upon moving, Salme remembered meeting a pleasant woman who lived in Dresden, the capital of the kingdom of Saxony, and wrote her a letter. The woman responded with a friendly letter of her own, and Salme went to visit her. She took an immediate liking to the city, situated in a lush green valley on both sides of the River Elbe. Filled with baroque-style architecture, museums, gardens, and parks, Dresden offered a moderate climate and a spacious, relaxed feel that reminded her a little of Zanzibar.

With the help of her friend, Salme soon found a place to live. It was just one floor with two rooms that she could rent out—she would have to live like a "bird in a cage"—but it was more affordable than anything she'd found in Hamburg.

A few weeks later Salme and her children moved. They were just beginning to settle in when their landlady invited her for coffee. Salme didn't want to go—she still had so much to do—but good manners prevailed. Entering the lady's home, she was astonished to find herself alone with her landlord. That in itself made her very uncomfortable, but then she learned that the invitation wasn't social; the couple wanted her rent money up front, an insult as far as Salme, who had never dealt with the business world before, was concerned.

She paid that first month's rent with almost all the ready money she had, and when her maid asked her for grocery money a few days later, was embarrassed to discover that she had nothing left. Mumbling an excuse, she escaped to her room, her heart pounding. With trembling hands, she opened her jewelry chest. She would have to sell some of her gems. She had anticipated this day, but the reality still came as a shock.

Feeling as if she were committing a crime, she chose a pair of earrings and went to a jeweler, a fashionably dressed gentleman, "looking somewhat Jewish." "Among us it is said that the cow-worshippers, the Banyans, are the worst cut-throats. This may be the case, but they are not the only ones, for such people are found everywhere and certainly not least in Europe," she wrote, again revealing her prejudices.

In the end, Salme sold the earrings for far less than they were worth. For the rest of the day, she could neither eat nor drink.

Many months later, Salme's landlady again invited her for coffee. She half-refused the invitation. But her landlady implored her. The proposed visit had been set up by a member of high society, the Baroness von Tettau, who badly wanted to meet the princess.

On the appointed day, Salme arrived at her landlady's home, to find the baroness already there. A warm and grandmotherly woman, she expressed no "vulgar curiosity" about the princess, and Salme, to her great surprise, took to her right away. The afternoon passed like a delicious dream—"one of the happiest hours of my life in Germany," Salme wrote. Some weeks later, the baroness visited the princess in her home, where she took great delight in meeting her children. Leaving that day, she said to Salme, "My dear, I think we understand each other." "Yes, indeed," the princess later wrote. She had found a true friend in Germany at last.

Salme considered the baroness to be the first truly religious Christian woman she had met, as well as the kindest and most understanding. Despite their difference in age, she felt she could tell the older woman everything. No matter what, the baroness always knew what to say and how to comfort her. Often, Salme would sit next to her on a footstool and the older woman would caress her head. "You appear to me as a transplanted palm tree, which, instead of being sheltered in a warm and well-kept greenhouse, must freeze outside in all weathers," the baroness said to her once. "But do not lose heart, my dearest, and be assured that the Lord will not leave you in the lurch."

Meanwhile, Salme's health was still troubling her. She was constantly nervous and irritable, and everyone had to wear slippers in the house so as not to disturb her. Finally, her doctor suggested that she get away for a while. At first Salme rejected the idea as being too expensive, but then she had a stroke of good luck. She succeeded in subletting her apartment, and she and her children traveled to a resort area in Switzerland.

While there, Salme met her second true German friend—Professor Georg Schweinfurth. He came to call on her one day, dressed in a tailcoat, top hat, white necktie, and white gloves. Ordinarily he loathed such formalities, he later admitted, but had felt that they were the appropriate attire for meeting a princess.

The professor, who was also from Dresden, had come to Switzerland specifically to meet Salme. He had a six-hundred-year-old globe with markings in Kufic script—the oldest calligraphic form of Arabic, distinguished by straight lines and angles—which he could not read. Could she help? Salme was not very familiar with Kufic script, but said that she would be happy to do what she could. Thereafter, the two met on a regular basis, with the professor teaching her some basic astronomy along the way. When they were finished, the professor suggested Salme give him Arabic lessons in return for scientific ones. And so they did, twice a week.

At first, Salme did not accept much of what the professor taught her. She questioned everything he said, demanding proof, but he was an excellent teacher who enjoyed her challenges and often they spent far more time discussing science than they did Arabic. When Salme protested that that was not fair to the professor, he replied, "No, no, your questions interest me too much." He also helped the princess with her German, and encouraged her to attend scientific lectures now and again, which she greatly enjoyed. Like her father before her, Salme had an inquiring mind, and perhaps if circumstances had been different, would have pursued her interests more seriously.

Throughout this period, Salme's financial situation continued to worsen, and she began to suspect her lawyer of being incompetent at best and unscrupulous at worst. On one of her visits to Hamburg, when she asked him where he kept her records, his reply was a vague: "It depends, Madam; sometimes I keep them with my banker, sometimes in my office." Then friends in Hamburg wrote to Salme to say that her lawyer's precarious financial position was well-known there and that he had recently fallen extremely ill. If he was to die, Salme would be reduced to begging.

The princess appealed to Professor Schweinfurth for help, and he advised her to contact the Royal Saxon Law Court. Now that she was living in Dresden rather than Hamburg, different laws applied, and the court could take over the trusteeship of her capital. However, the court oversaw only minors' accounts. Was Salme prepared to transfer most of her inheritance to her children? Absolutely! she replied—her children's future was her main concern.

As it turned out, Salme's worries about her finances were well founded. When the court requested the bonds that she owned from her lawyer, he could not produce them right away—meaning that he had probably sold them. It took him weeks to "find" them, and when they arrived, they included a considerable number of Hungarian Northeastern Railway bonds, which the Saxon court refused to accept because they were too insecure.

Salme took the bonds as her portion of the inheritance and deposited them in a bank. But only a short time later, when she went to the bank to withdraw interest from the bonds, she was told that they had depreciated greatly in value and that the railway's bankruptcy was near. Sell as soon as possible, the bank advised. Salme went home, spent a sleepless night, and sold the bonds the next day, at a loss of 30 percent. "Be just glad that you are the happy owner of a plantation, and avoid having to do with government or industry securities!" she wrote home.

After Seyyid Majid's death, Salme had written her brother Seyyid Barghash, the new ruler of Zanzibar, to renew her request for an allowance and permission to visit the island. Given the important role that she'd played in Barghash's attempted coup, she felt certain of success. But she was sorely disappointed—Barghash refused her.

In her memoirs, Salme ascribed Barghash's "obduracy" to his "spiteful resentment" of her friendship with Majid following the ineffectual revolt. But the truth was more complicated. Salme had rejected Islam, which under Muslim law is punishable by death. She had also deeply humiliated the royal Al Busaidi family. And, perhaps most important,

Barghash could remain in power only through the support of his subjects—even if he had wanted to pardon his sister, it would have been political suicide.

With her request for an allowance turned down, Salme took a different tack: she pressed her brother for inheritances that she claimed were hers. A number of her relatives had died since her flight from Zanzibar and ordinarily, under Muslim law, she would have been entitled to a portion of their estates. However, since she was no longer a Muslim, the law no longer applied to her—a technicality that she apparently hoped her brother would overlook.

But again, Barghash turned her down. Salme was devastated, and deeply angry. She had committed no crime. Her brother must have a heart. She would change his mind. After all, he owed her. . . .

And so the princess began what would be a sixteen-year-long campaign to claim her disputed inheritances. As a princess, she had access to high levels of German society, who in turn had access to high levels of English society, and she began using every contact she could think of to further her cause.

Many she approached were quite eager to help. Salme was a Christian convert and a victim of Muslim intolerance. She had suffered disastrous bad luck. Her case had great appeal.

Salme's first step was to travel to Berlin in 1872 to see Count von Bülow, Germany's secretary of state for foreign affairs. The count may have suggested that she become a citizen of the newly formed German Empire in order to further her case, because she did so shortly thereafter. She also wrote to Germany's first chancellor, Otto von Bismarck, which led to the German consul in Zanzibar speaking to Barghash on her behalf—several times. But each time, Barghash refused to discuss the matter.

In the spring of 1873, and again in 1875, Salme's good friend the Baroness von Tettau used her connections to contact the Crown Princess Victoria, Queen Victoria's eldest daughter and the consort of the German crown prince, on Salme's behalf. In the summer of 1873, the baroness used other connections to contact Ismail Pasha, the khedive of Egypt, who had good relations with Seyyid Barghash. Neither avenue was successful.

In 1874, the German foreign affairs office took Salme's case a step further by asking the British government to get involved. Subsequently, the British foreign office sent a letter to the acting British consul in Zanzibar, instructing him to give unofficial support to Salme's petition. But again, the plea led nowhere.

In early 1875, with the help of various German aristocrats, Salme convinced Ernst II, duke of Saxe-Coburg-Gotha, of the validity of her case, and he sent a courteous letter directly to Seyyid Barghash. It was a tactical error. The sultan was extremely offended by the unofficial communiqué and complained to both German and British officials. Chancellor Bismarck was also annoyed with the duke.

Then in the spring of 1875, Salme was astonished to read in the newspapers that her brother was planning to visit London that June. The idea was extraordinary—no Omani ruler had ever visited the West before. She toyed with the idea of trying to meet him, but initially dismissed it. He had made his position toward her painfully clear. But friends convinced her that she had to go—this could finally be her chance—and Count von Bülow assured her that the German ambassador to England, Count Munster, would be there to support her in her claim.

Salme spent the next two months studying the English language, and arrived in London a week before her brother was expected. She wanted to familiarize herself with the city before he arrived and to call on Count Munster. He received her graciously and promised to help in any way he could.

On Salme's fifth day in London, she was relaxing in the drawing room of her hotel suite when she received a calling card from Colonel R. L. Playfair and his wife. A member of Parliament, the colonel had been the English consul to Zanzibar in 1863–65, shortly before Salme left the island. The Playfairs had come to invite her to stay with them—an invitation she gratefully accepted. She knew almost no one in London and finding her way around the city had been a challenge.

A day or two later, Sir Bartle Frere came to call. The former governor of Bombay and a member of the Council of India, a government advisory body, he had visited Zanzibar three years earlier to try to negotiate a new anti–slave trade treaty with Barghash. He was also a member of the highest class of the Order of the Star of India, a chivalric order founded by Queen Victoria to reward outstanding service in India. Salme was probably unaware of Frere's knighthood, but if she had known about it, she would have laughed bitterly. To her mind, Frere was anything but chivalrous. It was on the day she met him, she later wrote, that "my most ardent hope and the future of my children were buried. An indescribable discomfort befell me when I caught sight of the great diplomat, who had Zanzibar and my brother so to speak in his pocket."

An imposing man with piercing eyes, a lean face, and long drooping mustache, Sir Bartle Frere began by asking Salme what she was doing in London—even though, she wrote, he "seemed fully informed in this respect." She answered him directly: she was seeking reconciliation with her family. Frere then asked: what is closer to your heart, reconciliation with your family or your children's future? The question shocked the princess, but she gave the only possible answer: her children, of course.

Sir Bartle Frere then said that the British government was not inclined to act as a mediator between her and her brother. The sultan was a guest in their country and must be spared all unnecessary annoyances. However, if the princess promised to keep away from Barghash, the English government would see to it that her children were provided for. Frere's proposal distressed and angered Salme, but not knowing what Barghash's reaction to her presence would be, or what the British might do to prevent her from meeting him, she accepted the diplomat's terms.

A disastrous mistake, as it turned out, at least according to Salme, who gave the following, and only known existing, account of the subsequent turn of events: During her brother's stay in London, she assiduously avoided him, and after he left, she drew up—at Frere's request—a detailed memorandum of her case with the help of English-speaking friends. The document was sent to the governor of Bombay for approval. Salme returned to Germany and several months passed. Finally, an envelope from London arrived. Enclosed was a copy of a letter that the British government had sent to Count Munster. The letter was a short rejection of her case. The reason? Her husband had been German and she was a German citizen—it was up to Germany, not Britain, to represent her.

"Ridiculous!" a distraught Salme railed in her memoirs. Sir Bartle Frere had known full well that she was German; he had deceived her into keeping away from her brother, to save his government trouble and embarrassment. "Inexperienced as I was, it could not possibly occur to me that people might be capable of depriving even helpless widows of their entire hopes in such a disgraceful and deceitful way," she wrote.

"Whether such behaviour towards an unhappy woman is worthy of a power like England, I leave to be judged by anyone who thinks rightly."

John Gray, a well-known twentieth-century British historian who wrote extensively about East Africa, believed that Salme's account of these events should be taken with "very considerable reserve." Sir Bartle Frere had an excellent reputation; he was a man of character. However, it seems quite unlikely that Salme would have made up the entire sequence of events. Her memoirs may not always be entirely accurate, but she had gone to London on a specific mission and something derailed it.

Meanwhile, Seyyid Barghash's visit to England had gone smoothly. He had traveled from Zanzibar on board the steamship *Canara*, owned by the East India Navigation Company. It was the most modern of journeys—the age of ocean-going steamships had just arrived—and the *Canara* passed from the Red Sea into the Mediterranean through the Suez Canal, completed six years before.

The *Canara* arrived at Gravesend, a port on the Thames outside London, on a sunny Wednesday morning at about nine a.m. The scarlet Omani flag flew from its mast, and sailors and Arab dignitaries crowded its decks.

The royal party debarked—elegant *dishdashas* blowing in a gathering wind—to board another, much smaller steamer that conveyed them to the steps of Westminster Palace. Waiting for them there were Salme's new nemesis, Sir Bartle Frere, and Britain's undersecretary of state for foreign affairs. Members of Parliament crowded the palace's terrace and throngs of curious citizens watched from Westminster Bridge. A band played "God Save the Queen" as rain began to fall.

Covering the event was *The Illustrated London News*, whose editors wrote, in a rather superior tone: "It is perhaps difficult to gauge, even in imagination, the importance of [Zanzibar] as it will one day be. As a gateway into the interior of Africa for the trade both of the United Kingdom and India it cannot but hereafter become a rich and thriving territory. [Seyyid Barghash] is most welcome here. . . . He should gain from his visit to this land an enlightened perception of the superior advantages both to the ruler and the ruled which would follow upon the extinction of a barbarous and cruel traffic in flesh and blood."

Traveling with Seyyid Barghash were various members of the Arab elite, an Indian merchant who represented Zanzibar's commercial interests, a secretary, a cashier, four cooks, two barbers, and John Kirk, the British consul to Zanzibar. Then in his mid-forties, Kirk was a Scottish physician and naturalist who'd accompanied the missionary-turned-explorer Dr. David Livingstone on his Zambezi Expedition into Central Africa over a dozen years before. A determined opponent of the slave trade, Kirk had been instrumental in negotiating an important 1873 anti–slave trade treaty with Barghash, and while in London, would help to convince him to sign a supplementary slave trade ban.

The next morning at ten a.m., two open landaus, each pulled by four horses, rolled up to the Alexander Hotel in Hyde Park, where the Zanzibaris were staying. The landaus had come to take them to Ascot to watch the Gold Cup, and as the carriages drove off, cheers rose from an onlooking crowd.

All was not quite as it seemed, however. The landaus were but ordinary carriages, and when Barghash and Kirk arrived at the races, they were not invited into the royal enclosure. The queen was not happy with the sultan—she considered his treatment of his sister to be a disgrace. Barghash noticed the slight immediately and unaware of its cause, or of Salme's presence in London, asked Kirk to find out if there was a boat traveling back to Zanzibar the next day.

Kirk soothed the ruler, and then went off to pace and fret. Two military-looking men approached and one began to harangue him about the sorry way in which the sultan was treating his sister. "I don't know what business you have to speak like that to me, Sir!" shot back Kirk and turned away. Afterward, he found out that the two men were the duke of Cambridge and Count Gleichen; at a reception for Barghash at the duke's residence later in the week, Kirk was asked to wait outside.

The matter of Salme's claim did not end there, either. A few days later, the British foreign office instructed Kirk to get in touch with Count Munster, the German ambassador, who handed him a letter. Addressed to Barghash, it was from Salme, who apparently did not feel that her agreement with Sir Bartle Frere not to contact her brother extended to the written word. Reading the letter, Kirk told the count that he could not show it to Barghash, as "it was couched in language that would only induce its rejection, and contained a definite demand as of right for a large sum of money." The count asked Salme to replace the letter with a more appropriate one, which she did, but Kirk did not give it to the Omani ruler until they were back in Zanzibar.

Seyyid Barghash stayed in England for six weeks. While there, he traveled to Birmingham, Liverpool, Manchester, and Brighton; visited the Woolwich Arsenal, the General Post Office, the Aquarium, the Crystal Palace, and the British Museum; attended many musical and theater performances, including *Bluebeard* and *Lohengrin;* and was a guest of honor at a wide variety of social events, including dinners, balls, and garden parties. The general public took a liking to him, and he in turn liked the British people. "How can I help it?" he exclaimed in one speech he delivered while in England. "It is the fault of the English people. You all welcome me. You all tell me I have done something for the abolition of the Slave Trade and you hope I shall do more. What can I say but thank you, thank you, thank you?"

Salme may have agreed to keep away from Barghash during his visit, but her friends had made no such promise. Her host Colonel Playfair and others continued to appeal to Kirk on her behalf until at last, worn down by their requests, he agreed to speak to the sultan. After apologizing for mentioning a female relative by name—considered to be extremely rude behavior by traditional Muslims—Kirk brought up her case. The sultan not only declined to discuss the matter, but told Kirk never to mention the subject again if he wanted to remain his friend.

In late 1876, nearly a year and a half after Barghash's visit to London, the German consul in Zanzibar approached the sultan with a message from Germany's foreign office: Salme was living in very reduced circumstances and was in desperate need of help. Barghash did not respond.

At this final refusal, an exhausted Salme decided to give up. Over the past six years, she had pulled every string she could think of, hounded every important personage she knew, to the point of embarrassment. She had no hope left—for the moment at least.

Dresden was a less expensive city than Hamburg had been, but Salme was still having a hard time making ends meet. In addition, her children were growing older, and she did not have the means to send them to the city's private schools.

And so Salme decided to move again, this time to the much smaller
city of Rudolstadt, where both daily life and private schools would be
less expensive. Beautifully situated in a wooded valley near the
Thuringian Forest in central Germany, Rudolstadt hugged the banks of
the lazy, winding River Saale, a tributary of the Elbe. On a small hill
above the town rose a glistening baroque palace, the Castle Heidecks-
burg, the ancestral home of the ruling Schwarzburg-Rudolstadt princes.

Arriving in Rudolstadt in the spring of 1877, Salme noticed a small
gathering of people on the railroad platform. Later, she asked an acquaintance if something important had been taking place, and the
woman laughed. The gathering had been for Salme. Her arrival had
been announced in the local paper. Everyone must be very disappointed, Salme thought. She and her children had traveled third class
and she had been dressed in an "anything-but-modern" Scottish over-
coat.

Local custom demanded that Salme call on the dignitaries of the
town, and she started with a visit to the princely family, where she was
warmly received by Princess Adolph, mother-in-law of the grand duke
of Mecklenburg-Schwerin, himself a nephew of the German emperor.
A high-ranking male in the Rudolstadt castle apparently also took a
fancy to the princess. Her friend the Baroness von Tettau described
him as a man "much talked-of, who in his appearance bears the expression of great materialism." But Salme herself mentioned no such person
in either her memoirs or letters, and seems to have closed off that part
of her life.

The following winter, illness stalked Salme's house. Her nine-year-
old son, Said, caught a severe case of diphtheria in November and almost died. The doctor had already given up on him when he suddenly
spit up blood, opened his eyes, and recognized his mother for the first
time in days.

Said was just beginning to recover when Salme, worn down from
nursing him, became sick with what must have been malaria, in her
bloodstream from a mosquito bite years before. She took quinine for
three months to overcome her shivers and regain her strength. And
then, her two daughters caught scarlet fever. Said had to be isolated
from them, and was taken to a teacher's boardinghouse to live.

For the next six weeks, Salme was completely alone with her two sick children. Fear of contamination kept all others away. Her only visitors were the doctor and an old seamstress who came now and then to assist in the kitchen. "Our fatalism is often jeered at here," a dejected Salme wrote home, "but I do not know whether it is not more this alarm here which should be pitied. . . . I was abandoned by all."

Now Salme began to seriously consider teaching Arabic as a way to make ends meet. The idea had occurred to her before, but she had resisted it. The very thought of working for a living felt degrading, no matter the Western attitude. But her children were continuing to grow, and she needed money more now than ever before. She could see no other way out.

There would be no demand for an Arabic teacher in a small town like Rudolstadt. Berlin was her best bet. And so, in the spring of 1878, after living in Rudolstadt only one year, Salme and her children moved yet again.

Salme liked Berlin, even more than Dresden. She felt welcomed by the people she met, and found her first student through an acquaintance. Later, other pupils followed, and she talked to them about a wide variety of subjects, including African culture, flora and fauna, and Islam. But the topic that interested them the most was slavery. "The amazement did not come to an end . . . ," wrote Salme, before lapsing into her usual defense of the institution. "As if our field- and house-slaves had to exert themselves even half as much as the so-called free people in the mines and factories of Europe." Even after living over a decade in the West, Salme still did not grasp the importance of being one's own master.

Said had missed a great deal of school due to health problems, and Salme could not help him with his studies. She began to consider the unthinkable—sending him to a military academy, where he could receive a good education for little money. Friends had recommended the idea, and although Salme had been resisting it, the memory of her husband once again intervened.

Writing to the "noble and affable Emperor William I," she requested that Said, now thirteen years old, be admitted into the cadet corps on scholarship. She was half hoping the emperor would turn her down, but only three weeks later, she received an answer. Said was to report to the military academy in Bensberg on October 1, 1882. It was already September.

On the appointed day, mother and son traveled to Bensberg in silence, their hearts heavy. A friendly soldier met them at the gate of the military academy and showed them around, but Salme barely noticed anything. She never forgot the last look Said gave her. "I read so much grief in it. . . . My child appeared to me as a sacrifice that I had deposited on the altar of loyalty—to my deceased husband, his father," she wrote. "Oh, how often had I wished to be able to live far away from the complicated European outlook on life, where only on rare occasions does the individual person find the possibility to manifest himself. Everything here is stereotyped, the individual is nothing but a number amidst millions."

Salme may not have understood the importance of being one's own master, but she did understand the concept of freedom.

24

Tippu Tip

FOLLOWING THE DEATH OF SEYYID SAID IN 1856, THE SLAVE trade in Zanzibar had continued to flourish. Slaves were still being imported to work the island's many clove plantations and to be smuggled farther north. One historian estimates that between 1859 and 1872, when the Indian Ocean slave trade was at its height, the flow of slaves from East Africa north each year was twenty to twenty-five thousand—a figure that rivaled the numbers shipped from West Africa to the Americas at the height of the Middle Passage.

The most remarkable of Zanzibar's slave and ivory traders, in business from the mid-1850s to the late 1880s, was Hamed bin Muhammad bin Juma bin Rajad al-Murjebi, better known as Tippu Tip. Unlike most Arab traders, who had little political power, Tippu Tip ruled over an extensive personal empire half the size of Western Europe in the Manyeuma region, now part of the Democratic Republic of Congo. During his thirty-odd years as a trader, he procured an astonishing amount of ivory—carrying back an unheard-of two thousand tusks on one extraordinary trip—and captured a prodigious number of slaves, depopulating parts of East and Central Africa. He also befriended many Westerners, most of whom sang his praises despite their abhorrence of his profession, and in 1887, King Leopold II of Belgium appointed him governor of the Congo Free State. In 1890, Tippu Tip retired to

Zanzibar, where he owned a reputed ten thousand slaves and seven plantations and, in his final years, wrote his autobiography.

Six feet tall, muscular, and imposing if not handsome, Tippu Tip was a courteous, well-bred, and intelligent man whose demeanor belied his profession. A forceful leader and astute businessman, he was always impeccably dressed, usually in a spotless white *dishdasha* with a silk sash and gold-filigreed *khanjar* at his waist. He considered himself to be a full-blooded Arab, though like many other so-called Arab slave traders, he looked more African than Arab, thanks to a great-great-grandmother on his father's side. His nickname probably came about because of the twitching of his eyelids, which was very apparent, though he attributed the name to the sound that his men's guns made when they were capturing slaves or wreaking revenge on a hostile village.

Bold and brave, Tippu Tip took chances that few other traders did, such as venturing into unknown, cannibal-inhabited territories, and though he was often cruel, he was seldom as wantonly brutal as many of his fellow slavers. A touch of mockery in his manner and language seemed to add to rather than detract from his appeal.

Upon meeting Tippu Tip for the first time, in the Congo in 1876, the Welsh-American journalist-turned-explorer Henry Morton Stanley wrote: "He was a tall, black-bearded man, of negroid complexion, in the prime of life, straight, and quick in his movements, a picture of energy and strength. He had a fine intelligent face, with a nervous twitching of the eyes, and gleaming white and perfectly formed teeth. . . . With the air of a well-bred Arab, and almost courtier-like in his manner, he welcomed me. . . . After regarding him for a few minutes, I came to the conclusion that this Arab was a remarkable man—the most remarkable man I had met among Arabs, Wa-Swahili, and half-castes of Africa."

Tippu Tip was born in Zanzibar around 1840, a few years before Salme. His father was Muhammad bin Juma, a prosperous ivory and slave trader, and his mother was Bint Habib bin Bushir, a full-blooded Arab from an upper-class family. At the time of his son's birth, Muhammad was away in Tabora in East-Central Africa—where he had a second home and second wife—and he did not see his firstborn until the child was a year old.

Tippu Tip and his mother lived on Kwarara, her family's coconut *shamba*, just outside Stone Town. The plantation teemed with children of all ages, and when Tippu Tip was six, he began to study the Quran under the tutelage of a religious teacher. He also helped out in the fields . . . and daydreamed—of joining his father, of leading great caravans, of fighting off huge armies, and of returning home a wealthy man.

When Tippu Tip was in his early teens, his uncle Bushiri bin Hamid invited him and his half brother Muhammad to accompany him on a short copal-trading trip to the coast. That expedition led to others, during which the boys watched and learned. Their dhows were sometimes stopped by British anti–slave trade cruisers, and the boys observed how their uncle deftly deflected any questions that were asked about the newly captured slaves who were sometimes on board. The boys also rescued an occasional escaped slave clinging to a piece of wood in the water—only to sell him or her when they returned to Zanzibar—and poked at other floating bodies with harpoons to see if they were still alive.

When Tippu Tip was eighteen, his father returned to Zanzibar on one of his periodic trading trips. As usual upon seeing his father, Tippu Tip begged to go to Africa with him, and this time, to the boy's great surprise, his father agreed. He assigned his son to travel behind him in a second caravan that left Zanzibar a few weeks after his.

The boy's journey lasted three months, covering five hundred miles, and he walked the whole way. He was not accustomed to walking such great distances—there were no great distances in Zanzibar—and at first, he found the going very difficult. But he was too proud to complain and even when the caravan stopped for the night, refused to collapse. Instead, he supervised the setting up of the camps, thereby both gaining a reputation for endurance and establishing a pattern that he would continue his entire life. Later, as a wealthy and powerful ruler, he liked to say that he always walked to show that in the eyes of God, he was still only a humble trader.

Tippu Tip's caravan stopped to regroup in Tabora, the Arab outpost where Burton and Speke had spent much time. Weeks passed, with painful slowness as far as Tippu Tip was concerned. But then, at last, the day that he had been waiting for since childhood arrived. Tabora teemed with activity that morning as he and his father oversaw the final preparations for their departure—dividing loads among porters, tying bundles on donkeys, and making sure that all of their guards were present and armed. Then finally the caravan started off on the first leg of a three-hundred-mile journey that would take them to Ugangi, an Arab outpost northeast of Lake Nyasa.

It was a peaceful and very successful trip, with father and son returning to Zanzibar ahead of schedule to sell their ivory and "other goods" for a handsome profit. Throughout his career, Tippu Tip never referred to his captives as slaves—they were always "other goods." The Africans weren't people. They were commodities.

At the slave market, Tippu Tip's father sold most of their captives in cages, a practice that his son would continue. For major traders who trafficked in hundreds of slaves at a time, it was the only efficient way. Each twenty-foot-square cage held about 150 people, and getting the right mix of men, women, and children in a cage was critical to making a good profit.

A few especially handsome young girls and boys were separated out from the cages, to be sold individually. The girls were destined to become concubines, and the boy, eunuchs—if they survived the surgery. As elsewhere in the Islamic world, many boys died on the operating table. Others died crawling in the streets after surgery. Tippu Tip's father tried to choose boys who had no parents, for he hated the crying that ensued when the children were separated from their mothers and fathers.

Whether Tippu Tip ever felt much sympathy for the Africans he captured is hard to tell, but it seems likely that he never seriously questioned the morality of what he was doing. He was a businessman after all—and he was saving the Africans' souls. As he explained to one critic: "My slaves don't want to leave me. They are too content with their lives. . . . There is no lack of dignity among slaves that leave the cruel tyranny of their African master for the enlightened tutelage of the Arab whose religion dictates benevolence and justice."

Tippu Tip's next expedition took him into Central Africa, where he was to spend much of the rest of his life. Father and son traveled first to

Ujiji, the Arab outpost on Lake Tanganyika. But the price of ivory in Ujiji was quite high, and the people there advised them to keep heading west to Urua, in Manyeuma country on the western side of the lake, then all but unknown territory to the Arabs. Tippu Tip's father was not interested. He had duties to attend to back in Tabora, and he missed his creature comforts. He advised his son to make the trip without him, under the supervision of an older, more experienced Swahili man.

But Tippu Tip would have none of that. He would go as the leader of the expedition, or not at all. "If you want to trust your wares to this Swahili, and I am to be under him, it is better I should go back with you," he said arrogantly, paying no attention to the fact that he himself was Swahili. His father argued with him, but Tippu Tip held his ground and said that should he fail in his self-appointed task, his father need not trust him to trade for him ever again. Reluctantly, his father finally agreed, and Tippu Tip and his party, including about twenty other Arabs and a retinue of slaves and porters, set off across the lake in dugout canoes.

Weeks later, the exhausted caravan arrived at Urua, where they did indeed find many tusks available for trade. Tippu Tip's companions coveted the larger tusks, which were sent to Europe and America, where they were used to make such things as billiard balls and piano keys. The small ones were sent to India, to make less expensive bangles and ornaments. But during his last stay in Zanzibar, Tippu Tip had noticed that there was a glut of large tusks on the market, and so snapped up the small tusks instead. His gamble paid off. Once back in Zanzibar, he sold the ivory for a record $55 per *frasila*, earning a handsome profit. His reputation was made.

For the next few years, Tippu Tip remained in Zanzibar, trading for his father and conducting a few small trading trips of his own to the coast. He did not yet have the credit he needed for a longer expedition, which had to be underwritten by one or more of the island's Banyan banker-merchants.

Staying in Zanzibar allowed Tippu Tip to spend time with his first wife, Bint Salum, a full-blooded Omani Arab, whom he'd barely seen since their wedding. Bint Salum was the mother of his oldest child; arrangements for their marriage had been made before his first trip into the interior. Like his father, Tippu Tip would ultimately live most of his life apart from his first wife and acquire innumerable concubines, but it was important that his first wife be Arab and that his first son be born to an Arab mother.

A physically fit man who never smoked or drank and always observed his religious duties, Tippu Tip reportedly visited his concubines twice a day. However, women were never more than a secondary interest for him. His first love was the hunt.

By 1867, the year that Salme arrived in Germany, Tippu Tip had at last accrued enough credit to finance an expedition into the interior, although he still had to use his wife's plantation as collateral against the $30,000 worth of goods he needed to buy. Assembling his caravan on the mainland, he and his followers marched inland. Lake Tanganyika was their destination. A short distance in, they stopped to rest for two days, and Tippu Tip paid his seven hundred porters six days' advance rations. The men then scattered into the surrounding villages, as was the custom.

When it came time to leave, the drums sounded to call the porters back. But no one returned; they had realized that Tippu Tip did not intend to follow the usual route into the interior, but was instead heading south, into unknown territory. There was also famine in the land.

Many other traders would have turned back, but a furious Tippu Tip—"I lost my temper," he later said—took eighty of his remaining men and marched from one village to the next, plundering, burning, and capturing men as he went. At the end of five days, he had eight hundred prisoner-porters—and a new nickname, "The Leopard," because "the leopard attacks indiscriminately, here and there."

The caravan then traveled to Urori, where they found good trading conditions, with ten to fifteen pieces of cloth buying a *frasila* of ivory. But Tippu Tip heard rumor of an even richer country farther west and, leaving one man behind to continue trading, pushed on to Itawa, west of Lake Tanganyika. The ruler there, Sultan Nsama, was said to be a brutal, bloodthirsty tyrant, and everyone the caravan met along the way advised them to turn back. But Tippu Tip paid no heed—the siren of ivory called.

Crossing a large river and entering Itawa country, Tippu Tip and his followers immediately saw its wealth: it was filled with great plantations, populous towns, and haughty people, who acknowledged them with a thinly veiled hostility. Disconcerted, but far from intimidated, the intruders marched on, traveling for six days until they reached a mountain. At its foot stood Sultan Nsama's capital, fortified with stockades, thorn hedges and ditches. The men pitched their camp outside town and sent messengers bearing gifts and messages of peace to the sultan. But before the emissaries could reach the town's gates, they were showered with arrows.

The next day, Sultan Nsama apparently had a change of heart, for he summoned the traders to come see him—and bring presents. Tippu Tip and three Arabs entered the town bearing gifts of beads and cloth. They were led to a large round hut where the sultan lay reclining on a pile of skins, surrounded by elders, warriors, and women. He was about eighty-six or even ninety years old, Tippu Tip wrote in his autobiography, and enormously fat—so fat that he almost couldn't walk and had to be carried about on a stretcher—with a belly swollen from drinking too much *pombe* beer. He signaled to his slaves to show him the visitors' gifts, and his eyes darted greedily about. But otherwise he did not acknowledge the Arabs, or speak a word. After all the presents had been displayed, the sultan signaled again to his slaves, who carried him to another, larger room, the Arabs following behind, and flung open its doors to reveal piles upon piles of ivory tusks. Only then did Sultan Nsama look directly at Tippu Tip, who was blinking uncontrollably. The African smiled a malevolent, toothless grin, and clapped his hands. The doors to the treasure room slammed shut and the ruler was borne away.

Tippu Tip was stunned. He didn't know what to make of the African chief or of the fact that he had been offered no ivory—most chieftains gave him at least a tusk or two in friendship. Hurrying, he caught up with the bobbing stretcher and forced himself to smile: "Sultan, you are so rich and powerful, can't you even spare a tusk for an honest trader?"

At that, Sultan Nsama became enraged and, shaking with anger, ordered his warriors to throw the Arabs out. Excited crowds gathered and followed as the intruders were shoved out of town.

The men retired to their camp, to spend an uneasy night. But the next morning, another messenger arrived with another apparently friendly missive: the sultan wanted to invite the Arabs to come back to town to get their tusks. However, they were to bring no weapons. Naturally, Tippu Tip was suspicious.

Nonetheless, he gathered together his Arab companions and a dozen slaves, and entered the town. The gates closed, and spears and arrows began to fly. Tippu Tip was badly wounded by three arrows, and another Arab was also hit. Two slaves were killed.

The visitors had not entered the town unprepared, however. Under their robes, their guns were at the ready. They opened fire. "At a shot they fell like birds. . . . 200 people fell at once; others were trampled down, and so died. They hurriedly took to flight. Within an hour 1,000 were dead . . . ," wrote a crowing Tippu Tip. "They took their Sultan with them. At last, by two o'clock there was not a soul left in the city, except blind people and such as had had their noses or arms cut off, for he was very cruel."

The Arabs remained in the town that night, and after darkness fell, the sultan's followers crept back, to surround them in great numbers. Tippu Tip was bleeding profusely but had the presence of mind, he later claimed, to order his men to build large fires in front of each city gate and to man each gate with ten guards. The fires prevented the Africans from seeing the guards, and as they drew near, the Arabs began to shoot and kill by the score. The Africans had no experience with firearms and within minutes, over six hundred warriors lay dead, their spears and weapons scattered around them.

The next afternoon, the Africans advanced again, and again the Arabs let the crowd draw near before opening fire. In minutes, 150 were dead. The Africans tried again the next day, and this time, lost 250 men. Thereafter, they did not return.

Some time later, Tippu Tip and his followers left their stronghold, carrying with them a whopping 1,950 *frasilas* of ivory, 700 *frasilas* of copper, and a large quantity of salt. With them too were over a thousand prisoners—captured followers of Sultan Nsama. The traders proceeded very cautiously at first, expecting an ambush at every turn, but it soon became evident that the people of the country were terrified of them. Chieftains of tribes large and small came out to welcome them, and they were offered gifts at every turn.

An especially warm reception awaited them at Urungu at the southern end of Lake Tanganyika: "I am very happy you defeated [Sultan Nsama]," the ruler there said. "He was my enemy and rival. . . . Stay in my country and we will fight him together." Tippu Tip agreed, and for

the next two months, the men's combined forces combed the countryside, flushing out their enemy until a badly defeated Sultan Nsama surrendered.

Tippu Tip's first solo expedition had taught him a valuable lesson:
defeat a region's most powerful chief first, and all the area's lesser chieftains will follow.

When Tippu Tip finally returned to the East African coast with his
enormous spoils of war, he was surprised to find Seyyid Majid and many
of Zanzibar's elite in Dar es Salaam, the port opposite Zanzibar. The
sultan intended to make the "harbor of peace" his new capital, and was
overseeing the construction of a new palace and other major buildings.
He had offered free land to all Zanzibaris willing to make the move
with him, and those who had accepted the offer were busy clearing land
and erecting makeshift homes.

As fate would have it, Seyyid Majid would die only a few years later,
before his new palace was completed, and Seyyid Barghash would have
no interest in moving to the harbor. It was left abandoned, to be taken
over first by the African jungle and then by the Germans, who developed it into the capital of their East African colony, established in the
late 1880s. Such are the vagaries of history. Perhaps if Majid had successfully transferred his capital to Dar es Salaam, the Germans would
never have gained a foothold in East Africa and the Omanis would have
retained their control over the coast.

Once back in Zanzibar, Tippu Tip relaxed for a time, reveling in his new
wealth and reputation. But he was a restless man, and before long he
was heading into the interior again. He stopped to visit his father in
Tabora, and then traveled deeper into Africa, to first enter Urua country, west of Lake Tanganyika, and next, Irande, still farther west, where
no Arab had set foot before. The area had little to offer in the way of
ivory, but Tippu Tip was amazed by much of what he saw. The Irande
towns were "astonishingly large," with rows of houses "like rows of
clove-trees," where one could walk for seven or eight hours before coming to their end, he wrote. In each town center was a big *baraza* where

craftsmen wove grasses into *viramba*—long skirts worn by both men and women.

From Irande, Tippu Tip and his companions headed northwest in the direction of Utetera, conquering various tribes along the way, but before they arrived at their destination, four emissaries from that country came to meet them. Tippu Tip's reputation had preceded him, and their chief, Kasongo Rushie, wanted to invite him to come trade with his people. To which the canny slaver replied, "It is well. Utetera, you must know, is my home. Kasongo is my [uncle]." The astonished emissaries asked how. And Tippu Tip replied:

Ages ago there was in Urua a Sultan, Rungu Kabare Kumambe, who made war on all countries, and amongst others came against Utetera. There he took captive two women, Kina Daramumba and Kitoto, and took them with him to Urua. There my grandfather, Habib bin Busher el Wardi, my mother's father, who had also come to Urua, met them, and he bought one of the women and made her his wife. In this way my mother was born. When I was born she said to me: "In my own country I am a great Princess, and there is very much ivory there. And our elder brother is called Kasongo Rushie Mwana Mapunga." Then I decided to come, and fought with everyone who came in my way, with the object of reaching my home.

The emissaries listened agape. But Tippu Tip had made the whole story up. He had heard about Utetera from others, most notably one of his concubines, who had told him about its plentiful ivory, its peace-loving people, its elderly ruler, and his two favorite sisters, who had been sold into slavery when young and never heard from again.

Tippu Tip's story sounded credible. His complexion and features were African, he knew Utetera's history, and he even spoke a few words of the language, which he had learned from his concubine. In addition, hundreds of Utetera men, women, and children were traveling with him. He had rescued them from a rival tribe and was bringing them safely back home, he said.

Marveling at the trader's story, the emissaries left and the caravan proceeded though a region of fertile lands and tall African oak and teak trees. Arriving in Utetera, they were welcomed by thousands of excited people. Banana-leaf arches lined the road and young women proffered baskets filled with fruits and vegetables. The sultan's chief adviser, a very old man almost completely covered in monkey skins, took them to a compound to rest, saying, "My master will visit you after you have eaten and refreshed yourself."

Tippu Tip and his Arab companions changed out of their travel-worn garments and into their ceremonial best—*dishdashas* of brilliant white, worn with gold embroidered coats and elaborately rolled turbans. Then they heard a wild drumming and blowing of horns. Sultan Kasongo was arriving.

The elderly man entered the compound, surrounded by his procession—a half-dozen drummers, thirty or forty spearmen, and a half-dozen women bearing shields, as well as family members and village headmen. Like his chief adviser, the ruler was dressed in long-haired monkey skins, while most of his followers wore grass skirts.

Sultan Kasongo considered only the sun and elephant to be his social equals. He showed respect for the former by never looking at the sunrise or sunset, and for the latter, by never eating its flesh or touching its tusks.

The two leaders exchanged elaborate formal greetings, and then retired to a *baraza* to discuss the future of Utetera. When they emerged, they were smiling, and the people stamped and screamed with pleasure, wrote Tippu Tip. Holding up his hands, the sultan quieted them, saying, "Tomorrow we will have a great *baraza* in my village and my people will hear what I propose."

The next day, the sultan delivered a bombshell—perhaps not entirely of his own volition. He was getting old and tired, he said, and couldn't fight his enemies properly anymore. Yet now, the powerful grandson of his sister had arrived, just in time to take his place. "Obey him," Sultan Kasongo told his surprised people. "As I am chief, he is chief with me. . . . For protecting us against our enemies he will only ask for the teeth of the elephant. Give them to him, and all that he requires."

Three or four years after his first solo expedition in 1867, Tippu Tip was now virtually king of one of the largest and wealthiest regions of East-Central Africa. Wasting no time, he appointed subordinate rulers, ordered them to pay him tribute, and settled down to a life of prosperous trading. Thanks to Sultan Kasongo's scruples, he could claim all the region's ivory for himself, and within his first fortnight in power had acquired over two hundred tusks.

Slaves built Tippu Tip and his Arab companions simple but comfortable huts on a small hill, and villagers provided the men with all their basic necessities, including food, women, and *pombe* beer. Wrote the explorer V. Lovett Cameron, who visited the area, in 1873: "The only drawback I experienced to the comfort of Tipo-Tipo's camp was the number of slaves in chains who met my eyes at every turn; but, except being deprived of their freedom and confined in order to prevent their running away, they had a tolerable easy life, and were well fed."

Three years passed, most peacefully. Tippu Tip was an excellent administrator and strong leader, who dealt fairly with his subjects but pitilessly with his enemies. Periodically, he sent trading expeditions into the surrounding districts to track down more ivory and slaves, and these scouting parties were usually treated with great respect by everyone they met.

Until, that is, one horrific trip when a scouting party led by Tippu Tip's beloved uncle Bushiri—the man who had taken him on his first trading expeditions to the coast—was attacked, killed, and eaten by cannibals. Tippu Tip was devastated—and furious. With the help of his benefactor Sultan Kasongo, he gathered together thousands of Africans and sent them on the warpath. For weeks, the warriors marched determinedly from village to village, plundering, murdering, and eating their enemies as they went—most of Tippu Tip's subjects were cannibals. They had "a hearty appetite, two of them eating up a whole man," he commented, but the smell of the burning flesh made him sick.

Even Tippu Tip drew the line somewhere.

25

Dr. Livingstone

ON JULY 29, 1867, WHILE HUNTING DOWN THE LAST REMAINING
warriors of the morbidly obese Sultan Nsama, Tippu Tip came upon a
most curious sight—one almost as curious as the sultan himself: a tall,
ill, emaciated Scotsman wandering about in the village of Ponda, southwest of Lake Tanganyika. The stranger was traveling with no other
white men, had only ten porters, and was near starvation. Despite his
vulnerable position, however, he was busy taking measurements, asking
questions, and writing everything down in a "big book."

He was Dr. David Livingstone, the missionary, explorer, and passionate anti–slave trade crusader. By then world-renowned, Dr. Livingstone
had left Zanzibar eighteen months earlier to trek inland along the
hippo-infested Ruvuma River, which marks the border between today's
Tanzania and Mozambique.

Tippu Tip gave Livingstone a goat, a piece of white calico, four large
bunches of beads, a bag of sorghum, and guides to lead him safely out
of the region. In true Arab fashion, too, he apologized for not being able
to give him more. Livingstone, in turn, was greatly impressed by Tippu
Tip's generosity, friendliness, and good manners.

Two months later, despite his profound revulsion for the slave trade,
the explorer traveled with the slaver for three months. The two became
friends, and when they parted, Livingstone gave Tippu Tip a letter of
thanks, "in acknowledgment of his good services," to serve as an introduction to the British powers in Zanzibar.

Tippu Tip was neither the first nor the last of the Arab slavers that Dr. Livingstone befriended. Until, that is, one fateful morning in 1871.

A true legend in his own time, Dr. David Livingstone turned Britain's attention to East Africa and the Indian Ocean slave trade. His ideas about the African continent, which involved ending slavery and other "backward" tribal customs through the introduction of Western-style commerce, colonization, and Christianity, changed the way much of Europe viewed Africa, and continued to influence international politics for decades after his death. Among those who would be most deeply affected by Livingstone's ideas were the sultans, slavers, merchants, and bankers of Zanzibar.

Livingstone was born in a tenement in Blantyre, Scotland, just south of Glasgow, in 1813. His father, Neil Livingstone, was a traveling tea merchant and a deeply religious man. The family lived in a single fourteen-by-ten-foot room with no indoor plumbing.

Neil Livingstone greatly admired book learning, but financial need forced him to put David to work at the Blantyre cotton mills at age ten. The boy worked from six a.m. until eight p.m. Mondays through Saturdays, and was employed as a "piecer," which involved crawling and stooping under and around the spinning frames to piece together breaking threads. Piecers, who were almost all children, walked or crawled up to twenty miles daily, and when the end of their shift finally came, most were too tired to do anything but go home and sleep. Even as a child, however, David had an extraordinary will; after the factory whistle blew, he went to the company school from eight to ten p.m. Fewer than 10 percent of the children who worked the mills ever learned to even read or write, but David spent his factory years studying Latin and the classics. After school was done, he usually read until midnight.

Not all of David's reading time was spent on serious tomes, however. Travel books were a family favorite, and he devoured the adventures of such Scottish explorers as Mungo Park, the first Westerner to discover Africa's Niger River, and James Bruce, who had braved extraordinary dangers while following the Blue Nile in Ethiopia, only to die after falling down a flight of stairs in his home. He was also greatly inspired by missionary Karl von Gützlaff's *Journal of Three Voyages Along the*

Coast of China. Unlike most religious men and women of the day, Gützlaff advocated sending medical missionaries—then virtually unheard of—into the field to minister to both the mind and the body. David already had a strong interest in studying medicine, but his father was insisting that he use his talents for a religious purpose; here was a way for him to do both.

In his early twenties, Livingstone put himself through medical school in Glasgow and, after graduating, entered the London Missionary Society's seminary. There, he was regarded as a plodding, uninspired, but nonetheless worthy student, and in 1841, he was posted to the mission station of Kuruman in Southern Africa, about six hundred miles north of Cape Town.

To have finally achieved his long-dreamed-of goal after so many years of hardship and intense study must have been a heady experience for the earnest, idealistic young man. He immediately fell in love with Africa and its wide, open spaces—so different from his cramped existence in Glasgow and London. But within months of his posting, he was frustrated and bored. The mission station was much smaller than he had expected, having converted only forty Africans in twenty years, and its director was in England for an indefinite period, meaning that no one knew what to do with the new arrival. The young doctor requested permission to "go forward into the dark interior" to hunt for new mission sites. His request was granted.

Livingstone spent the next ten years exploring Southern Africa. He opened a new mission station at Mabotsa in 1843 and married Mary Moffat, the daughter of a fellow missionary, in 1845; the couple would have four children. Together with Mary and their oldest children, he crossed the Kalahari Desert in 1849; and he discovered the Upper Zambezi River for the West in 1851. In the mid-1850s, he crossed south-central Africa from coast to coast along the course of the Zambezi, and in 1855, discovered a spectacular waterfall, which he named "Victoria Falls," in honor of his queen. "The most wonderful sight I have seen in Africa," he called it, and measured its length by creeping to the precarious edge of the thundering falls and lowering a weighted rope into its abyss.

Early in his African wanderings, Livingstone was attacked by a lion, a transformative encounter that left him with a permanently crooked left arm and taught him, he later wrote, to be unafraid of death. Also early in his travels, he ran into his first slave traders, a second transformative experience that shocked him to the core. Slavery had been abolished in Britain's colonies and protectorates in 1834, and the young missionary was horrified to find it still thriving among the Arabs, Swahili, Portuguese, and Africans themselves. He began sending reports and articles back to England describing the unspeakable cruelty he was witnessing: miles upon miles of burned-down villages, dozens of slaves roped or chained together at the neck, children herded into tiny holding pens, slaves too weak to travel being left for dead, mutilated bodies heaped up into mounds, babies' skulls bashed in because they were too heavy for their captured mothers to carry.

By the time Livingstone returned to England in 1856, after fifteen consecutive years in Africa, he was famous. The general public was fascinated by his wildly romantic, adventurous life—their interest in the slave trade was secondary—and they eagerly drank up every new detail about him. Starstruck crowds mobbed him everywhere he went, and on one occasion he was almost crushed to death by rabid admirers on Regent Street.

In 1856, Africa and slavery had been off Britain's radar for decades. The British Parliament had passed the historic Slave Trade Abolition Act almost fifty years earlier, and the nation's campaign against the Oman-India slave trade had ended more than thirty years earlier. Slavery no longer existed in the British colonies, and even the transatlantic slave trade was nearing its end.

But Livingstone's passionate anti–slave trade speeches, delivered in churches and assembly halls throughout England, ignited Britain's interest in Africa and slavery once more. Once again, the country had the chance to save the ravaged continent and deliver liberty and justice to all.

As always in politics, however, Britain's sudden interest in East Africa and the Indian Ocean slave trade was not as simple or altruistic as it first appeared. Livingstone's reports may have ignited the interest of the general public, but the politicians were more interested in the fact that the continent offered a treasure trove of raw materials needed for industrial production; it was the dawn of the industrial age. Britain's politicians were also careful not to direct their anti–slave trade fervor toward the powerful nations of Spain and Portugal, which still owned massive slave-labor colonies. Attacking the Arabs was a far safer proposition. They were a much weaker target. They were also non-white, and thus, uncivilized.

One year after his return, Livingstone published his first book, *Missionary Travels and Researches in South Africa*, which was an overnight sensation, selling seventy thousand copies. And shortly thereafter, he resigned from the London Missionary Society, in order to concentrate on ending the slave trade. His new credo was the "three C's"—Christianity, commerce, and colonialism. His new employer was the British foreign office.

The Livingstone Tippu Tip met in 1867 was a far different person than the one who had been fêted by London eleven years earlier, however. Failure and tragedy had transformed the former golden boy adventurer into a man old before his time.

The change had occurred during Livingstone's 1858–63 Zambezi expedition, when he returned to Africa to explore the Zambezi River and its watershed. He had been firmly convinced—to the point that he had promised his backers—that the river could be developed into a major international waterway, and its shores into fertile agricultural and even industrial lands. But Livingstone's dreams had no basis in reality. The river was much too shallow for easy navigation, and slavery and famine had decimated the countryside.

Throughout the expedition, Livingstone and his half-dozen white traveling companions were constantly at one another's throats. He preferred to travel without other white men—but the British foreign office had insisted. His companions made fun of him behind his back, and except for John Kirk, a fellow Scottish doctor who later became the British consul to Zanzibar, they couldn't keep up with him. They resented his style of exploring, which involved much aimless wandering about, and his motto, "never give up," which they felt put their lives in danger.

Livingstone, in turn, was an abysmal leader. Aloof and taciturn, he often lost his temper and was incapable of rallying his men's spirits during the expedition's many dark days.

Then in 1862, Livingstone's wife, Mary, joined the expedition. Since crossing the Kalahari Desert with her husband over a decade earlier, she had spent many lonely years without him in England, raising their children and falling into depression. Finally, she couldn't stand it any longer. Placing her children in the care of family and friends, she sailed to Africa to meet her husband in Shupaga, a small port on the lower Zambezi River. But within a week of her arrival, she was ill with malaria, and within two weeks, she was dead. Livingstone was devastated.

The next year, the Zambezi expedition was recalled. Wrote the editor of *The Times* of London on January 20, 1863, reflecting the mood of his countrymen and women: "We were promised cotton, sugar and indigo . . . and of course we got none. We were promised trade; and there is no trade. . . . We were promised converts and not one has been made. In a word, the thousands [of pounds spent] have been productive only of the most fatal results."

Livingstone spent most of the next two years living in seclusion in Scotland with his children, whom he hadn't seen in seven years. But his heart remained in Africa, and when in 1865 the Royal Geographical Society invited him to head up a new expedition to find the source of the Nile—still a mystery—he accepted. The trip would both allow him to attempt to solve the age-old geographic riddle and, more important as far as he was concerned, take him into the heart of East Africa's slave-trade country. "The Nile sources are valuable only as a means of enabling me to open my mouth with power among men," he told a friend. "It is this power which I hope to apply to remedy an enormous evil"—i.e., the slave trade.

Traveling via Bombay, where he hired thirteen *sepoys*, or Indian soldiers, for his expedition, Livingstone arrived in Zanzibar on January 28, 1866. Seyyid Majid received him with great courtesy and gave him a letter of introduction addressed to all his subjects in the interior, asking that they aid the explorer in his travels. The letter was *pro forma*—but it was also extraordinary. Seyyid Majid and his subjects all knew that Livingstone's mission was to abolish the very trade that was their livelihood.

While in Zanzibar, Livingstone hired more men, bought supplies, and arranged for a second, essential shipment of goods to be transported to Ujiji on Lake Tanganyika later via Arab caravan. He also visited the island's famed slave market, where he saw three hundred slaves being sold. Zanzibar was nothing but "a great slave emporium," he wrote to the foreign office.

On March 19, the explorer debarked for the mainland. His plan was to hike west along the Ruvuma River to Lake Nyasa, and then head north to Lake Tanganyika and, hopefully, the Nile. It was a route that lay three hundred miles south of the one taken by Burton and Speke ten years earlier; Livingstone believed that the Nile's source lay in "fountains" in or near small Lake Bangweulu, southwest of Lake Tanganyika.

Livingstone had chosen an exceptionally difficult route to follow. There was no trail along the Ruvuma—his men had to hack their way through jungle—and the air was heavy and foul. The caravan made painstakingly slow progress, covering just four miles a day, and trouble dogged every step. The pack animals, which included buffalos and camels as well as donkeys and mules, began dying of sleeping sickness. The *sepoys*, who had never traveled in Africa before, dawdled, refused to carry goods, stole from the villagers, and badly mistreated the animals. The porters began to pilfer supplies and to desert. And two hundred miles in, drought, famine, and evidence of the slave trade began to show in the travelers' surroundings.

Battling depression, Livingstone made things even worse by all but abdicating his leadership role and leaving his men on their own while he wandered ahead, taking notes on all that he saw. He wrote of an orphaned girl, left behind by the slavers because she was too weak to travel, and of a well-dressed woman with a new "very heavy slave-taming stick" around her neck, whom he freed by purchasing her with a piece of cloth. He also wrote of local people rescuing sick or rejected slaves, caring for them until they were well, and selling them again.

Livingstone had always been horrified by the Africans' callous involvement in the very trade that was decimating their society, and now he spent many hours telling the chiefs that "if they sell their fellows, they are like the man who holds the victim while the Arab performs the murder." But he couldn't get through: "They were rather taken aback. . . . If they did not sell, the Arabs would not come to buy," he wrote.

Finally, in August 1866, after six months of travel, Livingstone and his party reached Lake Nyasa. But the triumph of the moment was muted by the fact that the caravan now numbered only 26, down from an original number of about 40, which had been few to begin with; most explorers traveled with caravans of at least 120. Livingstone had been forced to dismiss the *sepoys* one month earlier, for their disobedience and unwillingness to work, and over a dozen porters had deserted.

Livingstone's next task was to reach Lake Bangweulu and find a link between it and Lake Tanganyika. Due to tribal hostilities, however, he could not continue directly north. Instead, he had to circle around Lake Nyasa to the south before traveling north.

Fearing that the hostilities had also spread south, fourteen more men then deserted, leaving Livingstone with a dangerously small party of eleven. Still, he pressed determinedly onward, climbing four-thousand-foot-high mountains and descending to the Loango River. A severe famine was upon this land as well, and the men survived largely on goat milk—until their animals all died in early January. Livingstone took his belt up three holes, and the rains of winter began, increasing the party's misery still more.

Then on January 20, 1867, the caravan suffered a devastating blow. Two more porters deserted, taking with them all that they could carry, including the medicine chest.

Many other explorers would have given up at this point and returned to the coast, or at least traveled to Ujiji or Kilwa to obtain more supplies. To travel without quinine in Central Africa was to court death. But Livingstone did not even consider the possibility. His journey had already taken too long and brought him too far. Now in his fifties and in increasingly poor health, he knew that this trip would be his last. He couldn't afford to waste time on detours.

The caravan trekked on, entering dense woods and sprawling swamps where there was nothing to eat but mushrooms, leaves, occasional pieces of bitter elephant meat purchased from villagers, and rats. Livingstone became ill with rheumatic fever.

It was then, when things were at their worst, that Livingstone was saved by the very people he detested: slave traders. On February 1, 1867, a slaver named Magaru Mafupi came upon the forlorn caravan and rescued them with a generous supply of food. Magaru, who was headed for the coast, also promised to deliver a letter from Livingstone to John Kirk, now the British consul in Zanzibar, asking for a second relief caravan to meet him in Ujiji.

Two months later, having bypassed Lake Bangweulu by mistake, Livingstone reached another major milestone—the southern end of Lake Tanganyika. He was preparing to continue north along the western shore of the lake to look for the river that he felt sure connected Bangweulu to Tanganyika, when he heard that a full-scale war had broken out between the Africans and the Arabs in that region. It was the war that Tippu Tip had begun against Sultan Nsama, now joined by others. Livingstone had no choice but to retreat south.

In May the Livingstone party reached an Arab encampment, and there they remained through August, waiting for the war to end. When it did, they joined an Arab caravan heading west toward Lake Bangweulu. Leading that caravan was Tippu Tip.

Scholars have long puzzled over Livingstone's friendship with the Arab slavers. How could he, an ardent abolitionist, have spent so much time with people whose profession he so reviled? How could he have witnessed—and recorded—their constant wanton cruelty day after day and still accepted their help?

Necessity had much to do with it. Without the slavers' assistance, Livingstone probably would have starved to death or been killed. Without their help, too, he could not have gathered as much information as he did about the slave trade.

But his friendship with the traders was more complicated than that. While in Zanzibar, he had seen how intrinsic slavery was to its Arab-Swahili-Indian-African society—everyone from the sultan to simple shopkeepers to slave-owning slaves was involved. And the Europeans, Americans, and Indians of the subcontinent were complicit as well. It was their demand for ivory that had helped develop the trade in the first place. The vile institution could not be blamed on the traders alone.

Also while in Zanzibar, Livingstone had seen how well most slaves on the island were treated—far better than he had been treated as a boy working in the Blantyre cotton mills. Slavery and the slave trade *had* to be abolished, on that point he never wavered, but he was only too well aware of the harsh inequities that Western-style capitalism would create in the Arab-African world.

Finally, Livingstone had the rare ability to see people as individuals separate from their culture and beliefs. The slavers were products of their time and place and should be "judged by the East African Moslem standard . . . and not by ours," he wrote. The traders whom he befriended were gracious, hospitable, and intelligent men—the best of their kind. He also met far cruder slavers during his travels, and these he wanted nothing to do with. "If one wanted to see the slave trade in its best phases," he wrote at one point, "he would accompany the gentlemen subjects of the Sultan of Zanzibar. If he wished to describe its worst form he would go with the Kilwa traders." The latter, along with the Portuguese, were "the vilest of the vile. [Theirs] is not a trade, but a system of consecutive murders; they go to plunder and kidnap."

Even while overlooking Tippu Tip's more unpleasant qualities, Livingstone was growing impatient with the progress of his caravan. They were proceeding at a snail's pace, thanks to the trader's constant search for ivory. But finally, after about a month, they reached the shores of Lake Mweru, near Lake Bangweulu, which Livingstone badly wanted to explore. While waiting out the war at the Arab encampment, he had heard of a large river, the Lualaba, that flowed out of Lake Mweru to the northwest. *This* had to be the source of the Nile, he became convinced as soon as he saw the river. Now, all he had to do was follow it northward.

For the moment, however, that was impossible. He had only nine followers left, and virtually no supplies. For him to proceed, it was imperative that he get to Ujiji, 250 miles to the northeast, to pick up the goods that he had arranged to have delivered before leaving Zanzibar.

Tippu Tip had no intention of traveling to Ujiji at that time, but Livingstone soon met another Arab trader who did: a man named Muhammad bin Gharib, whom Livingstone called Bogharib. The two would travel together for over a year, and become close friends.

When Livingstone contracted pneumonia just before reaching Ujiji, it was Bogharib who kept him alive. The Arab personally cooked for, fed, and nursed the explorer, and ordered his porters to carry him. When Livingstone met with crushing disappointment in Ujiji—his relief caravan had indeed arrived but had been ruthlessly plundered—it was Bogharib who found him a hut in which to stay and provided him with food and medicine. And when Bogharib left Ujiji four months later, he took the explorer with him. He couldn't leave him behind in Ujiji, where the other slavers might let him die. He was also heading into Manyeuma country, where Livingstone was eager to go. Manyeuma was the land through which the Lualaba River flowed.

Livingstone's plans were to travel quickly to the town of Nyangwe on the banks of the Lualaba, in the heart of Manyeuma country, and from there trace the river north to the Nile—a journey that he expected to take six months. But as usual, his estimations were wildly optimistic. A year after leaving Ujiji, he had still completed only half of the three-hundred-mile journey to Nyangwe.

Part of the reason for the delay was the Manyeuma terrain, which was both exquisitely beautiful and extremely rugged, with steep forested slopes that at times had to be climbed on all fours. But the main reason for the delay was Livingstone's failing health. Still recovering from pneumonia, he couldn't walk for more than a few hours at a time. Dysentery was a recurring problem and, worst of all, he had developed painful ulcers on his feet. The ulcers "eat through everything—muscle, tendon, and bone, and often lame permanently if they do not kill," he wrote.

Halfway to Nyangwe, Livingstone decided to rest for a while in the town of Bambarre, and there he remained, except for occasional side excursions, from July 1870 to February 1871, while Bogharib continued on to pursue his trading activities. With only three of his followers left, Livingstone was alone and idle much of the time, and fell into a deeper depression. He was now fifty-seven years old, and had been in Africa five long years. Time, he felt, was running out. "I am very old & shaky—My cheeks fallen in—space round the eyes—the mouth almost toothless . . . a smile is that of a hippopotamus—a dreadful old Fogie," he wrote in a letter to his daughter.

Finally, in late January 1871, Livingstone was able to leave Bambarre, and two months later he arrived in Nyangwe. Sprawled over the right bank of the Lualaba, Nyangwe was by far the largest town in the region and was divided into two parts, one inhabited by wealthy Arab traders and merchants, and the other by the poor. Manyeuma was one of Africa's richest ivory-producing territories, and the Arabs had been pouring into the region ever since discovering it a few years before.

Livingstone took to Nyangwe right away. Laid out along long red streets with palm trees in its center, it teemed with Arabs in long white *dishdashas*, slaves tied together at the neck, and stunning African women who wore next to nothing and wove their hair into elaborate basket-like shapes in back. Many of the women were also excellent swimmers who could dive to the bottom of the Lualaba for freshwater oysters.

Livingstone was certain that he was on the cusp of success at last. At Nyangwe, the Lualaba was an impressive mile wide—and it flowed north. Where else could it be going but to the Nile? All he had to do was rent a canoe and prove it.

In actuality, the Lualaba led to the Congo River. It bent westward shortly after leaving Nyangwe. Some of the townspeople informed Livingstone of that fact, but he was too lost in his own dreams to listen.

Still too weak to walk far, let alone go exploring, Livingstone spent the next few months resting and trying to rent a canoe. But both the Arabs and the Africans distrusted him—the Arabs because they thought he was there to spy on their activities (as indeed he was), and the Africans because they thought he was involved in the slave trade.

To pass the time, Livingstone spent many hours in the Nyangwe marketplace, where everything from sweet potatoes and millet to white ants and dried snails to fishing nets and grass mats were for sale. Anywhere from two thousand to three thousand villagers, mostly women, came there on market days, and the scene enchanted Livingstone. "With market women it seems to be a pleasure of life to haggle and joke, and laugh and cheat," he wrote. "Many come eagerly and retire with careworn faces; many are beautiful and many old; all carry very heavy loads of dried cassava and earthen pots which they dispose of very cheaply for palm oil, fish, salt, pepper, and relishes for their food."

Livingstone hoped that his presence in the marketplace would lead people to trust him. Time was passing, and he needed to make plans. But still, no one would rent him a canoe. Finally, he approached the leading Arab in town, a cruel, vulgar, and greedy trader named

Dugumbe bin Habib, offering him four hundred pounds and all of the supplies that he was expecting to arrive in Ujiji, via the second relief caravan that he had requested in a letter to Kirk. Dugumbe said he would think it over.

On July 15, however, Livingstone ceased thinking about canoes.

It was an unusually hot and sultry morning, and the explorer was sitting in his usual shady spot in the marketplace. He was a strange sight— a bearded, near-toothless figure now much overweight, thanks to months of inactivity and plentiful food. Gunshots were sounding periodically from the far side of the Lualaba, and smoke was spiraling upward from the forests there. Somewhere nearby, the Arabs were burning another village, and enslaving and murdering more Africans.

The tension of that operation could be felt in the marketplace, but otherwise, everything was proceeding as usual, with Africans and a few Arabs mingling over the wares. Livingstone noted with surprise, however, that three of the Arabs, new to the town, were carrying guns. Guns were not allowed in the marketplace and he "felt inclined to reprove them," but did not.

When the heat of the day became unbearable, Livingstone got up to leave. As he did so, he heard two of the Arab newcomers haggling with a vendor over a chicken, and trying to grab the chicken without paying. That was not unusual, and he continued on his way. But before he had gotten very far, "the discharge of two guns in the middle of the crowd told me the slaughter had begun," he wrote. "Crowds dashed off from the place, and threw down their wares in confusion, and ran. At the same time . . . volleys were discharged from a party down near the creek on the panic-stricken women who dashed at the canoes. These, some fifty or more, were jammed in the creek and the men forgot their paddles in the terror that seized all."

Many of the Manyeuma people, who had little knowledge of firearms, had come to the market in canoes, and even as the gunshots continued, they rushed for the boats, or tried to swim. Men, women and children "leaped and scrambled into the water shrieking" while the Arabs stood emotionless by—aiming, firing, reloading. Only three of the canoes got away, and these were capsized by terrorized people in the water, trying to pull themselves on board.

Livingstone could see a long line of heads drifting downstream. But few of these survived. "Shot after shot continued to be fired on the helpless and perishing. Some of the long line of heads disappeared quietly, whilst other poor creatures threw their arms high, as if appealing to the great Father above, and sank."

He could do nothing: "As I write I hear the loud wails on the left bank over those who are there slain, ignorant of their many friends who are now in the depths of the Lualaba. Oh, let Thy kingdom come! No one will ever know the exact loss on this bright sultry morning. It gave me the impression of being in hell."

Later, the Arabs would estimate that four hundred Africans had been killed, though the number was probably closer to six hundred. And later still, Livingstone's published account of the massacre would enflame the British and help lead to the passage of a new and much stronger anti–slave trade treaty with Zanzibar.

In a state of shock, Livingstone vowed to never again accept the Arabs' help—not even if they offered him a whole fleet of canoes with which to explore the Lualaba. His four-year-long dependence on them was over. He would return to Ujiji, pick up his expected supplies, and travel independently once again.

He spent the rest of the day helping the survivors find their kin. The local chiefs were so impressed that they asked him to stay on. "But I told them I was so ashamed by the company [I had kept] that I could scarcely look the Manyeuma in the face," he wrote.

He left a few days later. The Arabs saw him off. They didn't think he would make it back to Ujiji alive. Thanks to their bloodbath, hostilities in the region had reached a feverish pitch, and the explorer didn't know his way through the virgin forest.

But three grueling months and several near-misses on his life later, Livingstone reached his goal. He had been sick most of the way with stress, dysentery, feet ulcers, and temporary blindness, but his strong will had prevailed.

Dragging himself into Ujiji on October 23, 1871, the explorer's only thoughts were for his expected supplies, which should have been there by now. And they would have been, had they not been pilfered by the very Arab who had brought them out. All that was left was a few yards of calico.

Livingstone sank into despair. His journey was all over. He was sick, old, near friendless, and penniless. "I felt in my destitution as if I were the man who went down from Jerusalem to Jericho and fell among thieves; but I could not hope for Priest, Levite or good Samaritan to come by on either side," he wrote.

Yet he was wrong. Against all odds, a good Samaritan was on his way.

Several weeks later, a volley of shots came from outside the town announcing the arrival of a caravan. "Susi came running at the top of his speed and gasped out, 'An Englishman! I see him!' and off he darted to meet him," wrote Livingstone. "The American flag at the head of a caravan told of the nationality of the stranger. Bales of goods, baths of tin, huge kettles, cooking pots, tents, etc., made me think 'This must be a luxurious traveler, and not one at his wits' end like me."

Crowds began to gather outside Livingstone's hut as columns of men from the caravan reached the town. Most were Arabs dressed in *dishdashas* and turbans, but then out from among them stepped a white man, immaculately attired in a pressed flannel suit, shiny boots, and a white helmet. He lifted his hat.

"Dr. Livingstone, I presume?" said Henry Morton Stanley, uttering what would become the most famous phrase in the annals of African exploration. His voice was trembling with excitement.

26
Stanley Meets Tippu Tip

HENRY MORTON STANLEY HAD BEEN BORN JOHN ROWLANDS ON January 28, 1841, in Denbigh, Wales, a village southwest of Liverpool, England. His mother was an unwed housemaid and his father, at least according to town records, a drunk. His birth was entered in the St. Hilary's Church register as "John Rowlands, Bastard"—a shame that he spent his entire life trying to live down.

John's mother abandoned him shortly after his birth, leaving him with her father to raise. The older man adored the child, taking him with him everywhere he went, but dropped dead of a heart attack when the boy was five. John had two prosperous uncles who could have supported him, but instead they unceremoniously deposited him at the St. Asaph workhouse, run by an alcoholic former coal miner. The workhouse children slept two to a bed, a younger child paired with an older one. Young John was fondled and violated by teenage boys as he slept, resulting in a fear of sexual intimacy that would last his entire life. He thrived in the classroom, however. He loved books and arithmetic, and was fascinated by geography.

At age fifteen, John was released from the workhouse, to embark on a youth filled with yet more mind-numbing misery. A chubby, awkward, and defiant boy, he stayed with a succession of relatives who wanted nothing to do with him and worked a succession of short-term jobs, each drearier than the last. His escape was books.

One day when he was seventeen and working as a butcher-shop delivery boy, John was sent to the Liverpool docks. Here, he was immediately caught up in the romance of the sea, and when the captain of an American merchant ship offered him a job, he accepted eagerly. Seven cold, miserable, seasick weeks later, he arrived in New Orleans. It was February 1859.

According to Stanley, shortly after arriving he at last ran into a stroke of good fortune, in the form of a cotton merchant in a tall hat and dark alpaca suit sitting outside a warehouse. The merchant was reading a newspaper, and when John approached him and asked him for a job, the man had him prove his literacy by reading a few lines and writing on a sack. The man then recommended him to a friend, who hired him as a clerk.

The cotton merchant's name was Henry Hope Stanley. John idolized him and began visiting him in his stately home on Charles Street. The older man was flattered by the attention and the two spent many happy hours together talking about books. The merchant's beautiful wife was quite taken with the young man, too, and soon the couple invited him to live with them.

Then tragedy struck, in the form of a yellow fever epidemic. The lovely wife succumbed, and the bereft husband clasped John to his breast, saying, "In future you are to bear my name, 'Henry Stanley.' "The two then spent an idyllic two years traveling the Mississippi River— conducting cotton business, reading out loud to each other, and talking about religion and books. Sadly, however, the merchant too fell seriously ill and died in 1861.

There is only one problem with Stanley's story: it wasn't true. It was a fantasy woven by a lonely youth desperate for a family. City records show that although Henry Hope Stanley was a real person, he and his wife lived until old age, and John Rowlands never resided at their home. It is even possible that the boy never met Henry Hope Stanley face-to-face, but only admired him from afar, so much so that he adopted his name.

Stanley fought for the Confederate Army in the Civil War, and after it was over, headed West, where he covered the American Indian Wars in an impressive series of articles for the *Missouri Democrat*. His articles were picked up by papers in the East, and in 1867, the year Salme moved to Germany and Tippu Tip led his first caravan into Africa, he arrived in New York City, intent on getting a job at the *New York Herald*, the city's most famous paper. His goal was to obtain an assignment to go to Africa and meet and write about Livingstone. He had been fascinated by the missionary ever since reading his bestselling book, *Missionary Travels and Researches in South Africa*, shortly after leaving the St. Asaph workhouse.

With no appointment or introduction, Stanley talked his way into the office of the *Herald*'s editor, James Gordon Bennett, a brash, imperious twenty-six-year-old known for both his bad-boy behavior and his determination to put out the greatest newspaper in the world. Bennett had no interest in Africa at first, but after Stanley proved himself with a sensational journalistic coup—scooping other journalists on a major story about the rescue of British hostages held by an Abyssinian emperor—followed by many solid stories, he finally sent the hungry reporter to track down Livingstone, missing for years by then and presumed by many to be dead. In a remarkably quick expedition made doubly remarkable by his complete lack of experience in Africa, Stanley found Livingstone in a mere eight months, a feat that foreshadowed his subsequent career as one of Africa's greatest explorers.

One day about three years after Stanley and Livingstone met in Ujiji, a chieftain came up to Tippu Tip, still ruling over his quasi-kingdom of Utetera, to complain about Arab raiding parties invading his territory. They were coming from the town of Nyangwe on the Lualaba River, he said.

"You mean there are Arabs now in Nyangwe?" Tippu Tip asked, astonished.

"A great settlement of Ujiji Arabs, Sultan," the chieftain replied. "Will you protect us against them, even if they are coast people and brothers to you?"

Tippu Tip assured him that he would, but his mind was racing. It had been many years now since he'd been in contact with other Arabs. He had no idea that they had moved into territories so far west, and was hungry to spend time with his kinsmen and to hear news from home.

He left for Nyangwe as soon as he could. Arriving there in August 1874, he could scarcely believe his eyes. After his many years in the hinterland, the town seemed like a sophisticated capital to him. The streets teemed with people, and Arab-style homes built around courtyards lined a central square. Cultivated gardens filled with all kinds of fruits and vegetables from Zanzibar surrounded the town, and extensive rice fields flourished in the wet lowlands below. Tippu Tip and his followers hadn't tasted rice in years. Evidence of the massacre that Livingstone had witnessed three years earlier had long since disappeared.

Eagerly, Tippu Tip soaked up the news from Zanzibar. For the first time, he heard that Seyyid Majid had died and that Seyyid Barghash was now sultan. The two brothers had never reconciled but Majid had had no heirs and the British approved of Barghash—a critical factor. As early as 1868, the future British consul Kirk had written, "Barghash is now a very intelligent liberal man, outspoken and quick, but a man of energy, and very well disposed to us."

Tippu Tip also learned about the ferocious hurricane of 1872 that had destroyed most of Zanzibar's clove plantations, wreaking havoc with its economy. Many of the Arab plantation owners, their crops destroyed, couldn't make their annual payments to the island's customs master and were sinking into disastrous debt. By the 1880s, about two thirds of the island's plantations would be mortgaged for their full value. The center of clove production moved to Pemba, which the hurricane had largely spared.

No one told Tippu Tip, however, about the new 1873 anti–slave trade treaty, passed in the wake of the Nyangwe massacre—perhaps because it hadn't greatly affected the inland trade. Up until that year the Arab traders had been legally allowed to transport slaves within the sultan's East African dominions by land or by sea; trade farther north was illegal, but continued mostly by sea from Zanzibar. The new treaty banned all trade in slaves by sea, meaning that no new slaves could even arrive in Zanzibar. It was a huge step forward, but the slavers, ever resourceful, had found a way around it. They were now transporting slaves to the coast and farther north via long, arduous inland routes. Coming from as far away as Lake Nyasa, Manyeuma, and the Upper Congo, more slaves were dying en route than ever before, but supplying East Africa's mainland plantations and points farther north with labor was as easy as ever. Only supplying the islands had become more difficult. The cost of slaves in Zanzibar had doubled and then tripled.

Some time after his first visit to Nyangwe, Tippu Tip decided to move there, and later still, he took up residence in a village on the Lualaba about thirty miles south of Nyangwe. His old benefactor in Utetera, Kasongo Rushie, was very unhappy to see him go—he had greatly enjoyed the peace that his protector had provided—but Tippu Tip reassured him by leaving a contingent of soldiers behind.

Once in his new home, Tippu Tip again conquered the area chieftains. Tributes, ivory, and slaves came pouring in. The rich and powerful slaver became even richer and more powerful, and his fame spread.

One afternoon in October 1876, Tippu Tip was going about business as usual in the village of Mwana Mamba, not far from Nyangwe. He and a number of other Arab traders had just returned from an expedition into the forest to avenge the murder of a colleague and his caravan of ten. More details are not known, but can easily be imagined.

Suddenly, the sound of a drum and trumpet was heard, and the Arabs looked up in astonishment to see a sweaty, red-faced white man arriving, accompanied by a caravan of about 130 men, women, and children. Caravans seldom arrived without notice, and Mwana Mamba was off the main caravan trail. What were they doing here?

Some of the Arabs rushed forward to welcome the white man, while others began preparing a place for him and his followers to stay. Last to acknowledge the newcomers was Tippu Tip, now an imposing, black-bearded man in his mid-forties. He approached the stranger only after he had been comfortably settled on a wide *baraza*.

"With the air of a well-bred Arab, and almost courtier-like in his manner, Tippu Tip welcomed me to Mwana Mamba's village, and his slaves being ready at hand with mat and bolster, he reclined vis-à-vis, while a buzz of admiration of his style was perceptible from the onlookers," wrote Henry Morton Stanley.

By the time Stanley and Tippu Tip met, five years had passed since Stanley's famed encounter with Livingstone in Ujiji. The two Western men had spent five months together, exploring the northern shores of Lake Tanganyika and traveling to Tabora, where Stanley promised the older man that if he failed in his mission to find the source of the Nile, he would carry on the search.

During their time together, the two men had become close. Livingstone felt profound gratitude toward Stanley, who had rescued him from near-certain death, and Stanley, whose quest to find the explorer had taken on an almost religious fervor, idolized the older man—the father he had never had. The two spent many hours in deep conversation, and when they parted—Livingstone to continue his explorations in Africa and Stanley to return to England—Stanley had to turn his face away to hide his tears.

The doctor died just over a year later. His faithful followers, Chuma and Susi, who had been with him for seven years, found him near dawn one morning, kneeling on the floor by his bed as if in prayer. He was sixty years old.

Chuma and Susi could have buried Livingstone in Africa, but knowing that he had wished to be buried in England, they prepared his body for transit. They made a small incision in his abdomen, through which they expertly removed his organs and intestines. His heart was placed in the tin box that he had used for storing his journals and buried at the base of a mpundu tree—his heart would always remain in Africa. Then they poured salt into the open cavity of the body and allowed it to dry in the sun for fourteen days, wrapped the corpse in calico, encased it in a cylinder of bark, sewed a large piece of sailcloth around it, tarred the whole bundle to make it watertight, and slung it from a pole that could be carried by two men.

Their eleven-month trek back to the coast was brutal. Ten men in their caravan died, and everyone suffered acutely from disease. But Chuma's and Susi's extraordinary loyalty to Livingstone never faltered, and his well-preserved body reached England in April 1874, eight years after he had departed for his last expedition.

All of England mourned. A special train provided by Queen Victoria transported the body from the coast to London, where it lay in state in the Map Room of the Royal Geographical Society. The next day, enormous silent crowds gathered on the streets to watch as the funeral procession made its way to Westminster Abbey. Livingstone was buried in a simple ceremony. Among the pallbearers was Stanley.

The epitaph on Livingstone's gravestone reads:

Brought by faithful hands over land and sea here rests David Livingstone, missionary, traveler, philanthropist, born March 19, 1813
at Blantyre, Lanarkshire, died May 1, 1873 at Chitambo's village,
Ulala.

For 30 years his life was spent in an unwearied effort to evan-
gelize the native races, to explore the undiscovered secrets, to
abolish the desolating slave trade, of Central Africa, where with his
last words he wrote: "All I can add in my solitude is may Heaven's
rich blessing come down on everyone, American, English or Turk,
who will help to heal this open sore of the world."

Livingstone's prayers would soon be answered. The end of the
African slave trade was near.

After leaving Livingstone at Tabora, Stanley had returned to Zanzibar.
Arriving there after a remarkably quick journey of less than two
months, he carried with him Livingstone's journals and a letter that the
explorer had written to the *Herald* about the Nyangwe massacre. That
letter was published, to great public outrage, one week before Britain's
House of Commons held hearings on the East and Central African slave
trade and thus helped lead directly to the passage of the 1873 anti–slave
trade treaty.

In Zanzibar, Stanley received a hero's welcome, complete with
cheering crowds and twenty-one-gun salutes. But his reception in England was more complicated. At first, some experts were skeptical of his
claim to have found Livingstone, and even after his story was accepted,
he was given only grudging praise. Britain had sent its own expedition
to find Livingstone, and many were exasperated to learn that Stanley—
a self-proclaimed American!—had reached the explorer first. Furthermore, Stanley was a commoner, and a grubby, ink-stained journalist to
boot. Most British explorers were gentlemen.

Livingstone may have told Stanley about his travels with Tippu Tip, but
the two younger men didn't meet until Stanley stumbled into the
Mwana Mamba village during his second trip to Africa, an 1874–77 ex-

pedition jointly and lavishly funded by the *New York Herald* and the London *Daily Telegraph*. Stanley's goal on this journey was to finally prove the source of the Nile—and to gain more fame and fortune in the process.

To settle the question of the Nile once and for all, Stanley had to accomplish three tasks: circumnavigate Lake Victoria to determine if the stream at Ripon Falls was its only outlet and thus the probable source of the Nile, as John Speke had believed; circumnavigate Lake Tanganyika to see if it had an outlet that might eventually lead to the Nile, as Richard Burton had posited; and follow the Lualaba River to see if it led to the Nile, as Livingstone had believed.

While in Zanzibar assembling his caravan, Stanley noticed an important change from his earlier visit: the slave market had been torn down, and the United Universities' Mission to Central Africa was building an Anglican church on its site. The mission had been formed by Cambridge and Oxford universities over a decade earlier, following an especially stirring speech delivered by Livingstone at Cambridge.

The slave market had been torn down because the slave trade had ended, officially at least. However, slavery itself was still legal on the island and would not be abolished until 1897. At the time of Stanley's visit, Seyyid Barghash alone owned about 4,000 slaves, while leading Arab and Swahili citizens owned between 500 and 2,000 slaves each, and the Indian community owned a total of about 8,000 slaves.

While in Zanzibar, Stanley met Seyyid Barghash, of whom he formed a most favorable impression: "It is impossible not to feel a kindly interest in Prince Barghash, and to wish him complete success in the reforms he is now striving to bring about in his country. Here we see an Arab prince, educated in the strictest school of Islam, and accustomed to regard the black natives of Africa as the lawful prey of conquest or lust, and fair objects of barter, suddenly turning round at the request of European philanthropists and becoming one of the most active opponents of the slave-trade."

Like his father before him, Barghash was a man of his word. He had been fiercely opposed to the 1873 anti–slave trade treaty at first, but once he had signed the document, he did his best to enforce it.

By the time Stanley met Tippu Tip, he had already completed the first two parts of his mission. He had circumnavigated Lake Victoria, where he determined that Ripon Falls was indeed its only outlet, and Lake Tanganyika, where he found no outlet large enough to lead to the Nile. He was now convinced that the mighty river rose in Lake Victoria, but he kept his opinion to himself. He still had one more task to complete: follow the Lualaba. If it was not the source of the Nile, where did it go?

Upon his arrival in Manyeuma country, Stanley immediately sought out Tippu Tip. He knew of the trader's reputation—"there was no person at Nyangwe whose evidence was more valuable than Tippu Tip's," he wrote—and desperately needed his help. Hostile tribes lined the Lualaba's banks for hundreds of miles, and without a powerful local ally at his side, his followers would desert.

But at first, the Arab trader turned Stanley down, saying, "If you Wasungu (white men) are desirous of throwing away your lives, it is no reason we Arabs should. We travel little by little to get ivory and slaves, and are years about it—it is now nine years since I left Zanzibar—but you white men only look for rivers and lakes and mountains, and you spend your lives for no reason, and to no purpose. Look at that old man who died in Bisa [i.e., Livingstone]! What did he see year after year, until he became so old that he could not travel?"

"I know I have no right to expect you to risk your life for me," Stanley replied. "I only wish you to accompany me sixty days' journey, then leave me to myself."

Tippu Tip said that he would think it over, and the next evening, brought up the subject again. Where exactly did the explorer wish to go?

"I would like to go down the river in canoes until I reach the place where the river turns for good," Stanley said.

"How many days' journey on land would that be?" Tippu Tip asked.

"I don't know. Do you?"

At that, Tippu Tip called in a young Arab, who professed to know all about the river. It flows "north, and north, and north, and there is no end to it," he said. "I think it reaches the salt sea, at least some of my friends say so."

An excited Stanley asked to hear more and the young Arab went on to describe a journey that he had taken into a rich ivory country north of Nyangwe. The country was filled with dwarfs, he said, who had been very curious to know what the traders wanted the ivory for, since they killed elephants for their meat only and threw away the tusks. But the dwarfs had also been hostile and fought the intruders ferociously, firing poisoned arrows at them from behind bushes and trees. The traders had collected more ivory than they could carry, but were forced to leave it all behind in order to escape with their lives. Out of the huge caravan that had departed Nyangwe, only thirty men returned.

Tippu Tip motioned for the young man to leave the room. He had made up his mind; he would travel with the explorer. Stanley was vastly relieved. Like Livingstone before him, and many other Europeans after him, he felt drawn to Tippu Tip and believed he could trust him.

The two men signed an agreement. Tippu Tip would supply Stanley with porters and an escort for a distance of sixty camps in exchange for $5,000. He wasn't doing it for the money, but out of kindness, he said. He didn't mention his real reason for accompanying the explorer: the opportunity to explore an unknown territory reputedly rich with ivory.

And so it was that on November 5, 1876, a caravan of about 450 people left Nyangwe, to trek north along the Lualaba's eastern bank; they would not put into the river until they had bypassed a series of waterfalls. Stanley's caravan only numbered about 145, but traveling with Tippu Tip were a dozen other Arab traders, 140 guards, and numerous porters, slaves, women, and children.

After only a day's march, the caravan entered the "dreaded black and chill forest called Mitamba," where "every leaf seemed to be weeping," wrote Stanley in his typically overwrought but compelling and fast-paced prose. "Down the boles and branches, creepers and vegetable cords, the moisture trickled and fell on us. Overhead the wide-spreading branches, in many interlaced strata, each branch heavy with broad thick leaves, absolutely shut out the daylight. . . . We marched in a feeble solemn twilight."

With each passing day, the way became more difficult. A party was organized to cut a path through the woods, but there were many fallen giant tree trunks that could not be removed, and slippery clay clung to the travelers' every step.

Finally, on November 19, the caravan came upon the Lualaba again, "gentle as a summer's dream," with black forests on either side of its mile-wide expanse. Most of the party set up camp on the river's grassy bank, while a few men put together the *Lady Alice*, a forty-foot-long steel-and-cedar boat that could be broken down into sections to make it easier to carry. The boat was named after Stanley's fiancée, Alice Pike, a seventeen-year-old American heiress. The two had signed a marriage pact before he left and even fixed a wedding date. But not surprisingly, it was not to be. Alice was a flighty girl whose world revolved around debutante balls, and she knew nothing of the rigors of traveling in Africa. "You never write to me any more, and I just want to know why??? I am really angry with Central Africa," she wrote her betrothed at one point. Alice would marry someone else long before Stanley returned. He never saw her again.

A small dugout canoe with two men approached from the opposite shore. Summoning an interpreter, Stanley asked the men for canoes to transport his entire party across the river, where the forest was less dense. He would give the men plenty of shells and beads in return, he said. But they refused.

"Go back, Wasambye; you are bad!" they said. "Wasambye are bad, bad, bad! The river is deep, Wasambye! You have not wings, Wasambye! Go back, Wasambye!"

"Wasambye" was the African name for the slave traders from Nyangwe.

The men then uttered a wild, weird cry—"Ooh-hu, ooh-hu-hu-hu"—which was answered by others up and down the river.

"That is a war-cry, master," Tippu Tip said as he loaded his gun.

"Nonsense, don't be foolish. What cause is there for war?" Stanley asked.

A short time later, Stanley, Tippu Tip, and a handful of others boarded the now-reassembled *Lady Alice* and crossed the river, where they approached a small village and again asked for canoes. After bribery and threats, the villagers reluctantly agreed to help them, and the entire expedition was successfully transported across the river. But when the explorers went back to the village the next morning, in the hopes of "a kindly interchange of gifts," the village was deserted. As were all the other villages nearby. Afraid that the intruders had come to enslave them, the Africans had fled. The explorers walked through the eerie empty settlements casting nervous glances over their shoulders. "Each village street had its two rows of bleached trophies of eaten humanity," wrote Stanley; they were in the heart of cannibal country.

Stanley and about thirty of his party then boarded the *Lady Alice* and departed downriver. The rest of his caravan set out on foot, under the leadership of the expedition's only other surviving white man, Frank Pocock. Tippu Tip and his caravan also traveled by land. The three parties kept in touch with drums, and their progress was marked by the beating of other drums and war cries warning villagers downstream of the approaching intruders. At night, the expedition camped onshore.

For those traveling on land, the way was very difficult. Thorns penetrated their feet and legs, causing painful ulcers, and smallpox and dysentery broke out. A makeshift floating hospital was constructed out of six abandoned canoes lashed together.

In early December, about a month after leaving Nyangwe, a flotilla of war canoes attacked Stanley's camp and he retaliated with gunfire, "doing terrible execution." He had hoped to remain on good terms with the river's people, but that was proving to be impossible. Convinced he was a slaver, they let fly hundreds of poisoned arrows whenever he or his followers drew near.

One day, Stanley was alone in camp with just forty men when he saw dozens of war canoes approaching, carrying a dense mass of five hundred to eight hundred Africans. His men fired at them, but they did not retreat and probably would not have retreated had not Tippu Tip's caravan suddenly appeared. Blowing their war horns, the Africans rowed away, but only to the far side of a nearby island, where they began to prepare for the next day's assault.

That night, Stanley and some of his men rowed quietly to the island. It was a rainy, gusty night, and they could hear the warriors talking by their campfires, their canoes safely secured with stakes—or so they thought. Gliding silently by, Stanley's men cut the stakes and pushed the canoes into the river, where they were retrieved by Frank

Pocock and his men. The next morning, the Africans were ready to negotiate.

On December 22, Tippu Tip announced that it was time for him to leave the expedition. Stanley raised no objections, even though, according to their earlier agreement, the trader still owed him eight camps, or marches.

Stanley and Tippu Tip had much in common. Both were courageous, larger-than-life men who did not hesitate to tell outrageous stories to enhance their reputation or further their cause. Both were also single-minded, ambitious egotists intent on accruing fame and fortune, no matter what the price to others or the violence involved.

But neither man liked sharing the leadership role and both were privately relieved to be parting company. They were jealous of each other. Stanley complained of Tippu Tip's undisciplined people and boasted about his own generosity, while Tippu Tip claimed that Stanley was not at all generous, and that it was he who made sure the explorer's followers were paid. The two would work together again over a decade later, rescuing a British governor surrounded by hostile forces in the Sudan, and then the rancor between them would become so extreme that Stanley filed suit against the trader. He later withdrew his case, but the two never reconciled.

On December 28, the two groups separated. Downriver floated the *Lady Alice*, followed by a flotilla of twenty-three canoes, while from the shore, Tippu Tip's men sang a farewell. "Ranged along the bank in picturesque costume the sons of Unyamwezi sang their last song," wrote Stanley. "We waved our hands to them. Our hearts were so full of grief that we could not speak. Steadily the brown flood bore us by, and fainter and fainter came the notes down the water, till finally they died away, leaving us all alone in our loneliness. . . ."

The next day, Tippu Tip sent scouting parties into the forest to determine which way back to Nyangwe would be best. But, as he had promised Stanley, he waited a month before leaving, to make sure that the explorer was safely on his way.

Later, when he did leave, Tippu Tip found the region to be as rich with ivory as had been reported. In addition, the local people had no idea the tusks were valuable and were using them for the most mundane of tasks, such as building fences and making kitchen utensils.

Sometimes, the Africans even threw the tusks into the bush where they were gnawed by animals or left to rot. Tippu Tip was in paradise.

Stanley's expedition had been fraught with difficulty from the day it left Zanzibar, but there was much, much worse to come. Ahead of him lay every possible disaster, including cataracts, disease, starvation, attacks, mutiny, theft, and the death by drowning of his last remaining white companion and friend Frank Pocock. Many others in their party would perish as well. Of the 143 people, including 16 women and 8 children, who waved good-bye to Tippu Tip on that day in late December, only 114 would make it to the coast and 5 more would die within days of their arrival.

After leaving Tippu Tip, the expedition followed the Lualaba due north for four hundred miles, passing numerous settlements and fighting off small-scale attacks along the way. Then came an unwelcoming sound—the roar of a cataract ahead. Disassembling the *Lady Alice* and hoisting the heavy dugout canoes, the party portaged around it, down slippery, rocky gorges lined with jungle. The backbreaking work seemed as if it would never end. The biggest canoe stretched fifty-four feet and weighed three tons, and the cataract extended for several miles. And yet, it was only the beginning: the cataract was just the first in a chain of seven, later to be known as Stanley Falls, now known as Boyoma Falls, extending over 60 miles. Even more mind-boggling, Stanley Falls was nothing compared to what the expedition would encounter at the end of the river: a 220-mile stretch of thirty-two cataracts interspersed with dangerous rapids.

While portaging around the falls, the expedition was forced to live on land, where they were vulnerable to attack. And despite Stanley's hope to maintain good relations with the area's tribes, his river journey turned bloody fast. With the Africans convinced that he was a slave trader, he often had no choice but to kill or be killed. But Stanley also seemed to revel in the bloodshed, boasting in his journal at one point that "we have attacked and destroyed 28 large towns and three or four score villages." Stanley probably killed hundreds of Africans during his expedition, in what was hardly a fair fight; he and his men were equipped with the latest rifles and a gun with exploding bullets designed to kill elephants. The Africans fought with spears and bows and arrows.

Stanley's battles with the riverside tribes mirrored other ugly incidents that had occurred earlier on Lake Victoria and Lake Tanganyika. He seemed to take every act of hostility as a personal affront and reacted to anything resembling mockery with great rage—due in large part, no doubt, to the pain of his childhood. On Lake Victoria, he coldly killed or badly wounded thirty-three Africans in retribution for an earlier hostile encounter, and later expressed no regret for his actions. Following an incident on Lake Tanganyika, he wrote: "The beach was crowded with infuriates and mockers. . . . I opened on them with the Winchester Repeating Rifle. Six shots and four deaths were sufficient to quiet the mocking."

Stanley has come to epitomize the cruelty, violence, and raw greed of the imperialistic Westerner operating in foreign lands. And yet, paradoxically, as biographer Tim Jeal writes in *Stanley: The Impossible Life of Africa's Greatest Explorer,* Stanley was one of the least racist of Africa's explorers. He became angry when a white man called a black man "nigger"—"that ugly derisive word"—and admonished his young white followers to "relax those stiff pallid features; let there enter into those chill icy eyes, the light of light and joy, of humour, friendship, pleasure"—i.e., the light of the Africans.

Stanley was also one of the few white men to fully acknowledge the invaluable help of his African followers. "The execution & fulfillment of all plans, and designs was due to the pluck and intrinsic goodness of 20 [African] men . . . take these 20 men out and I could not have proceeded beyond a few days journey," he wrote in one typical passage.

After passing Stanley Falls, the expedition followed the Lualaba due west, where, for the first time, they heard the river referred to as the "Ikuta Yacongo." There was no longer any doubt. The Lualaba was the Upper Congo. It led not to the Nile, but to the Congo and the Atlantic.

Stanley's 1874–77 expedition proved that the Nile rose in Lake Victoria, to flow north to Egypt and the Mediterranean, and that the Lualaba joined the Congo, to flow west to the Atlantic. The search to find the source of the Nile had finally ended. The lakes and rivers of Central Africa had been mapped.

Stanley had performed a superhuman feat, overcoming dozens of seemingly insurmountable obstacles along the way, any one of which would have felled a less determined or less courageous man. He had also opened up the Congo River Basin to the West, setting the stage for what historians and journalists would dub the "Scramble for Africa." With the scramble would come the end of the Omanis' rule of East Africa.

27

Seyyid Barghash

EVERY MORNING AT FOUR A.M., SEYYID BARGHASH ENTERED THE *baraza* of his palace, carrying a Quran in one hand and a lamp in the other. Taking a seat in his chair of state, he recited various passages from the holy book. At four-thirty a.m., twelve religious scholars joined him, and together the men said morning prayers. At six a.m., as the sun rose, the men broke their fast with tea and light cakes, and the religious scholars departed.

At seven a.m., the state treasurer, customs master, and other officials entered the *baraza* to give reports and get instructions for the day. Then Barghash retired to his private apartment and ate his first meal. Unlike his father, he always ate alone, at a large table covered with all kinds of foods—he was a gourmand.

His dining habits notwithstanding, Seyyid Barghash, who ruled Zanzibar for eighteen critical years, from 1870 to 1888, was a man much like his father. Ambitious, honorable, enlightened, and shrewd, he was a just sovereign, adroit negotiator, and talented administrator who modernized his state and greatly augmented its economy. Zanzibar under Barghash entered a golden era.

Barghash's reign began inauspiciously, with two events that seemed to spell economic doom for the island—the devastating 1872 hurricane and the 1873 anti–slave trade treaty. But Barghash, a born businessman like Seyyid Said, succeeded in rapidly refocusing Zanzibar's economy. The opening of the Suez Canal in 1869 meant that scheduled steamship travel—just recently developed—between the island and the outside world could begin, and that smaller merchants as well as larger ones could trade with foreign markets. British and European steamship lines began making regular stops at Zanzibar, and Barghash organized his own fleet of six vessels as well. He also connected the island to the world with underwater telegraph cables. During his reign, state revenues increased fourfold.

Barghash's exile in Bombay had given him a larger worldview than either his brother Majid or even his father, and with his new revenues he brought many much-needed reforms to the island. He built new roads, a stone aqueduct, and piping to supply freshwater to Zanzibar's inhabitants and its public baths. He connected his palaces with telephones and in the 1880s brought electric light to the harbor area— a first for the sub-Saharan region. He put more police on the streets and minted the island's first coins. Surprisingly, however, he did little to improve the town's sanitary conditions, which had become worse than ever, due to a population that had grown to about eighty thousand. Neither did he do anything to develop the port, which still operated without docks or cranes.

Inspired by what he had seen in Bombay and later in England, Barghash also constructed five new palaces for himself, each with innovative architectural details. The Beit al-Chuini was built over a river whose waters flowed through the complex's many baths on its way to the sea. The Beit al-Marhubi was surrounded by a wall much like the park walls of England, and contained an avenue of Indian mangoes, water-lily ponds, and stone aqueducts carrying water from Chemchem spring. The Beit al-Chukwani was connected to the town by a short railway—the first for the island.

Barghash's greatest architectural feat, however, was the Beit al-Ajaib, or House of Wonders, a palace built on the harbor waterfront in 1883 for ceremonial purposes. An enormous square block with a distinctive clock tower that continues to dominate Stone Town today, it featured a large central courtyard surrounded by broad verandas, wide teak staircases, black-and-white marble floors, and many carved Zanzibari doors, glittering mirrors, ornate clocks, and electrically powered chandeliers.

With a greater taste for luxury than either his brother Majid or his father, Barghash also furnished the House of Wonders with exquisite ebony tables and chairs, the most intricate of Persian carpets, and fine fabrics and silks. He preferred gold to silver—unusual for an Arab ruler—and reveled in the personal luxury goods imported for him from London, Paris, and Bombay.

During his 1875 visit to London, Barghash made a stop in Cairo, where he delighted in hearing *taarob* (Arabic for "joy, pleasure"), a type of secular music performed for the court. Thereafter, he sent a musician, Muhammad bin Ibrahim, to Cairo to study *taarob*. When he returned, he became the sultan's court singer and taught others what he had learned. *Taarob* was then performed at the palace every afternoon and during mealtimes—and became one of Barghash's most important legacies. Only the royal family and guests could attend the actual performances, but many others gathered outside the palace to listen to the hypnotic, mellifluous music, sung in Arabic. Two generations later, in the 1920s and 1930s, *taarob* was popularized by Siti binti Saad, who sang *taarob* in KiSwahili for the first time. Her recordings flooded the airways of the East African coast, and *taarob* remains wildly popular throughout the region today.

Barghash had only one legal wife, but like his father before him, he owned dozens of concubines—forty-four at the time of his death. For their enjoyment, he laid out a large English-style garden, surrounded by high walls. Now known as Victoria Gardens, the park was converted for public use in the late 1890s.

An 1870s picture of Barghash, who was Seyyid Said's seventh son, born to an Abyssinian concubine, shows a round-cheeked, smooth-complexioned man with warm brown skin, a frizzy black beard, heavily lidded eyes, and an aquiline nose. He is dressed in a fine, shiny, embroidered black cloak worn over a white *dishdasha*, and the *khanjar* at his waist appears to sit a bit uncomfortably on his solid paunch. A multicolored, striped turban is elaborately entwined around his head, with a tail jutting out in back. His expression is benign, but one can sense power and perhaps superiority behind it. Barghash's detractors criticized him for his autocratic manner, saying that, despite his reputation for fairness, if he wanted a plantation, he forced its owner to sell it to him at his price, and that if he coveted a subject's piece of jewelry or other personal possession, he simply confiscated it on the spot.

Barghash was more strictly religious than either his brother Majid or his father, and he appointed many more *qadis* and other Islamic officials to the East African coast than had his predecessors—a system that would continue long after his death. He provided free annual passage to Mecca to any pilgrim unable to pay his or her way, and proffered generous public feasts on Islamic holidays.

Early in his reign, Barghash also had close ties with the Mutawwah, stern Ibadhi reformers, and through their influence tried to gain some degree of independence from Britain, mostly by initially refusing to sign the 1873 anti–slave trade treaty. The Mutawwah wanted to excise Zanzibar's many non-Ibadhi influences, reinstate the strict principles of Sharia that had been ignored during Majid's reign, and reunite the sultanates of Oman and Zanzibar, so that one powerful imam could once again be both their political and religious leader. But Barghash's efforts to break loose from Britain's control died before they even started. He was strong-armed into signing the 1873 treaty under the threat of a blockade, and thereafter distanced himself from the Mutawwah.

Because of Barghash's strong interest in religion, Zanzibar under his rule began to attract some of East Africa's foremost religious scholars, turning it into an important Islamic cultural and intellectual center. In a chronicle of the island's *ulema*, Shaykh Abdalla Saleh Farsy provides biographies of more than 170 religious scholars who were connected with Zanzibar at some point in their careers, many during Barghash's reign. Access to a basic Quranic education became available to anyone who wanted it, and advanced lessons became available to select sons— although not daughters—of powerful Arab families. Literacy spread, both on the island and along the East African coast.

Barghash's religious devotion did not mean, however, that he was any less tolerant of other faiths than his forefathers had been. In fact, ever since Livingstone's last journey into Africa, Christian missionaries had been pouring into Zanzibar. The Universities' Mission to Central

Africa, the Holy Ghost Fathers, the Church Missionary Society, the London Missionary Society, the White Fathers—all were there.

Dominant among them was the Universities' Mission, a presence in Zanzibar since 1864. The Anglican church that they had constructed on the site of the old slave market was enormous. Designed by the mission's Bishop Edward Steere and built of portland cement, the church stood about sixty feet tall, combined Gothic and Arabic elements, had an unusual unsupported roof that spanned nine yards, and could seat six hundred. Its marble pillars had been specially imported from Italy, but were installed upside down, as the bishop had been on the mainland when they were erected. The altar was said to stand where the old whipping post of the slave market had once stood, and the crucifix on the north wall was made of wood from the tree at Chitambo's village where Livingstone's heart was buried.

A man of many talents, Bishop Steere tried to get Muslims involved in his new church by addressing them in KiSwahili every Friday in an adjoining chapel and including a gallery for veiled women in the church. He also compiled an English-KiSwahili dictionary, recorded many Swahili folktales, and was the first to translate the New Testament into KiSwahili.

Another of Steere's projects was a community for freed slaves, situated on the coast a few miles outside town. Known as Mbweni, the community included separate schools for boys and girls (the latter run by Caroline Thackeray, a cousin of William Makepeace Thackeray, author of *Vanity Fair*), homes for couples and families, shops, a church, and a printing press. Everyone had a small plot of land on which to grow their own food, and all were expected to attend church on Sunday. When Mbweni opened in 1874, it housed 23 men and women; ten years later, it held 250 men, women, and children.

Seyyid Barghash encouraged Bishop Steere in his endeavors, even donating the clock for the slave-market church. The sovereign greatly respected the Englishman and could afford to be generous. The Christians had been an active presence on the East African coast for over a hundred years—more if the Portuguese invasion of the sixteenth and seventeenth centuries was included—but had had virtually no religious impact on its people. The Arabs did not permit the Westerners to convert Muslims, just pagan Africans, and few Muslims were interested in converting anyway. For one thing, conversion was punishable by death.

Even those Africans who converted were seldom Christians in the true sense of the word. Unlike Islam, with its emphasis on the community rather than the individual, and its enthusiasm for polygamy, Christianity went against many traditional African customs. Most "converts," even at a mission like Mbweni, still practiced their tribal faiths when at home. Their attendance at church on Sundays was for show only. Mbweni and other communities like it aided the freed Africans considerably when it came to physical needs and education, but when it came to changing religious beliefs, they were failures.

In June 1866, while Seyyid Majid was still in power, the future British consul John Kirk had arrived in Zanzibar. The tall, slim, round-shouldered Scotsman who had accompanied Livingstone on his Zambezi expedition had been appointed the British consulate's doctor, on the recommendation of Livingstone.

Kirk ministered mostly to the island's European and Indian communities, but one day he received an unusual request. Barghash, recently returned from exile in India, asked him to make a house call on a beloved older half-sister who lived about five miles outside town. "[I] went prepared to do all I could: for Barghash is a good jolly fellow, I would willingly do what I can for his sake," wrote Kirk in a letter to his fiancée.

That house call laid the groundwork for what was to become an important relationship. Kirk was appointed the British consul to Zanzibar shortly after Barghash rose to power, and he remained in office for the duration of the sultan's reign. A soft-spoken, patient, and logical man who was adept at diplomacy, Kirk genuinely liked and trusted Barghash, who in turn genuinely liked and trusted Kirk. They worked closely together for eighteen years.

It was Kirk who persuaded Barghash to sign the 1873 anti–slave trade treaty—an accomplishment for which he was later knighted. Earlier attempts by other diplomats, including Sir Bartle Frere, had failed; Barghash had found the treaty's terms to be untenable at first. During one meeting with Kirk, he declared: "We cannot sign the new treaty on account of the hardship it involves to us, on account of dread of insurrection, and on account of the ruin it would cause to the plantation of our subjects. . . . In one word, No!" And in a letter to Kirk he wrote: "But it may be that the exalted English government is not aware of Zanzibar's need for slaves. The people of Zanzibar can do nothing, not even clip their whiskers, without the servants and slaves they own; if they were deprived of them they would be impoverished and their possessions worth nothing."

But slowly, Kirk brought the sovereign around, largely by persuading him that he had no choice. Britain's power was too great.

All that Kirk could offer Barghash in return for signing the treaty was his personal promise to help him keep his empire intact. Kirk kept his promise, but in the end, it didn't matter. Britain withdrew its support of both him and Barghash.

It was also Kirk who persuaded Barghash to sign another all-important anti–slave trade proclamation on April 18, 1876, shortly after their return from London. Filling in the gaping loophole left by the 1873 treaty, the proclamation read: "To all whom it may concern of our friends on the mainland of Africa, the island of Pemba, and elsewhere . . . Be it known that we have determined to stop and by this order do prohibit all conveyance of slaves by land under any conditions. And we have instructed our Governors on the coast to seize and imprison those found disobeying this order and to confiscate their slaves."

At long last, the centuries-old East African slave trade was unequivocally illegal on both land and sea. The slavers had met their match. Smuggling did continue for some time, and the trade would revive again, in the mid- to late 1880s, as Zanzibar lost control of the coast, but the large-scale slave-trade system was no more. Barghash kept his word and began punishing the treaty's offenders so harshly that his people muttered that he was worse than the British. He put down pro–slave trade rebellions at Kilwa and Mombasa, imprisoned a sheikh for harboring slaves, and declared that the end of slavery itself was near.

Barghash's commitment to ending the trade was made clear in one especially dramatic incident. One of his relatives, a man named Said bin Abdulla, was governor of Kilwa, where an attempt to reopen the trade was made in 1877. There was some evidence that Said had been involved, and Barghash dismissed him from his post. Said returned to

Zanzibar and, despite his disgrace, was sitting in a public *baraza* with Barghash one day when Kirk appeared with thirteen slaves and the agents who had been attempting to smuggle them from the mainland. The agents confessed to the deed, and said that they were in Said's employ; the slaves were his. Barghash had Said arrested on the spot and imprisoned in a common jail.

Helping Barghash enforce the new anti–slave trade agreement was a European-styled Zanzibari army—a first for the island. Trained by a British naval officer, the army began as a force of three hundred African soldiers led by Arab and Comorian officers, but soon grew to include over a thousand men. The army had been Kirk's idea.

One day in 1879, Seyyid Barghash sent a letter to Tippu Tip, whom he had never met, requesting that he return to Zanzibar. It had been a dozen years now since the trader had visited his island home and his creditors were asking for him to come settle his accounts. Barghash also wanted Tippu Tip to return for political reasons, and with his letter he sent various flattering gifts, including the latest development in firearms—what Tippu Tip called a "repeating gun."

Tippu Tip decided that the ruler was right. It *was* time for him to go home. His stocks of ivory had become enormous and he needed to take them to market. Over the next year, he organized his administration for his absence and arranged for two thousand porters and a thousand guards to relay his ivory to Mtoa, on the western shore of Lake Tanganyika, for shipment to Ujiji on the eastern shore.

Tippu Tip had not been in Ujiji since visiting it with his father over twenty years before, and he was astonished by what he found there. The town had grown tenfold, and all manner of goods were for sale in its market. The London Missionary Society had arrived, the French Catholics were also nearby, and, most ominously, as the savvy Tippu Tip realized, the International African Association had a station in the town.

Founded in 1876 by King Leopold II of Belgium and three dozen notable European philanthropists, scientists, and explorers, the association proclaimed the noble goal of "abolishing the slave trade, establishing peace among the [African] chiefs, and procuring them just and impartial arbitration." But, unbeknownst to the association's other founders, King Leopold also had a covert political agenda—to establish a Belgian colony in the Congo and reap the profits. Stanley's successful expedition down the Congo River had led the association to greatly intensify its activities in the area, and Stanley himself was back. Employed as an envoy of King Leopold, he was overseeing the construction of a road around the river's rapids and founding towns, while also secretly working to organize a Congo state for his employer.

Stanley's road would be used by the Belgians to transport ivory and other goods from Central Africa to the West Coast, thereby ending the Arabs' monopoly over the Manyeuma region. By helping Stanley travel down the Lualaba, Tippu Tip had sown the seeds of his own destruction.

Tippu Tip finally reached Bagamoyo in November 1882. Accompanying him, he later wrote, was a caravan of 2,000 porters bearing 70,000 pounds of ivory, which he would later sell for 70,000 pounds—enough to support him in royal style for the rest of his life. He also made a handsome profit on the sale of his porter-slaves. The slave trade in all its forms had been illegal for six years now, but Tippu Tip was an old master who knew how to operate outside the reaches of the law.

On Zanzibar, Seyyid Barghash was anxiously awaiting the trader's arrival. The Europeans' presence on the mainland seemed to be growing daily. Christian mission stations had been established in virtually all of the continent's Arab outposts, and Western explorers, scientists, and speculators were popping up everywhere. Politicians and military men were sure to follow. The only one who could save Zanzibar's interests on the mainland was Tippu Tip.

Kirk agreed with Seyyid Barghash. True to his promise to protect the sultan's interests, he had even proposed to the ruler that he empower Tippu Tip to control all the territories between the coast and Lake Tanganyika.

On the morning after Tippu Tip's arrival in Zanzibar, he went to visit the customs master, where he ran into a Belgian whom he had met before in Tabora.

"I want to make us a pact," said the Belgian, and offered him a share in the administration of the Upper Congo.

"I am a subject of the Sultan, Seyyid Barghash," said Tippu Tip, astonished at the proposition; since when did the Belgians control the Upper Congo? "And the country of Manyeuma over which I rule, both it and I are under the authority of Seyyid. I can do nothing without his sanction."

"I am not concerned with the Seyyid," said the Belgian. "You are the chief of Manyeuma who has all authority. If you agree, well and good; if you don't, no matter, leave it."

"I can do nothing except on the authority of my ruler," Tippu Tip said stiffly and left.

When Tippu Tip told Barghash about his conversation with the Belgian, the shocked ruler instructed Tippu Tip to return to Manyeuma "with all speed, Hamed. You must protect our interests there against these European expansionists' designs." He then instructed the customs master to give Tippu Tip all the financial help he needed to assemble a caravan as quickly as possible.

In late 1883, Tippu Tip left Zanzibar with the largest caravan its people had ever seen. Among the goods and supplies it was carrying were a thousand guns.

Upon his arrival in Manyeuma country, Tippu Tip set up headquarters in Stanley Falls, the new Belgian trading post established by and named after the explorer, where he did his best "to look out after all manner of things," as Seyyid Barghash had instructed him. Less than three years later, however, the ruler again summoned the trader back to Zanzibar.

"Hamed, be not angry with me," a weary Seyyid Barghash said when he arrived. "I want to have no more to do with the mainland. The Europeans want to take Zanzibar here from me; how should I be able to keep the mainland? Happy are those who did not live to see the present state of affairs."

"When I heard these words I knew that it was all up with us," wrote Tippu Tip.

28
Endings

IN 1883, THE SAME YEAR THAT TIPPU TIP LEFT ZANZIBAR TO SET up headquarters in Stanley Falls, Seyyida Salme sent a long letter to Seyyid Barghash. It was her first attempt to contact him in nearly eight years, and in the letter, she reiterated her earlier requests for reconciliation, financial assistance, and permission to return home. But the letter also contained several extraordinary passages that revealed the princess's new grasp of politics. She was no longer a naïve young woman from Zanzibar:

> I also wish you to understand, my brother, that all the English only wish to diminish your power and rule in your realm, and they cannot wait until the time has come to seize from you Zanzibar and what is in it. . . .
>
> Nor should you think, my brother, that strangers may be of greater benefit to you or may advise you better than your sister who loves you really and truly. . . . My Lord God knows that I have no other intention than to be useful to you with all the arts of Europe which I have seen and acquired. . . . In the same way, if you need me to settle matters with the German government, I can go to the ruler personally and speak with him for you. He is an extremely good lord. . . .
>
> I also wish to God, then to you, that you keep secret the information which I have given you [here] regarding the English. I have only informed you of it because of my great love of you and of my sincere advice to you and your entire family.

At the request of the crown princess of Germany, the British government instructed Kirk to deliver Salme's letter to Barghash and to speak to him on her behalf. True to form, however, the ruler refused to discuss the matter and never answered the letter.

Salme's grasp of politics went beyond what she revealed in her letter; she was not being completely honest with Barghash. She had neglected to mention another country with far more immediate designs on East Africa than Britain—Germany.

Up until the early 1880s, Germany had had no interest in establishing colonies in Africa or anywhere else. Only unified into a modern nation-state in 1871, it had been more concerned with cementing its new position and acquiring more power in Europe than with imperialistic expansion. In the early 1880s, however, Chancellor Otto von Bismarck began to realize that colonies could help Germany achieve both those goals while also providing it with valuable economic resources. Turning his sights on West Africa, he soon acquired German South West Africa (now Namibia), Togoland (now divided between Togo and Ghana), and Cameroon, all of which became German protectorates in 1884.

Salme followed Bismarck's actions in West Africa "with warm interest," and on June 17, 1884, the year after writing Barghash, sent the chancellor a letter saying that in return for his support of her claims in Zanzibar, she could be of assistance to him in East Africa. Bismarck listened. He wanted to establish an official German consulate in Zanzibar and believed that the princess could help him in that matter. Salme also suggested that she be sent to Zanzibar on a German warship because, she said, diplomacy alone would not work with Barghash. And again Bismarck listened—he had already been thinking of sending warships to Zanzibar, in the hopes of intimidating Barghash into giving him what he wanted. Salme was summoned to the chancellor's official residence in Berlin to discuss the mission, but it was delayed for a year. No warships were available until then.

Also in 1884, Salme became an enthusiastic supporter of the *Gesellschaft für Deutsche Kolonisation*, or German Colonization Society. The society was headed by a thin, young, bespectacled intellectual-adventurer named Carl Peters. Raised in a vicarage, Peters knew almost nothing about the world outside books, but following an 1882 visit to England, then much richer and more developed than the still-fledgling, struggling Germany, declared, "I got tired of being accounted among the pariahs, and wished to belong to the master race."

One way for Germans to join the British in the master race, Peters believed, was to acquire colonies, and so he founded his society, together with other obscure provincial intellectuals and professionals. Studying a map of Africa, the men considered various locations for their colony at first, but then read Stanley's *How I Found Livingstone*, which described the potential wealth of the coast opposite Zanzibar.

In September 1884, twenty-seven-year-old Peters and three companions left Germany for their great adventure. They had no financial or political backing, and upon landing in Zanzibar, found a telegram from Bismarck waiting for them. Germany did not support them in their endeavors, the chancellor warned.

Nonetheless, Peters and his companions blithely hired thirty-six porters and a half-dozen servants—all they could afford—and set off for the mainland, intent on signing treaties with the local tribes. Because their caravan was poorly equipped, they had to conduct their business as quickly as possible and soon developed a system: arrive at a village, listen to the chieftain's welcoming speech, hand over a treaty to be signed, hoist the black cross of the German flag, shake hands, and rush off to find the next chieftain. Within a few weeks, the adventurers had "negotiated" a dozen treaties, all signed with X's. The chieftains couldn't read or write and had no idea what they were signing.

Treaties in hand, Peters returned to Berlin, arriving there in February 1885, shortly before the end of the months-long Berlin Conference. Organized to resolve some conflicting European claims to West Africa, the conference is today regarded as the first formal move in the "Scramble for Africa," the greedy campaign by Western nations to establish colonies in Africa. Less than twenty years after the Berlin Conference, 90 percent of Africa would be under European control, with only one native African state—Abyssinia, or Ethiopia—retaining its sovereign power.

A dramatic Peters, sobbing at times, presented his case to Bismarck, fully expecting to be rebuffed. His mission had not been sanctioned; he had no real status; and Germany might not want to challenge Britain's authority in Zanzibar. But Bismarck was quite taken with Peters's story and not only accepted the questionable, unofficial treaties, but also gave Peters a charter for a German East African protectorate—a fact that was not publicized until after the Berlin Conference ended. The protectorate included only four undefined areas opposite Zanzibar, but Peters regarded it as license to take over most of the Al Busaids' empire, as far west as Lake Tanganyika.

While Peters was in Berlin, a well-known German explorer named Friedrich Gerhard Rohlfs arrived in Zanzibar under Bismarck's orders. Rohlfs hoped to become the first German consul to Zanzibar, and to convince Seyyid Barghash to turn Zanzibar into a German protectorate. Despite the longtime presence of the British on the island, they had no real legal status there and a mistaken rumor, promulgated in part by Salme, had it that the Zanzibaris were "tired" of the British. All Germany had to do was pursue a more energetic campaign, and Zanzibar, along with much of East Africa, would fall under its reign.

No diplomat, Rohlfs began pressuring Barghash immediately after his arrival. Did the sultan want German protection? The astonished ruler turned him down. Rohlfs continued to press. Barghash didn't budge. And then word arrived of Bismarck's acceptance of Peters's treaties.

Barghash was horrified. But except for sending a letter of protest to Germany, there was little he could do without the backing of the British, and this, he learned to his even greater horror, he didn't have. Britain needed Germany's help against the French, who were taking over much of North Africa, and in other delicate diplomatic matters. Literally overnight, the Al Busaids' near-century-long cooperation with the British became worthless. As the Italian doctor Vincenzo Maurizi had warned Seyyid Said in Oman many years before, "when two nations, the one powerful, the other weak, entered into a lasting alliance, the latter, in the course of time, always became subject to the former."

Consul Kirk was also horrified. For eighteen years, he had promised Barghash that as long as he cooperated with the British, they would protect Zanzibar. But now his country was asking him to betray all that he had stood for. He tried to counteract Germany's actions by advising Britain to increase its presence on the mainland between Mombasa and Kilimanjaro, where British missionaries and Zanzibar already had a small interest, but received no support from the foreign office. Instead he was abruptly ordered to cooperate with the Germans and not "convert a mere commercial speculation into a political question."

More drama soon followed. On August 7, 1885, much to the astonishment of the Zanzibaris, a squadron of five German navy vessels steamed into their harbor and trained their guns on Seyyid Barghash's House of Wonders. Four interminable days passed. Then finally, on August 11, the squadron's commander, Commodore Carl Paschen, delivered a twenty-four-hour ultimatum. Seyyid Barghash must either withdraw his protests against the claims of the German Colonization Society or face the consequences.

Kirk succeeded in convincing the Germans to extend their ultimatum one more day, but on August 13, Barghash reluctantly surrendered. He had no choice.

In the interim, another German ship, the *Adler*, which had been waiting off the north end of the island, arrived. On board was Emily Ruete.

Bismarck had initially planned to use Salme as an opening sacrificial pawn in his negotiations with Barghash. Speaking to the head of the German admiralty one year earlier, the chancellor had stated that "if Frau Ruete should be killed or ill treated, the Commandant would be authorised and would in duty be bound to take measures of reprisal. If the Sultan should reject his sister, the Commandant had power to compel him." Bismarck's secretary later elaborated: "[Salme] was to go out to Zanzibar and press her claim, and an accident might possibly occur to the lady—her brother might have her strangled." In such a case, Germany could justifiably seize control of Zanzibar.

Peters's treaties with the African chieftains had diminished Salme's importance to the chancellor, but she was still a valuable asset—and possible pawn. As Bismarck wrote to the German consul at Zanzibar shortly before her arrival: "Frau Ruete is for us solely an excuse for making demands upon the Sultan. . . . Just as military force may be necessary for dealing with the Sultan in regard to other matters, so also the German citeness Ruete and her rights are a useful argument for us in the justification of the use of force. . . . It does not matter if her brother does nothing *a l'amiable* towards her."

Salme's presence also carried other significance. Traveling with her was her sixteen-year-old son, Said, now known as Rudolph Said-Ruete, and rumor had it that Germany wanted to establish a German-Zanzibari dynasty.

The boy's presence was certainly giving the British pause. Wrote one senior British official: "This boy has been carefully educated in Germany, and his mother has never ceased to intrigue in order to bring about his recognition. . . . [She cannot] fail to be alive to the opportunity which has now arisen for interesting Germany in her son's claim to the Zanzibar sultanate; and, should she succeed in doing so, which is not unlikely, firm and prompt action on our part will possibly be the only means of preserving Zanzibar from a German protectorate, which would inevitably be the prelude to its becoming a German colony."

In later years, Salme dismissed the rumor of a German-Zanzibari dynasty as preposterous. But her son intimated otherwise. As a young lieutenant stationed at Torgau on the Elbe River in the summer of 1893, he was invited to lunch with the then-retired Bismarck. When their conversation inevitably turned to Zanzibar, Bismarck remarked that if Barghash had not cooperated with the Germans, Rudolph might now be sultan of Zanzibar. To which the young man reportedly replied that he would rather be an officer in a remote provincial garrison.

Accompanying Salme to Zanzibar that August was not only her son but her two teenage daughters and a German traveling companion, who would later publish her account of their journey in a Hamburg newspaper. Traveling incognito so as not to arouse British suspicion, the party had sailed via Alexandria, Egypt, where Salme had been overcome with the delicious feeling of being home—the city's many palm trees, its minarets, the bustle of its shrouded crowd.

Exactly nineteen years had passed since she had fled Zanzibar, and when her beloved island finally came into view, she ran to her cabin "as quickly as possible" to "thank the Almighty for His great kindness!" The events of her youth passed vividly before her mind's eye, momentarily erasing the hardships of the ensuing years.

Three days after Barghash's surrender, Commodore Paschen sent him a letter on Salme's behalf. A few days later, Admiral Ernst von Knorr, who had arrived to take over the "friendly negotiations" with the sultan, did the same. The German government had no intention of interfering in the ruler's private affairs, the men wrote, but it did wish to bring Salme's claims to his attention. Barghash did not reply to the letters for several days, and when he did, it was via a curt note signed by his secretary: "We have understood the contents of the secret letter you have transmitted to us, but please be so kind as to excuse us. We cannot answer you because she left us many years ago with somebody who is not of a similar rank as ourselves."

As a German citizen in good standing, Salme had the right to go ashore daily, with or without Barghash's permission, Admiral von Knorr then decided. And to ensure that she would not run into trouble, he or one of his officers would accompany her.

On her first visit to town, Salme shocked its inhabitants, both by her mere presence and by her unveiled face, European dress, and male escort. But then, she wrote, with what must have been great excitement, "right and left the crowd pressed around us to call out to me in Arabic and in Swahili: 'How are you, my mistress?' When we entered a stall to go shopping, an immeasurable crowd assembled. . . . Day by day our escort increased in the street and the welcome of the inhabitants became more cordial."

A throng of Africans, hanging around on the beach, began accompanying Salme on her daily walk, and a few Arabs joined in as well. Mothers lifted up their children to see the princess pass, and secret letters were handed to her. A few elite Arab women waited behind doors to whisper out hellos, and even Barghash's wives welcomed Salme by opening their harem shutters and lifting their hands to their veiled foreheads in greeting.

Barghash responded to the princess's reception with great anger. He had some people flogged and, according to Salme, personally whipped one of his Circassian concubines so harshly that she died a few days later, as he begged her forgiveness. For this reason, Salme wrote, she did not return any greeting personally and did not respond to any of the invitations sent to her by relatives and former friends.

Barghash could not stamp out his people's enthusiasm for his way-ward sister entirely, however, and every evening as he stood on his bal-cony, listening to his band playing Zanzibar's British-inspired national anthem, he was forced to endure the sight of a large crowd gathering on the beach. "*Kuaheri, Bibi! Kuaheri, Bibi!*"—"Good-bye, mistress! Good-bye, mistress!"—they would call as the princess returned to her ship.

Now in his late forties, Barghash still had the black hair and black beard of his youth, and bright, intelligent brown eyes. His hands were small and slender and he moved lightly and elegantly on his feet, though he was already suffering from the elephantiasis that would kill him a few years later. On his little finger flashed a big diamond ring.

Attending Barghash was a personal valet who tasted everything be-fore the sultan ate it, poison being a constant concern during his reign. Barghash himself was suspected of poisoning at least two prominent en-emies, and would later be accused by the Germans of poisoning a pow-erful underling who was sympathetic to the German cause.

Like Barghash, Counsel Kirk strongly disapproved of Salme's visits to the island. Her warm welcome by some of its citizens notwithstand-ing, he believed that the majority of the Zanzibari Arabs were outraged by her presence and that she was hurting rather than helping her cause—especially since she was pushing hard against forbidden bound-aries. She tried to enter the palace on several occasions, to be turned away at the door, and once approached Barghash's *baraza*, forcing him to quickly dismiss the assembly and disappear.

To get rid of the princess as quickly as possible, Kirk suggested to Barghash that he agree to give her some sort of settlement. But this, the ruler steadfastly refused to do. When Salme heard the news, she reacted angrily. She would not return to Europe empty-handed or abandon the chance given to her by the German government, she emphatically told von Knorr. Rather, she would take up residence in a French hotel on the island until her brother changed his mind. Nonplussed, the admiral cabled his superiors in Berlin for instructions.

The answer came quickly. Frau Ruete must leave the island at once. And so it was that on October 4, 1885, after six weeks in Zanzibar, a fuming Salme and her party were forced to leave their hotel and em-bark on the *Adler* once more. They sailed for Aden that very day and were back in Hamburg in mid-November. Salme must have been in despair—to have lost such a chance and to be back in the xenophobic city that had shunned her after her husband's death.

After her departure, von Knorr broached the subject of the princess with Barghash once more, and this time, the ruler responded somewhat more amiably. Salme had been guilty of a shameful act and was not entitled to any inheritance, he said, but he was willing to give the German government a sum of money out of friendship to use as it saw fit. Salme had asked her brother for 20,000 pounds, but von Knorr found that excessive, and suggested 6,000 pounds. Instead Barghash sent 6,000 rupees, or only 500 pounds. Salme refused to accept the small sum; Germany said that it would take it "provisionally."

That "provisional" acceptance meant that Germany was keeping Salme's claim alive in case they ever had to use it again. But for Salme, sixteen long years of fighting were finally over.

Shortly after Salme's visit to Zanzibar, Britain and Germany formed a commission to determine the future of East Africa. Barghash protested vehemently, but the Europeans were no longer interested in his wishes and organized a commission to visit East Africa's largest ports to study the extent of his power. A desperate Barghash tried to impress the visitors by sending as many ships as he could to the harbors in advance of their arrival, but the Europeans didn't pay much attention to them or to any of the facts they collected. They had already made their decision.

By the end of October 1886, an agreement had been reached. Barghash and his successors would retain control over Zanzibar, Pemba, the Mafia islands, and a ten-mile-wide strip along the East African coast between the Miningani River to the south and the port of Kipini to the north. But all the rest of Zanzibar's dominions, extending thousands of miles into the African interior, would be divided between the British and the Germans. Britain took the northern section, between the Tana and Umba rivers, which became British East Africa (later Kenya), and Germany took the southern portion, between the Umba and Ruvuna rivers, which became German East Africa (later Tanganyika). In addition, the British agreed to help the Germans negotiate with Zanzibar to gain control over Dar es Salaam, the harbor opposite the island.

For Barghash, as for Salme, it was the end. Disillusioned and humiliated, he lost all interest in governing and withdrew from public life. Hitherto a lively, courteous, and often entertaining man, he became moody, impatient, and listless. He died on March 27, 1888, of consumption and elephantiasis, a form of leprosy caused by microscopic worms that invade the body, blocking the lymphatic system and causing tissue to thicken.

Life as he knew it was over for Kirk as well. After twenty years in Zanzibar, he had seen much of what he had worked for come to nothing. In early 1886 he was knighted for his services, and that July he departed for a leave in England. When he arrived, he was told that he would not be asked to return to Zanzibar. He didn't object.

Barghash was succeeded by his younger brother Khalifa, Seyyid Said's seventeenth son, born to an Abyssinian concubine. A gentle and inexperienced man, Khalifa knew little about the world outside Zanzibar but was considered to be the most able of Seyyid Said's surviving sons. Had he lived in a different era, he might have evolved into an effective ruler, but by 1888, it scarcely mattered. The Al Busaids had lost their power. Shortly after taking the throne, Khalifa was forced to sign away most of what little remained of his forefathers' empire, and in 1890, Zanzibar became a British protectorate. The Al Busaidi sultan was nothing more than a figurehead, and would remain so for the next seven decades, until the tumultuous years of 1963–64, when Zanzibar gained independence from the British, underwent a bloody revolution that nationalized much of its economy, threw out its elite—including the sultan—and joined with the former mainland colony of Tanganyika to become Tanzania.

The end of the Omanis' rule of East Africa marked the beginning of a whole new era. The Muslims' domination of the region was finished; full-scale Christian intervention was about to start.

During Barghash's final years, when the fate of East Africa was uncertain, a substantial revival of the slave trade took place, beginning in 1884 and lasting four or five years. The cause was threefold: Britain's attention was deflected from patrolling the coast, there was a shortage of labor on Zanzibar, and a devastating famine had hit the mainland.

Africans were so desperate that they were selling their children and
even themselves in order to survive, though for some that survival did
not last long. As had been true throughout the century, a startling number of slaves died shortly after their capture for no apparent reason.
"The strangest disease I have seen in this country seems really to be
broken-heartedness, and it attacks free men who have been captured
and made slaves," wrote David Livingstone in one of his most evocative
passages years before.

Slavery was not abolished on Zanzibar until 1897.

Seyyida Salme returned to Zanzibar one final time the year after
Barghash's death, to make her plea to the island's new ruler, Seyyid
Khalifa. But this time she went without the support of the German
government, and must have known how futile her journey was. She lin-
gered in Zanzibar for five months, waiting for Khalifa to receive her, before finally giving up and saying good-bye to her homeland.

The princess spent the next twenty-five years living on the Syrian
coast, mostly in Beirut. Fed up with both Germany and Zanzibar, she
wanted nothing more to do with either of them and made no more
public appearances. By the time World War I broke out, she was almost
penniless. News of her condition reached Zanzibar; she was now the
sole surviving child of Seyyid Said, and the next generation of Al Busaids forgave her. In 1923, her nephew Seyyid Khalifa bin Harub bestowed a civil pension on her, but it was too late. She died just one year
later, on February 29, 1924, at age eighty, in the home of her daughter
Rosalie in Jena, Germany. Her ashes were buried in Heinrich's grave in
Hamburg, mixed together with sand from the Zanzibar beach, found
among her belongings.

Seyyida Salme, like her father, Seyyid Said, had been a person ahead
of her time. She lived in the nineteenth century, but behaved more like
a woman living in the twentieth, for which she paid a steep price. Societies, be they Muslim or Christian, do not appreciate those who stray
too far outside their place.

Seyyida Salme, like her father, Seyyid Said, had the rare ability to
look beyond her immediate world and not only envision another way of
being, but also—through extraordinary courage—turn that vision into

reality. In Seyyid Said's case, that ability had brought him enormous reward; in Seyyida Salme's case, through no fault of her own, it brought her great unhappiness. Fate had dealt her a cruel blow from which it was all but impossible to recover.

Salme ended her memoirs with an account of her first return visit to Zanzibar and a haunting farewell poem. It had been sent to her by friends, she wrote, but it could also be read as a message that she herself sent to those she loved, or as a message that the Omanis could have sent to the world they had lost:

> *They went away but did not tell me they were going;*
> *That tore my heart, and left fire in my insides;*
> *Oh, that I had clung to them the day they left . . .*
> *Oh, if I were a bird, I would fly for longing,*
> *But how can it fly when its wings are clipped?*

Acknowledgments

First and foremost, I would like to thank my three wonderful editors at Random House: Nancy Miller, for her unfailing confidence in me and in the viability of this project; Laura Ford, for her excellent suggestions on how to streamline and refocus parts of my manuscript; and Courtney Moran, for her meticulous reading of my book and further sharpening of my prose. A heartfelt thanks, too, to Abdul Sheriff and the staff of the Zanzibar National Archives for their help when I was in Zanzibar; to my agent, Neeti Madan of Sterling Lord Literistic; and to Holly Webber, for the care that she took in copyediting my work. To Calvin Allen of Shenandoah University, who read the Oman portions of this book in manuscript and gave me invaluable suggestions, I owe a special debt. I also wish to thank Melissa Marie Brown, for her advice on transliterating words from Arabic into English, and everyone at Random House who helped shepherd this book through the publishing process.

Notes

Preface

xv   He then used her as a pawn   Bismarck's use of Salme is described in various history books, including Reginald Coupland, *The Exploitation of East Africa 1856–1890* (London: Faber and Faber, 1939), pp. 437–39, and E. van Donzel, ed., *An Arabian Princess Between Two Worlds* (New York: E. J. Brill, 1993), pp. 64–70.

xvi   when she was thirty-one years old   There is some doubt regarding the year of Salme's birth. She states that she was born on August 30, 1844, the date also used by van Donzel, but Patricia Romero, in her introduction to the reissued 1888 edition of Seyyida Salme/Emily Ruete, *Memoirs of an Arabian Princess from Zanzibar* (Princeton, N.J.: Markus Wiener Publishers, 1996, reprint), p. vii, states that the princess was four years older than she claimed. For simplicity's sake, I have used Salme's date throughout.

xvi   "Nine years ago I made up"   Ruete, *Memoirs*, Patricia Romero, ed., p. xviii.

PART ONE: OMAN

In re-creating episodes of Omani history, I drew from two classic Omani sources: Sirhan ibn Said ibn Sirhan (al Izkawi), *Annals of Oman to 1728*, E. C. Ross, tr. (New York: The Oleander Press, 1984, reprint) and Salil ibn Razik (Humaid ibn Muhammad ibn Ruzayq), *History of the Imams and Seyyids of Oman*, George Percy Badger, tr. (New York: Burt Franklin, 1967, reprint). Both contain much legend and lore as well as fact. Ibn Razik was also the panegyrist for Seyyid Said and his history reflects that connection.

Other essential, more objective sources on Oman included Wendell Phillips, *Oman: A History* (New York: Longmans, 1967); Calvin H. Allen, Jr., *Oman: The Modernization of the Sultanate* (Boulder, Colo.: Westview Press, 1987); Reginald Coupland, *East Africa and Its Invaders: From the Earliest Times to the Death of Seyyid Said in 1856* (London: Oxford University Press, 1938); and M. Reda Bhacker, *Trade and Empire in Muscat and Zanzibar* (New York: Routledge, 1992).

1: Beginnings

3   The time is 1806   The story of Sultan Said's ascent to power has several variations; the narrative here is an amalgam of the accounts in ibn Razik, *History of the Imams*, pp. lxx–lxxi; Abdalla Saleh Farsy, *Seyyid Said bin Sultan* (New Delhi: Lancers Books, 1942), p. 30; Vincenzo Maurizi, *History of Seyd Said, Sultan of Muscat* (New York: The Oleander Press, 1984, reprint), pp. 10–11; and Rudolph Said-Ruete, *Said bin Sultan (1791–1856): Ruler of Oman and Zanzibar* (London: Alexandre-Ousley, 1929), pp. 14–15.

Farsy puts an even greater emphasis on the role of Said's aunt than the version I relate; he says that it was Bibi Mouza who told Said how and when to commit the murder, and then accompanied him and his companions on their homicidal ride. In contrast, Maurizi's account, reputedly told to him by the Nubian slave at the scene, doesn't mention Bibi Mouza at all, but instead rather suspiciously credits the Nubian with killing Bedr. All the accounts of the event agree on the main facts of the case, however: the young Said treacherously killed (or had killed) his cousin on the outskirts of Barka with the approval of his advisers and brother Salim, and was proclaimed ruler of Oman.

6   "one of the most picturesque places in the world"   George Nathaniel Curzon, *Persia and the Persian Question* (London: Longman & Co., 1892), vol. 2, p. 433.

8   "Now the people of Oman"   Sirhan al Izkawi, *Annals of Oman*, p. 45.

10   But the great migration of the Azd   A second major wave of Arab tribes is believed to have arrived in Oman in the early 300s A.D. Coming from the north this time, they may have been fleeing Shapur II (A.D. 310–330), a Persian ruler who had invaded central Arabia on a putative mission, to eradicate the Arabs who had been attacking Persian trading vessels. In contrast to the earlier Azd settlers, the newer displaced tribes were mostly of Adnani stock and they settled mostly in northern Oman.

The division between the Azd and the Adnani tribes is one that permeates all of Arab history. According to traditional genealogies (which are disputed by some modern scholars), every Arab can trace his or her roots back to one of two ancestors: Qahtan or Adnan, both descended from Shem, the son of Noah of Noah's Ark fame. The people of southern Arabia, including the Azd, are believed to be descended from Qahtan, who may have lived around 700 B.C., about four hundred years before Adnan. The Arabs of northern Arabia trace their ancestry back to Adnan, who is believed to be a descendant of Ishmael. The prophet Muhammad was of the twenty-second generation from Adnan.

10   an early collapse   The dam also broke on at least four other major occasions (circa A.D. 370, 449, 450, and 542) before its final collapse around 570, but Arab legends attribute their peoples' great migrations to the break that occurred during the late second/early third century A.D.

10   Malik bin Fahm   All descriptions and dialogue regarding Malik and the founding of Oman are from Sirhan al Izkawi, *Annals of Oman*, pp. 4–5.

11   war elephants   Trained by humans for combat, the elephants were primarily used to charge the enemy, trampling them and breaking their ranks. The first war elephants were probably used in India between the eighth and fourth centuries B.C.; they were also used in the West, by the ancient Greeks and by the Carthaginians.

2: Muscat

14   "the most wonderful that nature"   Engelbert Kaempfer, a German traveler who visited Muscat in 1688, in Philip Ward, *Travels in Oman* (New York: The Oleander Press, 1987), p. 4.

14   "thick as gnats"   James Baillie Fraser, *Narrative of a Journey into Khorassan* (London: Longman & Co., 1826), p. 12.

14   When the sea was calm   Paraphrase of a description in James Raymond Wellsted, *Travels in Arabia* (London: John Murray, 1838), pp. 10–37.

15   "the most agreeable and polite"   Francis Erskine Loch, in Ward, *Travels in Oman*, p. 11.

15   "mild yet striking countenance"   J. R. Wellsted, in Ward, *Travels in Oman*, p. 15.

15   "so much firmness, honesty"   William A. Shepard, *From Bombay to Bushire and Bussara*, in Phillips, *Oman: A History*, p. 131.

15   "as shrewd, liberal and enlightened"   Richard F. Burton, *Zanzibar: City, Island, and Coast* (New York: Johnson Reprint Corp., 1967), vol. 1, p. 304.

17   "The people of Muscat seemed"   James Silk Buckingham, *Travels in Assyria, Media and Persia* (London: H. Colburn, 1830), vol. 2, p. 413.

17   "a leathern girdle which keeps"   Maurizi, *History of Seyd Said*, pp. 23–24.

19   From Muhammad the Messenger   Letter is as quoted in Isam al-Rawas, *Oman in Early Islamic History* (Reading, UK: Ithaca Press, 2000), p. 205. Some scholars have expressed doubts about the authenticity of this letter and other similar letters addressed to other rulers in the region.

23   The early Ibadhis elected   For centuries, the imam was elected irrespective of his family descent or material fortune. But during the reign of the Yaarubi dynasty, 1624–1749, a change occurred. The elected imams began to pursue personal wealth, and the office of the imam began to pass from father to son. Later, during the reign of Imam Said bin Ahmed Al Busaid in the late 1700s, the responsibilities of the imam's office were split in two, with the religious duties retained by the imam and the administrative/military duties taken over by a "seyyid." I cover the subject briefly in "Chapter Six: War with the Wahhabis."

23   "white spot on the body"   Phillips, *Oman: A History*, p. 10.

24   "Since they are in my charge"   Al-Rawas, *Oman in Early Islamic History*, p. 150.

24 **"the hallway to China"** The medieval Arab geographer al-Muqaddasi, in Shirley Kay, *Enchanting Oman* (Dubai, UAE: Motivate Publishing, 1999), p. 37.

24 **"It is not possible"** Ibid., p. 37.

3: Slavery

For background information on the history of slavery in the Muslim world, Bernard Lewis, *Race and Slavery in the Middle East: An Historical Inquiry* (New York: Oxford University Press, 1990); Murray Gordon, *Slavery in the Arab World* (New York: New Amsterdam Books, 1989); and Ronald Segal, *Islam's Black Slaves: The Other Black Diaspora* (New York: Farrar, Straus and Giroux, 2001) were invaluable.

25 ***It begins when one finds things*** Adbulaziz Y. Lohdi, *The Institution of Slavery in Zanzibar and Pemba*, Research Report No. 16 (Uppsala, Sweden: The Scandinavian Institute of African Studies, 1973), p. 3.

26 **"well-oiled to show off"** . . . **"Number one"** Sir John Malcolm, *Sketches of Persia by a Traveller* (London: John Murray, 1828), vol. 2, p. 17.

26 **as a "good" slave system** Frederick Cooper, *Plantation Slavery on the East Coast of Africa* (Portsmouth, N.H.: Heinemann, 1997), p. 153.

26 **"At Muskat, it is certain"** William Heude, *A Voyage up the Persian Gulf* (London: Longman, Hurst, Rees, Orme, and Brown, 1819), p. 25.

26 **Another Englishman noted** William Gifford Palgrave, *Narrative of a Year's Journey Through Central and Eastern Arabia* (London: MacMillan and Co., 1865), vol. 2, p. 272.

27 **The Arabs' use of African slaves** Numbers relating to the extent of the slave trade in North and East Africa from Segal, *Islam's Black Slaves*, pp. 56–57; Gordon, *Slavery in the Arab World*, pp. 148–49, 187–89; Sheriff, *Slaves, Spices & Ivory in Zanzibar*, p. 60; and Cooper, *Plantation Slavery on the East Coast of Africa*, pp. 39–43.

28 **"As to your slaves"** Prophet Muhammad at the Farewell Pilgrimage, in Gordon, *Slavery in the Arab World*, p. 19.

29 **"And such of your slaves"** As translated by Mohammed Marmaduke Pickthall in *The Meaning of the Glorious Koran* (New York: Penguin Group, n.d.); I have used his translations throughout.

31 **She had lived peacefully** Seyyida Salme/Emily Ruete, *Memoirs of an Arabian Princess*, in *An Arabian Princess Between Two Worlds*, van Donzel, ed., p. 152.

32 **"indirect and unintended consequence"** Lewis, *Race and Slavery in the Middle East*, p. 41.

33 **"fight on the road"** . . . **"God would save"** Bernard Lewis, *The Arabs in History* (New York: Harper & Row, 1958), p. 104.

35 **"The Zanj have an elegant language"** G.S.P. Freeman-Grenville, *The East African Coast: Select Documents from the First to the Earlier Nineteenth Century* (Oxford, UK: Clarendon Press, 1962), p. 16.

36   **"Kilwa is one of the most"**   Freeman-Grenville, *The East African Coast*, p. 31.

36   **"The Zanj are in great fear"**   Gordon, *Slavery in the Arab World*, p. 111.

37   **As the story goes**   Story is as told by the Persian Gulf sailor Buzurg bin Shahriyar in his mid-tenth-century collection of sailors' tales, *Kitab al-Ajaid al-Hind*, P. A. Van der Lith, tr., in Freeman-Grenville, *The East African Coast*, pp. 9–13.

4: The Portuguese Invasion

To bring to life the era of the Portuguese in the Indian Ocean, I depended on G. Correa, *The Three Voyages of Vasco da Gama to India*, Henry E. J. Stanley, tr. (New York: Burt Franklin, n.d., reprint); Richard Hall, *Empires of the Monsoon: A History of the Indian Ocean and Its Invaders* (London: HarperCollins, 1996); Reginald Coupland, *East Africa and Its Invaders*; Genesta Hamilton, *In the Wake of Da Gama* (New York: Skeffington and Son, 1951); and Phillips, *Oman: A History*.

42   **"We shouted with joy"** . . . **"The men of this land"**   Hall, *Empires of the Monsoon*, p. 162.

44   **Ahmed bin Majid**   Some historians question whether Ahmed bin Majid was originally from Oman; others believe that da Gama's navigator was someone else altogether.

45   **"I have exhausted"**   Hall, *Empires of the Monsoon*, p. 181.

45   **"Oh, had I known"**   Ibid., p. 183.

46   **"The Moors were very powerful"**   Correa, *The Three Voyages*, p. 155.

46   **"many other saints were painted"**   Ibid., p. 157.

49   **"Sir you have nothing"** . . . **"Alive you shall"**   Ibid, pp. 313, 315.

49   **"to cut off the hands"** . . . **"so that the people"**   Phillips, *Oman: A History*, p. 34.

50   **"a great city . . . a noble city"**   Ward, *Travels in Oman*, p. 143.

51   **"courage"** . . . **"Antonio do Campo . . . pursued"**   Phillips, *Oman: A History*, pp. 38–39.

51   **"For four days your men"**   T. F. Earle and John Villiers, eds. *Albuquerque, Caesar of the East: Selected Texts by Afonso de Albuquerque and His Son* (Warminster, UK: Aris & Phillips, 1990), p. 17.

51   **"Muscat is a large"** . . . **"The town burned"**   Ibid., p. 59.

52   **"Allah keep you, Said Ali"**   Hall, *Empires of the Monsoon*, p. 207.

53   **"God bestowed [Nasir]"**   ibn Razik, *History of the Imams*, p. 74.

54   **"If you do not give"** . . . **"forces as numerous"**   Ibid., pp. 81–82.

5: The Al Busaids Come to Power

56   "discreet in judgment" . . . "Where are you going?"   This and the following dialogue are from ibn Razik, *History of the Imams*, p. 133.

58   "so that his renown spread"   Ibid, p. 134.

59   "This is a grievous calamity"   Ibid., pp. 139–40.

59   "plundered all they could lay hands on"   Ibid., p. 142.

60   "This is my castle and my grave"   Ibid., p. 149.

60   "Anyone who has a grudge"   Ibid., p. 153.

61   "O, Imam of Oman" . . . "By Allah!" . . . "Welcome, O Imam"   Ibid., p. 157.

62   "There are at present such immense"   A. Parsons, *Travels in Asia and Africa* (London: Longmans, 1808), p. 287, in Bhacker, *Trade and Empire*, pp. 29–30.

6: War with the Wahhabis

My synopsis of the Wahhabi faith is drawn primarily from Gary Troeller, *The Birth of Saudi Arabia: Britain and the Rise of the House of Saud* (London: Frank Cass, 1976); Molly Izzard, *The Gulf: Arabia's Western Approaches* (London: John Murray, 1979); George Rentz, "Wahhabism and Saudi Arabia," in Derek Hopwood, ed., *The Arabian Peninsula: Society and Politics* (Totowa, N.J.: Rowman and Littlefield, 1972); and Zamil Muhammad Al-Rashid, *Su'udi Relations with Eastern Arabia and 'Uman* (London: Luzac & Co., 1981). Also helpful were Bhacker, *Trade and Empire*, and ibn Razik, *History of the Imams*.

64   the twosome had plotted against   As sons of the ancient Jiboor tribe on their mother's side, Saif and Sultan considered themselves to be of nobler birth than their older brother Said, whose mother was of more lowly origins, and therefore thought that they were more worthy of succeeding their father.

64   "His indolence and extortion"   George Percy Badger, introduction to ibn Razik, *History of the Imams*, p. lii.

65   "nothing for the number"   ibn Razik, *History of the Imams*, p. 214.

66   "I am writing this letter to you"   Phillips, *Oman: A History*, p. 71.

66   "In the name of God, the merciful"   ibn Razik, *History of the Imams*, p. 230.

67   "a mass of incoherent sentences"   Ibid.

67   "The Christians and the Jews"   Said-Ruete, *Said bin Sultan*, p. 14.

69   "Restless and bold"   Palgrave, *Narrative of a Year's Journey Through Central and Eastern Arabia*, vol. 2, p. 39.

69   "God preserve us from them"   Malcolm, *Sketches of Persia*, in Phillips, *Oman: A History*, p. 92.

70   "Had he remained at Habra"   ibn Razik, *History of the Imams*, p. 234.

70   "Here I am, O my God"   Albert Hourani, *A History of the Arab People* (New York: Warner Books, 1991), p. 150.

71   "the mountains closed in"   ibn Razik, *History of the Imams*, p. 234.

71   "War threatens us on all"   This and the following dialogue are from ibid., pp. 235–36.

72   "roaring . . . at all times" . . . "the vilest of the vile"   Ibid., pp. 239–40.

72   "Wonders never cease"   Bhacker, *Trade and Empire*, p. 43.

7: Seyyid Said in Muscat

74   "The ministers, who had never thought"   Ruete, *Memoirs*, in *An Arabian Princess*, p. 277.

75   "Everyone and everything was put to use"   Ibid., p. 278.

76   "seized the hilt of his dagger"   ibn Razik, *History of the Imams*, p. 253.

77   "I suspect that Muhenna"   Ibid., p. 270.

77   "His constant love of justice"   Maurizi, *History of Seyd Said*, p. 18.

78   "Begun amidst unfavourable omens"   J. G. Lorimer, *Gazetteer of the Persian Gulf, Oman and Central Arabia* (New York: Cambridge University Press, 1986, reprint), vol. 1, p. 440.

78   "Peace be with you; return home"   ibn Razik, *History of the Imams*, p. 297.

79   "circumstances of horrid solemnity"   J. R. Wellsted, *Travels to the City of the Caliphs*, quoted in Bhacker, *Trade and Empire*, p. 58.

79   "Seyd Said is a good looking"   Maurizi, *History of Seyd Said*, p. 18.

80    $75,000 came from slave taxes   Ibid., p. 29.

80   in 1831, a British visitor estimated   Sheriff, *Slaves, Spices & Ivory in Zanzibar*, p. 38.

80   "The battle, or rather massacre"   Maurizi, *History of Seyd Said*, p. 66.

80   "Active personal courage"   Ibid., p. 76.

81   "I took the liberty to suggest"   Ibid., pp. 73–74.

81   "when two nations, the one powerful"   Ibid., p. 75.

82   "Philosophers and Poets have alike observed"   Ibid., p. 91.

PART TWO: ZANZIBAR

For general background information on Zanzibar, I am indebted to Norman R. Bennett, *A History of the Arab State of Zanzibar* (London: Methuen & Co., 1978) and John Gray, *History of Zanzibar from the Middle Ages to 1856* (London: Oxford University Press, 1962). Also essential were Reginald Coupland, *East Africa and Its Invaders*; Coupland, *The Exploitation of East Africa*; and Sheriff, *Slaves, Spices & Ivory in Zanzibar*. My re-creations of palace life are drawn from Ruete, *Memoirs*, in *An Arabian Princess*.

8: A Princess Is Born

89   had probably begun trading with Zanzibar   *Periplus of the Erythraean Sea,*
the seafarer's guide written about A.D. 100, refers to an island called Menouthias,
which many historians believe to have been Zanzibar.

90   "Of all the most beautiful places"   Horace Putnam, in Norman R. Bennett
and George E. Brooks, Jr., eds., *New England Merchants in Africa: A History Through
Documents, 1802 to 1865* (Boston: Boston University Press, 1965), p. 402.

91   "woe to the person"   Ruete, *Memoirs,* in *An Arabian Princess,* p. 148.

92   "every time one of his concubines"   Farsy, *Seyyid Said,* p. 12.

92   "They are the most beautiful girls"   Putnam, in Bennett and Brooks, *New
England Merchants,* p. 402.

92   "Above middle-height"   Ruete, *Memoirs,* in *An Arabian Princess,* pp. 150–52.

93   "extremely imperious" . . . **"she possessed"**   Ibid., p. 154.

93   "Not one of us was spoiled"   Ibid., pp. 204–5.

93   "What so many people"   Ibid., p. 155.

9: Clove Fever

Cooper, *Plantation Slavery on the East Coast of Africa,* was an invaluable re-
source for information on Zanzibar's clove plantations and the slaves who worked
them. Sheriff, *Slaves, Spices & Ivory in Zanzibar,* was also especially helpful.

95   "a perfect Frenchman"   Fortene Albrand, in Sheriff, *Slaves, Spices & Ivory,*
p. 49.

96   the real reason behind Saleh's ouster   Sheriff, *Slaves, Spices & Ivory,* pp.
49–50.

97   "After a short time"   W. H. Ingrams, *Zanzibar: Its History and Its People*
(London: Frank Cass and Company, 1967), p. 206.

97   also known as Stone Town   Around the time of Salme's arrival in the town
of Zanzibar, it began dividing into two parts: Stone Town, the more historical and
wealthier section, and Ng'ambo, where poorer Africans, Arabs, Swahili, and freed
slaves lived.

97   the sultan's plantations produced   Sheriff, *Slaves, Spices & Ivory,* pp. 50–51.

98   "Almost everyone on the island"   W.S.W. Ruschenberger, *A Voyage Round
the World Including an Embassy to Muscat and Siam in 1835, 1836 and 1837* (London: Dawsons of Pall Mall, 1970, reprint), vol. 1, p. 51.

98   Zanzibar was exporting 9,000   Cooper, *Plantation Slavery,* p. 52.

98   No accurate population statistics   Ibid., pp. 54, 42.

98   a sharp decline in price   Ibid., p. 52.

99   "The slave knows very well"   James Christie, *Cholera Epidemics in East
Africa* (London: Macmillan, 1876), pp. 42–43.

100 "do less work, on the average" J. Ross Browne, *Etchings of a Whaling Cruise* (Cambridge, Mass.: Harvard University Press, 1968, reprint), pp. 434–35.

100 "Strictly speaking they are not" Putnam, in Bennett and Brooks, *New England Merchants*, p. 427.

101 island probably held fewer than 15,000 Slave population estimates from Cooper, *Plantation Slavery*, p. 56.

101 the relatively humane treatment Cooper, *Plantation Slavery*, pp. 153–213.

102 "None obtains" . . . "How many have [been] seen" Farsy, *Seyyid Said*, pp. 75–76.

10: *The Move to Town*

103 Salme was her only child Djilfidan had given birth to another daughter, but she died very young, before Salme's birth.

103 "Intellectually speaking, my mother" Ruete, *Memoirs*, in *An Arabian Princess*, p. 153.

104 "Do you have no heart" . . . "Oh, my friends" . . . "In a real Arab house" Ibid., p. 160.

106 "More than forty children" Ibid., p. 183.

107 "The higher the tenement" Richard F. Burton, *Zanzibar: City, Island, and Coast* (New York: Johnson Reprint Corp., 1967), vol. 1, p. 86.

108 But just because Seyyid Said's control Norman R. Bennett, *Arab Versus European: Diplomacy and War in Nineteenth-Century East Central Africa* (New York: Africana Publishing Company, 1986), p. 122.

109 "silent wanderers of the sea" Anne K. Bang, "Sufis and Scholars of the Sea," (Dissertation: University of Bergen, 2000), p. 12.

109 "Each boat is crowded" Gray, *History of Zanzibar*, pp. 137–38.

111 "bleached and ghastly skeletons" Joseph Barlow Feitz Osgood, *Notes of Travel, or, Recollections of Majunga, Zanzibar, Muscat, Aden, Mocha, and Other Eastern Ports* (Salem, Mass.: George Cramer, 1854), p. 33.

11: *On the Streets*

Burton, *Zanzibar*, is filled with evocative descriptions of nineteenth-century life in Zanzibar. Cooper, *Plantation Slavery on the East Coast of Africa*, and Lohdi, *The Institution of Slavery in Zanzibar and Pemba*, offer fascinating detail about what daily life was like for the island's town slaves.

113 "How ghastly appears his blanched face" This and the following quotes are from Burton, *Zanzibar*, pp. 108–9.

117 "safe, easy, and profitable" Bartle Frere, in Cooper, *Plantation Slavery*, p. 185.

118 In a society where the size Ibid., p. 198.

118   But color was regarded as only   Ibid., p. 199.

118   "tried to possess the most handsome"   Ruete, *Memoirs*, in *An Arabian Princess*, p. 251.

119   A heavenly reward was coveted   Cooper, *Plantation Slavery*, p. 245.

119   "In my continual endeavours"   W. P. Johnson, in E. A. Alpers, *The East African Slave Trade*, Historical Association of Tanzania, Paper No. 3 (Nairobi: East African Publishing House), p. 26.

119   Around the time of Salme's birth   W. F. Baldock, "The Story of Rashid Bin Hassani of the Bisa Tribe, Northern Rhodesia," in *Ten Africans*, Margery Perham, ed. (Evanston, Ill.: Northwestern University Press, 1964).

12: A Day in the Life

123   "Salme, tell me"   Ruete, *Memoirs*, in *An Arabian Princess*, pp. 173–74.

124   "Our mothers walked about"   Ibid., pp. 175–76.

125   "without a doubt" . . . "no decency"   Ibid., p. 176.

125   eunuchs   The history of the use of eunuchs in Muslim society is covered in Segal, *Islam's Black Slaves*, various references; Gordon, *Slavery in the Arab World*, pp. 89–99; and Phillips, *Oman: A History*, pp. 126–28.

126   "copper-coloured" . . . "more richly dressed"   John Lewis Burckhardt, *Travels in Arabia* (Beirut: Librarie du Libon, 1972, reprint), p. 343.

128   "fish of so large a size" . . . "thirty to forty porters"   Ruete, *Memoirs*, in *An Arabian Princess*, p. 172.

129   "Arabs born in Arabia"   Ibid., p. 193.

130   "negro music played" . . . "People over there"   Ibid., p. 194.

130   "indescribably agreeable"   Ibid., p. 191.

13: Gatherings

132   "From His Highness the Imam"   Gray, *History of Zanzibar*, p. 146.

132   "Under Seyyid Said torture"   Burton, *Zanzibar*, vol. 1, p. 258.

134   "Do tell me, please"   Ruete, *Memoirs*, in *An Arabian Princess*, p. 188.

135   "But it still remains an open"   Ibid., p. 211.

135   "In my opinion, learning"   Ibid., p. 214.

136   "an appropriate punishment" . . . "In a thrice"   Ibid., p. 180.

136   "without which even the most skilled"   Ibid.

136   "such times, unfortunately"   Ibid., p. 183.

137   "intense relish of seeing"   Burton, *Zanzibar*, vol. 1, p. 302.

137   "more rude in mind and action"   Ruete, *Memoirs*, in *An Arabian Princess*, p. 186.

138   "Her heart belonged" . . . "Such a scene"   Ibid., p. 186.

138   "it often was revolting indeed"   Ibid., p. 185.

138   "this did not trouble me" . . . "oh how often have I"   Ibid., p. 187.

14: The Slave Trade

Helpful resources for compiling this chapter included Alpers, *The East African Slave Trade;* Coupland, *East Africa and Its Invaders;* Coupland, *The Exploitation of East Africa;* Gray, *History of Zanzibar;* Sheriff, *Slaves, Spices & Ivory in Zanzibar;* Cooper, *Plantation Slavery on the East Coast of Africa;* Gordon, *Slavery in the Arab World;* and R. W. Beachey, *The Slave Trade of Eastern Africa* (New York: Harper & Row, 1976).

140   "by what one has heard" . . . "innumerable people"   Ruete, *Memoirs,* in *An Arabian Princess,* p. 328.

140   **slave trade began in earnest**   Slave trade estimates from Gordon, *Slavery in the Arab World,* pp.148–49, 187–89; Sheriff, *Slaves, Spices & Ivory in Zanzibar,* p. 60; and Cooper, *Plantation Slavery on the East Coast of Africa,* pp. 39, 43.

141   **The sight and smell of dead bodies**   David Livingston, in Phillips, *Oman: A History,* pp. 118–19.

141   **four or five lives were lost**   Coupland, *The Exploitation of East Africa,* p. 140.

142   **The wicked end of the lash**   Salim C. Wilson (Hatashil Masha Kathish), *I Was a Slave* (London: Stanley Paul & Co. Ltd., 1833). Of the Dinka tribe, Salim was born in the Sudan in 1859 and freed by the English. He converted to Christianity and was a missionary in Africa for a period before settling in England.

142   **"The Arab dhows are large"**   Captain Fairfax Moresby, in Coupland, *East Africa and Its Invaders,* pp. 230–31.

144   **grain as it took to fill a hat**   Coupland, *The Exploitation of East Africa,* p. 138.

145   **"barbarously put to death"**   Gray, *History of Zanzibar,* p. 227.

145   **He was an ardent abolitionist**   Ibid., p. 238.

145   **out of political self-interest**   Gordon, *Slavery in the Arab World,* p. 191.

146   **"The governor might blow away"**   Gray, *History of Zanzibar,* p. 230.

147   **"Whosoever receives this letter"**   Ibid., p. 235.

147   **"the Imam of Muscat had issued"**   Beachey, *The Slave Trade of Eastern Africa,* p. 45.

148   **"for beneath its protecting shade"**   Robert Nunez Lyne, *Zanzibar in Contemporary Times* (London: Hurst and Blackett, 1905), p. 20.

148   **A dozen or so ships . . . Mozambique was sending**   Estimates from Beachey, *The Slave Trade,* p. 13.

149   **"the surest, if not the only"**   Coupland, *East Africa and Its Invaders,* p. 231.

149   "made up his mind"   Gray, *History of Zanzibar,* p. 116.

149   "mild and gentlemanly manners"   Coupland, *East Africa and Its Invaders,* p. 231.

150   "I thought I observed"   Ibid., p. 231.

150   "to put down the slave trade"   Gray, *History of Zanzibar,* p. 117.

151   "in a most awful state of delirium"   Anonymous quote, in Lyne, *Zanzibar in Contemporary Times,* p. 26.

151   one British captain estimated   Beachey, *The Slave Trade,* p. 48.

152   "forbid all slave trade"   Coupland, *East Africa and Its Invaders,* p. 505.

152   "muttered about one thing" . . . "It is the same"   Gray, *History of Zanzibar,* p. 245.

152   "That these countries will be totally"   Ibid., p. 246.

152   "like the British and other European"   Beachey, *The Slave Trade,* p. 52.

152   "The Sultan has neither officers"   Ibid., p. 53.

152   "You will take every opportunity"   Gray, *History of Zanzibar,* p. 250.

153   "Abyssinian girl-slaves and eunuchs"   Coupland, *East Africa and Its Invaders,* p. 516.

153   he may have seen it as an evil   Gray, *History of Zanzibar,* p. 226.

153   "remonstrate with the Imam"   Beachey, *The Slave Trade,* p. 53.

154   "In my time a good many Europeans"   Ruete, *Memoirs,* in *An Arabian Princess,* p. 300.

15: Americans in Zanzibar

Norman R. Bennett covers the history of Americans in Zanzibar in two excellent articles: "Americans in Zanzibar, 1825–45," Essex Institute *Historical Collections,* vol. 95, 1959, pp. 239–62; and "Americans in Zanzibar, 1845–64," Essex Institute *Historical Collections,* vol. 97, 1961, pp. 31–56. A compelling account of Naaman's visit to New York is Herman Frederick Eilts, "Ahmed bin Na'man's Mission to the United States in 1840, The Voyage of the Al-Sultanah to New York City," Essex Institute *Historical Collections,* vol. 98, pp. 219–77.

156   "To the most high and mighty"   Phillips, *Oman: A History,* p. 106.

156   "the reverse of pleasure" . . . "commenced by saying"   Bhacker, *Trade and Empire,* p. 111.

156   "Mr. Edmund Roberts"   Ibid., p. 112.

157   "a disaster befell the *Peacock*"   This and the following quotes are from a letter from Edmund Roberts to John Forsythe, in Bennett and Brooks, *New England Merchants,* pp. 160–61.

158   "star-spangled banner"   Nathaniel Isaacs, in Coupland, *East Africa and Its Invaders,* p. 365.

159 "the great tide of the East India trade" Eleanor Putnam, *Old Salem* (New York: Houghton Mifflin, 1887), p. 106.

160 the east coast of Africa Captain G. I. Sulivan, *Dhow Chasing in Zanzibar Waters* (Zanzibar: The Gallery Publications, 2003, reprint), pp. 11–12.

162 "No, Mr. Waters" Captain H. Hart, in Gray, *History of Zanzibar*, pp. 197–98.

162 "I expect you will be" Letter from Elbridge G. Kimball to George West, Jr., in Bennett and Brooks, *New England Merchants*, p. 226.

162 "I have desired" Excerpt from Waters's journals, in Bennett and Brooks, *New England Merchants*, p. 189.

162 "This city is a depot" Ibid., p. 192.

163 "I left the Sultan quite pleased" Ibid., p. 195.

163 "We were preceded by a guard" Ibid., p. 201.

163 "These people remind me" Ibid., pp. 197–98.

164 Capt. Hassan & the Imaun secretary Letter from William B. Smith to Daniel Webster, in Bennett and Brooks, *New England Merchants.*, pp. 233–34.

165 "The Consul is supposed" Bennett, "Americans in Zanzibar, 1845–64," p. 54.

166 "Respecting the letter" Bennett and Brooks, *New England Merchants*, p. 347.

166 "They were tormented continuously" British consul Hamerton, in Bennett, "Americans in Zanzibar, 1825–45," p. 37.

167 "The Arabs look around" *Morning Herald*, May 5, 1840, in Eilts, "Ahmad Bin Na'man's Mission to the United States," p. 240.

167 "naivete and intelligence" *Morning Herald*, May 20, 1840, in Eilts, "Ahmad Bin Na'aman's Mission to the United States," p. 246.

167 "looks quite cool and contented" *Morning Herald*, June 25, 1840, in Eilts, "Ahmad Bin Na'aman's Mission to the United States," p. 246.

16: The Swahili

For background information on the Swahili in this and the following chapter, I am indebted to John Middleton, *The World of the Swahili: An African Mercantile Civilization* (New Haven, Conn.: Yale University Press, 1992), and Derek Nurse and Thomas Spear, *The Swahili: Reconstructing the History and Language of an African Society, 800–1500* (Philadelphia: University of Pennsylvania Press, 1985). W. H. Ingrams, *Zanzibar, Its History and Its People* (London: Frank Cass and Company, 1967), was also especially helpful.

173 By the eleventh century Middleton, *The World of the Swahili*, p. 37.

175 "The kings of these isles" Freeman-Grenville, *The East African Coast*, pp. 14, 133–34.

17: Seyyid Said's Last Journey

179   "The proud Omani ladies"   Ruete, *Memoirs*, in *An Arabian Princess*, p. 230.

180   "Setting aside what I know"   Gray, *History of Zanzibar*, p. 244.

180   "placed his son's hand in mine"   Ibid., p. 274.

180   "there reigned a kind of loneliness"   Ruete, *Memoirs*, in *An Arabian Princess*, p. 231.

181   "the eyes of the population"   Ibid., p. 232.

181   "succeeded in winning hearts"   Ibid.

181   "The Prince Majid has given"   Gray, *History of Zanzibar*, p. 277.

181   "of a quite unnatural corpulence"   Ruete, *Memoirs*, in *An Arabian Princess*, p. 233.

185   "I proceeded about midnight"   Ingrams, *Zanzibar*, pp. 469–70.

187   "But man proposes"   Ruete, *Memoirs*, in *An Arabian Princess*, p. 235.

187   "But then, who could describe"   Ibid., p. 237.

188   "Good-bye Mother, I do not think"   Farsy, *Seyyid Said*, p. 83.

188   "I have the honour"   Gray, *History of Zanzibar*, p. 279.

189   "a very peculiar, lively"   Ruete, *Memoirs*, in *An Arabian Princess*, p. 240.

18: The Explorers

Edward Rice, *Captain Sir Richard Francis Burton: A Biography* (New York: Da Capo Press, 1990), along with Alan Moorehead, *The White Nile* (New York: Harper & Row, 1960), and Martin Dugard, *Into Africa: The Epic Adventures of Stanley & Livingstone* (New York: Broadway Books, 2003), provided me with fascinating, dramatic background material about Richard Burton. The explorer's own writings, especially *Zanzibar* and *The Lake Regions of Central Africa* (New York: Dover Publications, 1995, reprint) inform descriptions throughout the chapter.

190   "Earth, sea, and sky"   Burton, *Zanzibar*, p. 28.

192   "questing panther eyes"   Moorehead, *The White Nile*, p. 15.

193   "Of the gladdest moments"   Ibid., pp. 16–17.

194   "I can even now distinctly"   Ibid., p. 35.

195   "an undeveloped and not to be developed"   Rice, *Captain Sir Richard*, p. 362.

195   "He works on principle"   Ibid., pp. 369–70.

196   "walnut and velvet-slipper men"   Burton, *The Lake Regions*, p. 34.

197   "disorderly mob" . . . "The normal recreations"   Ibid., p. 242.

197   "the lads and lasses of the neighboring villages"   Ibid., p. 248.

198   "where modest young maidens beckoned"   Ibid., p. 51.

198   "a mortal smell of decay"   Ibid., p. 65.

198   "animals of grisliest form"   Ibid., p. 74.

200   "What is that streak" . . . "I am of the opinion"   Ibid., p. 307.

200   "mobbed by a swarm"   Ibid., p. 309.

200   "I felt sick at heart" . . . "the mystery remains"   Rice, *Captain Sir Richard*, pp. 393–94.

201   "I no longer felt any doubt"   Ibid., p. 401.

201   "We had scarcely, however, breakfasted"   Burton, *The Lake Regions*, p. 409.

201   "Jack changed his manners"   Rice, *Captain Sir Richard*, p. 403.

202   "everything had been done for"   Ibid., p. 407.

202   "incompetence, malice, cowardice"   Ibid., p. 491.

202   "unfit for any other"   Moorehead, *The White Nile*, p. 64.

203   "He looked at Richard and me"   Dugard, *Into Africa*, p. 27.

203   "I have to apologize"   Ibid.

203   "I saw by the workings"   Ibid., pp. 27–28.

19: Rebellion

205   "African tribes from the interior"   Bennett, *A History of the Arab State*, p. 63.

206   The longer-lasting effect   Ibid., p. 65.

206   "so categorically demanded"   Ruete, *Memoirs*, in *An Arabian Princess*, p. 264.

206   "shot down his own unsuspecting father"   This account of Tueni's death is taken from Seyyida Salme's *Memoirs*. In *History of the Imams*, ibn Razik states that Tueni was murdered in his sleep.

206   "Surely a sad picture"   Ruete, *Memoirs*, in *An Arabian Princess*, p. 267.

207   "if it had to be"   Ibid., p. 334.

207   "At the age of barely fifteen"   Ibid., p. 334.

207   "some two thousand cholera corpses"   James Christie, *Cholera Epidemics in East Africa* (London: Macmillan, 1876), pp. 384–85.

208   "the filthiest quarter in Zanzibar"   Ibid., p. 366.

208   "She was a remarkably handsome woman"   Ibid, pp. 377–79.

210   "Believing as they did"   Ibid., p. 387.

210   "acquitted themselves nobly"   Ibid., p. 385.

210   "prudent and clever"   Ruete, *Memoirs*, in *An Arabian Princess*, p. 245.

211   "For months I found myself"   Ibid., p. 336.

212   "On account of my ability to write"   Ibid, p. 344.

212   "like a little fortress"   Ibid., p. 346.

212   "a good talking-to"   Ibid., p. 347.

213   "Like a fleeing column"   Ibid., pp. 348–49.

214   "Panic seized our house"   Ibid., p. 353.

215   "Thus ended our enterprise"   Ibid., p. 355.

20: Elopement

Essential for understanding the story of Salme's elopement were John Gray, "Memoirs of an Arabian Princess," *Tanganyika Notes & Records*, 37 (1954), pp. 49–70, and van Donzel, *An Arabian Princess Between Two Worlds*, pp. 9–20.

216   "high waves of enmity"   Ruete, *Memoirs*, in *An Arabian Princess*, p. 357.

216   each daughter had received   Freeman-Grenville, ed., in *Memoirs of an Arabian Princess* by Emily Said-Ruete (London: East-West Publications, 1994, reprint), p. xi.

217   "My domestic animals"   Ruete, *Memoirs*, in *An Arabian Princess*, p. 358.

218   "Thinking back on these beautiful"   Ibid., p. 363.

218   "Oh, Salme, I never thought"   This and the following dialogue are from ibid., p. 366.

219   "much-loved, much-envied"   Ibid., p. 248.

220   "confine his payments to sums"   Bennett, *A History of the Arab State*, p. 80.

220   "Good morning, Salme"   This and the following dialogue are from Ruete, *Memoire*, in *An Arabian Princess*, p. 368.

221   Heinrich Ruete   Salme's husband spelled his last name "Reute," but Salme changed it to "Ruete" about fifteen years after his death. I have used Salme's spelling throughout to avoid confusion.

221   "the head, if not the sole" . . . "adequately educated" . . . "borne a character"   Gray, "Memoirs of an Arabian Princess," p. 51.

221   "knows a little English"   van Donzel, *An Arabian Princess*, pp. 10–11.

222   "During this troubled time"   Ruete, *Memoirs*, in *An Arabian Princess*, p. 371.

222   "There had long been half"   van Donzel, *An Arabian Princess*, p. 14.

223   "She'd have been killed"   Daniel Liebowitz, *The Physician and the Slave Trade*, p. 134.

224   "bellowing up the street"   van Donzel, *An Arabian Princess*, p. 16.

226   "on no account be permitted" . . . "Every effort has been made"   Gray, "Memoirs of an Arabian Princess," p. 53.

PART THREE: GERMANY AND AFRICA

My account of Seyyida Salme's life in Germany and her voyages home to Zanzibar is drawn from her own writings: Ruete, *Memoirs* and *Letters Home*, in *An*

Arabian Princess. Throughout the Africa section, I depended on Bennett, *A History of the Arab State,* and Coupland, *The Exploitation of East Africa,* for background material.

21: Hamburg

231   "And here you wish to pass"   Seyyida Salme/Emily Ruete, *Letters Home,* in *An Arabian Princess,* p. 411.

232   "as if they had invisible wings"   Ibid., p. 437.

233   "Here it became clear to me"   Ibid., p. 412.

233   "I was seized by such fear"   Ibid., p. 410.

234   "in the kindest manner"   Ruete, *Memoirs,* in *An Arabian Princess,* p. 372.

234   "horrible chicken feathers"   Ruete, *Letters Home,* in *An Arabian Princess,* p. 417.

234   "slight feeling of horror"   Ibid., p. 412.

235   "rightly or wrongly"   Ibid., p. 430.

235   "Such a situation"   Ibid., p. 429.

235   "endless smiles"   Ibid., p. 413.

235   "If at home you are"   Ibid., p. 410.

236   "exotic people"   Ibid., p. 421.

236   "In fact I led two lives"   Ibid., p. 423.

236   "badly knocked"   Ibid., p. 426.

237   "Oh, how often did my husband"   Ibid., p. 440.

237   "With the sadness of winter"   Ibid., p. 425.

237   "most melancholy reflections"   Ibid., p. 428.

238   "Nothing else was required"   Ibid., p. 411.

238   "Conviction? Indeed, from whom"   Ibid.

238   "I left my home"   Ibid., p. 389.

239   "Why discuss a problem"   Ibid., p. 412.

239   "into one of them internally"   Ibid., p. 411.

239   "I found so few good examples"   Ibid., p. 427.

240   "Occidental rites"   Ibid., p. 434.

240   "I was very disillusioned"   Ibid., p. 435.

22: Alone

241   "You, on your peaceful island"   Ruete, *Letters Home,* in *An Arabian Princess,* p. 441.

241   "European states all suffer"   Ibid., p. 441.

241   "For what does it mean"   Ibid., pp. 441–42.

242   "The Lord be praised"   This and the following dialogue and inner thoughts are from ibid., pp. 443–46.

245   "Wait a minute, Bibi"   This and the following dialogue and inner thoughts are from ibid., pp. 449–50.

246   "Just go to the hospital"   Ibid., p. 452.

246   "The mere thought of having"   Ibid., p. 452.

246   "Off, off homewards!"   Ibid., p. 454.

247   "Nowhere was there a ray"   Ibid., p. 459.

248   "hardly had we changed greetings"   This and the following dialogue and inner thoughts are from ibid., pp. 461–63.

248   "naturally, because [Salme] had named"   Ibid., p. 463.

248   "but as is well known"   Ibid., p. 464.

23: Changes

250   "I had now taken"   Ruete, *Memoirs*, in *An Arabian Princess*, p. 373.

251   "I experienced for the first time"   Ruete, *Letters Home*, in *An Arabian Princess*, p. 464.

251   "an able housewife"   Van Donzel, *An Arabian Princess*, p. 30.

251   "Most people, though having taken"   Ruete, *Letters Home*, in *An Arabian Princess*, p. 468.

252   "Lord, God, protect me"   Ibid., p. 469.

252   "an honourable person"   Ibid., p. 470.

252   "He who does not know"   Ibid., p. 471.

252   "bird in a cage"   Ibid., p. 471.

253   "looking somewhat Jewish" . . . "Among us"   Ibid., pp. 475–76.

253   "vulgar curiosity" . . . "the happiest hours" . . . "My dear"   Ibid., p. 477.

253   "You appear to me"   Ibid., p. 478.

254   "No, no, your questions interest"   Ibid., p. 480.

254   "It depends, Madam"   Ibid., p. 481.

255   "Be just glad that you are"   Ibid., p. 483.

255   "obduracy" . . . "spiteful resentment"   Ruete, *Memoirs*, in *An Arabian Princess*, p. 374.

256   **inheritances that she claimed were hers**   How much money Salme thought due her in the early 1870s is unclear, but by 1888, she was claiming a substantial amount—about 360,000 German marks or 18,000 pounds. From van Donzel, *An Arabian Princess*, p. 31.

256   **Her case had great appeal**   Gray, "Memoirs of An Arabian Princess," p. 56.

258 "my most ardent hope" Ruete, *Memoirs*, in *An Arabian Princess*, p. 376.

258 "seemed fully informed" Ibid., p. 376.

258 "Inexperienced as I was" Ibid., p. 380.

259 "very considerable reserve" Gray, "Memoirs of an Arabian Princess," p. 57.

259 "It is perhaps difficult to gauge" *The Illustrated London News*, June 19, 1875.

260 important 1873 anti–slave trade treaty I discuss the treaty in more depth in "Chapter 24: Tippu Tip."

260 "I don't know what business" van Donzel, *An Arabian Princess*, p. 42.

260 "it was couched in language" Gray, "Memoirs of an Arabian Princess," p. 57.

261 "How can I help it?" Coupland, *The Exploitation of East Africa*, p. 240.

262 "anything-but-modern" Ruete, *Letters Home*, in *An Arabian Princess*, p. 486.

262 "much talked-of" van Donzel, *An Arabian Princess*, p. 44.

263 "Our fatalism is often jeered at" Ruete, *Letters Home*, in *An Arabian Princess*, p. 492.

263 "The amazement did not come" Ibid., p. 500.

263 "noble and affable Emperor" Ibid., p. 502.

264 "I read so much grief in it" Ibid., pp. 505–6.

24: Tippu Tip

My account of Tippu Tip's life is taken from two different translations of his autobiography—Heinrich Brode, *Tippu Tip: The Story of His Career in Zanzibar and Central Africa* (Zanzibar: The Gallery Publications, 2000); and Tippu Tip, *Maisha ya Hamed bin Muhammed El Murjebi, yaani Tippu Tip*, W. J. Whitely, ed. (Nairobi: East African Literature Bureau, 1966)—and from a biography, Leda Farrant, *Tippu Tip and the East African Slave Trade* (New York: St. Martin's Press, 1975).

265 One historian estimates Frederick Cooper, in Bennett, *A History of the Arab State*, p. 66.

266 "He was a tall, black-bearded man" Henry M. Stanley, *Through the Dark Continent* (New York: Dover Publications, 1988), p. 95.

268 "My slaves don't want" J. Becker, *La Vie en Afrique II*, in Liebowitz, *The Physician and the Slave Trade*, p. 152.

269 "If you want to trust" Brode, *Tippu Tip*, p. 9.

270 "I lost my temper" . . . "the leopard attacks" Tippu Tip, *Maisha ya Hamed*, p. 19.

270 Sultan Nsama This is the proper name used by Brode in his translation. Whitely and Farrant call the tribal leader "Suma."

271   "Sultan, you are so rich"   Farrant, *Tippu Tip*, p. 39.

272   "At a shot they fell"   Brode, *Tippu Tip*, p. 16.

272   "I am very happy you defeated"   Farrant, *Tippu Tip*, p. 42.

273   "astonishingly large" . . . "rows of clove-trees"   Brode, *Tippu Tip*, p. 41.

274   "It is well. Utetera, you must"   Ibid., p. 43.

275   "My master will visit you"   Murjebi Family Papers, in Farrant, *Tippu Tip*, p. 64.

275   "Tomorrow we will have" . . . "Obey him"   David Livingstone, *Last Journals*, in Farrant, *Tippu Tip*, p. 65.

276   "The only drawback I experienced"   V. Lovett Cameron, *Across Africa*, in Farrant, *Tippu Tip*, p. 71.

276   "a hearty appetite"   Brode, *Tippu Tip*, p. 46.

25: Dr. Livingstone

For biographical information on Livingstone and descriptions of his last journey into Africa, I depended on Tim Jeal, *Livingstone* (New York: G. P. Putnam's Sons, 1973), and David Livingstone, *The Last Journals of Dr. David Livingstone, in Central Africa, from 1865 to His Death*, vols. 1 and 2, Horace Waller, ed. (The Project Gutenberg eBooks). Also most helpful were Moorehead, *The White Nile*, and Dugard, *Into Africa*.

277   "big book"   Farrant, *Tippu Tip*, p. 43.

277   "in acknowledgment of his good services"   Melvin E. Page, "David Livingstone, the Arabs and the Slave Trade," in *Livingstone: Man of Africa, Memorial Essays 1873–1973*, Bridglal Pachai, ed. (London: Longman Group, 1973), p. 140.

279   "go forward into the dark interior"   Dugard, *Into Africa*, p. 34.

279   "The most wonderful sight"   Ibid., p. 99.

282   "We were promised"   Jeal, *Livingstone*, p. 269.

282   "The Nile sources are valuable"   F. Debenham, *The Way to Ilala*, in Jeal, *Livingstone*, p. 287.

283   "a great slave emporium"   Page, "David Livingstone, the Arabs and the Slave Trade," p. 138.

283   "very heavy slave-taming stick"   Livingstone, *The Last Journals*, vol. 1, June 26, 1866 entry (p. 45 in eBook edition).

283   "if they sell their fellows"   Ibid. (p. 46 in eBook edition).

285   But his friendship with the traders   Discussion of the reasons behind Livingstone's friendship with the traders from Jeal, *Livingstone*, pp. 298–99.

286   "judged by the East African"   Livingstone, *The Last Journals*, vol. 2, pp. 75–76, in Page, "David Livingstone, the Arabs and the Slave Trade," p. 142.

286   "If one wanted to see"   Jeal, *Livingstone*, p. 307.

286   "the vilest of the vile"   Livingstone, *The Last Journals*, vol. 2, May 26, 1869 entry (p. 12 in eBook edition).

287   "eat through everything"   Ibid., July 23, 1870 entry (p. 34 in eBook edition).

287   "I am very old & shaky"   Jeal, *Livingstone*, p. 327.

288   "With market women it seems to be"   Livingstone, *The Last Journals*, vol. 2, April 10, 1871 entry (p. 72 in eBook edition).

289   "felt inclined to reprove them"   This and the following quotes from that day are from ibid., July 15, 1871 entry (p. 82 in eBook edition).

290   Later, the Arabs would estimate   Jeal, *Livingstone*, p. 334.

290   "But I told them I was"   Livingstone, *The Last Journals*, vol. 2, July 16, 1871 entry (p. 84 in eBook edition).

291   "I felt in my destitution" . . . "Susi came running"   Ibid., Oct. 24, 1871 entry.

291   "Dr. Livingstone, I presume?"   Many question whether Stanley actually said these words. He swore he did, but the corresponding page of his journals is torn out. The issue is discussed at length in Jeal, *Livingstone*, pp. 117–20.

26: Stanley Meets Tippu Tip

For biographical information on Stanley, I relied on two fascinating sources: Tim Jeal, *Stanley: The Impossible Life of Africa's Greatest Explorer* (New Haven, Conn.: Yale University Press, 2007) and Stanley's own writings, especially, *Through the Dark Continent*, vol. 2. Also offering intriguing insight were Adam Hochschild, *King Leopold's Ghost: A Story of Greed, Terror, and Heroism in Colonial Africa* (New York: First Mariner Books, 1999); Moorehead, *The White Nile*; and Dugard, *Into Africa*.

292   his father, at least according   Doubt exists as to who Stanley's father was. In *Stanley: The Impossible Life*, p. 25, Jeal convincingly argues that he may have been a prominent local lawyer named James Vaughan Horne.

293   "In future you are"   Henry M. Stanley, *The Autobiography of Sir Henry Morton Stanley* (Boston: Houghton Mifflin Co., 1901), p. 113.

294   "You mean there are Arabs" . . . "A great settlement"   Murjebi Family Papers, in Farrant, *Tippu Tip*, p. 66.

295   "Barghash is now a very"   Bennett, *A History of the Arab State*, p. 90.

296   "With the air of a well-bred"   Stanley, *Through the Dark Continent*, vol. 2, p. 95.

298   "Brought by faithful hands"   Epitaph quoted in Moorehead, *The White Nile*, pp. 128–29.

299   "It is impossible not to feel"   Stanley, *Through the Dark Continent*, vol. 1, p. 40.

300   "there was no person at Nyangwe"   Ibid., vol. 2, p. 96.

300   "If you Wasungu"   This and the following dialogue are from ibid., vol. 2, pp. 98–99.

301   "dreaded black and chill"   Ibid., vol. 2, p. 130.

302   "gentle as a summer's dream"   Ibid., vol. 2, p. 148.

302   "You never write to me"   Hochschild, *King Leopold's Ghost*, p. 51.

302   "Go back, Wasambye"   This and the following dialogue are from Stanley, *Through the Dark Continent*, vol. 2, pp. 152–53.

302   "a kindly interchange" . . . "Each village street"   Ibid., vol. 2, p. 156.

303   "doing terrible execution"   Ibid., vol. 2, p. 74.

304   neither man liked sharing   Farrant, *Tippu Tip*, p. 87.

304   "Ranged along the bank"   Stanley, *Through the Dark Continent*, vol. 2, p. 197.

305   "we have attacked and destroyed"   Hochschild, *King Leopold's Ghost*, p. 49.

306   "The beach was crowded"   Ibid., p. 49.

306   "that ugly derisive word"   Jeal, *Stanley*, p. 11.

306   "relax those stiff pallid features"   Ibid.

306   "The execution & fulfillment"   Letter from Stanley to Edward King, in ibid., p. 204.

27: Seyyid Barghash

313   "[I] went prepared to do"   Coupland, *The Exploitation of East Africa*, p. 50.

313   "We cannot sign the new"   Liebowitz, *The Physician and the Slave Trade*, p. 170.

314   "But it may be"   Ibid., p. 175.

314   "To all whom it may"   Coupland, *The Exploitation of East Africa*, p. 225.

315   "abolishing the slave trade"   Hochschild, *King Leopold's Ghost*, p. 45.

316   "I want to make us a pact"   This and the following dialogue are from Tippu Tip, *Maisha ya Hamed*, p. 113.

317   "with all speed, Hamed"   Farrant, *Tippu Tip*, p. 102.

317   "to look out after all manner"   Ibid., p. 103.

317   "Hamed, be not angry" . . . "When I heard"   Brode, *Tippu Tip*, p. 93.

28: Endings

When describing Germany's early colonization efforts in Africa and how they affected Zanzibar, I consulted Bennett, *A History of the Arab State*, and Thomas Pakenham, *The Scramble for Africa: The White Man's Conquest of the Dark Conti-*

3577

Notes

nent from 1876 to 1912 (New York: Random House, 1991). Gray, "Memoirs of an Arabian Princess," and van Donzel, *An Arabian Princess Between Two Worlds;* both discuss Salme's visits home in detail.

318   I also wish you to understand   van Donzel, *An Arabian Princess,* pp. 51–57.

319   "with warm interest"   Ibid., p. 63.

320   "I got tired of being"   Pakenham, *The Scramble for Africa,* p. 290.

321   "tired" of the British   van Donzel, *An Arabian Princess,* p. 67.

321   Busaids' near-century-long cooperation   Bennett, *A History of the Arab State,* p. 127.

321   "when two nations"   Maurizi, *Seyyid Said,* p. 75.

322   "convert a mere commercial"   Bennett, *A History of the Arab State,* p. 128.

322   "if Frau Ruete should be killed"   Gray, "Memoirs of an Arabian Princess," p. 61.

322   "[Salme] was to go out to Zanzibar"   Ibid., p. 61.

322   "Frau Ruete is for us"   Ibid., pp. 62–63.

323   "This boy has been carefully"   Frederic Holmwood, in van Donzel, *An Arabian Princess,* p. 69.

323   the young man reportedly replied   Heinz Schneppen, "Zanzibar and the Germans: German Interests and Diplomacy, 1844–1966," lecture delivered at the Palace Museum in Zanzibar, Sept. 26 and 29, 1997.

323   "thank the Almighty"   Ruete, *Memoirs,* in *An Arabian Princess,* p. 389.

324   "friendly negotiations"   Coupland, *The Exploitation of East Africa,* p. 437.

324   "We have understood"   van Donzel, *An Arabian Princess,* p. 74.

324   "right and left the crowd"   Ruete, *Memoirs,* in *An Arabian Princess,* p. 391.

326   "provisional" acceptance meant that Germany   van Donzel, *An Arabian Princess,* p. 80.

327   Had he lived in a different   Bennett, *A History of the Arab State,* pp. 138–39.

328   "The strangest disease I have seen"   Livingstone, *Last Journals,* quoted in Jeal, p. 327.

329   "They went away but did not"   Ruete, *Memoirs,* in *An Arabian Princess,* p. 405.

Bibliography

Allen, Calvin H., Jr. *Oman: The Modernization of the Sultanate.* Boulder, Colo.: Westview Press, 1987.

Al-Maamiry, Ahmed Hamoud. *Oman and East Africa.* New Delhi: Lancers Publishers, 1980.

Alpers, E. A. *The East African Slave Trade,* Historical Association of Tanzania, Paper No. 3. Nairobi: East African Publishing House, 1967.

———. *Ivory and Slaves in East Central Africa.* London: Heinemann, 1975.

Al-Rashid, Zamil Muhammad. *Su'udi Relations with Eastern Arabia and 'Uman (1800–1871).* London: Luzac & Co., 1981.

Al-Rawas, Isam. *Oman in Early Islamic History.* Reading, UK: Ithaca Press, 2000.

Anonymous. "R. P. Waters: A Sketch." Salem, Mass.: Reprint from the *Bulletin of the Essex Institute,* vol. 20.

Baldock, W. F. "The Story of Rashid Bin Hassani of the Bisa Tribe, Northern Rhodesia." In *Ten Africans,* edited by Margery Perham. Evanston, Ill.: Northwestern University Press, 1964.

Beachey, R. W. *The Slave Trade of Eastern Africa.* New York: Harper & Row, 1976.

Beguin Billecocq, Xavier. *Oman: Twenty-Five Centuries of Travel Writing.* Paris: Relations Internationales & Culture, 1994.

Bennett, Norman R. "Americans in Zanzibar, 1825–45." Essex Institute *Historical Collections,* vol. 95, 1959, pp. 239–62.

———. "Americans in Zanzibar, 1845–64." Essex Institute *Historical Collections,* vol. 97, 1961, pp. 31–56.

———. *Arab Versus European: Diplomacy and War in Nineteenth-Century East Central Africa.* New York: Africana Publishing Company, 1986.

———. *A History of the Arab State of Zanzibar.* London: Methuen & Co., 1978.

———. *Studies in East African History.* Boston: Boston University Press, 1963.

Bennett, Norman R., and George E. Brooks, Jr., eds. *New England Merchants in Africa: A History Through Documents, 1802 to 1865.* Boston: Boston University Press, 1965.

Bhacker, M. Reda. *Trade and Empire in Muscat and Zanzibar: Roots of British Domination.* New York: Routledge, 1992.

Bidwell, Robin. "Bibliographical Notes on European Accounts of Muscat 1500–1900." *Arabian Studies IV* (London: C. Hurst & Company, 1978), pp. 123–59.

Brode, Heinrich. *Tippu Tip: The Story of His Career in Zanzibar and Central Africa.* Translated by H. Havelock. Zanzibar: The Gallery Publications, 2000.

Browne, J. Ross. *Etchings of a Whaling Cruise, with Notes of a Sojourn on the Island of Zanzibar.* Cambridge, Mass.: The Belknap Press of Harvard University Press, 1968, reprint.

Buckingham, James Silk. *Travels in Assyria, Media, and Persia,* vol. 2. London: Henry Colburn and Richard Bentley, 1830.

Burton, Richard F. *The Lake Regions of Central Africa.* New York: Dover Publications, 1961, reprint.

———. *Zanzibar: City, Island, and Coast,* vols. 1 and 2. New York: Johnson Reprint Corp., 1967.

Buxton, Meriel. *David Livingstone.* New York: Palgrave, 2001.

Carter, J.L.R. *Tribes in Oman.* London: Peninsular Publishing, 1982.

Christie, James. *Cholera Epidemics in East Africa.* London: Macmillan, 1876.

Cooper, Frederick. *Plantation Slavery on the East Coast of Africa.* Portsmouth, N.H.: Heinemann, 1997.

Correa, Gaspar. *The Three Voyages of Vasco Da Gama and His Viceroyalty.* Translated by Henry E. J. Stanley. New York: Burt Franklin, n.d., reprint.

Coupland, Reginald. *East Africa and Its Invaders: From the Earliest Times to the Death of Seyyid Said in 1856.* London: Oxford at the Clarendon Press, 1938.

———. *The Exploitation of East Africa 1856–1890: The Slave Trade and the Scramble.* London: Faber and Faber, 1968.

Crofton, R. H. *The Old Consulate at Zanzibar.* London: Oxford University Press, 1935.

Dugard, Martin. *Into Africa: The Epic Adventures of Stanley & Livingstone.* New York: Broadway Books, 2003.

Earle, T. F., and John Villiers, eds. *Albuquerque, Caesar of the East: Selected Texts by Afonso de Albuquerque and His Son.* Warminster, UK: Aris & Phillips, 1990.

Eilts, Herman Frederick. "Ahmed bin Na'man's Mission to the United States in 1840, The Voyage of the Al-Sultanah to New York City." Essex Institute *Historical Collections,* vol. 98, pp. 219–77.

Else, David, and Heather Tyrrell. *Zanzibar, The Bradt Travel Guide.* Guilford, Conn.: The Globe Pequot Press, 2003.

Farrant, Leda. *Tippu Tip and the East African Slave Trade.* New York: St. Martin's Press, 1975.

Farsy (Farsi), Abdalla Saleh. *Seyyid Said Bin Sultan.* New Delhi: Lancers Books, 1942.

Fraser, James Baillie. *Narrative of a Journey into Khorassan*. London: Longman, Hurts, Rees, Orme, Brown, and Green, 1825.

Freeman-Grenville, G.S.P. *The East African Coast: Select Documents from the First to the Earlier Nineteenth Century*. Oxford, UK: Clarendon Press, 1962.

Gates, Henry Louis, Jr. *Wonders of the African World*. New York: Alfred A. Knopf, 1999.

el-Gheithy, Said. "Past and Future Exhibitions." Monograph prepared by the Princess Salme Institute, London, to accompany museum exhibit.

Gordon, Murray. *Slavery in the Arab World*. New York: New Amsterdam Books, 1989.

Gray, John. *History of Zanzibar from the Middle Ages to 1856*. London: Oxford University Press, 1962.

——. "Memoirs of an Arabian Princess." *Tanganyika Notes and Records* 37 (1954), pp. 49–70.

A Guide to Zanzibar. Zanzibar: Government Printer, 1952.

Hall, Richard. *Empires of the Monsoon: A History of the Indian Ocean and Its Invaders*. London: HarperCollins, 1996.

Hamilton, Genesta. *In the Wake of Da Gama*. New York: Skeffington and Son, 1951.

Heanley, R. M. *A Memoir of Edward Steere*. London: George Bell and Sons, 1888.

Heude, William. *A Voyage up the Persian Gulf, and a Journey Overland from India to England, in 1817*. London: Longman, Hurst, Rees, Orme, and Brown, 1819.

Hill, Ann, and Daryl Hill. *The Sultanate of Oman: A Heritage*. New York: Longman Group, 1977.

Hochschild, Adam. *Bury the Chains: Prophets and Rebels in the Fight to Free an Empire's Slaves*. New York: Houghton Mifflin, 2005.

——. *King Leopold's Ghost: A Story of Greed, Terror, and Heroism in Colonial Africa*. New York: First Mariner Books, 1999.

Hollingsworth, L. W. *Zanzibar Under the Foreign Office, 1890–1913*. London: MacMillan & Co., 1953.

Holmes, Timothy, ed. *David Livingstone Letters & Documents 1841–1872*. London: James Currey, 1990.

Hopwood, Derek, ed. *The Arabian Peninsula: Society and Politics*. Totowa, N.J.: Rowman and Littlefield, 1972.

Hourani, Albert. *A History of the Arab Peoples*. New York: Warner Books, 1991.

Hourani, George F. *Arab Seafaring: In the Indian Ocean in Ancient and Early Medieval Times*. Princeton, N.J.: Princeton University Press, 1995.

Ingrams, W. H. *Zanzibar, Its History and Its People*. London: Frank Cass and Co., 1967.

Izzard, Molly. *The Gulf: Arabia's Western Approaches*. London: John Murray, 1979.

Jayne, K. G. *Vasco da Gama and His Successors 1460–1580*. London: Methuen & Co., 1910.

Jeal, Tim. *Livingstone.* London: William Heinemann, 1973.

———. *Stanley: The Impossible Life of Africa's Greatest Explorer.* New Haven, Conn.: Yale University Press, 2007.

Kay, Shirley. *Enchanting Oman.* Dubai, UAE: Motivate Publishing, 1999.

Levtzion, Nehemia, and Randall L. Pouwels. *The History of Islam in Africa.* Athens, Ohio: Ohio University Press, 2000.

Lewis, Bernard. *The Arabs in History.* New York: Harper & Row, 1960.

———. *Race and Slavery in the Middle East: An Historical Inquiry.* New York: Oxford University Press, 1990.

Liebowitz, Daniel. *The Physician and the Slave Trade.* New York: W. H. Freeman and Co., 1999.

Livingstone, David. *The Last Journals of David Livingstone, in Central Africa, from 1865 to His Death,* vols. 1 and 2. Edited by Horace Wallace. Project Gutenberg Online Book Catalogue: eText No. 16672 (released Sept. 7, 2005) and eText No. 17024 (released Nov. 8, 2005).

Lohdi, Abdulaziz Y. *The Institution of Slavery in Zanzibar and Pemba,* Research Report No. 16. Uppsala, Sweden: The Scandinavian Institute of African Studies, 1973.

Lorimer, J. G. *Gazetteer of the Persian Gulf, Oman and Central Arabia,* vol. 1. New York: Cambridge University Press, 1986, reprint.

Lyne, Robert Nunez. *Zanzibar in Contemporary Times.* London: Hurst and Blackett, Limited, 1905.

Malcolm, John. *Sketches of Persia by a Traveller,* vol. 1. London: John Murray, 1827.

Maurizi, Vincenzo. *History of Seyd Said, Sultan of Muscat.* New York: The Oleander Press, 1984, reprint.

Mazrui, Alamin, and Ibrahim Noor Shariff. *The Swahili: Idiom and Identity of an African People.* Trenton, N.J.: Africa World Press, 1994.

Metz, Helen Chapin. *Persian Gulf States: Country Studies.* Washington, D.C.: Department of the Army, 1994.

Middleton, John. *The World of the Swahili: An African Mercantile Civilization.* New Haven, Conn.: Yale University Press, 1992.

Miles, S. B. *The Countries and Tribes of the Persian Gulf.* London: Harrison and Sons, 1919.

Moorehead, Alan. *The White Nile.* New York: Perennial, 2000.

Nurse, Derek, and Thomas Spear. *The Swahili: Reconstructing the History and Language of an African Society, 800–1500.* Philadelphia: University of Pennsylvania Press, 1985.

Osgood, Joseph Barlow Feltz. *Notes of Travel; or, Recollections of Majunga, Zanzibar, Muscat, Aden, Mocha, and Other Eastern Ports.* Salem, Mass.: George Cramer, 1854.

Owen, Captain W.F.W. *Narrative of Voyages to Explore the Shores of Africa, Arabia, and Madagascar,* vols. 1 and 2. London: Richard Bentley, 1833.

Page, Melvin E. "David Livingstone, the Arabs and the Slave Trade." In *Livingstone: Man of Africa, Memorial Essays 1873–1973*. Edited by Bridglal Pachai. London: Longman Group, 1973.

Pakenham, Thomas. *The Scramble for Africa: White Man's Conquest of the Dark Continent from 1876 to 1912*. New York: Random House, 1991.

Parsons, Abraham. *Travels in Asia and Africa*. London: Longman, Hurts, Rees, and Orme, 1808.

Pearce, F. B. *Zanzibar: The Island Metropolis of Eastern Africa*. London: Frank Cass & Co., 1967.

Phillips, Wendell. *Oman: A History*. London: Longmans, 1967.

Pickthall, Mohammed Marmaduke. *The Meaning of the Glorious Koran*. New York: Penguin Group, n.d.

Pouwels, Randall L. *Horn and Crescent: Cultural Change and Traditional Islam on the East Africa Coast, 800–1900*. New York: Cambridge University Press, 1987.

Putnam, Eleanor. *Old Salem*. New York: Houghton Mifflin & Company, 1887.

ibn Razik, Salil. *History of the Imams and Seyyids of Oman*. Translated and edited by George Percy Badger. New York: Burt Franklin, 1967, reprint.

Rice, Edward. *Captain Sir Richard Francis Burton: A Biography*. New York: Da Capo Press, 1990.

Risso, Patricia. *Oman and Muscat: An Early Modern History*. London: Croom Helm, 1986.

Roberts, Edmund. *Embassy to the Eastern Courts*. New York: Harper & Brothers, 1837.

Ruete, Emily (born Salme, Princess of Oman and Zanzibar). *Memoirs of an Arabian Princess from Zanzibar*. Introduction by Patricia W. Romero. Princeton, N.J.: Markus Weiner Publishers, 1996, reprint.

Ruschenberger, W.S.W. *Narrative of a Voyage Round the World, During the Years 1835, 1836, and 1837*, vol. 1. London: Dawsons of Pall Mall, 1970, reprint.

Russell, Mrs. Charles E., ed. *General Rigby, Zanzibar and the Slave Trade*. London: Allen & Unwin, 1935.

Said-Ruete, Emily. *Memoirs of an Arabian Princess*. Edited by G.S.P. Freeman-Grenville. London: East-West Publications, 1994, reprint.

Said-Ruete, Rudolf. "The Al-Bu-Said Dynasty in Arabia and East Africa." Lecture given at a joint meeting of the Royal Asiatic and Central Asian Societies, London, July 1, 1929.

———. *Said bin Sultan (1791–1856): Ruler of Oman and Zanzibar*. London: Alexandre-Ousley, 1929.

Schneppen, Heinz. "Zanzibar and the Germans: German Interests and Diplomacy 1844–1966." Lecture given at the Palace Museum, Zanzibar, Sept. 26 and 29, 1997.

Segal, Ronald. *Islam's Black Slaves: The Other Black Diaspora.* New York: Farrar, Straus and Giroux, 2001.

Sheriff, Abdul. *Historical Zanzibar: Romance of the Ages.* London: HSP Publications, 1995.

——. *Slaves, Spices and Ivory in Zanzibar.* Athens, Ohio: Ohio University Press, 1987.

——. *Zanzibar Stone Town: An Architectural Exploration.* Zanzibar: The Gallery Publications, 2001.

Sirhan ibn Said ibn Sirhan. *Annals of Oman to 1728.* New York: The Oleander Press, 1984. Translated and annotated by E. C. Ross.

Stanley, Henry M. *The Autobiography of Sir Henry Morton Stanley.* Boston: Houghton Mifflin Co., 1901.

——. *Through the Dark Continent,* vols. 1 and 2. New York: Dover Publications, Inc., 1988, reprint.

Sulivan, Captain G. I. *Dhow Chasing in Zanzibar Waters.* Zanzibar: The Gallery Publications, 2003, reprint.

Tippu Tip. *Maisha ya Hamed bin Muhammed el Murjebi, Yaani Tippu Tip.* Edited and translated by W. H. Whitely. Nairobi: East African Literature Bureau, 1966.

Troeller, Gary. *The Birth of Saudi Arabia: Britain and the Rise of the House of Saud.* London: Frank Cass, 1976.

van Donzel, E., ed. *An Arabian Princess Between Two Worlds: Memoirs, Letters Home, Sequels to the Memoirs, Syrian Customs and Usages,* by Sayyida Salme/Emily Ruete. New York: E. J. Brill, 1993.

Vine, Peter. *The Heritage of Oman.* London: Immel Publishing, 1995.

Ward, Philip. *Travels in Oman: On the Track of the Early Explorers.* New York: The Oleander Press, 1987.

Wellsted, James Raymond. *Travels in Arabia.* London: John Murray, 1838.

Wilkinson, John C. *The Imamate Tradition of Oman.* New York: Cambridge University Press, 1987.

Index

About the Author

CHRISTIANE BIRD is the author of *A Thousand Sighs, A Thousand Revolts: Journeys in Kurdistan; Neither East Nor West: One Woman's Journey Through the Islamic Republic of Iran;* and *The Jazz and Blues Lover's Guide to the U.S.* A graduate of Yale University and former travel writer for the New York *Daily News,* she lives in New York City with her family.

About the Type

This book was set in Berling. Designed in 1951 by Karl Erik Forsberg for the Typefoundry Berlingska Stilgjuteri AB in Lund, Sweden, it was released the same year in foundry type by H. Berthold AG. A classic old-face design, its generous proportions and inclined serifs make it highly legible.